GARDENS OF NORTH AMERICA AND HAWAII

GARDENS OF NORTH AMERICA AND HAWAII
A Traveler's Guide

*A handbook to gardens, arboreta, and conservatories
in the United States and Canada*

by

Irene Jacob
Education Coordinator, Phipps Conservatory

and

Walter Jacob

*With drawings by
Barnes Tilney and Walt Haglund*

TIMBER PRESS
Portland, Oregon
1985

© Timber Press 1985

All rights reserved.
Printed in the United States of America
ISBN 0-88192-017-7

Design: Sandra Mattielli
Maps: Kristine Elkin

TIMBER PRESS
9999 SW Wilshire
Portland, Oregon 97225

Table of Contents

Dedicated to our sons

Kenneth G. Jacob
Daniel B. Jacob

and their future

Preface

This is a guide to fourteen hundred gardens, conservatories, and arboreta of the United States and Canada, including Hawaii. Our book is intended for the casual traveler who would like to visit gardens and for those with a professional interest in gardening and horticulture.

The map of each state or province and the directions provided should make the gardens easy to reach. The information on the design, plant material and outstanding features will present an introduction to each site.

Every garden included in our book has been verified through two independent sources. We have visited many of the gardens. The remainder of the descriptions have been based on the sources available and we have tried to make them as accurate as possible.

Occasionally we have listed an unusual natural setting which might be overlooked by a traveler, but we have not generally included national or state parks. A few large nurseries with outstanding collections have also been included. Some of the numerous flower and blossom festivals have been noted.

We have purposely omitted the following categories unless there was a specific reason for their inclusion: nature centers, garden centers, private gardens, historic houses with very small gardens or remnants of former gardens, sites which have badly deteriorated.

Although we have made an effort to be comprehensive, some gardens have undoubtedly been missed. We look forward to hearing from our readers about gardens which we have omitted or whose descriptions should be changed. Please write to us at the address below.

We want to express our gratitude to more than two thousand helpful people associated with the institutions listed as well as many friends who have patiently answered our questions and assisted us with this project. We are especially grateful to our editor, Richard Abel, for his helpful suggestions.

Irene and Walter Jacob

September 1984.
303 Le Roi Road
Pittsburgh, PA 15208

How to Use This Book

Location—Gardens may be located by state or province through the numbers provided on the maps. The states are listed alphabetically. The index of place names and gardens may be useful if the precise location of a garden is not known.

Ratings and Symbols—The gardens, conservatories and arboreta have been rated according to the variety of specimens, the quality of the plantings, the landscaping, and the level of maintenance. The length and general description will also demonstrate which sites are better than others. We have tried to be conservative; some sites probably deserve an additional star, but we feel it is better to be surprised than to be disappointed.

A few sites barely qualify but have been included as there is so little in that area or because restoration and improved maintenance is underway. Regular maintenance is of primary importance to gardens. A few years of government neglect, foundation disinterest, change of management, or the death of the founder may make a major difference in the state of the garden. Occasionally this may have occurred without our knowledge.

The size of the garden and the date of founding will provide some idea of variety and maturity of plant material. Special collections have been noted. Institutions with libraries or a university connection will have a more academic orientation.

The symbols are listed on the next page.

Hours, Fees, Handicapped Access—The hours, seasons, and admission fees are subject to constant change. We have divided them by $3.- intervals with the hope of reasonable accuracy. When the fee is less than $1.-, it is listed as nominal. The vast majority of gardens are free or ask a low entrance fee. The telephone number provided should enable our reader to check on these matters.

Handicapped access has been noted in the symbols; partial handicapped access is noted in the text and may have a a variety of meanings. Fragrance gardens for the blind or those marked with braille have also been indicated through symbols.

No Admission Charge—The vast majority of institutions charge no admission. More than 900 free gardens have been listed. In addition to those marked "no admission" whenever nothing is said about admission, the garden is free.

Special Events—Whenever we have known of special facilities such as tram tours, picnic facilities, boat rides, ancillary programs, and annual festivals, we have noted them.

Nurseries—The nurseries listed do not indicate an endorsement, but rather a willingness on the part of the owners to accomodate visitors and an interest in beauty of display. Only nurseries which provide unusual collections have been listed. Those interested in other nurseries should inquire at local gardens and conservatories.

Other Sites to Visit—We have included only a few nationally known theme parks; local amusement parks are often beautifully landscaped and may be worth a visit. Some local cemeteries display outstanding collections of trees. Atriums and shopping malls sometimes feature unusual indoor landscaping interesting to the visitor.

Historic Houses—Many historic houses in the South and New England include gardens of varying size and quality. The gardens are usually the first to suffer when funds are diminished, so their maintenance is likely to be uneven from season to season.

Symbols

A number of abbreviations have been used along with the description of the gardens. They will identify some special features at a glance. 'How to Use This Book' provides the criteria for the ratings.

**** — superb gardens, conservatories, or arboreta.
*** — excellent gardens, conservatories, or arboreta.
** — very good gardens, conservatories, or arboreta.
* — good gardens, conservatories, or arboreta.
    — braille, raised beds, or fragrance garden for the blind and handicapped.
HA — handicapped access; partial access not included.
A — azaleas, rhododendrons.
B — Biblical gardens.
BO — bonsai.
BX — boxwoods.
BR — bromeliads.
C — cacti.
CA — camellias.
CH — chrysanthemums.
F — fruit trees, orchards.
FE — ferns.
G — greenhouses, conservatories, orangeries.
H — herb gardens.
HD — home demonstration gardens.
HH — historic houses.
J — Japanese gardens, Chinese gardens.
L — landscape designs.
O — orchids.
P — palms, tropical plants.
R — rose gardens.
RG — rock gardens.
S — specimen trees, shrubs, plant collections.
SH — Shakespearean gardens.
SU — succulents, agaves, aloes, yuccas.
T — topiaries, mazes, knot gardens.
W — water lilies, aquatic plants, bogs.
WF — wildflowers.

ALABAMA

TENN.

1. Tuscumbia
2. Athens
3. Huntsville
4. Phil Campbell
5. Gadsden
6-8. Birmingham
9-10. Tuscaloosa
11-13. Selma
14. Montgomery
15-16. Wetumpka
17. Auburn
18-22. Mobile
23. Theodore

MISS.

GA.

FLA.

TUSCUMBIA

1 Ivy Green and International Gardens ☆-HA-HH-BX
Helen Keller Shrine
Keller Lane, off N. Main St.

These lovely landscaped gardens contain plants which are the gift of 25 nations. boxwood, crape-myrtle, magnolia, iris, and ivy may be found here. The grounds around Helen Keller's home are well maintained.

8:30-4:30 Mon-Sat; 1-4:30 Sun; adults, under $3; 6-11 half; handicapped access; (205) 383-4066.

ATHENS

2 Brown's Ferry G
U.S. 31, 10 mi. southwest of Athens

Experimental greenhouses are located near this large nuclear power facility. A wide variety of tropical plants, annuals and perennials are grown.

Daily 9-5; no admission charge; (205) 729-0389.

HUNTSVILLE

3 The Burritt Museum
3101 Burritt Drive.

The grounds of this local museum have been developed into a small formal garden.

Old trees as well as flowering shrubs are its main features. Gardens appropriate to the pioneer cabins are displayed.

Daily 8:30-dusk, grounds only; museum has different hours; donations; (205) 536-2882.

PHIL CAMPBELL

4 Dismals Wonder Gardens ☆☆ CA-FE-L-WF
Rt. 43 between Russelville and Phil Campbell

Waterfalls and streams course through this sunken garden planted with Mountain Laurel, camellias, wild hydrangeas, *Decumaria*, dogwood, ferns, and wildflowers. This is an unusual setting. Many of the plants are labelled. Pamphlets are available.

Daily 8-sunset; adults, under $3; students $1; (205) 993-5537.

GADSDEN

5 Noccalula Falls Botanical Gardens ☆☆ A-HH

3 mi. off I-59

A fine array of dogwood with an unusual display of bulbs in springtime may be seen in this garden; there are more than 21,000 azaleas. Numerous annuals bloom later in season. The falls and the banks of the stream are beautifully planted. A pioneer village is located on the grounds.

Daily 8-dusk; adults, under $3; children half; train through park; picnic facilities; (205) 534-7412.

BIRMINGHAM

6 Birmingham Botanical Gardens ☆☆☆ HA-A-BO-BX-C-FE-G-J-O-R-S-SU-WF
2612 Lane Park Rd.

A 67-acre botanical garden, established in 1962. There are 12 distinctive areas which include a good Japanese garden with a waterfall, a tea house, a Zen garden, and a Bonsai exhibit. Noteworthy are the wildflower garden, 'touch' and see garden, rhododendron garden, the fern glade, and the 26 foot floral clock. The gardens feature good collections of roses - 2,000 bushes of over 140 varieties—irises, day-lilies, camellias, dogwood. The large conservatory contains an excellent collection of cacti, succulents, and orchids with more than 5,000 different plants. Three seasonal flower shows each year. Test and demonstration gardens for annuals and vegetables are maintained. There is a library.

Daily, dawn-dusk; no admission charge; handicapped access; (205) 879-1576.

7 Arlington Historic Home and Garden ☆ HA-HH-BX-R-S
331 Cotton Ave. S.W.

A Greek Revival mansion built in 1842 is surrounded by 6 acres of beautifully landscaped 19th century gardens. This is Birmingham's oldest home. There are clipped boxwood hedges, magnolias, a good rose garden, a perennial, and an old annual garden.

9-5 Tues-Sat; 1-5 Sun, April-Sept; 9-4:30 Tues-Sat; 1-4:30 Sun, rest of year; closed holidays; adults, under $3; 12-18 half; 4-11 less; handicapped access; (205) 780-5656.

8   **Advent Gardens**   B
    Episcopal Church of the Advent
    2019 Sixth Ave. N.

4 distinctive small gardens surround this church in downtown Birmingham. Plants of the Bible are featured in a children's garden. There is a formal rector's garden, and a miniature roof garden.

Daily 9-5; no admission charge; (205) 251-2324.

TUSCALOOSA

9   **Gulf States Paper National Headquarters**   ☆   A-HA-J-L-RG
    1400 River Road, off U.S. 82 at Holt exit.

The headquarters buildings of this large corporation are of Oriental design and are set in a large Japanese garden with a reflecting pool. There are rock gardens, azalea plantings, flowering shrubs, and fine walkways.

Tours 5-7 Mon-Fri; 10-7 Sat, holidays; 1-7 Sun; no admission charge; handicapped access; (205) 553-6200.

10   **University of Alabama Arboretum**   ☆   HA-S-WF
    3½ mi. east on 15th St., on Loop Rd.

This 60-acre arboretum, established in 1958, lies a few miles from the campus. Emphasis has been placed on indigenous trees, shrubs, and more than 250 kinds of wildflowers. The four sections of the garden are a native woodlands, an ornamental area, a wildflower garden, and an experimental garden. The campus itself is well landscaped. Test and demonstration gardens for annuals not usually grown in the South have been developed.

Daily 7-sunset; no admission charge; handicapped access; (205) 348-5960.

SELMA

11   **Sturdivant Hall**   HH-S
    713 Mabry St.

Behind the house lie formal gardens of native flowers and shrubs. There are some fine old specimen trees.

Daily 9-4; Sun 2-4; closed Monday; adults under $3; students half; (205) 872-5626.

12   **Joseph T. Smitherman Historic Building**   HH-S
    109 Union St.

A park with old trees, fountains, and brick walks surrounds the building.

9-4 Mon-Fri; 2-4 Sun; no admission charge; (205) 872-8713.

13   **Historic Pilgrimage**   HH

Each springtime on the fourth weekend of March many homes and gardens are open to the public.

For information call (205) 875-7241.

MONTGOMERY

14   **Ordeman-Shaw Townhouse**   HH
    310 N. Hull St.

A restored 1848 townhouse along with a small garden. This is part of a larger restoration in the area which includes several gardens.

Tours 9:30-3:30 Mon-Sat; 1:30-3:30 Sun; closed Jan 1, Thanksgiving, Christmas; adults, under $3; students half; under 6 free; (205) 263-4355.

WETUMPKA

15   William Bartram Arboretum ☆   HA-HH-WF
Fort Toulouse Jackson Park
Route 6, off U.S. 231.

This arboretum is planted with specimens found in the region by the famous colonial botanist, Bartram, 200 years ago. An upland and lowland forest, wildflowers, and a bog area may be enjoyed from wooden walkways. A replica of the original fort lies nearby.

Daily 6-9, April-Oct; 8-5 Nov-March; closed Christmas and New Year; no admission charge; handicapped access; (205) 567-3002.

16   Jasmine Hill Gardens ☆☆   L-A-S
Jasmine Hill Rd. east of U.S. 231.

This is a 17-acre garden with reproductions of Greek and Roman statuary established in the 1920's. The grounds contain a copy of Temple of Hera in Olympia. Fine hedges, shrubbery, pools, fountains, Flowering Cherries, azaleas, and rhododendrons provide a beautiful setting. There are good old specimen trees.

9-5 Tues-Sun, March 1-Nov 30; adults, under $3; 6-12 half; partial handicapped access; concerts and plays from late May to Oct; (205) 263-1440.

AUBURN

17   Auburn University Arboretum ☆   HA
Auburn University.

A 14-acre arboretum, founded in 1963, contains a Pitcher Plant bog, a sand dune area, an alkaline prairie soil garden, and an annual garden. Emphasis has been placed upon indigenous trees and shrubs; there are test and demonstration gardens for cultivars generally not grown in the South.

Daily, dawn-dusk; no admission charge; handicapped access; (205) 826-4830.

MOBILE

18   Conde-Charlotte House   HH
104 Theatre St.

This house built in 1822 is set in a walled Spanish garden of late 18th century design, which is beautifully planted with native trees and shrubs.

10-4 Tues-Sat; Sun by appointment only; closed holidays; adults, under $3; 6-18 half; (205) 432-4722.

19   Richards D.A.R. House   A-CA-H-HH
256 N. Joachim St.

An antebellum townhouse of the mid-1800's which has been restored along with its formal garden. There are numerous cultivars of azaleas and camellias as well as Sweet Olive. A Colonial herb garden has been established recently.

10-4 Tues-Sat; 1-4 Sun; closed holidays, Dec 24-26, 31-Jan 2; adults, under $3; under 12 half; (205) 438-7320.

20 Oakleigh House A-HH
350 Oakleigh Place.

The house is surrounded by 3½ acres of grounds dominated by stately old oaks. Hundreds of azalea bushes bloom in spring.

10-4 Mon-Sat; 2-4 Sun; closed Christmas and legal holidays; adults, under $6; 12-18 half; (205) 432-1281.

21 Mobile Botanical Gardens ☆☆ .-A-FE-H
Southern Alabama Botanical & Horticultural Society
Museum Drive, Municipal Park

This young garden was established in 1974 and development continues on its 64 acres. Its woodland area contains more than 600 different species. There is a fragrance and texture garden for the blind, a native azalea area, a camellia garden, a herb garden, a fern garden, and a nature trail. Plants are labelled. Mid-March to the end of May is the best time for seeing the garden in bloom.

Daily, dawn-dusk; no admission charge.

22 Mobile Historic Home Tour HH
During Mardi Gras many homes and gardens are open to the public.

For information call (205) 432-2229.

THEODORE

23 Bellingrath Gardens ☆☆☆☆ A-BR-CA-CH-G-HH-J-L-O-R-RG-S-W
Rt. 59 off U.S. 90.

A large mansion lies in a 1,000-acre estate overlooking the Isle-aux-Oies River. 65 acres have been developed into formal gardens along the French, Italian, and English styles. There is also an Oriental-American garden as well as a grotto garden, a rock garden, and a bamboo grove. Streams run through the grounds and there is a large pool. Spectacular displays of 250,000 azalea bushes represent 200 species and varieties. More than 4,000 camellias are displayed; all of them are labelled and some are more than 100 years old. They bloom from September to April. 2,000 rose bushes of many different kinds bloom in the late spring. In autumn and early winter millions of chrysanthemums bloom. The garden contains good collections of African violets, water-lilies, lilies, oleander, hydrangeas, gardenias, crape myrtles, hibiscuses, dogwoods, Mountain Laurels, chrysanthemums, caladiums, crocuses, and wisterias. The conservatory has an excellent collection of orchids and bromeliads. Demonstration and test gardens for roses are maintained. There is a library. The garden is a bird sanctuary in which more than 200 species may be seen.

Daily 7-dusk; adults, under $6; 6-11 half; home additional charge; partial handicapped access; tours; (205) 973-2365.

ALASKA

Arctic Ocean

1. Palmer
2. Anchorage
3. Juneau

CANADA

Bering Sea

Gulf of Alaska

PALMER

1 Agricultural Experiment Station
Palmer Research Center
7 mi. southwest of Palmer

This experimental farm with its very small display gardens of perennials, annuals, and vegetables lies in a rich and fertile vegetable and pasture area. It is at its best in August.

Daily 8-4:30, May-Sept; no admission charge; (907) 745-3257.

ANCHORAGE

2 Centennial Rose Garden   R
Park Strip.

This small rose garden displays plants which are able to survive in this climate.

Daily, dawn-dusk.

JUNEAU

3 Governor's Mansion
9th St. and Calhoun Ave.

A small garden of perennials and annuals has been planted on the grounds.

For hours call (907) 586-2201.

ARIZONA

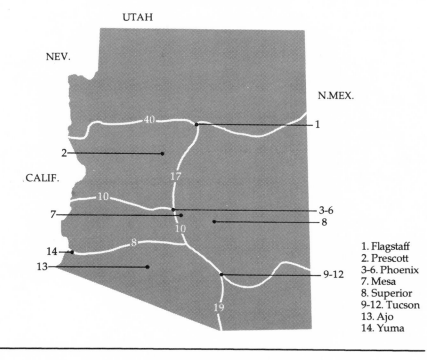

UTAH

NEV.

N.MEX.

CALIF.

1. Flagstaff
2. Prescott
3-6. Phoenix
7. Mesa
8. Superior
9-12. Tucson
13. Ajo
14. Yuma

FLAGSTAFF

1 Transition Zone Horticultural Institute C
Woody Mountain Road, off U.S. 66 southwest.

This new institution is located in a Ponderosa Pine forest at an elevation of more than 7,000 feet. It emphasizes plants of the Colorado Plateau and cacti of northwestern Arizona.

8-4:30 Mon-Fri, late May to Sept 30; no admission charge; call for touring information; (602) 774-1441.

PRESCOTT

2 Sharlot Hall Historic Society H-R
415 W. Gurley St.

A museum complex of frontier buildings which includes the Governor's Mansion with a pioneer herb garden and a memorial rose garden with 350 bushes honoring deceased Arizona women.

9-5 Tues-Sun, March 7-Oct 31; 10-4 Tues-Sun, Nov 1-March 6; 1-5 Sun; closed Mon, except national holidays; donation requested; partial handicapped access; (602) 445-3122.

PHOENIX

3 Desert Botanical Garden ☆☆☆☆ HA-C-SU
5800 E. Van Buren St. 6400 E. McDowell Rd. (Papago Park)

This is a world famous botanical garden; it contains desert plants and flora from arid lands. There are numerous agaves, cacti, Desert Fern trees, Creosote Bush, acacia, Boojam, Desert Spoon plants, aloes, yuccas. Approximately 4,500 specimens within 150 acres of desert land have been planted since the garden was established in 1935. There is a lath house display. Height of the blooming season from late March to May. Annual cactus show in February. Self-guided tours. Demonstration and test gardens for economic and landscape plants for arid areas.

7-sunset, May-Oct; 9-5 remainder of year; adults, under $3; children half; handicapped access; (602) 941-1217.

4 Encanto Park ☆ HA-P-SU
2705 N. 15th Ave. and W. Encanto Blvd.

Gardens with lagoon and islands which serve as waterfowl refuge have been established here; there are unusual trees and shrubs, many labelled as well as a tree walk of Mexican palms, African Sumac, bottle trees, and others.

Daily, sunrise-sunset, no admission charge; handicapped access.

5 Pinnacle Peak Village Desert Garden ☆ C-SU
Pinnacle Peak Road

A 3½-acre garden with two-thirds devoted to a naturally preserved area which include *Cercidum larrea*, and *Simmondsia*. The remainder of this garden established in 1980 is landscaped with drought resistant native species. Many cacti and succulents are labelled.

Call for hours; no admission charge; (602) 941-1217.

6 Valley Garden Center HA-R
1809 North 15th Ave.

This rose test center displays with 3,000 roses as well as seasonal flowers. There are test and demonstration gardens.

Daily 9-5; no admission charge; access for handicapped.

MESA

7 Mormon Temple Gardens ☆☆ C-L-P-SU
525 E. Main St.

In these Temple gardens we find 200 acres of unusual trees and shrubs with many species of attractive cacti, palms, citrus, flowering plants. Features a sunken garden, fountains, reflecting pools, beautifully landscaped.

9-9; no admission charge; guided tours each hour or half hour; partial handicapped access; (602) 964-7164.

SUPERIOR

8 Boyce Thompson Southwestern Arboretum ☆☆☆☆ C-G-HA-S-SU
3 mi. west on U.S. 60

1,076 acres of Sonoran desert and woodland with 1,500 desert species was established in 1929. Plantings include Saguaro, Palo Verde, yuccas, agaves, and Boojum trees. Many well-marked trails; plants labelled; eucalyptus grove with 50 species; natural desert area; greenhouses. Sister institute to Boyce Thompson Institute for Plant Research at Cornell University. Spring rains bring blooming lupines, poppies, penstemons. Some plants bloom all year round. There are demonstration and test gardens for ground cover. There is a library.

Daily 8-5:30 except Christmas; adults, under $3; children free; picnic area; handicapped access; (602) 689-2811.

TUCSON

9   **Saguaro National Monument** ☆ C
17 mi. east via East Broadway; 15 mi. west via Speedway Blvd.

Both sections of this park contain stands of the Saguaro Cactus and typify the Sonoran desert. Saguaro bloom in May, attain an age of 200 years and may reach a height of 50 ft.

Daily 8-5; admission under $3; visitor center at Rincon Mt.; nature walks in winter; picnic sites.

10   **The Arizona-Sonora Desert Museum** ☆☆ HA-C-L
Tucson Mt. Park
Ajo-Kinney Rd., 14 mi. west of Tucson, near Saguaro National Monument

This is an indoor and outdoor display of plants and animals indigenous to the Sonoran desert, includes limestone cave galleries, aquarium, landscaped garden, demonstration garden, cacti, and a Saguaro exhibit covering 10 acres.

Daily 8:30-sunset; adults, under $6; children 13-17 half; 6-12 less; handicapped access; picnic sites; guided tours; (602) 883-1380.

11   **Tucson Botanical Gardens** ☆☆ HA-C-G-H-R
2150 N. Alvernon

This well-landscaped estate has been managed by the city since 1964; rose, iris, herb, and demonstration gardens are found here along with a southwestern traditional crop conservancy garden. There is a greenhouse with botanical displays and a library.

8-5 Mon-Fri; 10-2 Sat; 12-4 Sun; no admission charge; handicapped access; tours by reservation; self-guided tours; (602) 326-9255.

12   **Gene C. Reid Park** R
900 S. Randolph Way

A rose garden is part of this park.

Daily, dawn-dusk.

AJO

13   **Organ-Pipe Cactus National Monument** ☆☆ HA-C-SU-WF
142 mi. west of Tucson, via Rt. 86 and 85;
140 mi. south of Phoenix via U.S. 80 and Rt. 85; on U.S. Mexican border.

516 square miles of Sonoran desert which contain thousands of the rare Organ Pipe Cacti as well as 30 other species, including Senita, Whisker Cactus, many varieties of cholla, ocotillo, paloverde, mesquite, Mountain Mahogany, Arizona Rosewood, Jojoba, and an abundance of wildflowers in years of good spring rains. Catalogue of plants available.

Daily 8-5; winter 8-4:30; no admission charge; visitor center; guided tours in winter; handicapped access; (602) 387-6849.

YUMA

14 Century House Museum and Gardens   C-HH-SU
240 Madison Ave.; Giss Parkway off I-8.

This 1870 home and garden is now maintained by the Arizona Historical Society; there is an aviary and a garden of native plants and those available at the turn of the century.

10-4 Tues-Sat except legal holidays; 12-4 Sun, Oct-April; no admission charge; guided tours; (602) 783-8020.

ARKANSAS

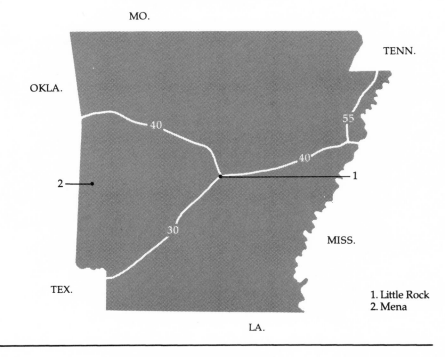

MO.

TENN.

OKLA.

40

55

40

2

1

30

MISS.

TEX.

1. Little Rock
2. Mena

LA.

LITTLE ROCK

1 Arkansas Territorial Restoration   BX-H-HA-HH
214 E. Third St.

A city block devoted to the restoration of thirteen, 19th century buildings with their surrounding gardens. There is a fine herb garden and a boxwood garden; annuals and perennials common in pre-Civil War period have been planted. A library is available.

9-5 Mon-Sat; 1-5 Sun; closed Jan 1, Easter, Thanksgiving, Christmas; adults under $3.00; over 64 under 17 nominal; free first Sun each month; handicapped access; (501) 371-2348.

MENA

2 Queen Wilhemina State Park

A garden of tulips was planted here; they are the remnants of a castle garden allegedly built for Queen Wilhemina. It was never completed. Thousands of tulips may be enjoyed high up on Rich Mt.

Daily, dawn-dusk.

16

CALIFORNIA

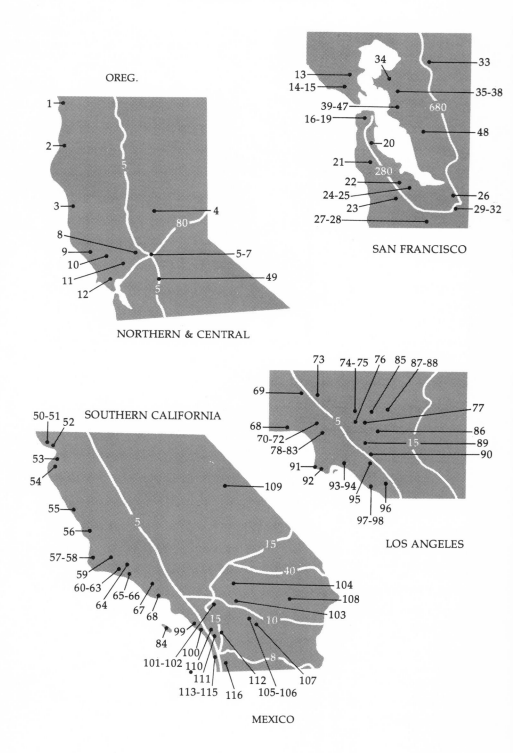

OREG.

1

2

3

4

5

8
9
10
11
12

5-7

49

5

NORTHERN & CENTRAL

34

13
14-15

33

35-38

680

39-47

16-19

48

20

21

280

22
24-25
23

26
29-32

27-28

SAN FRANCISCO

73 74-75 76 85 87-88

69

77

68
70-72
78-83

86

15

89
90

91
92

5

93-94

95

96

97-98

LOS ANGELES

50-51
52

SOUTHERN CALIFORNIA

53

54

109

55

56

5

57-58

59

60-63

15

65-66

64

67

40

68

104

108

99

15

103

84

10

100

101-102

110

111

8

112

107

113-115

116

105-106

MEXICO

1. Smith River
2. Arcata
3. Fort Bragg
4. Oroville
5-7. Sacramento
8. Davis
9. Plantation
10. Santa Rosa
11. Sonoma
12. Ross
13. San Rafael
14-15. Mill Valley
16-19. San Francisco
20. S. San Francisco
21. San Mateo
22. Redwood City
23. Woodside
24-25. Menlo Park
26. Santa Clara
27-28. Saratoga

29-32. San Jose
33. Martinez
34. El Cerrito
35-38. Berkeley
39-47. Oakland
48. Hayward
49. Stockton
50-51. Santa Cruz
52. Capitola
53. Pacific Grove
54. Monterey
55. San Simeon
56. San Luis Obispo
57-58. Lompoc
59. Solvang
60-63. Santa Barbara
64. Montecito
65-66. Carpenteria
67. Thousand Oaks
68. Malibu

69. Mission Hills
70-72. Beverly Hills
73. La Canada
74-75. Pasadena
76. San Marino
77. San Gabriel
78-83. Los Angeles
84. Santa Catalina
   Island
85. Arcadia
86. Whittier
87-88. Claremont
89. Fullerton
90. Anaheim
91. Palos Verdes
   Peninsula
92. Rancho Palos
   Verdes
93-94. Long Beach
95. Westminster

96. Irvine
97-98. Newport
   Beach
99. Laguna Beach
100. Laguna Niguel
101-102. Riverside
103. Cherry Valley
104. Lucerne Valley
105-106. Palm
   Springs
107. Palm Desert
108. Twentynine
   Palms
109. Furnace Creek
110. Vista
111. Encinitas
112. Escondido
113-115. San Diego
116. Citrus Heights

SMITH RIVER

1 Lily Fields

Large fields of Easter Lilies are grown here commercially, a magnificent sight in early spring.

ARCATA

2 Azalea Reserve   A
1 mi. east of U.S. 101; exit for RV. 200 from Rt. 299

This great natural plantation of azaleas is best viewed in June and July. Trails lead through the preserve.

Daily, sunrise-sunset.

FORT BRAGG

3 Mendocino Coast Botanical Gardens   ☆☆   A-FE-L-W
18220 Rt. 1, 2 mi. south

This 47-acre garden was established in 1961; trails lead to the ocean through a natural garden which contains 3,000 hybrid rhododendrons, azaleas, bulbs, heather, 30,000 dahlias, foxgloves, *Cistus*, gladiolas and many others; there is a 'rain forest' canyon, fuchsia walk, and woodlands with many varieties of ferns. Formal gardens and a lily pond are also part of this park.

Daily 8-dusk; adults, under $3; 12-18, over 64 half; (707) 964-4352.

OROVILLE

4 Chinese Temple Garden   ☆   A-J
1505 Broderick St.

A Chinese Temple built in 1861 in a courtyard garden planted with typical plants from China as ginkgo, persimmon, loquat, tallow trees, Chinese Flame trees, Dawn

Redwood, peach, bamboo, plum, pomelo, grapefruit, ginger, peony, rhododendron, Chinese Lily, and others. Many of them express Taoist ideas. This is a meditation garden.

Daily 10-4:30, Memorial Day-Labor Day; 10-4:30 Fri-Tues; 1-4:30 Wed, Thurs, rest of year; closed Dec 1-Jan 15; adults, under $3; under 12 free; (916) 533-1496.

SACRAMENTO

5   **C.M. Goethe Arboretum**   HA
California State University
6000 J St.

This 3-acre arboretum specializes in plants of central California along with a general collection of temperate ornamentals. Founded in 1959, the collection has grown steadily.

Daily; no admission charge; handicapped access; (916) 454-6494.

6   **State Capitol Gardens**   CA-HA
10th–12th and L and N Sts.

The capitol is surrounded by 33 acres of landscaped park with emphasis on camellias as well as some 5,000 other plants. There are fine seasonal displays of bulbs and annuals.

Daily; handicapped access; (916) 324-0333.

7   **Annual Camellia Show**   ☆   CA
Community Center
14th and L Sts.

A major camellia show has been held here for more than half a century in spring. More than 5,000 blossoms are displayed.

For dates and times call (916) 324-0333.

DAVIS

8   **University of California Arboretum (Davis)**   ☆☆   HA-S
University of California

This 100-acre arboretum lies along a 2-mile section of Putah Creek. It contains special collections of Californian, Australian, and Mediterranean native plants; there are fine specimens of eucalyptus, acacia, pine, and cypress. Also noteworthy is the Shields Oak Grove, the Weier Redwood Grove, the Storer Perennial Garden, and the Shields White Flower Garden. Emphasis has been placed upon drought-tolerant woody plants. There is a research station and a library.

Daily; no admission charge; handicapped access; docent-led tours most Sundays except during summer; (916) 752-2498.

PLANTATION

9   **Kruse Rhododendron State Reserve**   ☆   A
2 mi. west on Rt. 1.

A grand display of rhododendrons which is best seen during the blooming season in late May and early June. Some specimens are 30 ft high.

Daily, dawn-dusk.

SANTA ROSA

10   Luther Burbank Memorial Gardens and Home   ☆   C-CH-G-SU
204 Santa Rosa Ave.

Luther Burbank, the horticulturist, lived and worked here for 50 years; many of the 800 varieties of plants he introduced are displayed, including Spineless Cactus, Plum-cots (a cross between apricots and plums), agapanthus, canna, dahlia, and chrysanthemum. There are formal gardens as well as cacti and aloe gardens; lath house; greenhouse; library.

Daily 8-6; no admission charge except to house which has different hours; for tour information call (707) 576-5115.

SONOMA

11   Gen. Mariano Guadalupe Vallejo Home
Sonoma State Historic Park

A garden surrounds this 19th century home of an early northern California settler.

Daily 10-5; adults and children nominal; (707) 938-1578.

ROSS

12   Marin Art and Garden Center   ☆☆   A-C-O-S
Sir Frances Drake Blvd. and Laurel Grove Ave.

A 10-acre garden surrounds this center; there are numerous fine specimen trees including a 100-year-old magnolia, 45 species of sequoia, Dawn Redwood, Black Oak, and Japanese Maple. The wisteria walk, rhododendrons, and orchids are beautiful.

Daily 9-4; no admission charge; (415) 454-5597.

SAN RAFAEL

13   Marin County Civic Center   HA
North off U.S. 101

This complex of fairgrounds and theaters was Frank Lloyd Wright's last large project. It contains a water conservation garden with emphasis on drought-resistant plants.

8:30-4:30 Mon-Fri; closed holidays; handicapped access; (415) 499-6104.

MILL VALLEY

14   Edgewood Botanic Garden   A-S-WF
436 Edgewood Ave.

This botanical garden is in a beautiful location; large plantings of azaleas and rhododendrons remain along with wildflowers and good specimens of native trees and shrubs. The garden is, however, no longer properly maintained.

Daily, dawn-dusk.

15   Muir Woods National Monument   S
Rt. 1 and Panoramic Highway

This 550-acre national monument contains one of the most beautiful and accessible of the Redwood groves. There are many *Sequoia sempervirens* as well as 200 species of other plants; some are labelled.

Daily 8-sunset; no admission charge.

SAN FRANCISCO

16   Strybing Arboretum and Botanical Gardens   ☆☆☆☆   -A-B-C-G-HA-J-R-RG-S-SH-SU-WF
9th Ave. at Lincoln Way

Although this large metropolitan arboretum was established in 1935, its beginning goes back to the 19th century and John McLaren, a Scottish gardener who began to transform sand barrens into a park. 70 acres with more than 5,000 species flourish in various micro climates, so Alaska Cedars can be found with New Zealand Christmas trees and Himalayan Magnolias. Excellent collections of Malaysian Rhododendrons, Australian and New Zealand plants, echeveria, succulents, proteas, barberries, cotoneaster, crab apples, magnolias. Special gardens include Shakespeare, opera, Japanese stroll, Bible, rose, dwarf conifer, rock, native flora, Redwood, and a superb fragrance garden for the blind. Specimen trees include Campbell Magnolia, Mayden-tree, Rimu, Santa Lucia Fir; conservatory. There is a library. A large flower show is held each August.

8-4:30 Mon-Fri; 10-5 Sat, Sun, holidays; no admission charge; handicapped access; (415) 661-1316.

17   Japanese Tea Garden   ☆☆☆☆   A-J-L
Between Strybing Arboretum and de Young Museum

This 5-acre garden is one of the earliest Japanese gardens in the country as it was constructed in 1893. It is beautifully landscaped with walks, bridges, waterfall, streams, a large statue of Buddha, and a tea house. The fine selection of mature plants includes peaches, cherries, plums, and azaleas.

Daily 8-6:30; admission fee from 9-5; adults and children nominal; free 1st Wed of each month, Easter, Memorial Day, July 4, Labor Day, Thanksgiving, Christmas; (415) 661-1316.

18   Conservatory of Flowers   ☆   FE-HA-P
John F. Kennedy Drive
Golden Gate Park

This Victorian Conservatory contains a good collection of tropical plants. Continuous floral displays are maintained.

Daily 8-6:30; admission fee from 9-12 and 1-5; adults and children, nominal; free 1st Wed of each month. Easter, Memorial Day, 4th of July, Labor Day, Thanksgiving, Christmas; (415) 661-1316.

19   Japan Center   J
Post and Geary at Laguna and Filmore Sts.

A cultural and commercial center with a series of small Japanese gardens as well as many flowering plums and cherries.

Daily 9-5.

SOUTH SAN FRANCISCO

20   Acres of Orchids   ☆   G-O-R
1450 El Camino Real (U.S. 82)

A very large and continuously blooming display of orchids including *Cattleyas,* *Cymbidiums* and *Paphiopedilums* in 4 acres of greenhouses; there are also more than 80,000 rose bushes. The acreage is divided into an exhibit area and commercial area.

Daily 8-5 except Jan 1, Memorial Day, July 4, Labor Day, Thanksgiving, Christmas; tours; (415) 871-5655.

SAN MATEO

21   San Mateo Arboretum   ☆   HA-J-S
Central Park
Fifth Ave. and El Camino St.

A 16-acre arboretum which was established in 1974. It includes a fine Japanese garden done in the traditional manner. A good collection of California trees has been grown here. There are demonstration and test gardens for annuals.

Daily 9-9; Japanese Garden 9-4; no admission charge; handicapped access; (415) 342-1692.

REDWOOD CITY

22   Rose Gardens   R
Community Park

The rose gardens form part of a larger public park; a number of varieties are represented.

Daily, dawn-dusk.

WOODSIDE

23   Filoli   ☆☆☆☆   CA-L-R-T
Canada Rd.

This 654-acre estate contains 17 acres of landscaped gardens; some are most unusual such as formal knot garden, Chartres Cathedral window garden, and Dutch garden. There are unusually fine collections of camellias and roses.

Tours 10 and 1 Tues-Sat; closed mid-Nov to mid-Feb; adults, under $6; no children under 12 admitted; partial handicapped access; (415) 364-2880.

MENLO PARK

24   Allied Arts Guild
Cambridge Ave. off Rt. 82.

An Old World neighborhood setting for artists which contains courtyard gardens with numerous fountains.

9:30-5 Mon-Sat; no admission charge; partial handicapped access.

25   Sunset Gardens and Publishing House   ☆   HD
Middlefield and Willow Roads

A fine ranch-style building surrounded by well known experimental gardens. These are practical demonstration gardens for the home owner which primarily use local flora.

Daily 9-5; tours from 10 to 3; (415) 321-3600.

SANTA CLARA

26 Mission Santa Clara de Asis R-S
University of Santa Clara

Although the mission buildings have been rebuilt, portions of the original garden survive with some mature specimens. Best time for blooms is April-May. There is a small rose garden.

Daily 6:30-9:30 during school year; shorter summer hours; no admission charge; (408) 984-4023.

SARATOGA

27 Hakone Japanese Garden ☆ CA-J
21000 Big Basin Way

This Japanese Garden with many plants and artifacts was taken from the Japanese Exhibit of 1915 in San Francisco. There is a fine camellia collection as well as some other special plant collections.

10-5 Mon-Fri; 11-5 Sat-Sun; closed holidays; no admission charge; partial handicapped access; (408) 253-2506.

28 Villa Montalvo Center for the Arts S
Rt. 17, 4 mi. northwest on Rt. 9 to Montalvo Rd.

This 1911 Mediterranean-style villa is surrounded by a 175-acre arboretum crossed by trails; there are many mature specimens. A formal garden with statuary, shrubs, beds of annuals, and perennials lies on the grounds.

Daily 9-5; different hours for galleries; no admission charge; partial handicapped access; (408) 867-3421.

SAN JOSE

29 Japanese Friendship Tea Garden J
Kelley Park
1300 Senter Rd.

This garden contains some elements similar to the Kor-a-kuen Garden in Kyoto, Japan.

10-dusk Tues-Sun; no admission charge; partial handicapped access; (408) 286-3626.

30 Municipal Rose Garden HA-R
Naglee Ave. between Gardens Dr. and Dana Ave.

7,500 rose bushes have been planted in a 5½-acre garden with best viewing time in May-June. More than 150 varieties are to be found here.

Daily 10-8:30, April 26-Oct 25; 10-4:30 rest of year; no admission charge; handicapped access; (408) 277-5181.

31 Overfelt Botanical Gardens WF
Park Drive and McKee Rd.

A 37-acre garden planted with a wide variety of trees and shrubs as well as annuals, perennials, and wildflowers. There is a massive Chinese gate in an Oriental section.

Daily, dawn-dusk; (408) 259-5477.

32   Rosicrucian Egyptian Museum   P-W
Park and Naglee Aves.

This museum of Near Eastern art stands in a garden of palms and papyrus reminiscent of Egypt.

9-4:30 Tues-Fri; 12-4:30 Sat-Mon; closed Jan 1, Aug 2, Thanksgiving, Christmas; no admission charge; (408) 287-9171.

MARTINEZ

33   John Muir National Historic Site   HH-F
Alhambra Ave. and Rt. 4.

The 1882 home of the great naturalist, John Muir, has been restored. The grounds with their orchards and gardens are being restored.

Daily 8:30-4:30; closed Jan 1, Thanksgiving, Christmas; adults nominal; under 16 and over 61 free; special transportation up the steep hill available on request; (415) 228-8860.

EL CERRITO

34   Design Garden
944 Arlington Ave.

This private garden of Sundar S. Shadi contains 5 areas planted to represent Persian rug designs. Colorful annuals are used.

Daily 9-5; viewed from the street only.

BERKELEY

35   Berkeley Botanical Garden   ☆☆☆☆   A-C-FE-G-O-SU
University of California
Centennial Drive

This 32-acre garden was established in 1895 and contains more than 12,000 species, many of them mature. It is among the very best university botanical gardens in the country. Plants are arranged according to regions of origin within special gardens. There are collections of Indian plants rhododendrons, cacti, and succulents especially from South America, ferns, orchids; greenhouses; library.

Daily 9-5; some tours; closed Christmas; no admission charge; (415) 642-3343.

36   Regional Parks Botanical Garden   ☆☆   C-S-WF
Tilden Regional Park

7 acres of this large regional park have been devoted to an arboretum with special emphasis on California plants with more than 1,500 species. Special sections include dune, sea bluff, mountain meadow, alpine gardens. Fine specimens of Santa Cruz Ironwood, Santa Lucia Fir, California Nutmeg, Giant Sequoia, Redwood, and wildflowers. The plantings are arranged by regions so that one can take a walk from Oregon to the Mexican border; the Channel Islands are included.

10-6 April-Sept; 10-5 Oct-March except Thanksgiving, Christmas, New Year; no admission charge; (415) 841-8732.

37   Berkeley Municipal Rose Garden   ☆   L-R
Euclid Ave. and Bayview Place

Beautifully landscaped with an arbor view of the bay, this garden displays 4,000 rose bushes representing numerous varieties.

Daily, dawn-dusk.

38   Blake Garden   ☆☆   HA-L-S
70 Rincon Rd.
Kensington

A 10-acre estate garden founded in 1924 is well designed with numerous rare plants. This garden is part of the University of California Department of Landscape Architecture. It serves as an outdoor laboratory for plant identification and all phases of garden design. Some fine specimen trees stand on the grounds. There is a library.

Weekdays 8-4:30; no admission charge; handicapped access; (415) 524-2449.

OAKLAND

39   William Joseph McInnes Botanic Garden and the Campus Arboretum of Mills College   ☆   L-S
Seminary Ave. and McArthur Blvd.

A 120-acre arboretum established in 1948 along with a 2½-acre botanical garden. It is well landscaped with special emphasis on California native plants and South African bulbs; special collections include cypresses, *Ceanothus, Corylus* and *Arctosaphylos*. There is a library with a rare book collection.

8-4 weekdays, fall and spring semesters only; no admission charge; (415) 430-2158.

40   Lakeside Park   ☆   P
Park View Terrace

This 122-acre park contains an unusual palm garden with more than 67 species, dedicated in the summer of 1964. There are a series of trial and show gardens along with general recreational facilities.

Daily, dawn-dusk.

41   Lakeside Park Garden Center   ☆☆   .-CA-CH-H-J-L
666 Belleview Ave.

This fine series of gardens includes a fragrance garden marked with braille, a new herb garden, and a traditional Japanese garden with a temple and tori, the gift of the city of Fukuoko. There are plantings of fuchsias, dahlias, tuberous begonias, camellias, chrysanthemums as well as 80 varieties of trees and shrubs.

Daily 10-4:30; 10-3 winter; closed all major holidays; no admission charge; partial handicapped access; (415) 273-3208.

42   Regillus Apartment   G
240 Lakeside Drive

These apartments and the adjoining building have been erected on the former Schilling Estate which had a fabulous 19th century garden. Little of the original remains, but there are some pleasant plantings as well as greenhouses.

Weekdays 10-4.

43   Oakland Museum   W
10th and Oak Sts.

These gardens, in the form of terraces, are planted with many varieties of shrubs and trees including Liquidambar, White Alder, and Cork Oaks. There is a pond with lilies and papyrus.

10-5 Wed-Sat; 12-7 Sun; closed legal holidays; no admission charge; (415) 834-2413 or 273-3401.

44 Morcom Amphitheater of Roses L-R
Jean St. 1 block from Grand Ave.

400 varieties of roses are planted on 8 acres of well-landscaped gardens with reflecting pools. There are more than 8,000 bushes along with many trees and shrubs.

Daily 7-3:30; no admission charge; (415) 658-0731.

45 Kaiser Center ☆ HA
Lakeside Drive

A spectacular 3½-acre garden is located on the top of this 28-story building. The plantings are varied and the view excellent.

9-9 Mon-Sat; closed holidays; handicapped access; (415) 271-3300.

46 Mormon Temple Garden
4780 Lincoln Ave.

The gardens offer a fine view of the bay; a good selection of plants is represented in this formal garden.

Daily 9-9; no admission charge; (415) 531-1475.

47 Dunsmuir House HH-S
Hellman Park
2960 Peralta Oaks Ct.

This Colonial Revival Mansion has been restored and the garden is being rebuilt. The original garden contained a grotto, waterfall, orchards, as well as numerous exotic species. Many of the old trees remain and extensive other plantings are being carried out.

Sundays 12-4, Easter through Sept 12; no admission charge; (415) 562-7588.

HAYWARD

48 Japanese Garden J
22372 N. 3rd Ave.; off Crescent Ave.

A garden landscaped in the traditional Japanese manner, but utilizing California native plants; there is a tea house and a small lake. It is best seen in spring during cherry blossom time.

Daily 10-4; no admission charge; (415) 881-6715.

STOCKTON

49 Micke Grove Park and Zoo ☆☆ A-CA-J-R-S
11793 N. Micke Grove Rd.

This park with its giant oaks contains a camellia garden, an azalea garden, a rose garden, and a Japanese garden. The latter was designed by Nagao Sakurai of the Imperial Garden in Tokyo.

8-dusk; admission charge per vehicle, under $6; (209) 944-2444.

SANTA CRUZ

50 Arboretum
University of California, Santa Cruz

This site contains Australian gardens which feature 1,400 ornamental taxa. The South African gardens display 100 ornamental species of proteas. New Zealand and California native gardens are being developed. There are collections of rare plant material of scientific interest. Best visited from January through April.

Weekdays 9-4; 2-4 Wed, Sat, Sun, tours and plant sales; (408) 429-2301.

51 Antonelli Brothers Begonia Garden   G
2545 Capitola Rd.

This tuberous begonia nursery was established in 1935 and followed others in the area. Some new varieties have been developed here. There are large, colorful display beds.

Daily 9-5; closed Jan 1, Easter, Thanksgiving, Christmas; (408) 475-5222.

CAPITOLA

52 Shaffer's Tropical Gardens   G-O
1220 41st Ave.

An unusual commercial collection of orchids, including *Phalaenopsis* and *Cymbidiums*; best time to visit is from December to July.

9-5 Mon-Sat; 11-5 Sun; (408) 475-3100.

PACIFIC GROVE

53 Pacific Grove Museum of Natural History
165 Forest Ave.

This small garden founded in 1881 emphasizes plants of the Monterey Peninsula; a number of endangered species may be found here.

10-5 Tues-Sun; no admission charge; partial handicapped access; (408) 372-4212.

MONTEREY

54 Casa Amesti
Monterey History of Art Association
516 Polk St.

A formal Italian landscaped garden accompanies this house.

2-4 Sat-Sun; adults, under $3; partial handicapped access; (408) 372-2608.

SAN SIMEON

55 Hearst San Simeon State Historical Monument   ☆☆☆☆   L-R-S-SU
off Rt. 1.

85 acres of garden and arboretum with 5 acres of beautiful formal gardens surround this spectacular mountain-top house. Numerous pools, fountains, terraces, statues; about 300 varieties of annuals, perennials, and tropical plants used. There is a rose garden with 50 kinds as well as a mile-long pergola of fruit trees. Fine specimens of

Cedar of Lebanon, Italian Cypress, Redwood, Live Oak, eucalyptus, acacia may be found here.

8-4 June 1-Aug 31; 8-3:30 rest of year; closed Jan 1; adults, under $9; 6-12 half; advance reservations through Ticketron advised; (805) 927-4621.

SAN LUIS OBISPO

56 Mission San Luis Obispo de Tolosa
Chorro and Monterey Sts.

Known as the 'Prince of Missions', it contains a small garden.

Daily 9-5, June 1-Labor Day; 9-4 rest of year; closed Jan 1, Thanksgiving, Christmas; admission for adults and families nominal; (805) 543-9638.

LOMPOC

57 Lompoc Area   ☆
The surrounding area is responsible for half the world's supply of flower seeds. Thousands of acres of sweet peas, larkspur, petunias, asters, marigolds, and others bloom throughout the summer. The height of the season is marked by a festival in June. Three large seed companies are located here.

58 La Purisima Mission State Historic Park
Purisima Rd.

This mission and its garden have been restored to their 1820's character. It is set in a protective park area.

Daily 9-6, summer; 9-5 Oct-April; (805) 733-3713.

SOLVANG

59 Mission Santa Innes
1760 Mission Drive

The mission building has been restored after several earthquakes. The courtyard gardens are green and restful.

9-5 Mon-Sat; 12-5 Sun, holidays; winter closes at 4:30; closed Jan 1, Thanksgiving, Christmas; adults nominal; under 16 free; (805) 688-4815.

SANTA BARBARA

60 Santa Barbara Botanic Garden   ☆☆   S-WF
1212 Mission Canyon Rd.

A 56-acre garden beautifully located in the foothills of the Santa Ynez Mountains. Established in 1926 it contains over 1,000 types of plants; sections devoted to various California areas with informal plantings. There are good collections of California Poppies, Channel Island plants, and wildflowers. Fine specimens of cypress, wild lilacs, Chaparral plants, Coast Live Oak, and Douglas Fir. There is a library.

Daily 8-dusk; no admission charge; handicapped access; (805) 682-4726.

61 Alice Keck Park Memorial Garden
Micheltorena and Santa Barbara Sts.

This botanical garden covers 4½ acres and features more than 300 varieties of plants.

It is very well-landscaped with attractive flower beds, shrubs and trees.

Daily 24 hrs.

62 Alameda Park
Anacapa, Garden, Sola and Micheltoerna Sts.

A fine park with flower beds containing 300 varieties of plants.

Daily, dawn-dusk.

63 County Courthouse
1120- Anacapa St.

A grand Spanish-Moorish building with sunken gardens.

Daily; tours; (805) 966-1611.

MONTECITO

64 Lotusland   C-L-SU

A private estate of the opera star, Ganna Walska, contains large plantings of cacti, cycads, and aloes as well as formal gardens.

Plans to open to the public soon.

CARPINTERIA

65 Abbey Garden   C-G-SU
4620 Carpinteria Ave.

A very large cacti and succulent nursery with many unusual plants. This is one of a very large number of greenhouses in the area.

Daily 9-5; (805) 684-5112.

66 Armacost and Royston Orchid Farm   G-O
3376 Foothill Rd.

Excellent collection of orchids are displayed by this commercial grower. This area produces the largest number of *Cymbidiums* in the United States.

Daily 9-5; (805) 684-5448

THOUSAND OAKS

67 Gregor Mendel Botanic Foundation   HA

A 53-acre reservation with large plantings of native trees, shrubs, and flowers.

By reservation only; no admission charge; handicapped access; (805) 496-5750

MALIBU

68 J. Paul Getty Museum   ☆☆   H-S
17985 Pacific Coast Highway

A museum housed in the replica of a Roman villa in 12 acres of gardens; the formal gardens have a good collection of Mediterranean plants. There is a fine herb garden.

10-5 weekdays, summer; 10-5 Tues-Sat, winter; no admission charge; parking reservations required; partial handicapped access; (213) 459-2306.

MISSION HILLS

69 Mission San Fernando Rey de España
15151 San Fernando Mission Blvd.
Between I-405 and I-5.

This old mission green garden is well preserved and contains trees, shrubs, and flowers typical of other mission gardens.

9-5 Mon-Sat; 10-5 Sun, holidays; closed Jan 1, Thanksgiving, Christmas; adults and children nominal; (818) 361-0186.

BEVERLY HILLS

70 Greystone Park   L
905 Loma Vista Drive

This park includes 19 well-landscaped acres of formal gardens, ponds, and forest, which surround a former mansion. The plantings have been simplified for easy maintenance.

Daily 10-6 summer; 10-5 rest of year; closed holidays; no admission charge; (213) 550-4864.

71 The Gardens   C-R
Santa Monica Blvd.

A series of small parks along the boulevard within Beverly Hills provides various plant displays. There is a cacti park, a rose park, and others.

Daily, dawn-dusk.

72 Robinson Gardens Foundation   ☆☆☆☆   P-R-S
1008 Elden Way

This 6-acre estate of Virginia Dryden Robinson has recently been opened to the public. There are lush terrace gardens with subtropical plants, formal gardens, a palm grove, and a rose garden. The palm collection is very large; there are fine specimen trees.

10-3 Tues-Fri; by reservation only; (213) 446-8251 ext 35.

LA CANADA

73 Descanso Gardens   ☆☆☆☆   A-BO-CA-HA-J-O-R-S

Established in 1937 by Manchester Boddy for his growing camellia collection, this garden now has the largest camellia collection in the world with more than 100,000 plants representing 600 varieties and cultivars. Spectacular display of blooms may be seen in spring. The historic rose garden traces the history of the rose with 500 varieties. There is a Japanese garden, Chinese courtyard garden, large collections of lilacs, irises, lilies, rhododendrons, azaleas, *Cymbidiums*, fuchsias, begonias, daffodils, and Bonsai. Demonstration and test gardens are maintained as is an All-American rose selection.

Daily 9-4:30; closed Christmas; adults, under $3; 5-17, senior citizens half; under 18 must be accompanied by an adult; guided tram tours; handicapped access; (213) 790-5571.

PASADENA

74 Pacific Art Museum J
46 N. Los Robles Ave.

This museum is designed like a Chinese treasure house with a meditation garden in its courtyard.

12-5 Wed-Sun; closed holidays; adults, under $3; under 12 free; free to everyone on third Sat of each month; (213) 449-4100.

75 Earthside Nature Center
3160 E. Del Mar Blvd. Madre Exit off 210 Freeway.

Emphasis has been placed on California native plants with 453 species represented.

Weekdays 10-4; some weekends; adults, under $3; children half; (213) 796-6120.

SAN MARINO

76 Huntington Botanical Gardens ☆☆☆☆   A-C-CA-H-HA-J-R-P-S-SH-SU-W
1151 Oxford Rd.

The grand library and art museum of this estate are surrounded by 207 acres of gardens established in 1929. The magnificent formal and botanical gardens are among the best in the western world. They contain more than 9,000 types of plants. 10 acres of cacti and succulents are the best in the nation with 2,000 species with 25,000 plants; 1,500 camellia cultivars . Excellent collection of cycads, palms, Australian plants, conifers. Special gardens include a rose, Japanese, Shakespeare, herb, and desert garden. Fine specimen of Deodar Cedars, Queensland Kauri, Araucarias. Library; rare books.

11-4:30 Tues-Sun; reservations by mail needed for Sun; closed holidays; tours; no admission charge; handicapped access; (213) 449-3901.

Huntington Botanical Gardens

SAN GABRIEL

77 Fred A. Stewart Inc. G-O
1212 East Las Tunas

One of the largest orchid nurseries in the country; it introduces a number of new varieties each year. There are also fields of cut flowers. Flowers in bloom each month. The best orchid blooms may be seen from Feb to May.

8-5 Mon-Sat; 12-5 Sun; no admission charge; (213) 285-7195.

LOS ANGELES

78 Exposition Park Rose Garden ☆ R
South Figueroa St.

A 7-acre sunken rose garden lies in this civic center park composed of a number of museums. More than 16,000 bushes of 190 varieties have been planted.

Daily, dawn-dusk.

79 Mildred E Mathias Botanical Garden ☆☆ C-J-P-S-SU
University of California at Los Angeles Botanical Garden
Hilgard and Le Conte Aves.

This garden established in 1920 presents 8 acres with more than 3,500 different species. There are good collections of California plants, desert plants, palms, sub-tropicals, eucalyptus, acacias, aloes, gymnosperms, South and Central American *Melastomatacea* and *Ericaceae*. The nearby Japanese Garden is open only by appointment.

8-5 weekdays; 8-4 Sat, Sun; closed University holidays; no admission charge; partial handicapped access; (213) 825-4321.

80 Lawry's California Center ☆
568 San Fernando Rd.

This manufacturing center for Lawry's Foods stands in the midst of a lovely garden which has been planted with a wide variety of sub-tropical plants.

10-5 Mon-Sat; 11-9 Sun; no admission charge; (213) 225-2491.

81 Echo Park Lotus Garden ☆ W
Glendale Blvd. and Park Ave.

This unusual collection of lotus plants fills a large part of the lake. Plants bloom in June and July; seed pods dry in September.

Daily, dawn-dusk; no admission charge.

82 Fuchsia Land
4629 Centinela Ave.

A nursery which specializes in fuchsia and other exotic plants; owners go plant hunting in South America from November to February.

Weekdays 10-4:30; closed Nov 1-Feb 1; (213) 822-8900.

83 Elysian Park Arboretum S
Elysian Park
N. Broadway and Academy Rd.

This was the first botanical garden in Los Angeles. Some good old specimen trees may be seen here.

Daily, dawn-dusk.

SANTA CATALINA ISLAND

84 **Wrigley Memorial Botanical Garden**
2 mi. on Avalon Canyon Rd.
Tram from Island Plaza in Avalon

This small botanical garden concentrates upon the local flora; the collection is well displayed.

Daily 8-5; adults nominal; under 12 free; (213) 510-2288.

ARCADIA

85 **Los Angeles State and County Arboretum** ☆☆☆☆ B-C-G-H-HA-HD-P-O-R-S
W-301 N. Baldwin Ave.

This arboretum stands on the grounds of an old mission in the foothills of the San Gabriel Mountains. It was established in 1948 on 127 acres and now contains more than 4,500 different kinds of plants. 200 Indian peacocks descendent from those introduced in 1880 roam the grounds. Plants are grouped in geographical areas with Australian, Mediterranean, Asian, and African sections. Special collections of eucalyptus, palm, cassia, bottle-brush, holly, magnolia, and juniper are found here. There are good specimens of Mesa Oak, Coast Live Oak, Blue Gum, eucalyptus. The arboretum contains Biblical, rose, annual, perennial, demonstration, and ground cover gardens. Greenhouses display fine orchid and begonia collections. There is a new plant introduction site and a library.

Daily 9-4:30; closed Christmas; adults, under $3; senior citizens, children 5-17 half; under 17 must be accompanied by an adult; tram tours; handicapped access; (213) 446-8251.

WHITTIER

86 **Rose Hills Memorial Park** ☆☆ J-R
3900 S. Workman Rd.

A 3½-acre rose garden with thousands of bushes has been planted at the entrance of this large cemetery. There are more than 750 varieties of roses and new introductions are made each year. The park also contains a Japanese garden in the section of Oriental graves.

Daily 8-dusk; no admission charge.

CLAREMONT

87 **Rancho Santa Anna Botanic Garden** ☆☆ C-S-SU-WF
1500 N. College Ave.

This 100-acre garden which was founded in 1927 lies in the foothills; emphasis has been placed upon native California and desert plants with more than 1,300 species. There is a good collection of wildflowers as well as fine yuccas, Mariposa Lilies, Monkey Flowers, cacti, and cedars. There is a library.

Daily 8-6 Feb-June; 8-5 rest of year; closed Jan 1, July 4, Thanksgiving, Christmas; no admission charge; (714) 626-3922.

88 Claremont Tree Walks   S
Claremont Colleges

An extensive collection of trees is found on the campus of 7 colleges and nearby portions of the city. A guide map may be obtained at the colleges or at the Rancho Santa Anna Botanic Garden.

FULLERTON

89 Fullerton Arboretum   ☆   C-F-H-HD-P-SU-W
California State University

This 25-acre university arboretum was established in 1979; it has developed a number of special collections and groups them according to moisture requirements. There is a subtropical fruit grove, a carnivorous plant bog, a palm garden, a cactus and succulent garden, a herb garden, a conifer area, a historic area, and a series of community gardens.

Daily 8-dusk; closed Jan 1 and Christmas; no admission charge; tours; (714) 773-2071.

ANAHEIM

90 Disneyland   ☆☆   C-P-SU-T
1313 Harbor Blvd.

The theme park and the hotel areas are landscaped with a wide variety of tropical and sub-tropical plants. There are large garden areas with palms, cacti, succulents, spectacular water falls, and lakes. The grouping of plants is often unusual. Nearby is a motel which is surrounded by topiary animals.

9-midnight Sun-Fri; 9-1 a.m., mid-June to Labor Day; hours vary remainder of year; adults, under $15; 12-17 three-quarters; 3-11 two-thirds; horticultural tours by appointment; (714) 999-4565.

PALOS VERDES PENINSULA

91 South Coast Botanic Garden   ☆☆   C-HA-HD-R-S
26300 Crenshaw Blvd.

This landfill area of 87 acres was turned into a garden in 1960 with 2,100 different species. Emphasis has been placed upon native California species including cassias and other legumes, as well as Mediterranean and coastal plants. There are large collections of roses, myrtles, proteas, pines, and flowering fruit trees. The youth practice gardens are excellent. The test gardens deal with soil erosion and new introductions. The nature of the area has caused problems of land shifting and occasional odors.

Daily 9-4:30; closed Christmas; adults, under $3; 6-17 and students nominal; tram tours; handicapped access; (213) 772-5813.

RANCHO PALOS VERDES

92 Wayfarers Chapel
5755 Palos Verdes Drive South

The gardens surround the redwood, glass, and stone chapel designed by Frank Lloyd Wright. They overlook the ocean and feature collections of roses and orchids.

Daily 9-5; no admission charge; (213) 377-1650.

LONG BEACH

93 **Rancho Los Alamitos** ☆☆ C-HA-HH-R-SU
Historic Site Museum
6400 Bixby Rd.

A fine home and garden built in 1806 during the Spanish Colonial period. 5 acres of gardens include a courtyard of succulents, a cactus garden, and a fountain which reflects the Spanish-Moorish period. The Friendship Garden, formal terrace, arbor, rose garden, and native California garden are from later periods.

1-5 Wed-Sun; tours are given; closed all holidays; admission charged; handicapped access; (213) 431-2511.

94 **Rancho los Cerritos**
4600 Virginia Rd.

This 2-story Spanish-colonial adobe house is surrounded by gardens which were begun in 1850 and may have been the first formal gardens in California. Many of the old trees survive in the restored Victorian gardens.

1-5 Wed-Sun; no admission charge; (213) 424-9423.

WESTMINSTER

95 **Rose Garden** R
Civic Center
8200 Westminster Ave.

A rose garden with more than 75 varieties has been planted in formal beds around the civic center.

Daily, dawn-dusk.

IRVINE

96 **University of California at Irvine Arboretum** ☆ HA-SU
North Campus
Jamboree Blvd. between Birch and Campus Rd.

This university arboretum was established on 10 acres in 1965. There are special sections of narcissus, gladiola, aloe, haworthia, and African Cormous.

7:30-4 weekdays; no admission charge; handicapped access; (714) 833-5833.

NEWPORT BEACH

97 **Sherman Library and Gardens** ☆☆☆ C-HA-L-R-SU
2647 E. Coast Highway

This beautiful garden established on 2 acres in 1958 emphasizes tropical and sub-tropical plants; there are also fine collections of succulents and cacti. There is a rose garden, a tea garden, as well as several pools and fountains. The entire garden is well landscaped. There is a library.

Daily 10:30-4; closed Jan 1, Thanksgiving, Christmas; adults, under $3; 12-16 nominal; under 12 free; tours; handicapped access; (714) 673-2261.

98   Rogers Gardens   ☆   R
2301 San Joaquin Hill Rd.

A large nursery with an exceptionally fine display area stands on 7½ acres. Plants have been placed in a terrace setting. There is a Victorian garden, a rose garden, a perennial garden, along with other areas.

Weekdays 10-4; tours; (714) 640-5800.

LAGUNA BEACH

99   Hortense Miller Garden   ☆   S
This garden contains a very large range of plants; the 2½ acres display more than 1,200 species from temperate to sub-tropical. There are fine eucalyptus, *Tollons*, Monkey Flowers, *Pentstemons* and *Euphorbias*.

Tues-Sat by appointment; no admission charge; partial handicapped access; (714) 497-3311.

LAGUNA NIGUEL

100   Niguel Botanical Preserve
29751 Crown Valley Parkway

A 19-acre botanical preserve is being created; planting was begun recently. It forms part of a larger park.

Daily 9-5; no admission charge.

RIVERSIDE

101   University of California at Riverside Botanic Gardens   ☆☆   C-H-L-S-SU
Main Campus

This is another in the series of excellent university botanic gardens. It was established in 1963 on 37 acres. There are many Australian species with emphasis on desert and dry land plants. Sections deal with perennial grasses, cacti, and succulents. There is a herb garden and a California native garden. Good specimens of cypress, ficus, cycad, pine, and iris may be found here.

Daily 8-5; closed Jan 1, July 4, Thanksgiving, Christmas; no admission charge; partial handicapped access; (714) 787-4650.

102   Jurupa Mountains Cultural Center
7621 Highway 60.

This nature center and museum has a small botanical garden. There is also a sunken garden.

10-4:30 Tues-Sat; closed holidays; adults, under $6; children half; (714) 685-5818.

CHERRY VALLEY

103   Edward-Dean Museum of Decorative Art   T
9401 Oak Glen Rd.

A small courtyard garden with a pool and topiary hedges is part of this museum.

1-4:30 Tues-Fri; 10-4:30 Sat, Sun; closed legal holidays; adults nominal; (714) 845-2626.

LUCERNE VALLEY

104 Tegelberg Cactus Gardens ☆   C
South Rock Camp Rd.

This is one of the largest and best cacti nurseries in the United States. The displays are very well arranged.

Daily 9-5.

PALM SPRINGS

105 Moorten Botanical Garden ☆☆   C-HA-S-SU
1701 S. Palm Canyon Drive

More than 2,000 shrubs, trees, and desert plants are displayed in this 3-acre garden established in 1936. Emphasis has been placed on desert plants with fine specimens of Joshua trees and Saguaro cacti. The plants are arranged geographically.

Daily 9-5; adults, under $3; 7-17 half; handicapped access; (714) 327-6555.

106 Palm Canyon ☆   P
Agua Indian Reservation

Washington Palms, some 2,000 years old line the canyon. There are more than 3,000 trees. Trails lead through the area.

Daily 9-4, Oct 1-May 31; adults, under $3; 6-11 nominal; (714) 325-2086.

PALM DESERT

107 Living Desert Reserve   C-HA-SU
47900 Portola Ave.; 2 mi. south of Rt. 111

These 1,200 acres are intended to preserve the desert flora and fauna; 18 acres are developed with 6 mi. of trails. There is an aviary.

Daily 9-5; adults, under $3; 7-17 half when with an adult; handicapped access;(714) 346-5694.

TWENTYNINE PALMS

108 Joshua Tree National Monument ☆☆   S

Joshua trees from 10 to 40 feet in height as well as much other desert vegetation may be viewed.

Daily 8-5 mid-Oct to Memorial Day; no admission charge; camping; (714) 765-9921.

FURNACE CREEK

109 Furnace Creek Inn ☆   P
Death Valley National Monument

A beautiful oasis in the desert with palm-shaded terraced gardens overlooking Death Valley has been created around this hotel. Tropical plants, annuals, and a small stream are found here.

Daily, dawn-dusk; (619) 786-2345.

VISTA

110 Grisby Cactus Gardens ☆ C-G-S-SU
2326 Bella Vista Dr.

This nursery has a large display garden on its 4 acres of grounds. Aside from cacti and succulents, good specimens of unusual trees may be found here. There are 13 greenhouses.

8-4 Thurs, Fri, Sat; closed Sun-Wed; no admission charge; (619) 727-1323.

ENCINITAS

111 Quail Botanical Gardens ☆☆☆ A-BR-C-L-S-SU-WF
230 Quail Garden Dr.

1,000 varieties of plants divided into geographic categories are grown on this 26-acre estate. Emphasis has been placed on California and subtropical flowering plants. There are good collections of puyas, wildflowers, bromeliads, azaleas, acacias, bamboos, cacti, and succulents. There is a library.

Daily 9-6 summer; 8-5 rest of year; no admission charge; partial handicapped access.

ESCONDIDO

112 San Diego Wild Animal Park ☆☆ .-C-HA-P-S-SU
I-15 south to Via Rancho Parkway.

This 1,800-acre preserve is the home of 3,600 animals who live in natural settings which duplicate those of their African and Asian homelands. A wide variety of plants has been used with great care. A 10-acre Australian rain forest is a recent addition. A trail for the blind and handicapped has been created.

9-9 mid-June to Labor Day; 9-5 March to mid-June and Labor Day to Oct 9; 9-4 Nov-Feb; adults, under $9; 3-15 two-thirds; monorail through park; (619) 234-6541.

SAN DIEGO

113 Balboa Park ☆☆☆☆ C-CA-FE-G-HA-P-R-SU-W
Laurel St. and 6th Ave.

A 1,200-acre park and cultural center which began as the site of the California International Exhibit of 1915-16; the fine buildings of Spanish-Moorish architecture are surrounded by appropriate gardens: Casa del Rey Moro Garden, Alcazar Garden, English garden, rose garden. There is a lily pond, reflecting pools with lotus and aquatic plants, desert garden, and a camellia canyon. Many informal plantings are carried out throughout the park. The Botanical Building is constructed of lath and glass. It contains 500 cultivars including ferns and shade-loving tropical plants; seasonal exhibits are featured.

Daily, sunrise-sunset; Botanical Building 10-4:30 Sat-Thurs; closed holidays; no admission; handicapped access.

114 San Diego Zoo ☆☆☆☆ C-FE-HA-O-P-S-SU
Balboa Park

Among the largest zoos in the country with 5,000 animals exhibited over 128 acres. Special attention has been given to the flora which feature an extraordinary collection of rare trees and shrubs. 3,500 species represented; special collections of orchids, cycads, ferns, aloes, agaves, euphorbia, *Zingiber*, ficus, *Araceae*, and palms.

Daily 9-6 July 1 to Labor Day; 9-5 Labor Day to Oct 31 and March 1 to June 30; 9-4 rest of year; adults, under $6; 3-15 half; Skyfari; bus tours; handicapped access; (619) 231-1515.

115 Sea World HA-P
Mission Bay Park

This 100-acre marine life center and oceanarium uses 115 species of unusual plants including Natal Plum hedges, Cajeput trees, and palms. Pleasant beds of annuals.

Daily 9-dusk; adults, under $12; 3-11 two-thirds; handicapped access; (619) 224-3526.

CITRUS HEIGHTS

116 Rush Botanical Garden C-F-H-R-RG-SU
7801 Auburn Ave.

This garden, begun in 1978, is established on 2 acres with plantings divided into the areas of the five continents. There is also a miniature rose garden, herb garden, a cactus and succulent garden, a rock garden, a California native flower garden, and a dwarf fruit orchard.

By appointment only; (619) 725-1585.

COLORADO

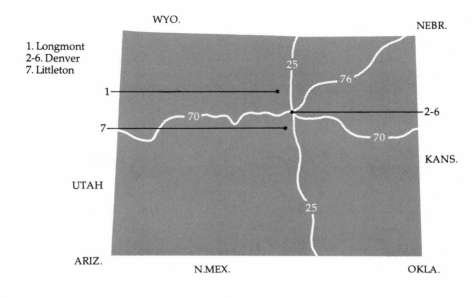

1. Longmont
2-6. Denver
7. Littleton

WYO.

NEBR.

N.MEX.

KANS.

UTAH

ARIZ.

OKLA.

LONGMONT

1 Memorial Rose Gardens R
Roosevelt Park

A rose garden with many varieties is part of this park.

Daily, dawn-dusk.

DENVER

2 City Park HA
17th and 23rd Sts. to York St. and Colorado Blvd
Entrance on Elizabeth St.

A large city park which contains gardens, pools, fountains, as well as special plantings of native trees and shrubs.

Daily; handicapped access; picnic area.

3 York Street Gardens ☆☆☆ B-BR-G-H-HA-HD-J-O-P-R-RG
Denver Botanic Garden
1005 York St.

Established in 1951, this botanic garden has steadily expanded and now has developed areas in four locations. Each of them is discussed separately here. The York Street Gardens, which contain the main collection on 20 acres, are most accessible. There is a rose garden with more than 400 varieties, Scripture garden, herb garden, Shofu-en, a classic Japanese garden, landscape demonstration garden, 18-acre test garden, Lew Hammer's low maintenance garden, rock garden, alpine house. The conservatory displays 800 tropical and subtropical plants and trees; the orchid pavillion has more than 1,000 species of orchids and 1,200 bromeliads. Large library. Illustrated guide booklet.

Daily 9-4:45; adults, under $3; children nominal; handicapped access; (303) 575-2547.

4 **Chatfield Arboretum**
Denver Botanic Gardens
Chatfield Dam, southwest of Denver

This 700-acre site lies in the foothills and is being developed into an arboretum of Rocky Mountain trees and shrubs.

Open at selected times; (303) 575-2547.

5 **Mount Goliath Alpine Unit**   WF
Denver Botanic Gardens
50 mi. west of Denver

160 acres of alpine and subalpine plants, includes two mile nature trail; large collection of native plants, many labelled.

Open during summer only; (303) 575-2547.

6 **Walter S. Reed Botanical Gardens**
Denver Botanic Gardens
West of Denver, near Evergreen

20-acre site in the montane zone which is being developed into a research and educational facility.

Open during selected times; (303) 575-2547.

LITTLETON

7 **War Memorial Gardens**   R
5804 S. Benis St.

A small rose garden stands as a memorial garden here.

Daily, dawn-dusk.

CONNECTICUT

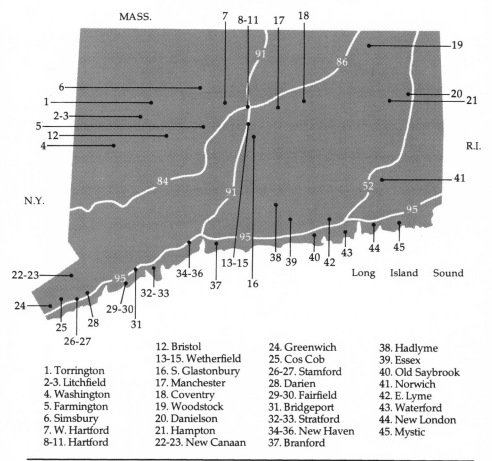

MASS.

N.Y.

R.I.

Long Island Sound

	12. Bristol	24. Greenwich	38. Hadlyme
	13-15. Wetherfield	25. Cos Cob	39. Essex
1. Torrington	16. S. Glastonbury	26-27. Stamford	40. Old Saybrook
2-3. Litchfield	17. Manchester	28. Darien	41. Norwich
4. Washington	18. Coventry	29-30. Fairfield	42. E. Lyme
5. Farmington	19. Woodstock	31. Bridgeport	43. Waterford
6. Simsbury	20. Danielson	32-33. Stratford	44. New London
7. W. Hartford	21. Hampton	34-36. New Haven	45. Mystic
8-11. Hartford	22-23. New Canaan	37. Branford	

TORRINGTON

1 Hotchkiss-Fyler House   G
192 Main St.

This grand Victorian mansion built in 1900 has a greenhouse with plants appropriate to the period.

Mon-Fri 8-4; no admission charge; (203) 482-8260.

LITCHFIELD

2 White Memorial Conservation Center   W-WF
2 mi southwest on US 202

This 4,000-acre nature center, which lies along Bantam Lake, is the largest in the state. There is a wildflower area and a wetland area; trails for the blind have been provided. A library is maintained.

Daily, dawn-dusk; (203) 567-0015.

3   **White Flower Farm** ☆ G
Rt. 63 south.

This large commercial nursery grows many unusual plants in 20 acres of fields which are at their peak blooming season in late summer. There are 8 acres of display gardens which are best viewed in May and June. The greenhouses specialize in giant tuberous begonias.

9-4 Wed-Mon; closed Tues, April 10 to Dec 23; (203) 567-8789.

WASHINGTON

4   **American Indian Archeological Institute** HA
Curtis Rd., Rt. 199; exit 16 from I-84

A museum of the woodland Indians of this region is surrounded by 15 acres which include a native American plant walk. This is a display of living native plants used by the American Indians of the Northeast.

10-4:30 Mon-Sat; 1-4:30 Sun; adults, under $3; children half; handicapped access; (203) 868-0518.

FARMINGTON

5   **Stanley Whitman House** H-HH
37 High St. Exit 39 from I-84

A beautifully restored Colonial homestead lies in the midst of a flower garden. There is also a herb garden.

1-4 Tues-Sun, May-Oct 31; 1-4 Sun, Nov-Dec; closed Jan-Feb, major holidays; adults, under $3; 6-14 half; (203) 677-9222.

SIMSBURY

6   **Massacoh Plantation** H-HH
800 Hopemeadow St.

The grounds contain a number of 18th century houses along with special exhibits. There is a herb garden.

Daily 1-4, May 1-Oct 31; adults, under $3; over 65, 5-15 half; (203) 658-2500.

WEST HARTFORD

7   **Noah Webster House** H-HH
227 S. Main St.

This 18th century farm house was the birthplace of the lexicographer Noah Webster. It has been restored along with a herb garden of the period.

10-4 Tues, Thurs; 1-4 Sun; also by appointment; closed Jan 1, Thanksgiving, Christmas; adults, under $3; 6-12 half; (203) 521-5362.

HARTFORD

8   **Elizabeth Park** ☆☆ G-HA-HD-P-R-RG-WF
915 Prospect Ave.; exit 44 from I-84.

This 102-acre park contains a grand rose garden with 500 varieties among its 15,000 bushes. It was established in 1903 as the first municipal rose garden in the country; some bushes are 75 years old. In 1912 it became the first rose test garden. The height of the rose season is reached toward the end of June. There is a rock garden, an annual garden of 46 beds, a wildflower, a lilac collection, and a perennial garden. The greenhouses display collection of tropical plants. Winter and spring flower shows are held annually.

The Knox Park Foundation dedicated to horticultural education provides a children's garden, a model school garden, a model community garden, a herb garden as well as a library and special children's programs.

Daily, dawn-dusk; greenhouses 9-4; stories for children, Wed at 2 in July and Aug; handicapped access; (203) 722-6541; Knox Foundation (203) 523-4276.

9   Harriet Beecher Stowe House   H-HH
77 Forest St.

The house has been restored along with its garden. There are perennials, annuals, woody ornamentals, and herbs with no cultivars dating after 1896 used. The nearby Stowe-Day Foundation has a library with a special collection of 19th century American seed and plant catalogues.

Daily 10-4:30, June 1-Aug 31; 9:30-4 Tues-Sat, 1-4 Sun, rest of year; closed Jan 1, Easter, Labor Day, Thanksgiving, Christmas; adults, under $3; 6-15 half; partial handicapped access; (203) 525-9317.

10   Butler-McCook Homestead   HH
396 Main St., Capitol Exit from I-91.

The house is a mixture of Colonial and Victorian architecture; the garden is Victorian.

Daily 12-4, May 15-Oct 15; closed holidays; adults, under $3; senior citizens half; children nominal; (203) 522-1806.

11   Flower Show
Hartford Civic Center

An annual flower show is held in February or March.

For information call (203) 722-6541.

BRISTOL

12   American Clock and Watch Museum
100 Maple St.

This museum is housed in a building erected in 1801; the restored small courtyard garden reflects that period.

Daily 11-5, April 1-Oct 31; adults, under $3; 8-15 half; (203) 583-6070.

WETHERFIELD

13   The Webb-Deane-Stevens Museum   H-HH
Main St. Exit 26 from I-91

This complex displays 3 authentically restored 18th century houses. Behind them lie 5 acres of land which have been planted with plants used in the 18th century. A flower garden has been laid out behind the Webb house and a herb garden behind the Stevens house.

10-4 Tues-Sat; 1-4 Sun, May 15-Oct 15 only; adults, under $3; (203) 529-0612.

14 **Isaac Stevens House** H-HH
Main St., exit 26 from I-91

This 1788 house has a small backyard herb garden planted with herbs of the period.

10-4 Tues-Sat, all year; 1-4 Sun, May 15-Oct 15; adults, under $3; children half; (203) 529-0612.

15 **Comstock, Ferre, and Co**
263 Main St.

This large seed company runs All-American Selection trials for flowers and vegetables.

Field days are Sat, Sun of second weekend in Aug; for times call (203) 529-3319.

SOUTH GLADSTONEBURY

16 **Welles-Shipman-Ward House** H-HH
972 Main St., Rt. 17

Rudy J. Favretti designed a Colonial kitchen garden in keeping with the 1755 period of the house in 1966. The garden contains culinary and medicinal herbs as well as some flowers.

2-4 Sun, June-Oct; also by appointment; (203) 633-6652.

MANCHESTER

17 **Wickham Park** HH-J-W
1329 W. Middle Turnpike, 4 mi. west on U.S. 6 and 44

A former estate surrounded by a 210-acre park with well kept grounds. There is an Oriental Garden, a lotus pond, and an aviary as well as recreational facilities.

Daily 9:30-sunset, 1st Sat in April to last Sun in Oct; each car, under $3; over 64 free.

COVENTRY

18 **Capriland Herb Farm** G-H
Silver St., off Rt. 44A

31 different herb gardens surround this 18th century farm house. More than 300 kinds of herbs are grown both outside and in commercial greenhouses.

Daily 9-5; garden tours April-Dec by reservation; (203) 742-7244.

WOODSTOCK

19 **Bowen House "Roseland Cottage"** HH
Rt. 169 on the Common

This Gothic revival house built in 1846 has a full complement of outbuildings and a parterre garden designed in 1850. Many of the plants in the garden are descendents of the original plantings.

12-5 Wed-Sun, June 1-Sept 15; 12-5 Fri, Sat, Sun, Sept 16-Oct 15; adults, under $3; under 12 half; (203) 928-4074.

DANIELSON

20 Logee's Greenhouses FE-G-S
55 North St.

8 commercial greenhouses display 1,800 different kinds of plants, including 100 different types of ferns, 150 varieties of geraniums as well as exotic plants. The original glass-house is more than a century old and contains old specimens of Angel's Trumpet, kumquat, a Japanese Persimmon, and a lemon tree.

9-5 weekdays; 1-4 Sun; (203) 774-8038.

HAMPTON

21 James L. Goodwin State Forest and Conservation Center W
Rt. 6

An arboretum is part of this 1,800-acre woodland and marsh preserve. Self-guided trails interpret the forest.

Daily, dawn-dusk; Education Center 1-5 Memorial Day to Labor Day; closed Mon, Tues; (203) 455-9534.

NEW CANAAN

22 Olive W. Lee Memorial Garden ☆ A-RG-WF
89 Chichester Rd.

¾-mile of paths stretch through this 3-acre woodland garden begun in 1940. 2,000 azaleas bloom in May; they represent 175 varieties including 40 of the Gable hybrids. There are also 280 types of rhododendrons including hybrids of Gable, Shammarello, Dexter, Amateis, Nearing, and Leach. A rock garden and good collection of eastern and west coast wildflowers is found here.

Daily 9-5; no admission charge; (203) 742-7244.

23 New Canaan Nature Center G-H
144 Oenoke Ridge

This nature center contains a small herb garden, a solar greenhouse as well as many nature trails. Specimen trees are to be found around the main building.

Weekdays 9-5; (203) 966-9577.

GREENWICH

24 Audubon Fairchild Garden WF
Riversville Rd., 8 mi north; Rt. 15 exit 28

This 135-acre garden is part of a larger preserve; it was established in 1945. It contains plants of Connecticut, the Blue Ridge mountains and Appalachia as well as a collection of medicinal plants and wildflowers.

9-5 Tues-Sun; closed holidays; adults, under $3; under 18 nominal; (203) 869-5272.

COS COB

25 Montgomery Pinetum ☆ A-G-WF
Greenwich Garden Center
Bible St.

The former estate of Robert H. Montgomery contains a good collection of conifers, rhododendrons, and azaleas, along with woodland wildflowers. There are greenhouses.

Daily 9-5; (203) 869-9242.

STAMFORD

26 Bartlett Arboretum ☆☆ A-HA-S-W
University of Connecticut
151 Brookdale St

This 63-acre arboretum was established in 1965; it has special collections of dwarf conifers, rhododendrons, azaleas, Witches'-brooms, nut trees, daffodils, and pollarded trees. There are good specimen of Japanese Umbrella trees, Stewartias, and columnar Sugar Maples. There is a bog area, a natural woodland, a demonstration garden for woody ornamentals, and a library.

Daily, dawn-dusk; handicapped access; (203) 322-6971.

27 The Champion Greenhouse G-HA
Champion International Corporation
One Champion Plaza, exit 8 from I-95

This leading forest products company has established a greenhouse at its headquarters. Seasonal horticultural displays are presented.

11-5 Tues-Sat; no admission charge; handicapped access; (203) 358-6688.

DARIEN

28 Bates-Scofield Homestead H-HH
45 Old King's Highway, North; exit 12 from I-95

A small good herb garden lies behind this classic 18th century house. 40 kinds of herbs as well as some ornamental shrubs are grown here.

2-4 Wed, Thurs; 2:30-4:30 Sun; also by appointment; donation; (203) 655-9233.

FAIRFIELD

29 Larsen Sanctuary HA-WF
Connecticut Audubon Society
2325 Burr St.; exit 21 from I-95

Although primarily a bird sanctuary, this 170-acre site has display plots of native plants particularly attractive to birds, an organic garden, and a nature walk for the blind and handicapped. There is a library.

9-5 Tues-Sat; 12-5 Sun; closed major holidays; handicapped access; adults, under $3; children nominal; (203) 259-6305.

30 Ogden House H-HH-WF
1520 Bronson Rd.

This mid-18th century farmhouse stands in a 2-acre garden with a fine collection of New England wildflowers. There is a demonstration kitchen and herb garden with more than 50 species of herbs.

Thurs and Sun 1-4; May 15-Oct 15; adults, under $3; children half; (203) 259-6356.

BRIDGEPORT

31 Beardsley Zoological Gardens G
Noble Ave.

The park contains greenhouses as well as woodland walks. There is a zoo and recreational facilities.

Daily 10-4:30; each car, under $6; state residents half; local residents free; (203) 576-8082.

STRATFORD

32 American Shakespeare Theatre SH
1850 Elm St., exit 32 off I-95

The grounds contain a Shakespearean Garden with more than 80 plants mentioned in his plays.

Daily 10-dusk; no admission charge; (203) 375-5000 or 375-1233.

33 Captain David Judson House F-H-HH
967 Academy Hill

The ¾-acre which surround this 18th century restored house have been planted with material typical of the period. There is a small orchard of Roxbury Russett apples, a kitchen herb garden along with some unusual plants.

11-4 Wed, Sat, Sun, April 17-Nov 1; adults, under $3; senior citizens, students half; (203) 378-0630.

NEW HAVEN

34 Marsh Botanical Garden ☆ C-G-HA-S-SU
Yale University
Prospect St.

This 5-acre botanical garden was established in 1900. It contains collections of conifers, oaks, and hemlocks. The greenhouse displays cacti and succulents. There are iris test gardens and a library.

Daily 9-dusk; no admission charge; handicapped access; (203) 436-8665.

35 East Rock Park R-RG
East Rock Rd., Willow St. exit from I-91

This city park contains a series of gardens and woodlands. The Pardee rose garden covers 2 acres with thousands of bushes representing many varieties. There is a rock garden, and a garden of perennials and annuals.

Daily, dawn-dusk.

36 Pardee-Morris House H-HH
325 Lighthouse Rd., exit 50 from I-95

A small formal garden and a herb garden lie behind this restored 1750 Colonial house.

1-4 Tues-Sun, June-Aug; closed Mon and major holidays; adults, under $3; children half; (203) 562-4183.

BRANFORD

37 **Harrison House** H-HH
124 Main St., exit 54 from I-95

A classical Colonial saltbox which has been restored along with its herb garden.

2-5 Wed-Sat, and by appointment June 1-Sept 30; (203) 488-5771.

HADLYME

38 **Gillette Castle State Park** G-HH
Off Rt. 82

The famous actor, Gillette's home is surrounded by landscaped grounds. There are formal plantings in the conservatory and on the patio.

11-5 Memorial Day to Columbus Day for castle; daily 8-dusk for park; adults nominal; under 12 free; (203) 526-2336.

ESSEX

39 **Pratt House** H-HH
20 West Ave., exit 3 from Rt. 9

Built in 1732, this center chimney Colonial house has a period herb garden which is well-labelled.

1-5 Tues, Thurs, Sun, June 1-Oct 1; adults, under $3; seniors half; under 12 free; (203) 767-8201.

OLD SAYBROOK

40 **General William Hart House** H-HH
350 Main St., Rt. 154

The home of this Colonial merchant was built in 1767; there is a herb garden.

11-3 Fri-Mon, May-Aug; 11-3 Fri-Sun, Sept-Oct; adults, under $3; seniors, 6-16 nominal; (203) 747-6577.

NORWICH

41 **Mohegan Park** R
Mohegan Rd., off Rt. 32

This 200-acre park contains a memorial rose garden which is in full bloom toward the end of June.

Daily, dawn-dusk.

EAST LYME

42 **Thomas Lee House** H-HH
Rt. 156; Turnpike exit 72

This Colonial frame house was built in 1660; a period herb garden lies behind the home.

Daily 10-5, except Tues, Memorial Day to Columbus Day; adults, under $3; 12-16 half; (203) 739-6070.

WATERFORD

43   Harkness Memorial State Park   ☆☆   BX-C-FE-G-HA-RG-T
Rt. 213

This mansion, built in 1902, is set in an estate with 2 acres of formal gardens. There is topiary, boxwood, a rock garden, a cutting garden as well as annual and perennial beds. The greenhouses contain tropical rooms, ferns, cacti, and a grapery.

Daily 8-sunset for grounds; 10-5 buildings; parking $1-Memorial Day to Labor Day; handicapped access; (203) 443-5725.

NEW LONDON

44   Connecticut Arboretum at Connecticut College   ☆☆   A-HA-S-WF
Williams St.; exit 83 from I-95

This 415-acre arboretum was established in 1931; more than 800 different kinds of plants are found here. There are 375 species of trees representing 116 genera with special collections of hawthorns, hollies, heaths, viburnums, and native trees. In addition there is the Nancy Moss Fine Rhododendron Garden, a laurel walk, the Edgerton and Stengel wildflower areas, the Caroline Black Botanical Garden, a tidal marsh, a bog garden, and several nature areas. Demonstration and test gardens are maintained along with a library.

Daily, dawn-dusk; no admission charge; handicapped access; (203) 447-1911.

MYSTIC

45   Denison Peqyotsepos Nature Center   WF

This 125-acre nature center contains marked trails, including one in braille.

9-5 Mon-Sat, 1-4 Sun, April-Nov; closed holidays; adults, under $3; 6-14 half; (203) 536-1216.

DELAWARE

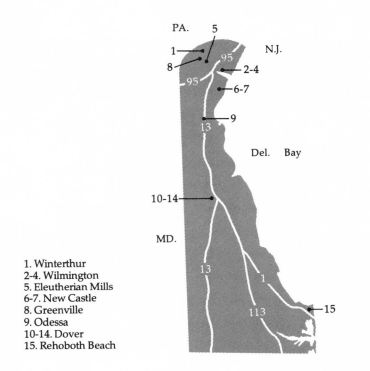

1. Winterthur
2-4. Wilmington
5. Eleutherian Mills
6-7. New Castle
8. Greenville
9. Odessa
10-14. Dover
15. Rehoboth Beach

WINTERTHUR

1 Winterthur Gardens ☆☆☆☆ A-HA-L-S-W-WF
Rt. 52, 6 mi. northwest of Wilmington

A magnificent 60-acre woodland garden on an estate which has belonged to the Du Ponts since 1839; at its center lies a great museum of decorative art and 200 period rooms. The gardens display a collection of thousands of trees and shrubs, many labelled, in a naturalized setting. There are unusual collections of azalea, dogwood, rhododendron, viburnum, primula, heather, wildflowers. The pinetum contains excellent specimens of Blue Atlas Cedar, Japanese Umbrella Pine, Dawn Redwood, tulip trees, Japanese maple, Japanese crab-apples along with numerous rare trees. A fine stand of eastern climax forest contains a 300-year-old Tulip Poplar, the William Penn Tree.

There are meadows, upland marshes and ponds with their special plantings. The remaining area is divided into a number of gardens; they include the heather garden, primula quarry, wildflower garden, and a formal sundial garden in the 18th century French style with a reflecting pool. There are grand displays of flowers in spring and autumn. The library is very good.

10-4 Mon-Sat; 12-4 Sun, holiday Mons; closed Mons, Jan 1, Thanksgiving, Dec 24, 25; admission, under $3; 25% discount for senior citizens, students over 12, groups of 25 or more; tram tours; handicapped access; (302) 654-1548.

WILMINGTON

2 The Nemours Foundation ☆☆☆☆ F-G-HH-L-RG-T-W
Rockland Rd. off Rt. 141

A Louis XVI style chateau placed on a 300-acre estate with French-style formal gardens. This beautiful garden is patterned on Versailles with intricately designed beds, statuary, fountains, cascades, topiary, clipped hedges, and allees lined with Horse-Chestnut, linden, and oaks. There is a maze, a colonade area, sunken garden, a rock garden, a dozen ponds, an orangery, greenhouses, a cutting garden, and orchards. The gardens extend ⅓-mi. and are surrounded by woodlands. 100 acres remain as a natural forest area. The mansion was built at the beginning of the century; the gardens were completed in 1932 and have recently been completely restored.

Admission by 2 hr. tour through reservation only; 9, 11, 1, 3 Tues-Sat; 11, 1, 3 Sun, May 1 - Nov 30; admission, under $6; under 16 not admitted; visitors should arrive 15 min. prior to tour; no handicapped access; (302) 573-3333 or 651-6912; P.O.Box 109, Wilmington, DE 19899.

3 Josephine Gardens HA-L-S
Brandywine Park
18th and Market Sts.

This park along the Brandywine River was designed by Frederick Law Olmsted; beautifully landscaped with a fine variety of trees and shrubs; 118 Japanese Cherry trees stand along a formal walk.

Daily 10-4; handicapped access; (302) 571-7788.

4 Rockwood Museum
610 Shipley Rd.

This nineteenth century rural Gothic style building is set in a fine setting of 'gardenesque' design reflecting mid-19th century style.

11-4 Tues-Sat; adults, under $3; children half; (302) 571-7776.

ELEUTHERIAN MILLS

5 Hagley Museum ☆☆ HA-HH-F-T
Rt. 100 at Rt. 141

225 acres of exhibits which deal with the industrial development along the Brandywine. The Georgian style home of E.I. DuPont built in 1803 is surrounded by a 2-acre formal garden restored in the 19th century manner. There are formal parterres and a good collection of fruit trees. Early 19th century cultivars are used as much as possible. The DuPonts conducted horticultural experiments on this estate.

9:30-4:30 Tues-Sat; 1-5 Sun and holiday Mons; closed Mons, Jan 1, Thanksgiving, Christmas; adults, under $6; students, over 62 half; under 14 with adult free; handicapped access; (302) 658-2400.

NEW CASTLE

6 The Read House HH-S
The Strand

This townhouse begun in 1797 is part of a street of such homes; it has a formal boxwood garden with fine old specimens; planted with bulbs in spring.

10-4 Tues-Sat; 12-4 Sun; adults, under $3; students and children half; under 6 free; partial handicapped access; (302) 322-8411.

7 Home and Garden Tour HH

This tour is conducted annually on the third Saturday of May; there are also summer walks.

For information call (302) 571-4088.

GREENVILLE

8 Mount Cuba Botanical Park
Barley Mill Rd.

A display and research garden with emphasis on the flora of the Piedmont is being established here.

Not open to the public yet.

ODESSA

9 Corbit-Sharp House ☆ BX-H-HH-S
2nd and Main St.

A series of homes maintained by Winterthur in Odessa includes this Georgian home begun in 1772 which has a formal garden of the period. The herb and flower gardens are done in geometrical design; there are evergreen hedges, huge old trees, and sweeping lawns. Fine flowering shrubs and bulbs bloom in spring.

Tours 10-4:30 Tues-Sat; 1-4:30 Sun; closed Jan 1, July 4, Thanksgiving, Dec 24, 25; adults, under $3; over 62, students over 12 half; partial handicapped access; (302) 378-4069.

DOVER

10 John Dickinson Mansion HH
Kitts-Hummock Rd., east of U.S. 113

A 1740 Delaware plantation mansion set in a restored English formal garden; the grounds contain specimen trees and shrubs. There is a lovely display of blooming bulbs in spring.

10-4:30 Tues-Sat; 1:30-4:30 Sun; closed Easter, Thanksgving, Christmas; no admission charge; (302) 734-9439.

11 The Green

This public square laid out in 1723 was turned into a formal Victorian park in the last century and has been maintained in that style.

Daily, dawn-dusk.

12 Woodburn ☆ BX-HH-T
Kings Highway

This Georgian mansion built in 1790 became the governor's official residence in 1966. The spacious grounds contain formal gardens which include a boxwood maze.

Sat 2:30-4:30 except holidays; no admission charge; (302) 678-5656.

13 Great Geneva BX-H-HH

Built before 1748, this home lies besides a formal herb garden and a boxwood garden.

Open during the old Dover Days only; (302) 736-4266.

14 Old Dover Days HH

This festival is held annually early in May; numerous old homes and their gardens are open to the public.

For information call (302) 736-4266.

REHOBOTH BEACH

15 The Homestead BX-H-HH
Henlopen Acres
Doods Lane

The grounds of this 1743 home contain a boxwood garden begun in 1930; it is divided into 5 sections. There is also a herb garden.

Daily 10-4, summer season; (302) 227-8408.

54

DISTRICT OF COLUMBIA

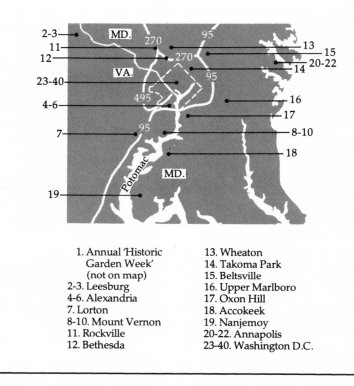

1. Annual 'Historic
   Garden Week'
   (not on map)
2-3. Leesburg
4-6. Alexandria
7. Lorton
8-10. Mount Vernon
11. Rockville
12. Bethesda

13. Wheaton
14. Takoma Park
15. Beltsville
16. Upper Marlboro
17. Oxon Hill
18. Accokeek
19. Nanjemoy
20-22. Annapolis
23-40. Washington D.C.

The gardens and arboreta of Washington and nearby areas in Virginia and Maryland are listed here. The gardens of those states are listed again with their state.

VIRGINIA

A large number of private homes and gardens are open during the annual spring 'Historic Garden Week', but they have not been included as the list changes each year. Also omitted are estates and other sites which contain very small gardens or remnants of formal gardens.

1 Annual 'Historic Garden Week'

A series of different gardens are open to the public each year throughout the state during this period.

For information call (804) 295-3141.

LEESBURG

2 Oatlands ☆ BX-HH-S
U.S. 15, 6 mi. south

A grand Federal style mansion with a Greek Revival portico, built in 1800 and completely restored along with its formal gardens. Terraced gardens with 150-year-old boxwood, gazebo, and reflecting pool have been developed on this 261-acre estate. There are fine plantings of tulips, daffodils, and perennials which bloom in spring and early summer. Specimen oaks planted by George Carter, the original owner, still stand along with magnolias, a boxwood allee, a bowling green, and forty species of trees. This is primarily a green garden and so interesting at all seasons.

10-5 Mon-Sat; 1-5 Sun, April-end of Oct; adults, under $6; students, senior citizens two-thirds; partial handicapped access; (703) 777-3174.

3 **Morven Park** ☆ BX-HH-S-W
Old Waterford Rd. and Morven Park Rd.

A fine old home with colonial gardens set in a 1,200-acre estate which continues to be farmed. There are boxwood gardens, and a reflecting pool surrounded by magnolias. Especially interesting are the parterre sundial garden, the boxwood allee, and the wildflower garden. The garden contains specimen miniature boxwood and yews.

10-5 Tues-Sat; 1-5 Sun, Memorial Day-Labor Day; 10-5 Sat; 1-5 Sun, May 1-Memorial Day and Labor Day-Oct 17; adults, under $3; senior citizens slightly less; 6-12 half; partial handicapped access; (703) 777-2414.

ALEXANDRIA

4 **Carlyle House** HH
121 N. Fairfax

This small garden lies in the section of old Alexandria which has been partially restored or renewed in the colonial style. The neighboring streets lead past various nicely planted miniature gardens.

Tues-Sat 10-5; Sun 12-5; closed January 1, Thanksgiving, Christmas; adults, under $3; over 59, 6-17 half; (703) 549-8454.

5 **Lee-Fendall House** HH
429 N. Washington St.

This historic home of the Lee family was built in 1785. It stands in a small colonial style garden.

10-4 Tues-Sat; 12-4 Sun; closed Jan 1, Christmas; adults, under $3; 6-16 half; (703) 548-1789.

6 **River Farm** ☆☆ BX-F-HD-R-WF
American Horticultural Society
7931 E. Boulevard Drive

These 25 acres were once part of George Washington's Mt. Vernon farm. The headquarters of the Society, acquired in 1973, display boxwood hedge gardens and wildflower plantings. The Society maintains large demonstration gardens for perennial borders, roses, dahlias, a fruit orchard and an idea garden. Official test gardens for numerous plant societies have been located here. There is a library.

8:30-5 weekdays; no admission charge; partial handicapped access; (703) 768-8882.

LORTON

7 **Gunston Hall** ☆ BX-H-HH-L-S
Rt. 242, east from U.S. 1

This Georgian colonial home, begun in 1755 by George Mason, stands in an 18th century garden. It presents excellent English boxwood parterres, some in an allee with 12 ft. high plants. There are 2 acres of formal gardens, a herb garden, a cutting garden as well as specimen trees and shrubs. The grounds provide a beautiful view of the Potomac.

Daily 9:30-5; closed Dec 25; adults, under $3; 6-15 half; partial handicapped access; (703) 550-9220.

MOUNT VERNON

8   **Mount Vernon**   ☆☆   BX-F-G-H-HH-L
Mount Vernon Memorial Highway

George Washington's home sited high above the Potomac has been restored along with its out-buildings and gardens in accordance with Washington's design. The grounds contain an orchard with native and exotic trees, a kitchen garden, and a large flower garden with boxwood hedges. There is a bowling green and greenhouses. Some of the original trees have survived. The gardens provide a good view of the Potomac.

Daily 9-5 March 1-Nov 1; 9-4 rest of year; adults, under $6; over 60 slightly less; 6-11 half; partial handicapped access; (703) 780-2000.

9   **Woodlawn**   ☆☆   HA-HH-R-S
9000 Richmond Highway (U.S. 1)

This estate, originally a part of Mount Vernon, contains an 18th century mansion along with magnificently restored 20 acres of gardens. The parterre gardens of old-fashioned roses are best seen toward the end of May. Nature trails lead through a portion of the 2,000-acre estate. There are specimen of Camperdown Elms and magnolias.

Daily 9:30-4:30; closed Jan 1, Thanksgiving, Christmas; adults, under $3; over 62 slightly less; 6-18 half; handicapped access; (703) 780-3118.

10   **Pope-Leighey House**   ☆   HH-FE-WF
U.S. 1, 14 mi. south of Washington

This home was designed by Frank Lloyd Wright in 1940. The native shrubs, ferns, and wildflowers blend with the house. The grounds contain a wildflower and a fern garden.

Sat and Sun 9:30-4:30, March-Oct; also by appointment; adults, under $3; children half; (703) 780-3118.

MARYLAND
ROCKVILLE

11   **Civic Center**
Edmonston Dr. and Baltimore Rd.

This 100-acre park contains an art gallery, a theater, and small formal gardens.

Daily 8-dusk.

BETHESDA

12   **Perkins Garden**   A-WF
Landon School
6101 Wilson Lane

A well-landscaped garden with a fine azalea collection; extensive hosta and wildflower plantings are found on this 4-acre garden established in 1937.

First weekend of May; other times by appointment only; no admission charge; (301) 320-3200.

WHEATON

13 Brookside Gardens ☆☆☆ A-FE-G-HA-J-R-W
1500 Glenallen Ave.

A 50-acre garden established in 1969 with numerous smaller fine gardens including a Japanese garden, a rose garden, a winter garden, an azalea garden, a fragrance garden for the blind, a formal garden with clipped hedges, and an aquatic garden. There are good collections of azalea, rhdodendron, dogwood, crab-apple, flowering Cherry, and ornamental grasses. Many rare trees and shrubs have been planted on these grounds. The greenhouses feature tropical plants, gesneriads and ferns. 3 seasonal flower shows are held. The gardens maintain demonstration and test gardens for roses and annuals.

Daily 9-5; closed Christmas; no admission charge; handicapped access; (301) 949-8230.

TAKOMA PARK

14 House and Garden Tour HH

Each May a series of homes and their gardens are open to the public.

For information call (301) 270-4048.

BELTSVILLE

15 U.S. Department of Agriculture Experimental Gardens ☆ CH-G-HA-R
Powder Mill Rd., off U.S. 1

Large experimental plantings of grain crops, vegetables, fruit as well as flowering plants may be seen here. There are fine beds of roses, chrysanthemums, lilies, gladiolas, flowers, and 6 acres of greenhouses.

8-4:30 Mon-Fri; closed holidays; self-guided tours; handicapped access; (301) 344-2483.

UPPER MARLBORO

16 Melwood Horticultural School G-HA
5606 Dower House Rd.

A horticultural training center for retarded children and adults. It presents a model program for rehabilitation through its greenhouse and ground programs.

By appointment only; (301) 599-8000.

OXON HILL

17 Oxon Hill Farm H-HH
Oxon Hill Rd., off I-95

A late 19th century exhibition farm along with its farm gardens of flowers and herbs.

Daily 8:30-5; closed Jan 1, Thanksgiving, Christmas; no admission charge; partial handicapped access; (301) 839-1177.

ACCOKEEK

18   **National Colonial Farm**   H
Bryan Point Rd.; exit 37 from I-495; Rt.210 south; also by ferry service
from Mt. Vernon

This demonstration farm utilizes colonial farming methods. There is a herb garden, a
kitchen garden, a woodland trail, and a grove of 500 chestnut trees. Demonstration
and test gardens for vegetables are maintained.

10-5 Tues-Sun, June 1-Labor Day; Fri, Sat, Sun only rest of year; adults, under $3;
children half; (301) 283-2113.

NANJEMOY

19   **Melwood Farm**   G-H-HA

An outdoor training and nature center for retarded children and adults. There is an
herb garden, a large greenhouse complex as well as nature trails.

By appointment only; (301) 599-8000.

ANNAPOLIS

20   **William Paca House and Garden**   ☆☆   BX-H-HH-R
186 Prince George St.

This mansion built in 1763 stands in a restored 18th century garden which uses only
plants known at that time. There are parterre terraces, a gazebo, a rose garden, and a
wilderness garden. The house contains a library.

10-4 Tues-Sat; 12-4 Sun; closed Thanksgiving, Christmas; garden only adults, under
$3; 6-18 nominal; partial handicapped access; (301) 267-8149.

21   **The Helen Avalynne Tawes Garden**   W
Rowe Blvd. and Taylor Ave.

6 acres of a new botanic garden are nestled among state office buildings. The gardens
emphasize the preservation of Maryland's natural resources; a section reproduces
each type of the state's flora. There are ponds and a sensory garden for the
handicapped.

Daily 8-dusk; no admission charge; (301) 269-2609.

22   **Home and Garden Tour**   HH

A tour of homes and gardens is held each spring.

For information call (301) 269-1714.

WASHINGTON D. C.

23   **Dumbarton Oaks**   ☆☆☆☆   BX-FE-G-L-R-S-T
1703 32nd St. N.W.

These gardens designed by Beatrix Farrand in 1940 spread over 16 acres of hilly
terrain which are beautiful at all seasons. This large estate is divided into the
following gardens: A green garden, a star garden which is very intimate, an Italian
garden, a pebble terrace garden, a beech terrace, a forsythia dell, a rose garden, a
fountain garden with a clipped circle of hornbeams, a boxwood walk, a walled
perennials and annual garden, and a terraced lawn. An orangerie built in 1810 is

covered with ficus which date from 1860. The gardens contain outstanding specimens of yew, holly, boxwood, magnolia, cherry and beech. There are two large greenhouses, one is entirely devoted to ferns. An excellent library and rare book collection are found here.

Daily 2-5; closed legal holidays; adults, under $3; under 12 must be accompanied by adult; senior citizens free; Nov 1-March 31 free; library, 2-5 Sat-Sun; museum 2-5 Tues-Sun; (202) 342-3290.

24 **U.S. Botanic Garden** ☆☆ BR-C-FE-G-HA-O-P-RG
Maryland Ave. S. W.

This conservatory was founded in 1842; the present building contains good collections of orchids, palms, as well as bromeliads, araceas, cacti, cycads, and ferns. Outside there is a rock garden along with plantings of perennials and annuals. Seasonal flower shows are held. There is a library and test gardens.

Daily 9-9, June 1-Aug 31; 9-5 rest of year; closed Christmas; no admission charge; handicapped access; (202) 225-7099.

25 **Victorian Garden** ☆ H
Office of Horticulture
Smithsonian Institute

This large Victorian garden lies behind the red-brick Castle and is planted in the authentic mid-19th century style with flowers and bushes of the period. There is a good collection of hosta and ivy.

Daily 10-9 April 1-Labor Day; 10-5:30 Labor Day-March 31; handicapped access; (202) 357-1926.

26 **Smithsonian Greenhouses** BR-O

These greenhouses contain outstanding collections of orchids and bromeliads as well as other tropical plants. There is a library and a rare book collection including Victorian nursery catalogues.

By appointment through a written request only; Smithsonian Institution, Washington, D.C. 20560; (202) 357-2700.

27 **Organization of American States Building**
Constitution Ave. and 17th St.

A tropical patio and an Aztec Garden are part of this lovely building.

9:30-4:30 Mon-Fri; closed holidays; no admission charge; (202) 789-3751.

28 **German American Friendship Garden**
Constitution Ave. behind White House

A special garden commemorating the friendship between the two countries is being built.

The garden is not yet open.

29 **White House Gardens** ☆☆ R-S
1600 Pennsylvania Ave.

The White House grounds contain a famous rose garden as well as a Children's garden, and the Jacqueline Kennedy Garden. More than 80 kinds of trees are found on the 18-acre grounds; many are fine specimens, many planted by prominent individuals.

Open one weekend in spring and fall; (202) 426-6700.

30 **National Zoological Park** HA
Smithsonian Institution
3000 Connecticut Ave.

A large zoo with good landscaping and general planting; in addition there are collections of ornamental grasses and bamboo.

Daily 6-8 April 1-Sept 30; 6-5:30 rest of year; closed Dec 25; different hours for buildings; no admission charge; handicapped access; (202) 673-4800.

31 **Bishop's Garden** ☆ BX-H-R-S
Washington National Cathedral Grounds
Wisconsin Ave. and Woodley Rd.

A 54-acre garden established 1916; there is an outstanding medieval herb garden, a 12th to 14th century garden, as well as a little garden, a Garth Garden, a Hortulus Garden, a rose garden, perennial and annual gardens, a yew walk, and woodland paths. The herb garden is labelled. The gardens contain fine specimens of yew, Cedar of Lebanon, Glastonbury Thorn, and old boxwood.

Daily all hours; no admission charge; partial handicapped access; (202) 537-6200.

32 **Decatur House** A-CA-HH
748 Jackson Place N.W.

This house, designed by Benjamin Latrobe in 1818, was the first on Lafayette Square. Behind it lie several inner-block gardens established in the 1960's. They contain plantings of evergreens, azaleas, and camellias.

10-2 Tues-Fri; 12-4 Sat, Sun; adults, under $2; 6-18 $1; (202) 637-4030.

33 **Woodrow Wilson House** HH
2340 S. St. N.W.

A Georgian revival townhouse built in 1915, which was the last home of Woodrow Wilson, has a 1920's style formal garden. It contains perennial borders on the terraces along with irises and peonies.

10-2 Tues-Fri; 12-4 Sat, Sun, holidays, March 1-Dec 31; 12-4 Sat, Sun only Feb 1-28; closed Thanksgiving, Christmas; adults, under $3; 6-18 and over 62, half; (202) 673-4034.

34 **Ippakutei** ☆ J
Ceremonial Tea House and Garden
Japanese Embassy
2520 Massachusetts Ave., N.W.

3 styles of Japanese gardens have been incorporated into this small garden with its tea house. The garden was designed by Nahiko Emori.

By appointment only, April-Nov; (202) 234-2266.

35 **Franciscan Monastery** ☆ A-G-R
1400 Quincy St.

These 40-acre grounds have been planted with thousands of daffodils, lilies, roses, as well as azaleas, rhododendrons, and dogwoods. Tropical plants are brought outside each summer. There is a greenhouse.

Daily 8:30-dusk; no admission charge; (202) 526-6800.

36 **Hillwood** ☆☆☆ G-HH-J-L-O-R
4155 Linnean Ave. N.W.

A mansion museum of 18th and 19th century French and Russian decorative art; it is surrounded by landscaped grounds which contain a formal French parterre, a rose garden, a Japanese garden, a rhdodendron walk, and greenhouses with 5,000 orchids. More than 3,500 species and cultivars may be found in this garden.

11-4 Mon, Wed, Thurs, Fri, Sat; reservation required; also house tours; adults, under $3; (202) 686-5807.

37   Potomac Park

More than 3,000 Japanese cherry trees bloom in April in the Tidal Basin and East Potomac park. They form a grand display.

38   Theodore Roosevelt Island   HA-WF
Potomac River

An 88-acre island nature preserve planted with more than 50 species of trees and 200 varieties of wildflowers.

Daily 8-dusk; closed Christmas; no admission charge; handicapped access.

39   U.S. National Arboretum   ☆☆☆☆   A-BO-BX-FE-H-HA-HD-J-R-S-T-WF
24th and R Sts. N.E.

This 444-acre arboretum established in 1927 contains more than 7,000 kinds of plants with many special collections. The Gotelli Dwarf Conifer Collection is among the best in the world with 1,500 specimens; the Morrison Azalea garden with its 400 varieties is spectacular in spring.
    The National Herb Garden covers more than 2 acres and contains a European knot garden and 10 specialty herb gardens. Among them are a Dioscorides garden with plants described by this ancient Greek botanical authority, an early American garden, an American Indian garden, a dye garden, and others.
    There is a historic rose garden with numerous old bushes. The Japanese garden and the National Collection of Bonsai are outstanding. The fern valley, native wildflower section and holly area represent good collections. Fine specimens of magnolias, camellias, dogwoods, boxwoods, maples, crab-apples, hibiscus, day-lilies, redwoods, crepe myrtles, cherries, rhododendrons, lilacs, bald cypresses and virburnums may be found here. The National Country Garden includes displays of home flower and vegetable gardens, some representing unusual ideas. The grounds contain woodland trails. Many special exhibits are held throughout the year. There is a library.

8-5 Mon-Fri; 10-5 Sat, Sun; Bonsai Collection daily 10-2:30; closed Christmas; no admission charge; handicapped access; (202) 475-4815.

40   Kenilworth Aquatic Gardens   ☆☆   HA-W
Anacostia Ave and Douglas St. N.E.

A 500-acre water garden established in 1938 with 14 acres of lotus and 2,000 water lilies representing some 70 kinds hardy varieties. There are also many tropical lilies some of which bloom at night. On hot days lilies should be viewed before noon as they will close later. Huge Victoria Regina lilies may be found here. Native aquatic plants and bog plants are well represented. There is a library.

Daily 7-sunset; no admission charge; handicapped access; (202) 426-6905.

FLORIDA

ALA.   GA.

Gulf   of   Mexico

1. Point Washington
2-3. Tallahassee
4. Gainesville
5-6. Jacksonville
7-9. St. Augustine
10. Palatka
11. Ormond Beach
12. Port Orange
13-14. Winter Park
15-18. Orlando
19. Lake Buena Vista
20. Kissimmee
21-22. Winter Haven
23. Lake Wales
24. Homassa Springs
25. Weeki Wachee
26-27. Tampa
28. Indian Shores
29. St. Petersburg
30-33. Sarasota

34. Fort Myers
35. Naples
36. Immokalee
37. Lake Placid
38. Melbourne
39. Stuart
40-41. Palm Beach
42. Boynton Beach
43. Delray Beach
44. Fort Lauderdale
45. N. Miami Beach
46. Miami Beach
47-51. Miami
52-55. Coral Gables
56-58. Homestead
59. Florida City
60. Largo
61. Islamorada
62-65. Key West

POINT WASHINGTON

1   Eden Gardens   ☆☆   HA-HH-R
Eden State Park
U.S. 98 north

A restored Greek Revival mansion, built in 1895, is set in a lovely series of gardens which cover more than 10 acres. Day lilies, roses, perennials, and annuals are planted against a background of moss-hung live-oak and magnolias.

Daily 8-sunset; different hours for house; no admission charge; handicapped access; picnic area; (904) 231-4214.

TALLAHASSEE

2   Alfred B. Maclay State Gardens   ☆☆   A-CA-HA-S
3540 Thomasville Rd. (U.S. 319)

This park of 308 acres presents 30 acres of massed plantings of azaleas and camellias;

the collections on this former estate are the best in the South. Formal gardens have pools and fountains. There are fine specimens of California Nutmeg, dogwood, and snowdrop trees. Demonstration gardens for camellias are maintained.

Daily 9-5; adults, under $3; 6-12 nominal; handicapped access; (904) 893-4232.

3 **LeMoyne Art Gallery and House** HH
Gadsden St. and Park Ave.

A garden lies behind this 1853 mansion.

Tues-Sat 10-5; Sun 2-5; adults, under $3; children half; (904) 224-2714.

GAINESVILLE

4 **Willmot Memorial Gardens** ☆☆ A-CA-G-HA-O-P
University of Florida

This natural garden, founded in 1953, contains fine collections of azaleas, palms, rhododendrons, camellias, hollies, and junipers. The greenhouses display many varieties of orchids. Best blooming season is mid-January through March.

Daily; greenhouses by appointment; no admission charge; handicapped access; (904) 392-1830.

JACKSONVILLE

5 **Cummer Gallery of Art**
829 Riverside Ave.

2½ acres of gardens lead from the museum to the river and are patterned after the Villa Gameraia Gardens near Florence. These formal Italian gardens are well designed. Lilies-of-the-Nile are extensively planted. Spring is the best time to visit.

10-4 Tues-Fri; 12-5 Sat; 2-5 Sun; closed major holidays; no admission charge; (904) 356-6857.

6 **Corner Oak Garden**
5939 Wesconnett Blvd.

This garden and commercial nursery specializes in daylilies; the gardens show hundreds of cultivars.

9-5 weekdays; no admission charge; (904) 771-0417.

ST. AUGUSTINE

7 **Oldest House** HH
14 St. Francis St.

This early 18th century house is built on the site of still earlier homes. A Spanish colonial garden lies in the patio.

Daily 9:30-5; adults, under $3; 6-12 half; closed Christmas; (904) 829-9624.

8 **San Augustin Antiguo** HH
St. George St.

6 buildings of an 18th century Colonial Spanish village have been restored here along with their gardens.

Daily 9-5:15; closed Dec 25; adults, under $3; 6-18 half; (904) 824-3355.

9 **Washington Oaks State Gardens** ☆ A-CA-R-S
Rt. 1, south of Marineland

390 acres of coastal scenery have been preserved in this park which extends from the ocean to the Matanzas River. There are hammocks with Live Oaks and magnolias along with tidal marshes. Formal gardens with reflecting pools have been planted with azaleas, camellias, and roses as well as exotic plants.

Daily 8-sunset; adults, children nominal; partial handicapped access; (904) 445-3161.

PALATKA

10 **Ravine Gardens** ☆☆ A
Twiggs St.

Azaleas are the main plantings of this 85-acre park; 100,000 bushes representing 50 varieties bloom January through April. There are more than 200,000 sub-tropical trees, shrubs, and flowers on the grounds. Emphasis has been placed on native plants. Sections of the gardens are formal; others use the informal settings of streams and ponds. An azalea festival is held each March.

Daily 8-dusk; no admission charge; (904) 328-4366.

ORMOND BEACH

11 **Rockefeller Gardens** HH
"The Casements"
25 Riverside Drive

The restored 2-acre garden overlooks the Halifax River. A patio, small pond, and some fountains are part of this simple garden planted with trees, shrubs, and annuals.

9-5:30 Mon-Fri; 10-12 Sat; no admission charge; (904) 673-4701.

PORT ORANGE

12 **Sugar Mill Gardens**
Herbert St.

This former Spanish mission contains a sugar mill; there is a small garden with a pleasant trail through it.

Daily 9-4; closed Jan 1, Christmas; no admission charge; (904) 767-1735.

WINTER PARK

13 **Kraft Azalea Gardens** A
Alabama Drive on Lake Maitland

This 11-acre garden contains numerous tropical plants and a large number of azaleas.

Daily 8-dusk.

14 **Central Park** R
Park Ave.

This park contains a large rose garden along with recreational facilities.

Daily, dawn-dusk.

ORLANDO

15 Harry P. Leu Gardens ☆☆ A-CA-HA-O-P-R
1730 Forest Ave.

The mansion on this estate has been restored and the 47-acre gardens are open. There is an azalea garden, a camellia garden, a rose ravine, a floral clock, a tropical and central Florida garden. Other gardens will be added in the future. Excellent collections of roses, orchids, and camellias are found here. An annual camellia festival is held in mid-February. A conservatory for unusual tropical plants lies near the entrance.

Daily 9-5; closed Christmas; adults, under $3; under 12 free; handicapped access; (305) 894-6021.

16 Eola Park
Robinson and Rosalind Sts.

The park is planted with beds of colorful perennials and annuals.

Daily, dawn-dusk.

17 Maitland Art Center
Packwood Ave.
Maitland

Cloistered courtyards with small gardens surround the buildings of this art center.

Tues-Fri 10-4; Sat, Sun 2-5; closed holidays; no admission charge; (305) 645-2181.

18 Tupperware Food Container Museum
Rts. 17 and 92 south of Orlando

The modernistic international headquarters building of this corporation is placed in landscaped gardens which use a wide variety of plants.

Weekdays, business hours; (305) 847-3111.

LAKE BUENA VISTA

19 Walt Disney World ☆☆ G-L-P-S

The grounds of Disney World feature themed landscapes which accent the architecture of each area. The 'Garden of the World Showcase' displays landscapes of 9 countries. Special plant material is labelled. There are collections of palms, bamboos, and flowering trees. Trial and display gardens are maintained.
   A controlled agricultural environment as well as greenhouses and experimental areas may be visited with horticultural seminars.

Daily 9-12, summer and some holidays; 9-6 rest of year; adults, under $18; 13-17 slightly less; 4-12 two-thirds; partial handicapped access; (305) 824-8000; for seminars (305) 828-1500.

KISSIMMEE

20 Gatorland Zoo W
3½ mi. north on U.S. 17 and 92

A boardwalk trail provides a leisurely view of the animals in a Cypress swamp. The trees and plants are labelled.

Daily 8-7, Memorial Day-Labor Day; 8-6 rest of year; adults, under $6; 3-11 half; under 3 free; narrow gauge railroad through grounds; (305) 855-5496.

Florida Cypress Gardens

WINTER HAVEN

21 Florida Cypress Gardens ☆☆☆☆ A-CA-FE-HA-J-O-P-R-S
Rt. 540 5 mi. southeast

This park with a variety of exhibits is set in beautiful gardens established in 1935 on 86 acres. More than 8,000 kinds of plants are found here. 13 theme gardens including Gardens of the World, the All-American Rose Garden, the Oriental Gardens, and the Living Forest. There are large collections of tropical and sub-tropical plants in a natural setting and massed plantings of azaleas, bouganvillias, and camellias. Good specimens of cucumber and various kinds of ficus trees. Test and demonstration gardens are maintained along with a library.

Daily 8-5:30; adults, under $9; 6-10 half; discount on garden admission; handicapped access; boat rides; (813) 324-2111.

22 Slocum Water Gardens ☆ W
1101 Cypress Garden Rd.

This is a commercial nursery which covers 7 acres and maintains 3 display gardens with ponds, pools, and fountains. The nursery deals exclusively in aquatic plants such as lotuses, bog plants, more than 100 types of water lilies, many night blooming varieties, papyrus, water-ferns.

Mon-Fri 8-12, 1-4; Sat 8-12; closed Sun and holidays; no admission charge; (813) 293-7151.

LAKE WALES

23 Bok Tower Gardens ☆☆ A-CA-FE-HA-S
Rt. 17A

128 acres of gardens established in 1929 were designed by Frederick Olmsted around this bell tower; beautiful plantings of azaleas, magnolias, camellias are found here. Thousands bloom at the appropriate season. There are good collections of subtropical landscape plants native to Florida. A tree fern grove, a Live-Oak grove, a reflecting pool, and a nature reserve lie on the grounds

Daily 8-5:30; under $3 per car; nature walks; handicapped access; (813) 676-1408.

HOMASSA SPRINGS

24 Garden of the Springs ☆ O
Junction U.S. 19 and 98

Numerous types of animals, birds and fish are displayed in beautifully planted areas. Many different kinds of tropical shrubs and flowers have been used. There is a good display of orchids.

Daily 9:30-5:30; adults, under $6; over 55 two-thirds; 5-11 half; partial handicapped access; (904) 628-2311.

WEEKI WACHEE

25 Weeki Wachee
Jnct. U.S. 19S and Rt. 50

Water and bird displays in a setting of a tropical rain forest with a good collection of plants. There are nature trails.

Daily 9-5:30; adults, under $9; 3-10 two-thirds; (904) 596-2062.

TAMPA

26 Busch Gardens ☆☆ P-S
Rt. 580 off I-75

This 300-acre park displays more than 1,000 African animals. There is also a fine landscaped tropical garden with thousands of tropical trees and shrubs. Grasses and bamboos of many varieties have been used. Each year more than 100,000 annuals are planted. A geodesic dome houses rare birds in a natural environment of tropical plants.

Daily 9:30-10, July 19-Aug 22; 9:30-6 rest of year; adults, children under $15; under 3 free; (813) 971-8282.

27 Lowry Park
North Blvd. and Sligh Ave.

Tropical trees and shrubs have been set in an informal landscape. Perennial and annual beds complete this garden.

Daily 8-dusk; (813) 935-5503.

INDIAN SHORES

28 Tiki Gardens ☆ W
196th Ave. and Gulf Blvd., off Rt. 694

These landscaped gardens utilize a Polynesian motif. A sunken garden and a mangrove swamp are found here. There is a good collection of tropical plants.

Daily 9:30-10; adults, under $3; over 65 two-thirds; 3-11 half; (813) 595-2567.

ST. PETERSBURG

29 Florida's Sunken Gardens ☆☆☆☆ G-HA-O-P-S
1825 Fourth St.

There are more than 7,000 different kinds of plants in this 7-acre garden established in an abandoned quarry in 1903 by George Turner. Good collections of tropical and sub-tropical plants have been gathered and are displayed in this natural setting. There are two large aviaries and an orchid house with more than 1,000 types which are labelled.

Daily 9-5:30; adults, under $6; 6-12 half; handicapped access; (813) 896-3186.

SARASOTA

30 Marie Selby Botanical Gardens ☆☆☆☆ BR-FE-G-HA-L-O
800 Palm Ave. at U.S.41

This 7-acre garden on a peninsula with a grand view of Sarasota Bay has been developed since 1973. It specializes in epiphytic plants like orchids, pineapples, and ferns and has been named as an orchid and bromeliad identification center. Good collections of aroids, ferns, bromeliads, and *gesneriacaea* are maintained. The greenhouses contain a fine orchid collection. A museum of botany and botanical art stands on the grounds. There are demonstration and test gardens for tropical fruit and vegetables. A library is available.

Daily 10-5; museum 10-4:30; closed Christmas; adults, under $6; under 12 free with adult; handicapped access; (813) 366-5730.

31 Sarasota Jungle Gardens ☆☆ B-BR-C-F-FE-P
3701 Bayshore Rd.

A striking display of birds and animals in a natural plant setting with more than 5,000 species and cultivars. There is a tropical rain forest, a collection of philodendron, a fern garden, fruit tree groves, and an exotic flower garden. The palm collection is large. A garden of plants mentioned in the New Testament has been created. A good display of hibiscus, bougainvillea, bromeliad, and cacti is maintained.

Daily 9-5; adults, under $6; 6-16 half; handicapped access; (813) 385-0011.

32 John and Mable Ringling Museums ☆☆☆ HA-P-R
U.S. 41

Fine formal gardens surround a Venetian style palace on 70 acres. The gardens were established in 1924; There is a formal rose garden, a parterre garden, a 'secret' garden, and an arboretum with emphasis on palms and ficuses as well as areas with fountains, pools, and statuary.

Mon-Fri 9-7; Sat 9-5; Sun, holidays 11-6; adults, under $6; under 12 free with adult; handicapped access; (813) 355-5101.

33 **Sarasota Garden Club**
1131 Blvd. of the Arts

The building stands in a small botanical garden.

Mon-Fri 9-1; no admission charge; (813) 955-0875.

FORT MYERS

34 **Thomas A. Edison Winter Home** ☆☆☆ HA-HH-O-P-S
2350 McGregor Blvd. (Rt. 867)

This was Edison's winter home from 1886 to 1931 with interesting displays of his inventions; it is surrounded by 14 acres of experimental botanical gardens with more than 6,000 kinds of plants collected from various parts of the world and frequently connected with inventions. There are fine specimens of ornamental figs, Kapok-trees, bamboos, Flame trees, palms, and Pagoda trees along with a massive Banyon-tree. The orchid collection is large. The demonstration and test gardens have been used to work with Goldenrod as a source of rubber.

9-4 Mon-Sat, holidays; 12:30-4 Sun; closed Christmas; adults under $3; 6-17 nominal; tours; partial handicapped access; (813) 334-3614.

NAPLES

35 **Jungle Larry's African Safari** S
1590 Goodlette Rd.

Wild birds and animals are displayed in a 70-acre jungle setting with many sub-tropical and indigenous plants; there is a Cyprus hummock.

Daily 9:30-5; adults, under $6; 12-15 two-thirds; 3-11 half; (813) 262-4053.

IMMOKALEE

36 **Corkscrew Swamp Sanctuary** ☆ S-W
Rt. 846, 16 mi. east

This is an 11,000-acre wilderness area which contains the largest remaining stand of virgin Bald-Cypress; some are 700 years old. A wet prairie area and a pine forest also stand on this site. A boardwalk leads through a representative section and some plants are labelled.

Daily 9-5; adults, under $6; students half; under 12 free; (813) 657-3771.

LAKE PLACID

37 **Caladium Nurseries**

The area has become a center for caladium growers and numerous nurseries have been established.

MELBOURNE

38 **Florida Institute of Technology** ☆☆ L-O-P-S

The campus consists of 146 acres of landscaped grounds; 40 acres are a lush tropical garden with palms, Water oaks, orchids, and tropical plants. The palm grove of 2,000 trees represents 100 species

Daily, dawn-dusk; (305) 723-3701.

STUART

39 Chrysanthemum Growers

This has become a center for growing chrysanthemums. Many varieties may be seen here.

PALM BEACH

40 The Society of the Four Arts ☆☆ J-H-HA-R
Four Arts Plaza off Royal Palm Way

A cultural complex with several fine gardens including a Chinese garden, a jungle garden, a formal garden, an urn garden, a Spanish facade, a rose garden, and a herb garden.

10-5 Mon-Sat; 2-5 Sun, Dec 4-April 18; 10-5 Mon-Fri, rest of year; no admission charge; handicapped access; (305) 655-7226.

41 Cluett Memorial Gardens
Bethesda-by-the-Sea
S. County Rd. and Barton Ave.

A Gothic church with formally landscaped gardens; there are good plantings of sub-tropical plants, perennials, and annuals.

Daily 9-5; no admission charge; (305) 655-4554.

BOYNTON BEACH

42 Alberts and Merkel Bros. Inc. O-P-SU
2210 S. Federal Highway

A nursery with an exceptional collection of sub-tropical and tropical plants, both flowering and foliage. There is a continuously blooming orchid display.

Weekdays 8-4:30; closed Sunday; (305) 732-2071.

DELRAY BEACH

43 The Morikami Museum of Japanese Culture BO-J
4000 Morikami Park Rd.

This Japanese style museum building is surrounded by a fine Japanese garden with waterfalls, lakes, and appropriate plantings. The courtyard garden is intimate. There is a Bonsai collection.

10-5 Tues-Sun and holidays; closed Jan 1, Easter, July 4, Thanksgiving, Christmas; no admission charge; partial handicapped access; (305) 499-0631.

FORT LAUDERDALE

44 Flamingo Gardens ☆☆ BR-F-FE-O-P
3750 Flamingo Rd.

This complex contains a botanic garden, citrus grove, Everglades museum as well as other attractions. The 45 gardens were begun in 1925 by Floyd Wray, a friend of David Fairchild. They have been extensively replanted within the last years; palms, ferns, cycads, bromeliads, orchids, as well as tropical economic plants may be found here.

Daily 9-5:30; adults, under $3; children half; tram rides; (305) 473-0064.

NORTH MIAMI BEACH

45 **Gardens and Cloisters of the Monastery of St. Bernard**
16711 West Dixie Highway

A 12th century Spanish Cistercian monastery has been reconstructed on these 20-acre grounds. Some of the gardens have also been restored.

Weekdays 10-5; Sunday 12-5; (305) 945-1461.

MIAMI BEACH

46 **Miami Beach Garden Center and Conservatory** ☆☆☆ BR-FE-O-P-S
2000 Garden Center Drive

A conservatory with a tropical rain forest of more than 2,300 different kinds of plants has been created here. There are good collections of bromeliads, orchids, and ferns. Seasonal displays are held. The conservatory is at its best from November through March.

Daily 10-3:30; no admission charge; (305) 673-7256.

MIAMI

47 **Japanese Teahouse and Garden** HA-J
Watson Park, across MacArthur Causeway

A garden in the classical Japanese style with lagoons, bridges, and a teahouse. Plants appropriate to the climate have been used. More than 110 varieties of trees have been planted in groves on the grounds.

Daily 9-6; no admission charge; handicapped access.

48 **Simpson Park** S
55 S.W. 17th Rd.

A good collection of hardwood hammock trees of the Caribbean and southern Florida has been established on this site. The 8-acre park was established in 1931. There is a library.

Daily 8-sunset; no admission charge; (305) 579-6947.

49 **Monkey Jungle** ☆ S
14805 S.W. 216 St.

A fine rain forest in which monkeys roam freely in their natural habitat has been created here. There are many unusual trees and shrubs.

Daily 9:30-6:30; adults, under $6; over 65 and military under $6; 5-12 under $3.00; (305) 235-1611.

50 **Vizcaya** ☆☆ HH
3251 S. Miami Ave.

This Italian style palace has been placed in 10 acres of formal gardens. There are terraces, parterres, a secret garden, a tea garden, a theater garden, and a water stairway.

Daily 9:30-5; closed Christmas; adults, under $6; senior citizens, military, students two-thirds; 6-12 half; reservations advisable; (305) 579-2708.

51 Jones and Scully Orchid Nursery   O
2200 N.W. 33 Ave.

A large display of orchids is presented by this orchid nursery; many hybrids have been developed here.

8-5 Mon-Fri; 8-4 Sat; closed Sun, holidays; (305) 633-9000.

CORAL GABLES

52 Fairchild Tropical Garden   ☆☆☆☆   BR-FE-HA-L-O-P-RG-S
10901 Old Cutler Rd.

2,500 kinds of plants may be studied in this beautifully landscaped 83-acre botanical garden established in 1936 by Col. Robert H. Montgomery and his friend the plant explorer David Fairchild. It contains the world's largest collection of palms with

Fairchild Tropical Garden

more than 500 different species represented. There are a number of special gardens including the L.H. Bailey Palm Glade, a Cycad Circle, the Montgomery Pinetum, a rock garden, a rain forest, and a vine pergola. Important collections of orchids, bromeliads, and ferns have been planted. There are good specimens of the Cannon-Ball tree, Triangle Palm, Mammey-Apple, Pony-Tail tree, Baobab, Sapodilla, Peach Palms. A Palm Products Museum and a library are part of this institution.

Daily 9:30-4:30; closed Christmas; adults $3; under 13 free; tram; guided walking tours; handicapped access; (305) 667-1651.

53   Parrot Jungle   ☆   BR-HA-O
Red Rd. (S.W. 57th Ave.) and Killian Dr. (S.W. 112th St.)

A sub-tropical jungle is the setting for a large display of unusual birds. Many flowering trees, bromeliads, and orchids may be seen here.

Daily 9:30-5; adults, under $6; 5-12 half; bird shows; handicapped access; (305) 666-7834.

54   Coral Gables House   HH
907 Coral Way

The former home of Solomon Meredith is set in a fine garden which has been restored.

Daily; no admission charge; (305) 442-6445.

55   Garden of Our Lord   B
St. James Luthern Evangelical Church
110 Phoenitia Ave.

A garden of plants of the Holy Land and those mentioned in the Bible has been planted alongside this church. The setting has been nicely landscaped.

Daily 8-5; no admission charge; (305) 443-0014.

HOMESTEAD

56   Orchid Jungle   ☆☆   G-O
26715 S.W. 157th St. at Newton Rd.

A natural jungle in which orchids are grown on Live-Oaks. This large collection of orchids is spread over this 23-acre site. Greenhouses and experimental laboratories stand on the grounds.

Daily 8:30-5:30; closed Thanksgiving, Christmas; adults, under $6; 13-17 two-thirds; 6-12 half; partial handicapped access; (305) 247-4824.

57   Everglades National Park   ☆☆   P-S-W
Rt. 27

Although not a garden or arboretum, this park contains an unusual variety of plants, especially bog and water plants.

Daily 8-5 for Royal Palm Interpretive Center; (305) 247-6211.

58   Redland Fruit and Spice Park   ☆   F-S
24801 S.W. 187th Ave.

This 20-acre park contains more than 313 varieties of fruit, nut, and spice trees. A grove of poisonous plants and medicinal plants may be studied.

Mon-Sat 8-4:30; Sun, holidays 9-5; guided tours recommended; no admission charge; tour nominal; (305) 247-5727.

FLORIDA CITY

59 Agricultural Guided Tour
32 Gateway Estates

A 3-hour tour of southern Dade county and its 150,000 rich acres travels through groves of 200 kinds of tropical and subtropical fruit as well as 50 different kinds of vegetable fields. There are more than 2,400 nurseries in this area.

9-1:30, Dec 1-April 1; for information call (305) 248-6798.

LARGO

60 Suncoast Botanical Gardens HA-S
10410 125th St. North

A 60-acre garden with a collection of native trees, other plants, and some special gardens. It has been neglected in recent years.

Daily 8-dusk; no admission charge; handicapped access; (813) 321-1726.

ISLAMORADA

61 Lignumvitae Key State Botanical Site ☆ HH-S

William Matheson's home built in 1919 stands in the midst of a West Indian hardwood hammock. There are many rare trees including the Pigeon Plum, Mastic, Poisonwood, Strangler Fig, Gumbo-Limbo, and *Lignumvitae*, as well as numerous ornamental blooming trees. It is best seen in spring or early summer.

Tours at 9, 1, 3; Wed-Sun; tour fee, under $3; under 6 free; accessible only by boat; limited to 50 visitors; (305) 664-4815.

KEY WEST

62 Audubon House and Garden ☆ HH-S
Whitehead and Greene Sts.

A home visited by John James Audubon in 1832 which has been restored along with its garden. The grounds contain a fine collection of tropical trees.

Daily 9-12, 1-5; adults, under $3; 5-11 half; (305) 294-2116.

63 Ernest Hemingway Home HH
907 Whitehead St.

This home built in 1851 was purchased by Hemingway in 1931; there is a lush tropical garden which mainly utilizes Caribbean plants.

Daily 9-5; adults, under $3; 6-12 half; (305) 294-1575.

64 Key West Garden Center
South side of White St.

A display of tropical plants is maintained here.

Weekdays 9-4:30.

65 West Martello Tower
3500 Roosevelt Blvd.

This Civil War Fort is the home of a museum and a garden of tropical plants.

10-12, 2-4 Tues, Thurs, Sat, Sun; closed Mon, Fri; no admission charge; (305) 296-2051.

GEORGIA

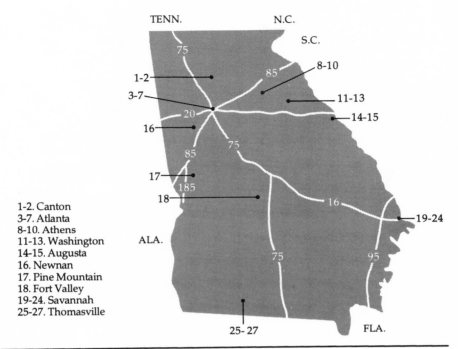

TENN. N.C. S.C.

1-2
3-7
16
17
18
8-10
11-13
14-15
19-24
25-27
ALA.
FLA.

1-2. Canton
3-7. Atlanta
8-10. Athens
11-13. Washington
14-15. Augusta
16. Newnan
17. Pine Mountain
18. Fort Valley
19-24. Savannah
25-27. Thomasville

CANTON

1 Gardens de Pajarito Montana
4 mi. west on Rt. 20

These gardens, begun in 1959, seek to preserve 59 acres of the north Georgia mountain area; native species are emphasized. There are 75 varieties of magnolias, 70 kinds of maples, 65 types of hemlocks, 125 kinds of rhododendrons; all types of native azaleas, 300 varieties of dwarf conifers. A grotto lies on the grounds; a small lake with an area devoted to bog plants has been planned.

For times call the Cline family; (404) 479-4471.

2 Woolford Memorial Garden
1815 S. Ponce de Leon Ave.

A small garden of shrubs, perennials and annuals has been developed here.

Daily, dawn-dusk.

ATLANTA

3 The Atlanta Botanical Garden ☆☆☆ H-HA-HD-J-R
Piedmont Park at S. Prado

This rather new 60-acre garden, established in 1977, possesses fine collections of indigenous plants. Already built are a rose garden, a herb garden, vegetable and demonstration gardens for the average home owner. An existing Japanese garden has been incorporated and renovated. There are also plantings of perennials and annuals.

9-4:30 Mon-Sat; 12:30-4:30 Sun; open till 8 during summer months; 12:30-8 Sun, during summer months; closed New Year, Thanksgiving, Christmas; tours; no admission charge; handicapped access; (404) 876-5858.

4 Fernbank Science Center ☆☆ A-C-G-HA-RG-S-SU-WF
Cator Woolford Memorial Gardens
156 Heaton Park Drive, N.E.

A 65-acre forest contains fine specimens of mimosa, White Oak, tulip, poplar, maple, and others. The 3-acre botanical gardens contain an excellent azalea collection, wildflowers, and ornamentals as well as perennials and annuals. The 10-acre Memorial Gardens have rockeries, fountains, a courtyard garden, and are planted with many ornamental shrubs. The greenhouses display tropical plants, succulents and cacti. Demonstration and test gardens as well as a library are found here.

Forest: 2-5 weekdays; 10-5 Sat; 2-5 Sun; Exhibit Hall: 8:30-5 Mon, Sat; 8:30-10 Tues-Fri; Sat 10-10:30; Sun 1-8; Greenhouses and gardens: 1-5 Sunday only; no admission charge; handicapped access; (404) 378-4311.

5 Atlanta Historical Society Grounds ☆☆ BX-H-HH-HA
3101 Andrews Drive, N.W.

This 23-acre preserve contains 2 restored homes and their gardens. The Tulie Smith house built in 1835 has a herb garden, vegetable garden, and informal flower garden; only authentic 19th century types of plants are used. The Swann House built in 1928 along Palladian lines has a formal boxwood garden with both English and American boxwood, terraced lawns, water cascades, and statuary. There is also a quarry flower garden.

10:30-4:30 Tues-Sat; 2-4:30 Sun; closed holidays and first two weeks in Jan; each house, under $3; 6-17 half; both houses under $3; 6-17 two-thirds; handicapped access; (404) 261-1837.

6 Governor's Mansion Gardens WF
391 West Paces Ferry Rd. N.W.

The grounds contain a wildflower garden. The gardens are open on special occasions.

For information call (404) 261-1776.

7 Dogwood Festival

Tours of residential areas and special gardens are featured during these weeks early in April. There are also many other activities.

For information call (404) 892-0539.

ATHENS

8 Founders Memorial Garden ☆ BX-HH-S
School of Environmental Design
University of Georgia
325 S. Lumpkin St.

3 acres of formal terraced boxwood gardens were established to honor the founder of the first garden club in America. There is a good perennial garden near the restored home. Fine specimens of Southern Magnolia, Double-Flowering Dogwood, Yellow-Wood, Dove Tree, and Short-Leaf Pine may be seen.

Mon-Fri 9-12; Sun 1-4; closed holidays; adults, under $3; partial handicapped access; (404) 542-3354.

9   **University of Georgia Botanical Garden**   ☆☆   HA-R-W-WF
S. Milledge Ave.; 1 mi. south of Athens

Established in 1968 on 293 acres this garden specializes in plants of Georgia's Piedmont. There is a bog and swamp section as well as a wildflower garden. Rare and endangered species are preserved in this garden. The annual and perennial garden as well as the rose garden are at their height from May to November. Many varieties of rhododendron and azalea have been planted. A new visitor center and other facilities are planned.

8-5 Oct-April; 8-8 May-Sept; no admission charge; partial handicapped access; (404) 542-1244.

10   **Taylor-Grady House and Garden**   HH
634 Prince Ave. U.S. 441 and 129

This Greek Revival home was built in 1839; its 13 pillars represent the original colonies. The home and the garden have been restored.

10-2 Mon, Wed, Fri; 2-4 Wed; adults, under $3; (404) 549-8688.

WASHINGTON

11   **Washington**   HH

This lovely old town contains many Greek Revival mansions and other interesting old homes with their gardens. They are open during the spring of odd numbered years through special tours.

For information call (404) 678-2013.

12   **Sunset Hill**   HH
North St.

A fine home surrounded by a well-maintained garden with old trees and shrubs.

By appointment only; (404) 678-2013.

13   **Pope Home**   HH
West Robert Thomas Ave.

This home has a widow's walk along the top, which is unusual for an inland house. The gardens contain beautiful plantings.

By appointment only; (404) 678-2013.

AUGUSTA

14   **Pendelton King Park**
1738 Pinetree Rd.

A touch and smell garden labelled in braille has been installed here by the city's garden clubs.

Daily 9-5; no admission charge; (404) 736-0715.

15   **Garden trails**   A

7 clearly marked trails with maps available lead through the various parks and residential areas with their interesting plantings. Springtime with its blooming

azalea, rhododendron along with many other kinds of shrubs and trees is the best period to take these walks.

For information call (404) 722-0421 or 724-2324.

NEWNAN

16 Dunaway Gardens J-RG
6 mi. northwest, off U.S. 29

20 acres of rocky terrain have been cleverly landscaped into a lovely series of gardens. Among them are hanging gardens, a sunken garden, a Japanese rock garden, and a cottage garden. Planned by Hetty Jane Dunaway Sewell, the gardens have been somewhat neglected during recent years; plans for their restoration are now being executed.

By appointment only; (404) 251-2109.

PINE MOUNTAIN

17 Callaway Gardens ☆☆☆☆ A-C-G-L-R-SU-WF
U.S. 27 south

This 2,500-acre resort and recreation area contains forest, lakes, vast landscaped areas and numerous trails. 8 acres have been developed into gardens with seasonal flowers including fine displays of azalea, dogwood, mountain laurel, crape-myrtle, hydrangea, rhododendron, crab-apple, rose, tuberous begonia, and holly. Vegetable gardens, a rock garden, and water falls may be found here. There are good collections of wildflowers, rhododenron, and azalea with more than 700 species and cultivars of wild plants grouped according to color. The greenhouses are filled with tropical and native plants. The new John A. Sibley Horticultural Center with its 5 acres of greenhouses and gardens has just been opened.

Daily 8:30-6 April 1-Aug 31; 9-5 rest of year; adults, under $6; 6-11 half; fees for other activities; partial handicapped access; (404) 663-2281.

FORT VALLEY

18 Camellia Gardens ☆☆ CA-G-HA
American Camellia Society Headquarters
Massee Lane; I-75 exit at Perry on 341 or Byron on 49

This peach center of Georgia in which the entire countryside blooms in April has been chosen as the national headquarters of the Camellia Society. The 10-acre gardens and greenhouses contain an excellent collection with many rare species; more than 1,000 kinds are to be found here. Flowers bloom from November to March. There is also a fine collection of Boehm porcelain, pictures of camellias, and a rare book library.

9-4 Mon-Fri; Sun afternoon during blooming season; no admission charge; handicapped access; (912) 967-2358.

SAVANNAH

19 Owens-Thomas House and Museum HH
Ogelthorpe Square at 124 Abercorn

A Regency style house built by William Jay of London in 1819 has a small formal garden planted with flowers and shrubs authentic for that period in Savannah.

10-5 Tues-Sat; 2-5 Sun, Mon; closed Sept and holidays; adults, under $3; students half; 6-12 nominal; (912) 233-9743.

20 **Juliette Gordon Low Birthplace**   HH-R
142 Bull St.

A restored Regency home with a garden of the 1870's; many favorite roses of the Victorian period may be found here. Other plants include climbing fig, crape-myrtle, verbena, and lilac.

10-4 Mon-Sat; 1:30-4:30 Sun; adults, under $3; children half; (912) 233-4501.

21 **Davenport Home and Garden**   HH
119 Habersham St.

This home built between 1815 and 1820 has been restored into a house museum. There is a fine garden.

10-4:30 Mon-Sat; closed major holidays; admission charge; (912) 236-8097.

22 **Bonaventura Cemetery**   ☆   A-S
330 Bonaventura Rd.

An old cemetery with fine hundred-year-old azaleas, dogwoods, camellias, wisterias, jasmines and two-hundred-year-old Live Oaks.

Daily 8:30-5.

23 **Forsythe Park**   .-A

This park has plantings of azaleas which are at their height in spring. There is a fragrance garden for the blind.

24 **Home and Garden tour**   HH

Held each March with many fine gardens open to the public.

For information call (912) 233-6651.

THOMASVILLE

25 **Rose Test Gardens of the American Rose Society**   ☆   R-HA
U.S. 84, east

More than 400 varieties of roses are represented here in plantings of over 2,500 bushes. Especially beautiful in March and April.

8-5 Mon-Sat; 2-5 Sun; mid-April to mid-Oct; no admission charge; handicapped access; (912) 226-9600.

26 **Pebble Hill Plantation**   HH-S

This plantation mansion is surrounded by an informal garden with many old trees and shrubs.

10-5 Tues-Sat; 1-5 Sun; closed day after Labor Day - Oct 1, Christmas, Thanksgiving; adults (grounds only), under $3; children half; children not admitted to house; (912) 226-2344.

27 **Rose Festival**   HH-R

This festival is held during mid April each year. Local homes and their gardens may be toured.

For information call (912) 226-9600.

HAWAII

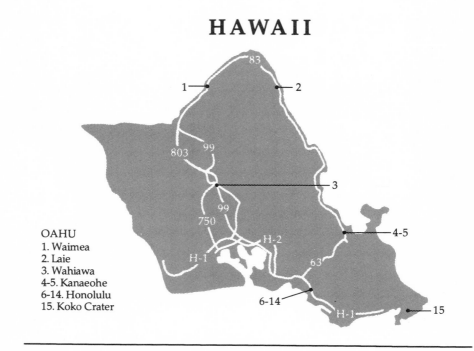

OAHU
1. Waimea
2. Laie
3. Wahiawa
4-5. Kanaeohe
6-14. Honolulu
15. Koko Crater

OAHU

WAIMEA

1 Waimea Arboretum and Botanical Garden ☆☆☆ HA-P-S
Waimea Falls Park
59-865 Kamehameha Highway

An 1,800-acre conservation zone situated in a protected valley; approximately 100 acres under intense cultivation has been developed into a botanical garden, bird sanctuary and nature park. A natural waterfall produces a medium-sized river which flows through the collections. The plant collections are arranged by genus, family, geographic origin or special use. 34 distinct collections are presently under cultivation including: palm, acanthus, begonia, coral tree, mallow, hibiscus hybrids, *Heliconia*, ginger. There are collections of plants from Guam, Malaysia, Madagascar, and the Mascarenes as well as the other Hawaiian islands. The gardens were founded in 1973; there is a library and a herbarium.

Daily 10-5:30; adults, under $9; 7-12 two-thirds; 4-6 half; under 4 free; tram tours and guided walks; handicapped access; (808) 638-8511 or 923-8448.

LAIE

2 Mormon Temple Gardens

Fine grounds of formal terraced gardens surround this temple. There are reflecting pools with a good selection of perennials and annuals as well as tropical plants around them.

Daily 10-4; no admission charge.

WAHIAWA

3 Wahiawa Botanic Garden ☆☆☆ FE-P-S
1396 California Ave.

Located at an elevation of a thousand feet, this area is full of palms, ornamentals, native plants, and ferns. There are more than a thousand varieties of aroids. The garden has an unusual collection of Pritchard Palms.

Daily 9-4; no admission charge; (808) 533-3406.

KANEOHE

4 Ho'omaluhia P

This ethno-botanical garden of the Hawaiian Botanical Gardens is devoted to environmental studies. 400 acres of wet wild tropical forest are developing into a collection of tropical areas around the world, with emphasis on the Pacific region. The garden contains no formal plantings and it presents the setting of a natural forest preserve.

Thurs-Mon 9-4; no admission charge; (808) 235-6636.

5 Byodo-in Temple J
47-200-Kahekili Highway (Rt. 83)

This replica of the ancient Japanese Temple at Uji stands in a Japanese garden by a small lake. There is a waterfall and a ceremonial tea house.

Daily 9-5; adults, under $3; students and children half; (808) 239-8811.

HONOLULU

6 Foster Botanical Gardens ☆☆☆ BR-FE-G-O
180 N. Vineyard Blvd.

2,600 species are found in this 17-acre garden. Some are the original plantings from 1855 when the garden was established by William Hillebrand adjacent to the king's botanic garden. It has and continues to play a vital role in the economy of the islands through plant introductions and experiments. There is an orchid garden with a collection of 10,000 plants, of which more than a hundred bloom each week, and a bromeliad garden with many species. The collection of palms and exotic trees is excellent and presents mature specimens.

Daily 9-4; adults, under $3; children half; free tours Mon, Wed afternoons; (808) 533-3406.

7 Harold L. Lyon Arboretum ☆☆☆ L-P-S
3860 Manoa Rd.

This old arboretum founded in 1918 is part of the University of Hawaii and covers 125 acres. Its altitude ranges from 450 to 1,300 feet with temperature variations from 55 to 85 degrees. Its 8,000 accessions include 4000 species of palms, ficus, taro clones, aroids, gingers, heliconias, *Marantaceae, Gesneriaceae*, ornamental ti, as well as native and endemic Hawaiian plants. The primary interest of the garden is tropical plant research, ethno-botany, and education.

Mon-Fri 9-3; free guided tours at 1 on 1st Fri of each month Jan-June; 1st Fri and 3rd Wed July-Dec; no admission charge; (808) 988-3177.

8 **Manoa Campus**
University of Hawaii
2444 Dole St.

560 types of plants have been used to landscape this campus; both tropical and sub-tropical plants have been used on these 300 acres which are beautifully maintained.

Daily, dawn-dusk; (808) 948-8369.

9 **Honolulu Academy of Arts** HA-J-O
900 S. Beretania St.

A series of patio gardens are part of this cultural center. They include a terrace garden, Hawaiian Garden, Oriental Court, and orchid garden.

10-4:30 Tues, Wed, Fri, Sat; 11-8 Thurs, 2-5 Sun; closed Jan 1, July 4, Labor Day, Thanksgiving, Christmas; no admission charge; handicapped access; (808) 538-3693.

10 **Kahameha Schools** S
Kapalama Heights

This school is located on 200 acres of very well-landscaped grounds with many fine specimen trees and native plants.

Daily; (808) 842-8211.

11 **Paradise Park** ☆ O-P
3737 Manoa Rd.

This is a jungle garden and aviary with a bamboo forest; there are a large number of orchids and tropical plants. Bird shows are featured.

Daily 9:30-5; closed Christmas; adults, under $9; 4-12 two-thirds; partial handicapped access; (808) 988-2141.

12 **Punahou School**
1601 Punahou St.

An old missionary school established in 1841 with beautifully landscaped grounds; there are several walls covered with Night Blooming Cereus which open about 8 p.m. July-Sept.

7:30-4 Mon-Fri; (808) 944-5711.

13 **Queen Kapiolani Rose Garden** R
Paki and Monsarrat Aves.

A large variety of roses are explained through a self-guiding tour; there are also numerous tropical flowering plants.

Daily 8-3.

14 **National Memorial Cemetery of the Pacific**
Punchbowl Crater at Puowaina Drive.

The floor of this extinct volcano, now a cemetery, has been beautifully landscaped with tropical trees, bushes, and flowering plants. The rim of the volcano provides an excellent view of Honolulu.

Daily 8-5:30, Sept 30-March 1; 8-6:30, March 2-Sept 29.

KOKO CRATER

15 Koko Crater Botanic Gardens ☆☆ C-SU

This preserve of 200 acres is very warm and dry; it has become the setting for a fine collection of cacti, *Euphorbia*, and *Plumeria*. More than 1,000 species are represented in a growing collection. The character of this garden is wild rather than formal.

Daily 9-4; no admission charge; (808) 533-3406.

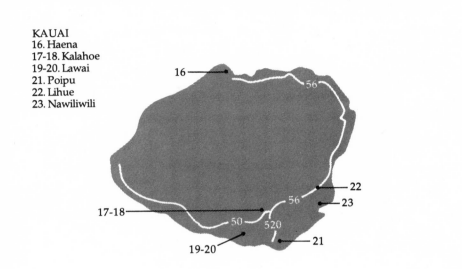

KAUAI
16. Haena
17-18. Kalahoe
19-20. Lawai
21. Poipu
22. Lihue
23. Nawiliwili

KAUAI

HAENA

16 Limahuli Preserve ☆☆ P-S-WF

This 1,000-acre preserve lies on the northern coast of Kauai in the Limahuli Valley. This lush area contains many newly discovered species of rare, native Hawaiian plants. A portion of it will be developed into collections of ethno-botanical, economic, and medicinal plants. This wetter site complements the Headquarters Garden at Lawai.

By reservation only; (808) 332-8131.

KALAHOE

17 Olu Pua Gardens ☆☆☆ C-HA-O-P-S-SU-W
½ mi. west on Rt. 50

Formerly a plantation manager's home built in 1932, this 12½-acre garden contains more than 4,000 species of sub-tropical and tropical plants. There are notable collections of tropical food plants, economic flowering foliage, hibiscus, palms, flowering trees and shrubs, aroids, *Calathea*, *Heliconia*, ginger, cacti, succulents, water lilies and orchids. There is a library.

Daily 8:30-5; closed Jan 1; adults, under $6; under 12 quarter; handicapped access; (808) 332-8182.

18   Kukuiolono Park   J
off Rt. 50

The former estate of Walter McBryde contains a Japanese garden.

Daily 6:30-6:30.

LAWAI

19   Pacific Tropical Botanical Gardens   ☆☆☆   H-P

This garden is especially interested in endangered tropical species. It has been developed around the well-landscaped former estate of Robert Allerton. The 186-acre gardens contain excellent collections of *Erythrina*, palms, Hawaiian native plants, rare fruit plants, medicinal and economic plants. There is a library. Several satellite gardens are maintained.

Tours, Mon, Tues, Thurs, Sat mornings by appointment only; adults, under $12; (808) 332-8131.

20   Allerton Gardens   ☆☆   HH-L-S
adjacent to the Pacific Tropical Botanical Garden
Hailima Rd.

This 100-acre estate has been turned into a beautiful, well-landscaped tropical garden. Begun by Queen Emma, the wife of Kamehameha IV in 1870, it has been much expanded by Robert Allerton and his son. The Queen's cottage remains on the grounds. The Three Springs Gardens lie nearby and form part of this complex.

Tours by appointment only, Mon, Tues, Thurs; (808) 332-8131.

POIPU

21   Moir's Gardens   S

This garden contains one of the largest collections of African aloes; there is a variety of other plantings.

Daily 8:30-4:30; adults, under $3.

LIHUE

22   Botanic Garden
Rice and Ewa Sts.

This small garden contains all the plants which were introduced to Kauai by the first immigrants. Plants are labelled and their use is discussed.

Daily, dawn-dusk.

NAWILIWILI

23   Menehune Gardens

A privately owned garden generally open to the public; it features hundreds of tropical species. Many of the plants are labelled. There is an enormous Banyon tree which covers one acre.

Daily 8:30-4:30; adults, under $3.

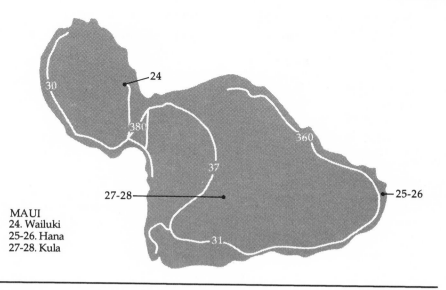

MAUI
24. Wailuki
25-26. Hana
27-28. Kula

MAUI

WAILUKU

24 Maui Zoological and Botanical Garden S
Kanaloa Ave.

This modern zoo is located on a 13-acre site; the gardens present an extensive collection of native Hawaiian plants. Many rare species may be found here.

Daily 10-4; adults, under $6; children half; (808) 244-9141.

HANA

25 Silversword Loop ☆ S
Haleakola National Park

These unusual members of the sunflower family take from 8 to 20 years to reach maturity; after blooming they die. Between 100 and 500 blooms are found on each stem.

Daily; bloom in July and Aug.

26 Kahanu Gardens ☆ HH-P-S

Breadfruit, coconut, and Loulo palm collections are found on this 120-acre preserve. It is the center for ethno-botanic collections of the Pacific Tropical Botanical Garden. The most ancient Hawaiian place of worship, the Piilanihale Heiau, stands on its grounds and is a National Historic Landmark.

By reservation only; (808) 332-8131.

KULA

27 Kula Botanical Garden Inc. ☆ H-HA-P-S
Upper Kula Rd.

This beautifully landscaped 23-acre garden was founded in 1971. It contains some striking waterfalls; there is a good collection of native Hawaiian plants, proteas, herbs, and flowering plants.

Daily 9-4; adults, under $3; 6-12 half; under 5 free; handicapped access; (808) 878-1715.

28 Maui Agricultural Research Station   R-S
Hawaii Institute for Tropical Agriculture
University of Hawaii at Manoa
Mauna Place off Copp Rd.

Located at an elevation of 3,000 ft, this station has a large collection of ornamentals in the *Proteaceae* family. There is also an All-American Rose Garden and an All-American Selection Garden.

7-3:30 Mon-Fri; closed weekends, holidays; no admission charge.

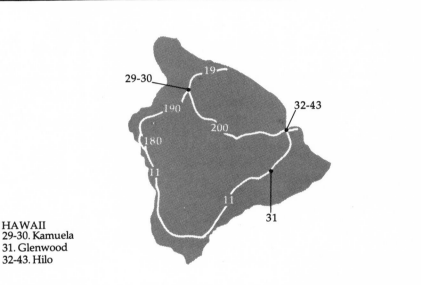

HAWAII
29-30. Kamuela
31. Glenwood
32-43. Hilo

HAWAII

KAMUELA

29 State Tree Nursery
1½ mi. south, near airport

This nursery provides a display of many species of young native trees.

Weekdays 7-3:30; no admission charge.

30 Hawaii Volcanoes National Park   ☆ FE-P

Large groves of tree ferns are to be found in these extensive rain forests.

Daily 8:30-5; no admission charge; (808) 572-7749.

GLENWOOD

31 Akatsuka Orchid Gardens   O
near Hilo

Hawaii's largest *Cymbidium* orchid farm exhibits more than 200 varieties. The plants are well displayed.

Daily 8:30-5; no admission charge.

HILO

32 Liliuokalani Garden Park ☆ J
25 Aupuni St.

A large Japanese garden which covers some 30 acres; it has been built in the Yedo-style with stone lanterns, pagodas, and bridges. A mixture of Japanese and indigenous trees and plants have been used. Coconuts and mangos are also found on the grounds.

Daily, dawn-dusk.

33 Nani Mau Gardens ☆☆ H-J-O
421 Makalika St.

This garden contains more than 2,000 varieties of orchids as well as 100 types of tropical fruit and more than 250 species of flowering plants. There is a herb garden with unusual tropical herbs a Japanese garden and a 3-acre collection of anthuriums and gingers. Large collection of Polynesian and Hawaiian flora are also displayed.

Daily 8-5; adults, under $3; 7-17 half; partial handicapped access; (808) 959-9442.

34 Tree Nursery
1643 Kilauea Ave.

This 19-acre site has been planted with a wide variety of tropical trees.

Weekdays 7:45-4:30; no admission charge; (808) 961-7221.

35 Hale Nui Flowers
Panewa Farm Lots

This nursery and garden specializes in anthuriums and possesses a very large collection.

Daily 9-5; closed Sunday; no admission charge; self-guided tours; (808) 959-9869.

36 Hawaii Mountain Orchid O
Panaewa Forest
Off Rt 11 near Macedonia Nut.

This large orchid nursery specializes in *Cattleyas* and *Cymbidiums*.

7:30-4 Mon-Fri; no admission charge; (808) 966-9120.

37 Hirose Nursery
2212 Kanoelehua Ave.

Many varieties of tropical plants and flowers are displayed here on a large site.

8-5 Mon-Fri; 8-4 Sat; 9-4 Sun; no admission charge; (808) 959-4561.

38 Kong's Floraleigh Gardens
1477 Kalanianaole Ave.

Tropical plants and flowers representing numerous varieties are represented here.

Daily 8:30-4; no admission charge; (808) 935-4957.

40   Orchidarium   O
524 Manono St.

This ½-acre orchid garden is utilized by orchid growers of the islands for displays. They are beautifully maintained.

Daily, dawn-dusk; donation nominal.

41   Kuaola Farms

62 acres feature exotic tropical flowers as well as numerous fruit and Macadamia nut trees.

Daily 8-4; no admission charge; (808) 959-4565.

42   Orchids of Hawaii
575 Hinano St.

A large variety of plants and flowers is displayed here.

Daily 8-4:30; adults, under $3; children half; guided tours; (808) 935-6617.

43   Tanaka's Anthurium Nursery
99 West Kahaopea St.

This nursery specializes in anthuriums and tropical flowers.

Daily 7-4; no admission charge; (808) 959-8212.

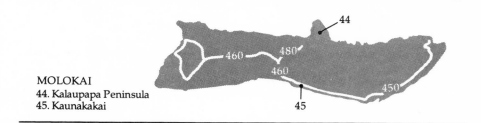

MOLOKAI
44. Kalaupapa Peninsula
45. Kaunakakai

MOLOKAI

KALAUPAPA PENINSULA

44   Palaau State Park
near Hilo.

This park contains a small arboretum with more than 40 species of trees; most are tropical and many are labelled.

Daily, dawn-dusk.

KAUNAKAKAI

45   Kapuaiwa Grove   P

More than 1,000 coconut palms cover this 10-acre beach and present a spectacular sight.

Daily, dawn-dusk.

IDAHO

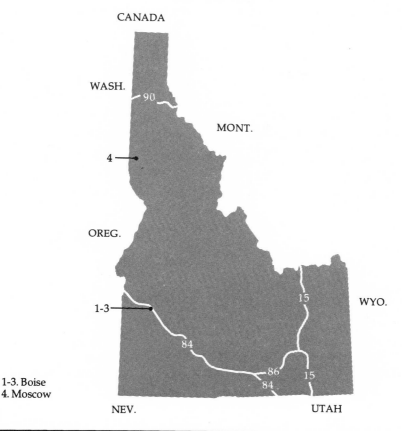

CANADA

WASH.

90

MONT.

4 —

OREG.

1-3 —

15

WYO.

84

86

15
84

1-3. Boise
4. Moscow

NEV.

UTAH

BOISE

1 Ann Morrison Memorial Park
1104 Royal Blvd/1000 Americana Blvd.
900 University Drive

This 153-acre park is the largest in Boise; it contains both formal and informal gardens planted with perennials and annuals. There is a tree-lined mall along with a reflecting pool with a water cascade. The park lies along a river bank.

Daily 6-midnight; no admission charge; picnic facilities; (208) 344-5515 or 384-4240.

2 Julia Davis Park   HA-R
700 S. Capitol Blvd.
Entrance on Capitol Blvd. or Myrtle St.

This 86-acre park contains a variety of cultural facilities. There is a lagoon with formal plantings as well as a rose garden.

Daily 6-midnight; no admission charge; picnic facilities; handicapped access.

3 **Howard Platt Gardens**
1633 S. Capitol Blvd.

These small well-groomed gardens of perennials, annuals and shrubs overlook the city and provide a fine view of the Sawtooth Mountains.

Daily; no admission charge.

MOSCOW

4 **Charles Huston Shattuck Arboretum** ☆ S
College of Forestry, University of Idaho

7 acres of this arboretum represent its old section. Its 200 species of trees and shrubs of the northern Rocky Mountains were planted in 1909 and are mature. The 35-acre new section, developed according to a master plan, now contains an Asian section begun in 1983 with trees, shrubs, and flowering plants.

Daily, dawn-dusk; no admission charge; partial handicapped access; (208) 885-6280.

ILLINOIS

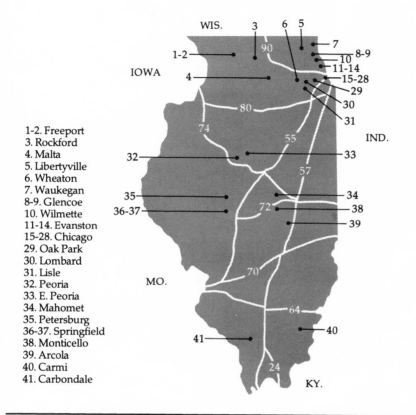

WIS. 3 6 5

IOWA

1-2
4

7
8-9
10
11-14
15-28
29
30
31

IND.

90
80
74
55
57
72
70
64
24

32
35
36-37
33
34
38
39

MO.

41
40

KY.

1-2. Freeport
3. Rockford
4. Malta
5. Libertyville
6. Wheaton
7. Waukegan
8-9. Glencoe
10. Wilmette
11-14. Evanston
15-28. Chicago
29. Oak Park
30. Lombard
31. Lisle
32. Peoria
33. E. Peoria
34. Mahomet
35. Petersburg
36-37. Springfield
38. Monticello
39. Arcola
40. Carmi
41. Carbondale

FREEPORT

1 Stephenson County Historical Society Arboretum R
1440 S. South Carroll Ave.

The grounds of this historical museum and farm museum form an arboretum with 75 species of trees and shrubs. Many of the mature specimens were planted in the last century. The Taylor Memorial Rose Garden specializes in hybrid tea roses.

1:30-5 Fri-Sun; donations; (815) 232-8419.

2 Don Opel Arboretum S
Highland Community College
Pearl City Rd.

This 210-acre arboretum is part of the college campus; when completed more than 5,000 plants representing 300 species will be planted. There also is a 3½-acre tall grass prairie with 50 species of native plants; best viewed in September and October.

Daily, dawn-dusk; no admission charge; (815) 235-6121.

ROCKFORD

3   **Sunken Gardens**   G-R
Sinnissippi Park
North 2nd St.

This sunken garden along with its lagoon are planted with roses, perennials, and annuals; another area contains hedges and trees. There are some fine crab-apples. A greenhouses with tropical plants lies on the grounds.

Daily 9-4; no admission charge.

MALTA

4   **Kishwaukee College**   F-G-HD

The campus contains an All-American Selection Trial Garden, one of 28 in North America. The Vaughan Seed Company also has trial gardens with more than 1,000 rows of flowers and vegetables on campus. There are greenhouses, orchards, and a 2-acre prairie restoration.

Weekdays 9-5 during summer months; 'Field Days' are held in July; no admission charge; (815) 825-2086 ex 294

LIBERTYVILLE

5   **Cook Memorial Park**   R
413 N. Milwaukee Ave.

A rose garden is part of this large park.

Daily, dawn-dusk.

WHEATON

6   **Catigny**   ☆☆   HA-L-R-RG-S
151 Winfield Rd.

10 acres of the 500-acre former McCormick Estate have been developed into formal gardens since 1966. There are 17 different gardens including a fountain garden, green garden, rose garden, rock garden, north scalloped garden, flowering and silver foliage shrubs, dryland garden, Alder-Birch collection, ornamental specimen tree collection, Douglas Fir grove, columnar and semi-columnar tree collection, south scalloped garden, ash, dogwood collection, maple, virburnum collection, linden and euonymous collection, and Burr Oak collection. The area is beautifully landscaped.

Daily, dawn-dusk; no admission charge; handicapped access; (312) 668-5161.

WAUKEGAN

7   **Haines House**   H
Bowen Park

The grounds of this house contain a small herb garden.

Daily 9-4; (312) 689-7500.

GLENCOE

8   **Chicago Horticultural Society Botanic Gardens**   ☆☆☆   HA-C-G-H-J-RG-SU-WF
Lake Cook Rd.

This is a garden was established on 300 acres of former marsh land in 1965. The Japanese Garden has been built around a series of small lakes. The gardens contain waterfalls, fountains, an alpine garden, a herb garden, a wildflower garden, and a prairie garden. There are good collections of native plants, *Ericaceae,* narcissus, and ornamentals. A demonstration garden is maintained along with greenhouses of tropical plants, succulents and cacti. There is a library.

Daily 9-4; no admission charge; handicapped access; (312) 835-5440.

9 **Everly Wildflower and Bird Sanctuary** WF
999 Greenbay Rd.

A variety of wildflowers are displayed here; some are labelled.

Daily 9-4; (312) 835-3030.

WILMETTE

10 **Baha'i Temple Gardens** ☆ R
Linden Ave and Sheridan Rd.

This 9-sided building is surrounded by 9 gardens; a good selection of roses, perennials and annuals as well as crab-apples and quinces may be found here.

Daily 10-10; May 15-Oct 14; 10-5 rest of year; no admission charge; partial handicapped access; (312) 256-4400.

EVANSTON

11 **Shakespeare Garden** SH
Northwestern University
Sheridan Rd.

A small Shakespearean garden has been created here. It is surrounded by hawthorn hedges and planted with herbs, perennials, and annuals known in Shakespeare's time.

Dawn-dusk while school is in session; (312) 492-7271.

12 **Merrick Rose Garden** R
Lake St and Oak Ave.

1,000 rose bushes representing 18 varieties have been planted in this garden.

Daily, dawn-dusk.

13 **Ladd Arboretum** ☆ HA-S
Emerson St. and McCormick Blvd.

A prairie restoration with a variety of grasses and other plants is the main feature of this 18-acre arboretum established in 1958. There is a collection of ornamental trees planted by family and an international friendship garden along with an ecology center.

Daily 9-9; 9-4:30 Tues-Sat for Ecology Center; no admission charge; handicapped access; (312) 864-5181.

14 **Center for Natural Landscaping** ☆ HA-S-WF
2603 Sheridan

10 acres are devoted to native plants with a collection of trees, shrubs, prairie grasses, and wildflowers of the woods and dunes. Demonstration and display gardens are maintained here.

Daily 9-9; no admission charge; handicapped access; (312) 328-2100

CHICAGO

15   Garfield Park Conservatory   ☆☆☆   HA-C-G-FE-P-SU
Garfield Park at Lake St.

This conservatory founded in 1892 has 4 acres under glass along with 20 acres of gardens. More than 4,000 different kinds of plants are represented; a collection of more than 125 species of palm, 175 species of fern, 400 varieties of succulent, 200 kinds of economic plants, as well as aroids, cacti, cycads, tropical fruit, and medicinal plants. The large exhibit greenhouses feature four major seasonal flower shows. This is one of the major conservatories of America. There is a library.

Daily 9-5; Fri to 9; 10-6 Fri, 9-9 during seasonal shows; no admission charge; handicapped access; (312) 533-1281.

16   Garfield Park Garden for the Blind   ☆☆
South of the Conservatory

This garden is formed by a very large raised bed. It is divided into 59 sections which display 1,500 species and cultivars. Labels are in braille and print. Flowers, scented plants, and vegetables make up this garden along with fountains.

Daily, dawn-dusk.

17   Garfield Park Formal Gardens   ☆☆   W
Central Park Blvd. and Hamlin Ave.

This 4-acre formal garden contains 2 water lily ponds with 200 plants representing 50 species and cultivars. The 56 flower beds with 25,000 annuals are arranged according to different patterns each year.

Daily, dawn-dusk.

18   Humboldt Park Flower Garden

Division St. and Sacramento Blvd.

20 flower beds form this sunken circular garden; 15,000 perennials and annuals are planted here.

Daily, dawn-dusk.

19   Douglas Park Formal Gardens   ☆   W
Ogden Ave. and Sacramento Blvd.

The lagoon of this park contains 60 species of water lilies, 40 day-blooming and 20 night-blooming. In addition 26 flower beds are planted with 18,000 annuals.

Daily, dawn-dusk.

20   Daniel L. Flaherty Memorial Rose Garden   ☆☆   R
Grant Park
Randolph St. and McFetride Drive

8,000 roses of hybrid tea, grandiflora, and floribunda types have been planted in 38 beds arranged in a formal design. There are fountains and pools along with statuary. This is a public rose test garden and displays new introductions along with older types.

Daily, dawn-dusk.

21   Court of Presidents in Grant Park   ☆
Congress Parkway

St. Gauden's statue of Lincoln stands in this very formal annual garden. 20,000 plants provide a colorful display each year.

Daily, dawn-dusk.

22 Lincoln Park Conservatory ☆☆☆ A-HA-FE-G-O-P
Stockton Drive

3 acres of greenhouse and 6 of gardens in the northern part of the city were established in 1891. The palm house, fernery, and tropical house contain excellent collections of palms, ferns, cycads, orchids, economic plants, ornamentals and azaleas. There are superb seasonal displays.

Daily 9-5; longer hours during flower shows; no admission charge; handicapped access; (312) 294-4770.

23 Lincoln Park Grandmother's Garden ☆
Stockton Drive and Lincoln Park West.

A garden of old-fashioned plants was begun here in 1893. 30,000 perennials and 10,000 annuals bloom in succession from spring to fall.

Daily, dawn-dusk.

24 Lincoln Park Main Garden and Rock Garden ☆ RG-S
South of the Conservatory

Large formal beds have been planted around a fountain; there are 25,000 perennials and annuals in this garden. The rock garden contains a collection of dwarf conifers, alpines, and annuals.

Daily, dawn-dusk.

25 Jackson Park Perennial Garden ☆ J
59th St. and Stony Island Ave.

Flowering shrubs, trees, perennials and thousands of annuals have been planted in this circular garden. More than 180 varieties of perennials and annuals are used here. There is a small Japanese garden with a bridge, tea house, and lanterns.

Daily, dawn-dusk.

26 Marquette Park Rose and Trial Gardens ☆☆ C-H-R-RG-SU-T
3540 W. 71st St.

The 1-acre garden has been designed in a contemporary free-form style. 4,000 roses of 80 varieties have been planted; another section contains 500 old-fashioned roses representing 85 cultivars. There is a cactus and succulent garden, a rock garden, a herb garden, and a topiary garden. The trial garden is used to test introductions of perennials and annuals.

Daily, dawn-dusk.

27 Rainbow Park Garden ☆ T
South Shore Drive and 77th and 78th Sts.

Large beds of perennials are the main feature of this garden. Annuals are added seasonally and some are trained in topiary forms.

Daily, dawn-dusk.

28 Washington Park Formal Gardens
55th St. and Cottage Grove Ave.

Geometrically arranged beds of annuals and perennials are displayed in this formal garden along with colored foliage plants. Annuals in mass planting complement this arrangement.

Daily, dawn-dusk.

OAK PARK

29　Oak Park Conservatory　☆　FE-G-P
Garfield St. and East Ave.

Built in 1929, this conservatory contains a tropical house, a desert house and a fern house with fine collections. Seasonal displays of foliage and tropical plants are offered throughout the year. There is a summer outdoor garden.

10-4 Tues-Sun; 2-4 Mon; no admission charge; (312) 386-4700.

LOMBARD

30　Lilac Park　☆☆　HA-S
Park and Maple Aves.

1,200 lilac bushes of 275 varieties have been planted in this 8½-acre garden founded by Col. Plum in the 19th century. They along with 43,000 tulips provide a grand display each spring.

Daily 9-9; adults, under $3; senior citizens half; admission charge during bloom time only; handicapped access; call for blooming period, approximately April 20-May 20; (312) 627-1281.

LISLE

31　The Morton Arboretum　☆☆☆　HA-HD-R-S
East-West Tollway, exit Rt. 53

This major arboretum was established in 1922 and now covers 1,500 acres with superb collections which represent 4,800 species. Plants are arranged botanically, geographically, or by landscape qualities. Outstanding collection and display of flowering crab-apples and lilacs which bloom in May. Fall foliage display is also unusual. A rose garden with more than 250 varieties of old-fashioned roses; prairie restoration with 140 species on 25 acres; hedge and street tree area; groundcover and, conifer areas. Test and demonstration gardens for hedges and dwarf shrubs are maintained along with more than 30 miles of walking trails; there is a library.

Daily 9-7 April 1-Oct 31; 9-5 rest of year; different hours for center; admission $3 per car; handicapped access; open-air bus tours; (312) 968-0074.

PEORIA

32　Glen Oak Botanical Garden　☆☆　HA-G-H-O-R
Prospect and McClure Aves.

A fine conservatory has been set in a formal garden of 6 acres. It contains a collection of orchids and tropical plants. The outside gardens have a collection of crab-apples and viburnum. There is a rose garden with 800 All-American selections, a herb garden, an all-seasons garden, a herbaceous perennial garden as well as test and demonstration gardens.

Daily, dawn-dusk; conservatory 8-4 weekdays; 12-4 Sat, Sun; no admission charge; handicapped access; (309) 685-4321.

EAST PEORIA

33 Ornamental Horticultural Land Laboratory ☆ S
Illinois Central College

An 8-acre series of gardens forms the entrance area of this college. There is a flowering crab-apple collection, a perennial flower garden, a landscape plant arboretum, and an All-American Selection Display Garden. July to October is the best season for visiting.

Daily, dawn-dusk; landscape and garden day sponsored on the last Sat of August; no admission charge; (309) 694-5011.

MAHOMET

34 Lake of the Wood Botanic Garden ☆☆ G-HA-H-R-WF
Early American Museum
Exit 172 from I-74

This pioneer life museum has an 8-acre botanic garden. The collection of native plants includes prairie grasses and wildflowers. There is a rose garden, a herb garden, and a dye plant garden along with a conservatory which houses tropical plants.

Daily 10-5 Memorial Day-Labor Day; 10-5 Sat and Sun May 1 to Memorial Day and Labor Day-Oct 10; adults, under $3; 11-17 half; 6-10 nominal; handicapped access; (217) 586-3360.

PETERSBURG

35 Starhill Forest HD
R.R. 1, Peterburg, Ill. 62675

This-20 acre arboretum established in 1976 emphasizes native plants and naturally-occuring varieties of exotics. There are demonstration gardens for food plants and ornamentals as well as a library.

By written appointment only; partial handicapped access.

SPRINGFIELD

36 Abraham Lincoln Memorial Garden ☆☆ HA-S-WF
2301 E. Lake Drive

80 acres have been used to reproduce the Illinois landscape as Lincoln knew it. Prairie flowers and wild meadow plants along with woodlands may be seen from the extensive trails. There is a collection of crab-apple, dogwood, redbud, wild plum, and grasses of the 1850's. The Nature Center has a library.

Daily, sunrise-sunset; Nature Center 10-4 Mon-Sat; 1-5 Sun; handicapped access; (217) 529-1111.

37 Washington Park ☆ G-R
S. MacArthur Blvd. and W. Fayette Ave.

The Thomas Rees Memorial Carillion is surrounded by several gardens; the rose garden presents many varieties of hybrid roses. Perennials and annual beds lie near the conservatory which contains a collection of tropical plants and has seasonal flower shows.

Daily, dawn-dusk; conservatory 10-4 weekdays; 2-4 Sat, Sun

MONTICELLO

38 Robert Allerton Park ☆ L

This 1,500-acre preserve and several additional large tracts of nearby land form a plant-life research center for the University of Illinois. There is a formal garden with sculpture, a sunken garden, ponds, a forest, and a wildlife reserve. Hiking trails are available.

Daily 10-sunset;

ARCOLA

39 Rockome Gardens ☆ H-HA-HH-R-RG-W
Rt. 2, 5 mi. west

An Amish house, barn and school have been set in a garden which uses natural rock formations. There are formal gardens, a rose garden, a perennial and annual garden, a herb garden, and lily ponds.

10-5 Wed-Sun May 1-25; Daily 10-5 May 26-Oct 17 and Oct 20-24; adults, under $6; 4-12 two-thirds; handicapped access; (217) 268-4216.

CARMI

40 Robinson-Stewart House G-HH-R
110 N. Main Cross St.

This 1815 house has a formal English garden on its grounds with 2,000 rose bushes; it is planted in the style of the period. There are 3 greenhouses.

10-12, 1-4 Tues-Sun, April 1-Oct 31; 1-4 Tues-Sun rest of year; adults, children nominal; partial handicapped access; (618) 382-7653.

CARBONDALE

41 Botanic Garden G-H
Southern Illinois University at Carbondale

A ½-acre garden lies alongside the university greenhouses. Several gardens are being developed; these include a Japanese garden, a rock garden, a herb garden, and others. Large prairie restoration units lie in the neighborhood, but have not been maintained in recent years.

Daily, dawn-dusk; no admission charge; (618) 453-3493.

INDIANA

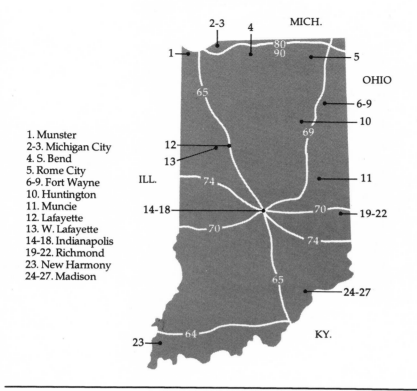

1. Munster
2-3. Michigan City
4. S. Bend
5. Rome City
6-9. Fort Wayne
10. Huntington
11. Muncie
12. Lafayette
13. W. Lafayette
14-18. Indianapolis
19-22. Richmond
23. New Harmony
24-27. Madison

MUNSTER

1 Carmelite Shrines
1628 Ridge Rd., 1 mi. west near U.S. 41

A monastery chapel is set in a small arboretum; there is also a grotto with Italian sculpture.

Daily 9-6; no admission charge; (219) 838-5050.

MICHIGAN CITY

2 International Friendship Garden ☆ HA-J-R-S
Pottawattomie Park, east on U.S. 12

Plants from many nations have been placed in special landscaped gardens. They extend over 130 acres. The park includes Dutch, English, Polish, Italian, Persian, Indian, and Asian gardens as well as a rose garden. There are collections of narcissuses, tulips, peonies, roses, poppies, as well as specimen trees.

Daily 9-dusk, May-Oct; adults, under $3; senior citizens two-thirds; 6-12 half; handicapped access; (219) 874-3664.

3 Barker Civic Center HH
631 Washington St.

This late 19th century mansion is placed in an Italian Garden planted with perennials and annuals.

Tours 10, 11, 12, 1:30, Mon-Fri; 12, 1, 2:30 Sat-Sun, June 1-Oct 31; 10, 11, 12 rest of year; adults, under $3; under 12 nominal; (219) 872-0159.

SOUTH BEND

4 **Conservatory** ☆ C-G-SU
Potawatomi Park
2105 Mishawaka Ave.

This conservatory contains an Arizona desert garden with 350 species and cultivars of cacti. Tropical and semi-tropical plants may also be found here. There are 3 annual flower shows.

Daily 9-3:30; no admission charge; (219) 284-9442.

ROME CITY

5 **Gene Stratton Porter State Memorial** HH-WF
off Rt. 9 south

A 2-story log cabin used by the author, Gene Stratton Porter is set in gardens and woods. Many wildflowers have been planted in the park.

9-5 Wed-Sat; 1-5 Tues, Sun; adults nominal; under 12 free; partial handicapped access; picnic area; (219) 854-3790.

FORT WAYNE

6 **Jaenicke Park** W
Greenwood Ave.

This park contains several acres of landscaped gardens, planted with perennials and annuals. Many terraces have been developed. Some lily ponds are maintained.

Daily, dawn-dusk.

7 **Lawton Park** G

Large plantings of chrysanthemums are the main feature of this park. The greenhouses contain a collection of tropical plants.

Daily, dawn-dusk.

8 **Lakeside Park** R

A display garden of 5,000 rose bushes representing 200 varieties covers 3 acres. The beds lie along a lagoon. Pergolas, reflecting pools and sunken beds are part of this garden.

Daily, dawn-dusk.

9 **The Foellinger-Freimann Botanic Conservatory** ☆☆ C-G-P-SU
1100 S. Calhoun St.

This new conservatory uses the latest techniques of energy conservation in its 3 display houses. One features tropical plants, the second desert plants, and the third is used for 6 annual flower shows. The collection of plants is being developed.

10-4:30 Mon-Sat; 1-4:30 Sun; (219) 422-3696.

HUNTINGTON

10   **Huntington College Arboretum and Botanical Garden**   ☆   H-S
Upper Wabash Basin Natural Research Center
2303 College Ave.

A 58-acre arboretum and research facility with more than 700 species and cultivars has been created here. The center has a large collection of medicinal plants. There is also a special collection of Indiana plants with many older specimens which were planted in the 19th century.

Daily 9-5; tour by appointment; no admission charge; (219) 356-6000 ext. 142.

MUNCIE

11   **Christie Woods of Ball State University**   ☆☆☆   HA-CH-O-S-W-WF
Riverside and University Aves.

Founded in 1918, this university arboretum extends over 18 acres and mainly emphasizes trees and wildflowers; more than 100 species of trees and 50 species of wildflowers may be found here. The grounds contain a bog area and some formal gardens with irises, peonies, and chrysanthemums. Fine collections of ash, oak, and hickory are found here. The greenhouses display the W.O. Wheeler Orchid Collection which consists of 7,000 plants representing 3,000 species. There is a library.

7:30-4:30 weekdays; 8-4:30 Sat; 1-4:30 Sun, fall, spring, summer quarters only; no admission charge; handicapped access; (317) 285-5341.

LAFAYETTE

12   **Jerry E. Clegg Botanic Garden**   ☆   HA-S-W-WF
1854 N. 400th East

This is a woodland and bog area founded in 1964 with extensive plantings over a 20-acre site; more than 300 different species (largely wildflowers and native trees) have been established here. The terrain is hilly and there are some nice views.

Daily 10-sunset; no admission charge; handicapped access; (317) 742-0325.

WEST LAFAYETTE

13   **Horticulture Park**   A
Purdue University
McCormick Rd and W. State St.

24 acres of woodland and landscaped areas are primarily used for instruction. Sections are devoted to crab-apples, rhododendrons, dogwoods, euonymuses, dwarf evergreens, and native woodlands.

Daily, dawn-dusk, no admission charge; (317) 494-6191.

INDIANAPOLIS

14   **Garfield Park Conservatory**   ☆☆   C-G-HA-SU
2450 Shelby St.

This early conservatory established in 1875 is located in a lovely park with sunken perennial gardens. The conservatory maintains a large collection of tropical plants and cacti. Three annual flower shows are presented.

Mon-Sat 10-5; Sun 12-5; closed major holidays; adults, children nominal; handicapped access; (317) 784-3044.

15 **The Holcomb Gardens** ☆ A-HA-WF
Butler University
4600 Sunset Ave.

A woodland area has been planted with more than 100,000 daffodils, along with
many species of peonies, lilacs, rhododendrons, gladioluses, hollies, and wildflowers. The grounds contain large beds of perennials and annuals.

Daily 7-sunset; no admission charge; handicapped access; (317) 283-8000.

16 **Hoosier Heritage Garden**
Governor's Residence
4750 N. Meridian St.

This garden is a living history of what Indiana authors have written about the state's
shrubs and flowers. There is a fountain surrounded by shrubs, perennials, roses, and
annuals in this small garden established in 1980.

Daily 8-dusk; end of May-Oct 21; no admission charge; (317) 283-8171.

17 **Indianapolis Museum of Art** ☆ HA
1200 W. 38th St.

This museum is placed on 120 acres of beautifully landscaped grounds with gardens
of perennials, annuals, sculpture, and fountains.

11-5 Tues-Sun; closed Jan 1, Thanksgiving, Christmas; no admission charge;
handicapped access; (317) 923-1331.

18 **Hillsdale Exhibition Rose Garden** ☆ R-RG
7800 N. Shadeland Ave, Fort Wayne Exit from I-465
Castleton.

This 63-acre commercial nursery has developed 5 acres as a series of display
gardens. There is a rock garden, a formal rose garden, and a rose display garden.
More than 7,000 rose bushes bloom each summer and large areas of spring bulbs
bloom in mid-April. An annual rose festival has been held here each June for more
than 4 decades.

Weekdays 9:30-4:30; no admission charge; (317) 849-2810.

RICHMOND

19 **The Hayes Regional Arboretum** FE-HA-S
801 Elks Rd.

Begun in 1915, this woodland arboretum of 300 acres contains all the woody plants
indigenous to the area. More than 150 species are represented. A beech-maple forest
as well as groves of Tulip Trees, White Oak, and White Ash have been established.
Some areas are planted close to demonstrate forest conditions, others widely spaced
to display specimen trees. There is a fern garden and a children's garden.

8-12 for scheduled groups; 1-5 for general public, Tues-Sun; closed Christmas to lst
Tues before Easter; no admission charge; handicapped access; (317) 962-3745.

20 **Hill Memorial Rose Garden** R
Glen Miller Park

More than 70 varieties of roses are represented in the plantings of this park.

Daily, dawn-dusk.

21 Hills Flora Products G-R
2117 Peacock Rd.

This is a large producer of cut flowers with more than 37 acres under glass. The neighboring area contains one of the main centers of commercial rose cultivation in the midwest.

Limited to groups by appointment only; no admission charge; (317) 962-2555.

22 Rose Festival R

A festival is held annually at the end of June.

For more information write Mr. L. Vance; P.O.Box 1332; 15 S. 17th St. 47374; (317) 935-7637.

NEW HARMONY

23 Robert Lee Blaffer Trust ☆☆ H-HA-HH-R-T

This Utopian community of the early 1800's has been preserved along with its period gardens which have been extensively replanted. The area contains small and large gardens both public and private. Numerous ornamental flowering trees bloom in spring. There are herb gardens, rose gardens, and a labyrinth, one of the few in North America.

Daily; no admission charge to gardens; private gardens by appointment only; handicapped access; (812) 682-4431.

MADISON

24 Dr. William Hutching Office and Hospital H-HH
120 W. 3rd St.

This 19th century private hospital has been restored along with its medicinal herb garden.

Daily 1-4:30, May 1-Nov 1; adults, under $3; children half; (812) 265-2956.

25 Jeremiah Sullivan House HH
Poplar Lane and E. 2nd St.

This 1818 Federal-style building lies in a small period garden.

10-4:30 Tues-Sat; 1-4:30 Sun, Mon; May 1-Nov 1; adults, under $3; children half; (812) 265-2956.

26 Schofield House H-HH
Poplar and E. 2nd St.

This early 19th century brick home has a small herb and flower garden behind it.

Weekdays 9:30-4:30; Sun 12:30-4:30; April 1-Dec 15; adults, under $3; children half; (812) 265-2956.

27 Talbott-Hyatt Pioneer Garden
Poplar and 1st St.

Originally established in 1820, the garden has been restored along its original lines.

Daily, dawn-dusk; (812) 265-2956.

IOWA

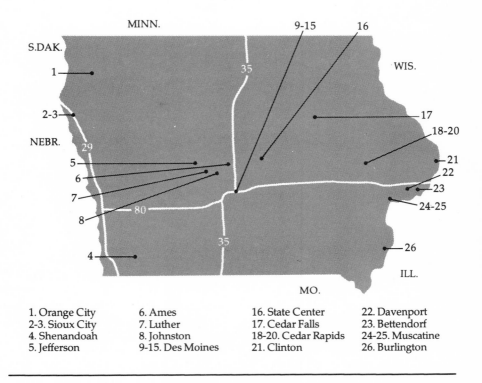

1. Orange City	6. Ames	16. State Center	22. Davenport
2-3. Sioux City	7. Luther	17. Cedar Falls	23. Bettendorf
4. Shenandoah	8. Johnston	18-20. Cedar Rapids	24-25. Muscatine
5. Jefferson	9-15. Des Moines	21. Clinton	26. Burlington

ORANGE CITY

1 **H.G. Kobes Rock and Flower Garden** HA-J-R-RG
403 Frankfort Ave N.E.

A beautiful garden created single-handedly on 1½ acres since 1949 with pools, waterfalls and fountains. There is an Oriental garden with a Japanese Tea house, rock garden, and a rose garden. They contain fine plantings of roses, tulips, dahlias, peonies, honey-suckles as well as some topiary. Thousands of tulips bloom in mid-May along with the Chinese May tree and the Jerusalem Joshua tree.

Daily 9-dark, May 1-frost; adults, children nominal; free admission during Tulip Festival and Thurs, Fri, Sat of 3rd week of month; handicapped access; (712) 737-4276.

SIOUX CITY

2 **Grandview Park** R
Douglas and 24th Sts.

A large rose garden with 3,000 bushes representing several hundred varieties; pleasant beds of annuals are to be found here also.

Daily, dawn-dusk.

3 **Latham Park**
1915 South Lemon St.

This park contains formal gardens of perennials and annuals surrounding sparkling fountains.

Daily, dawn-dusk.

SHENANDOAH

4 Earl May Seed and Nursery Co. Trial Gardens   HD
North Elm St.

76 acres of gardens display flowers and vegetables; there is a demonstration 'backyard' flower garden, a garden center, as well as nurseries and seed houses.

Weekdays 9-4; tours provided by appointment; (712) 246-1020.

JEFFERSON

5 Johnson Rose Garden   R
306 W. Lincolnway; 1 block w. Rt. 4.

This rose garden surrounds a private home; the area is well planted.

Daily June 1-Oct 15; lighted at night; no admission charge.

AMES

6 Horticultural Gardens   ☆☆   HA-R
Iowa State University

This 2-acre teaching garden contains more than 500 varieties of roses which is part of a rose breeding program begun in 1900; the garden has participated in the All-American Selection program since its beginning. Fine collections of lilies, geraniums, irises, peonies, heliotropes, and many annuals are maintained. Formal gardens are to be found on the campus near the Horticulture Bldg and the C.Y. Stephens Auditorium.

Daily, sunrise-sunset; no admission charge; handicapped access; (515) 294-2436.

LUTHER

7 Iowa Arboretum   ☆   S
2½ mi. west and 2 mi. south on Rt. E-57

This arboretum spreads over 340 acres and contains several hundred species of trees, shrubs and grasses. Plants are organized according to use, so there is a shade tree section, a wind-break section, etc. Trails lead through forest, meadow and prairie lands. Plants are labelled. Test and demonstration gardens for rare and endangered plants may be found here.

9-4 Mon-Sat; 1-6 Sun; free tours for groups; no admission charge; partial handicapped access; (515) 795-3216.

JOHNSTON

8 Garden of Men's Garden Clubs of America
North of I-80 and I-30

2 acres have been planted with perennials and annuals; the special garden of daylilies is being expanded.

Weekdays 8:30-5; no admission charge; (515) 278-0295.

DES MOINES

9 Arie den Boer Arboretum ☆☆☆ C-G-S-SU-W
Water Works Park 408 Fleur Drive

A beautiful arboretum spread over 30 acres which was begun in 1920; there are 2,000 crab-apples representing 215 species which bloom in early May and a small rare tree collection. The arboretum contains 180 kinds of hostas, peonies, ornamental shrubs, greenhouses with cacti and succulents collection. The park has lily ponds, lotus in fountains and pools.

Daily 9-4:30; no admission charge; partial handicapped access; (515) 283-8791.

10 Des Moines Botanical Center ☆☆☆ BO-C-G-HA-P-SU
900 East River Drive

This 14½-acre garden opened in 1979; the spectacular crystogon greenhouse displays 1,000 species and cultivars from all over the world. There is a good Bonsai collection. Six seasonal flower shows are held annually. The outdoor gardens are being developed. A library is available.

10-6 Mon-Thurs; 10-9 Fri; 10-5 Sat-Sun, holidays; closed Jan 1, Thanksgiving, Christmas; adults, under $3; senior citizens, children 6-18 nominal; handicapped access; (515) 283-4148.

11 Ewing Park ☆☆ HA-S
McKinley Rd. and Indianola Rd.

These 25 acres display the finest mid-western lilac collection with more than 1,800 French lilacs of 200 varieties. The garden also contains flowering crab-apple, dogwood, aspen, many ornamental shrubs.

Daily 8-sunset; no admission charge; handicapped access; (515) 283-4227.

12 Greenwood Park ☆ R
Grand Ave.

This park contains a good rose garden with more than 3,500 bushes representing 186 different varieties. The garden is formally planted.

Daily, sunrise-sunset.

13 Union Park
Saylor Rd. and E 9th St.

This park with its formal gardens lies on a promontory overlooking the Des Moines River. Perennials and annuals as well as flowering shrubs may be found here.

Daily, dawn-dusk.

14 State Capitol Park
Grand Ave. between 9th and 12th Sts.

A well-landscaped 80-acre park with plantings of perennials and annuals surround the capitol which lies on a hilltop.

Daily, dawn-dusk.

15 Living History Farms HH
Hickman Rd., exit 125 from I-80 and I-35

This working 1840 pioneer farm and 1900 horse-power farm features fine vegetable and flower gardens of the periods. Plants used during those times are displayed.

Daily 9-5 mid-April to Oct 31; adults, under $6; over 65 two-thirds; 4-16 half; (515) 278-5286.

STATE CENTER

16   Iowa Rose Society Garden   R
Old U.S. 30

This rose garden displays many varieties with several thousand bushes in bloom.

Weekdays 10-4; no admission charge.

CEDAR FALLS

17   Biological Preserves System   HA-S-W
University of Northern Iowa

7 tracts of land on and off campus have been set aside in this system of preserves which totals more than 150 acres. Each contains a study area and a public area. There is a lowland forest which displays more than 100 species of trees and shrubs, an upland forest preserve, a prairie preserve, a virgin tall grass prairie, a bog area, and a stream side forest.

Daily; permit required for some sections; no admission charge; handicapped access; (319) 273-2456.

CEDAR RAPIDS

18   Brucemore   F-HH
2160 Linden Drive SE

A Queen Anne style mansion built in 1884 stands in the midst of this 26-acre estate. The grounds contain formal gardens with perennials, annuals, an orchard, and ponds.

For times call (319) 362-6652.

19   Noelridge Park   G-P-R
Collins Rd NE

This 4-acre municipal flower garden includes a large variety of roses along with a test garden for annuals; 5 greenhouses display tropical and semi-tropical plants and have periodic flower shows.

Daily 9-4; Sun 2-4; no admission charge; (319) 398-5065.

20   Shakespeare Garden   SH
Ellis Park

The plants mentioned by Shakespeare, suitable to Iowa, have been grown in this garden founded in 1927.

Daily 9-dusk.

CLINTON

21   Bickelhaupt Arboretum   ☆   HA-S-WF
340 S. 14th St.

This 13-acre site contains a restored prairie section; more than 750 labelled native trees and shrubs. There are also collections of ground covers, vines, dwarf shrubs, and prairie wildflowers. The conservatory contains several hundred species. There is a library.

Daily, dawn-dusk; no admission charge; handicapped access; (319) 242-4771.

DAVENPORT

22 Municipal Rose Garden G-R
Vander Veer Park
Lombard and Main Sts.

This rose garden contains some 3,000 bushes representing 130 varieties; there are greenhouses with 4 seasonal flower shows.

Daily, dawn-dusk; greenhouses 9-5.

BETTENDORF

23 Municipal Rose Garden
2204 Grant St.

680 rose bushes representing 60 varieties have been planted in this garden.

Daily, dawn-dusk; handicapped access; (319) 359-1651.

MUSCATINE

24 Laura Musser Art Gallery and Museum ☆☆ J-L-WF
1314 Mulberry Ave.

There are 4 acres of beautifully landscaped grounds around this art center. A Japanese garden with small pools, a pagoda, and waterfalls are connected with the museum. A fine display of Iowa wildflowers is found here.

11-5 Tues-Fri; 7-9 p.m. Thurs; 1-5 Sat-Sun; closed holidays; no admission charge; (319) 263-0241.

25 Weed Park R
Off Rt. 22, east

Lilac and rose gardens are part of this recreational park.

Daily, dawn-dusk; no admission charge; (319) 263-0241.

BURLINGTON

26 Crapo and Dankwardt Parks S
Great River Rd.

Formal gardens as well as an arboretum are found in this park. The native tree collection is especially complete.

Daily 9-5; no admission charge; partial handicapped access.

KANSAS

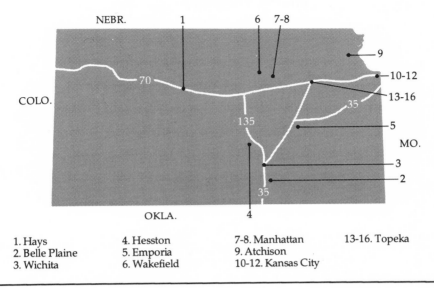

1. Hays
2. Belle Plaine
3. Wichita

4. Hesston
5. Emporia
6. Wakefield

7-8. Manhattan
9. Atchison
10-12. Kansas City

13-16. Topeka

HAYS

1 Fort Hays Kansas State College S
8th St. off Business I-70

This campus has been extensively landscaped in order to display native grasses, trees, and shrubs. There is a large collection of crab-apples. During the summer perennial and annual gardens are maintained.

Daily, dawn-dusk; (913) 625-5611.

BELLE PLAINE

2 The Bartlett Arboretum ☆☆☆ R-S
2½ mi. east of U.S. 81 on Rt. 55

This beautiful 20-acre garden and arboretum was established in 1910. Formal gardens surround small lakes planted with bulbs, irises, roses, tree peonies, annuals, and perennials. Numerous cypress, Japanese Table Pine, English Elm, pistachio, and various types of maple are grown here. Many of the trees are mature.

Daily 9-6, April 1 to mid-Nov; adults, under $3; high school, college half; grade school nominal; partial handicapped access; (316) 488-3451.

WICHITA

3 Sedgwick County Zoo ☆☆ HA-P-S-W
5555 Zoo Blvd.; 7 mi. northwest

A fine zoo which displays its large collection of animals in natural habitat areas. The 215 acres are well landscaped. The Jungle Building contains more than 1,400 species of tropical plants in its free flight aviary. The nature trail area runs through a short grass prairie and a long grass prairie as well as an evergreen grove, a swamp, and a marsh garden. There is a sensory garden for the handicapped which has been beautifully designed.

Daily 10-6 during DST; 10-5 rest of year; adults, under $3; under 13 free; handicapped access; (316) 942-2212.

HESSTON

4 Dyck Arboretum of the Plains WF
I-35

A 25-acre arboretum which specializes in native plants and wildflowers. There is a prairie grass and native grass area.

For times call (316) 327-8127.

EMPORIA

5 Hammond Park J
18th Ave. and Center St.

This 10-acre site contains a small Chinese garden with some fine trees and shrubs. It is part of an extensive municipal park system.

Daily, dawn-dusk.

WAKEFIELD

6 Kansas Landscape Arboretum ☆ CH-S-WF
½ mi. south on Milford Lake

A 193-acre site was established in 1970; it contains a large collection of native trees and is constantly expanding with some 800 introduced varieties already planted. There are special collections of pine, juniper, ash, oak, redbud, maple, flowering crab, dogwood, and nut trees. One section displays the various state trees. There is a wildflower garden as well as a meadow trail. The garden contains 90 varieties of day-lilies, 90 species and cultivars of irises, and 36 varieties of chrysanthemums.

Daily 8-dusk, summer only; no admission charge; partial handicapped access; tours; (913) 263-2540.

MANHATTAN

7 University Gardens ☆ C-G-P-SU
Kansas State University
17th and Anderson Sts.

The Department of Horticulture maintains a good conservatory built in 1902 with more than 300 species of tropical plants as well as a good selection of semi-tropicals from Hawaii. There is a desert section and a texture garden. Extensive outdoor gardens are under development.

Daily, May-Oct; (913) 532-6415.

8 City Park R
Poyntz Ave. between 11th and 14th Sts.

This park contains a small arboretum and a rose garden.

Daily, dawn-dusk.

ATCHISON

9   **International Forest of Friendship Trail**   HA
    Rt. 59, Warnock Lake

A trail winds through a forest planted to contain trees from all 50 states and 9 foreign lands. Some good specimens may be found here.

Daily, dawn-dusk; no admission charge; handicapped access; (913) 367-2427.

KANSAS CITY

10   **Municipal Rose Garden**   R
     Huron Park

The rose garden is part of this park.

Daily, dawn-dusk.

11   **'Flower and Gardens' Demonstration Garden**   HD-L
     4251 Pennsylvania Ave.

This garden of perennials, annuals, and vegetables covers 1-acre. Plants are labelled. The garden is an official display garden for All-America Selections. This garden lies on the grounds of the magazine publisher.

Daily 9-5; open garden days held on last Sun of June and Sept with magazine staff available; (816) 531-5730.

12   **Lenington-Long Gardens**

This private grower of daylilies is open to visitors during blooming season.

Call for times (816) 353-6666.

TOPEKA

13   **Reinisch Memorial Rose and Rock Garden**   ☆☆   HA-R-RG
     Gage Park between 6–10th St.

This 3-acre well-designed rose and rock garden was founded in 1930; it features an All-American rose selection of 7,000 plants representing more than 300 varieties. The test gardens are used by national growers.

Daily 6-11; no admission charge; handicapped access; (913) 272-6171.

14   **Doran Rock Garden**   RG-W
     4320 West 10th St.

This garden is adjacent to the rose garden; 2 brooks are planted with water and bog plants; around them is a rock garden containing more than 30,000 shrubs, trees, and flowering plants, many of them annuals. This 1-acre garden was founded in 1932.

Daily 6-11; no admission charge; partial handicapped access; (913) 272-6171.

15   **Topeka Zoological Park**   HA-P
     635 Gage Blvd.

This zoo of more than 400 animals, which are largely displayed in their natural environment, also contains an enclosed tropical rain forest with hundreds of varieties of plants and a large waterfall.

Daily 10-4:30; adults, under $3; 5-15, over 64 half; tours; handicapped access; (913) 272-5821.

16 Meade Park Gardens ☆ HA-HH-S
124 N. Filmore

The Meade Mansion serves as the center of this arboretum and garden with formal gardens and fountains. The arboretum contains more than 550 species of trees and shrubs whose blooms are best enjoyed in April and May; trees grown no taller than 30 feet. There are fine displays of more than 9,000 annuals and more than 5,000 tulips bloom in spring. Trial grounds for hardiness are maintained.

Daily 6-11; no admission charge; handicapped access; (913) 235-0806.

KENTUCKY

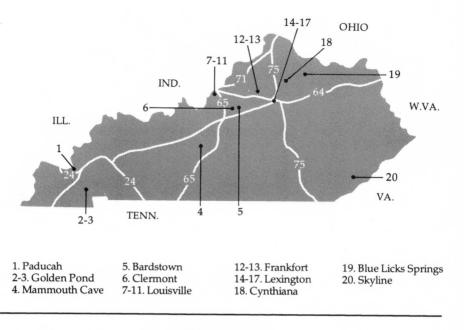

1. Paducah
2-3. Golden Pond
4. Mammouth Cave

5. Bardstown
6. Clermont
7-11. Louisville

12-13. Frankfort
14-17. Lexington
18. Cynthiana

19. Blue Licks Springs
20. Skyline

PADUCAH

1 Dogwood Trail Festival HH
This festival is held each April when thousands of dogwood trees bloom. Many homes and gardens are open for tours at this time.

For information call (502) 443-8783.

GOLDEN POND

2 Tennessee Valley Environmental Education Center HA-S
Land Between the Lakes
5 mi. north

Although not formally an arboretum, these 5,000 acres display the indigenous plants of the area and seek to preserve them. There are well-marked trails, demonstration plantings, and good specimens of local trees. This forms a small segment of the 170,000-acre wooded peninsula.

Daily 9-5; handicapped access; (502) 924-5602 ex 238.

3 Homeplace 1850 F-HH
A Living History Farm
5 mi. south

16 original log structures are located on this carefully restored farm which contains a tobacco plantation, an orchard, and a garden as well as a crop area.

Daily 9-5, March 1-Nov 30; no admission charge; partial handicapped access; (502) 924-5602.

MAMMOUTH CAVE

4 Mammouth Cave National Park   WF
I-65 west of Park City

This National Park is primarily visited for a tour of the caves, but the surface land contains an interesting array of wildflowers. 150 kinds species flowers flourish here, including irises, primroses, orchids, drifts, roses, violets, day-lilies, daisies, and many others. There are good trails; flowers bloom spring to August with the largest variety blooming in June and July.

Daily 7:30-7, summer; 8-5 winter; no admission charge; partial handicapped access; (502) 758-2328.

BARDSTOWN

5 My Old Kentucky Home State Park   HH
U.S. 150 southeast

This house was built in 1795 and visited by Stephen Foster; the garden is informal. A large variety of old-fashioned flowers are cultivated here.

Daily 9-5; closed Dec 31-Jan 16 and each Mon in Jan, Feb, Dec; adults, under $3; 6-12 half; partial handicapped access; (502) 348-3502.

CLERMONT

6 Bernheim Forest Arboretum   ☆☆☆☆   A-HA-S-WF
Exit 112 I-65 on Rt. 245

A 250-acre arboretum was created on this 10,000-acre forest preserve in 1950. More than 1,700 different species of plants are labelled on miles of trails. There are good collections of rhododendron, azalea, crab-apple, viburnum, redbud, dogwood, nut tree, and holly. Many special gardens including a sun and shade garden, quiet garden, hedge garden, fragrance garden, wildflower garden, and compact plant garden. There are also waterfowl ponds.

Daily 9-one hour before sunset, March 15-Nov 15; donation; handicapped access; picnic area; (502) 543-2451.

LOUISVILLE

7 Kentucky Botanical Gardens   ☆☆   C-FE-G-HA-O-SU
814½ Cherokee Rd.

This is a new botanical garden founded in 1980; it now contains a collection of 1,300 species of tropical plants in its greenhouses. Among them are 400 species of orchids and 200 varieties of ferns as well as numerous bromeliads, aroids, and carnivores. There is a good cactus and succulent collection. The garden has plans for expansion.

11-3 Mon, Wed, Thurs; 12:30-4:30 Sat, Sun; no admission; handicapped access; (502) 452-1121.

8 Cave Hill Cemetery   ☆☆   HA-S
701 Baxter Ave.

A beautifully landscaped 300-acre cemetery planted with fine specimen trees as well as numerous shrubs and flowers. It was founded in 1848.

Daily 8-4:45; no vans; handicapped access.

9 **Farmington Historic Home Museum** ☆ F-H-HA-HH
3033 Bardstown Rd., exit 16B I-264

Thomas Jefferson designed this home built in 1810; the gardens have been restored with plants known to have been used before 1820; the 17 acres contain a fine kitchen garden, herb garden, perennial garden, and 2-acre apple orchard.

10-4:30 Mon-Sat; 1-4:30 Sun; closed Jan 1, Easter, Derby Day, Thanksgiving, Dec 24, 25; adults, under $3; students half; handicapped access; (502) 452-9920.

10 **Locust Grove** HA-HH
561 Blankenbaker Rd., exit 22 I-264

This Georgian mansion built in 1790 has been restored along with its garden. The outbuildings are spread over 55 acres. A small 18th century border garden is planted with flowers and herbs.

10-4:30 Mon-Sat; 1:30-4:30 Sun; closed Jan 1, Easter, Derby Day, Thanksgiving, Dec 24, 25; adults, under $3; students half; handicapped access; (502) 897-9845.

11 **Audubon Park**

An annual dogwood festival is held here in April.

For times call (502) 452-1121.

FRANKFORT

12 **Liberty Hall** BX-HH-R
202 Wilkinson St.

A Georgian home built in 1801 with a Palladian window; the garden has been well restored with boxwood hedges and planted with old roses.

10-5 Tues-Sat; 1-5 Sun, March 31-Dec 31; closed major holidays; adults, under $3; under 12, half; partial handicapped access; (502) 227-2560.

13 **Kentucky Floral Clock**
Capitol grounds

This design contains 20,000 plants whch are changed seasonally. It is surrounded by a reflecting pool which is illuminated at night.

LEXINGTON

14 **Hunt-Morgan House** HH
Gratz Park
201 N. Mill St.

A fine Federal style home built in 1814; the small garden has been restored to antebellum style.

10-4 Tues-Sat; 2-5 Sun; closed Jan 1-31, Thanksgiving, Dec 25; adults, under $3; 6-12 half; (606) 266-8581.

15 **Ashland Henry Clay Mansion** H-HH
E. Main St. and Sycamore

This home of Henry Clay has a fine period garden along with a herb and vegetable garden; both are placed in parterres; 20 acres of woodlands.

Daily 9:30-4:30; adults, under $3; students with I.D. half; under 12 nominal; partial handicapped access; 606-266-8581.

16 Lexington Cemetery ☆☆☆ A-HA-R-S-W
833 W. Main St.

This is one of the most beautiful cemetries in the United States. In addition to fine plantings of specimen trees and shrubs, this cemetery, established in 1849, contains a series of gardens including a rose garden, iris garden, perennial garden, sunken garden, and pools with water lily and lotus. Many spring flowering trees have been planted; among them are flowering cherries, dogwoods, crab-apples, redbuds, and peaches. Thousands of bulbs bloom in the spring; perennials and annuals may be seen in the summer. There are special seasonal displays. Self-guided tour pamphlets for adults and children are available.

Daily 8-5; handicapped access; (606) 255-5522.

17 Open House in Kentucky

An annual tour of homes and gardens is held May 28 and 29th.

For information call (502) 491-6625.

CYNTHIANA

18 Iris Festival

An annual Iris festival is held here each spring.

For information call (606) 252-7565.

BLUE LICKS SPRINGS

19 Blue Licks Nature Preserve S
Blue Licks Battlefield State Park
U.S. 62 and 68

A nature preserve for rare and endangered species was established here in 1981. Many varieties of plants are being established here, including Short's Goldenrod.

Daily, dawn-dusk; April 1-Oct 1.

SKYLINE

20 Lilley Cornett Woods S-WF
Appalachian Ecological Research Station
Eastern Kentucky University
Rt. 1103, 8 mi. south of Ulvah

This forest preserves the remnants of millions of acres of forest which once covered the Cumberland Plateau. Fine native specimen trees may be found here along with numerous kinds of wildflowers. There is also a bird sanctuary.

Guided tours only; 9-4:30 weekends April-October; daily May 15-Aug 15. By appointment Mon-Fri April, May, Sept, Oct; 1½-hour and 3½-hour hikes; (606) 633-5828.

LOUISIANA

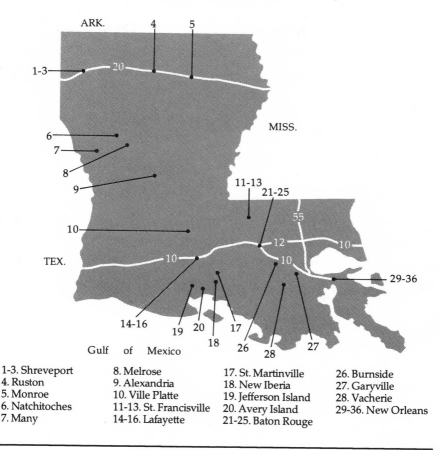

ARK.   4   5

1-3

MISS.

6
7
8
9

11-13
21-25

10

TEX.

29-36

14-16
19 20 17
18 26 28 27

Gulf of Mexico

1-3. Shreveport
4. Ruston
5. Monroe
6. Natchitoches
7. Many

8. Melrose
9. Alexandria
10. Ville Platte
11-13. St. Francisville
14-16. Lafayette

17. St. Martinville
18. New Iberia
19. Jefferson Island
20. Avery Island
21-25. Baton Rouge

26. Burnside
27. Garyville
28. Vacherie
29-36. New Orleans

SHREVEPORT

1   American Rose Society Garden ☆☆ A-CA-HA-R-S
Jefferson-Paige Rd., Rt. 80 exit from I-20

Although the headquarters of the American Rose Society was established in Shreveport in 1899, its garden dates back only a decade. Here thousands of roses bloom from April to December. Many old-fashioned roses are to be found along with the latest introductions. The garden is divided into special areas devoted to each variety of rose. There are also large plantings of camellias, dogwoods, crape-myrtles, flowering crab-apples, and azaleas. The test and trial gardens play an important role in the development of miniature roses. There is a library.

Daily 9-7, spring; 8:30-4:30 fall; adults, under $3; handicapped access; (318) 938-5402.

2   R. S. Barnell Memorial Garden and Art Center ☆ BR-G-HA-O
501 River Parkway

The botanical garden, founded in 1970, covers 7 acres on the banks of the Red River. Well landscaped, it possesses collections of bromeliads, orchids, ornamental trees and shrubs as well as tropical plants. There are greenhouses and a library.

9-4:30 weekdays; 1-5 Sat, Sun; no admission charge; handicapped access; (318) 226-6495.

3 Ford Municipal Park
Cross Lake, south shore

This park contains a large collection of redbuds; more than a thousand bloom in March.

Daily, dawn-dusk.

RUSTON

4 Louisiana Polytechnic Institute Arboretum S
Reese Hall
Tech Drive exit from I-20 to California Ave.

The arboretum, established in 1947, has been largely planted by students of the Department of Forestry. The collection is divided into three major sections devoted to native southern trees, as well as trees of other sections of the United States. A large number of fine specimens grow here.

8-5 Mon-Fri; no admission charge; partial handicapped access; (315) 257-3275.

MONROE

5 Louisiana Purchase Garden and Zoo P-S
Tichelli Rd.

A beautifully landscaped zoo and garden with more than 5,000 tropical and temperate plants. There is a collection of old trees.

Daily 10-dusk; partial handicapped access; (318) 329-2400.

NATCHITOCHES

6 Beau Fort Plantation HH
Rt. 119, between Natchitoches and Melrose

This antebellum home is surrounded by plantation gardens which have been restored.

Daily 1-4; adults, under $3; children half; (318) 352-6472.

MANY

7 Hodges Gardens ☆☆☆☆ A-BR-C-CA-FE-G-HA-L-O-S-W-WF
12 mi. south on U.S. 171

This huge reserve of 4,800 acres contains 70 acres of display gardens. The entire area is beautifully landscaped. The gardens contain 7 acres of roses with 3,000 bushes representing numerous varieties. Special gardens include azalea, camellia, Louisiana Iris, hibiscus, water lily, and wildflower. Fine specimen of crape-myrtle, Southern Magnolia, Long-Leaf Pine, and wisteria are found here. There are waterfalls, streams, a lake, a wild-life refuge, and trails through large areas. The greenhouses contain good collections of orchids, ferns, bromeliads, cycads, gesneriads, euphorbia, and cacti. There are test gardens.

Daily 8-sunset; closed Jan 1, Christmas; adults, under $6; under 14 free with parents; handicapped access; (318) 586-3523.

MELROSE

8   Melrose Plantation   HH
East on Rt. 493

A complex of 8 Colonial buildings is surrounded by large restored gardens.

2-4:30 Tues, Thurs, Sun; adults, under $3; 13-18 half; 6-12 less; (318) 379-0053.

ALEXANDRIA

9   Kent House State Commemorative Area   HA-HH
3601 Bayou Rapids Rd.

This park has preserved a plantation and series of outbuildings from the French-Spanish Colonial period of the late 18th century. The restored gardens accurately reflect that period in plant selection and style.

9-5 Mon-Sat; 1-5 Sun; closed Jan 1, Thanksgiving, Christmas; adults, under $3; 6-12 nominal; tours; handicapped access; (318) 445-5611.

VILLE PLATTE

10   The Louisiana Purchase Arboretum   ☆☆   A-S-WF
Chicot State Park
Rt. 3042, 8 mi. north

This woodland arboretum is being expanded to 600 acres with an excellent collection of indigenous trees, shrubs, and wildflowers; they include azaleas, redbuds, pawpaws, sourwoods, oaks, witch hazels, hickories, and spice-bushes. There are good specimens of Southern Magnolia and beech. The collections were established in 1961 and are growing rapidly. Spring and fall are the best seasons for a visit.

Daily 6-10, summer; 8-7 winter; no admission charge; handicapped access; (318) 363-6287.

ST. FRANCISVILLE

11   Rosedown Plantation and Gardens   ☆☆   A-CA-H-HH-S
U.S. 61 and Rt. 10

A grand mansion and garden was begun on these grounds in 1835 and was restored 30 years ago; there are two 10-acre gardens on this 2,000-acre estate. The formal French 17th century garden has been elaborately replanted in accordance with its original design. Many old azaleas, camellias, hydrangeas, cryptomerias, gardenias, crape-myrtles, and deutzias are found here. Specimen trees include a Live-Oak avenue of 150-year-old trees, Southern Magnolia, Empress tree, and Sawara Cypress. The plantation has a kitchen garden and a herb garden.

Daily 9-5 March 1-Nov 30; 10-4 rest of year; closed Christmas; adults, under $6; under 12, half with parents; gardens only, under $3; under 12 free; partial handicapped access; (504) 635-3332 or 524-8407.

12   Audubon State Commemorative Park   HH
3 mi. east on U.S. 61

This 100-acre park contains the Oakley mansion in which Audubon worked. The house has been restored to its Federal period style as have the formal gardens; there are large plantings of native shrubs and trees.

9-5 Mon-Sat; 1-5 Sun; adults, under $3; students nominal; under 6 free; partial handicapped access; (504) 635-3739.

13 Catalpa Plantation HH
U.S. 61, 5 mi. north

30 acres of grounds with specimen Live-Oaks and other native plants surround this old mansion.

Daily 9-5; adults, under $3; children half; (504) 635-3372.

LAFAYETTE

14 Ira S. Nelson Horticulture Center ☆ BR-HA-G-O
University of Southern Louisiana
U.S. 167 South

The center forms part of the campus and consists of a conservatory, several greenhouses as well as a large shade garden area. Good collections of woody ornamentals, orchids, bromeliads, and amaryllises are maintained. March, April and May are the best months for visiting.

8-5 Mon-Fri; no admission charge; handicapped access; (318) 231-5348.

15 Acadian Village and Gardens HH
Exit 97 from I-10 to Rt. 93

A restored 19th century Acadian town with 10 acres of gardens and woods; emphasis has been placed on tropical and semi-tropical plants. There are informal gardens typical of the period.

Daily 10-5; closed holidays; adults, under $3; 6-18, over 61, half; partial handicapped access; (318) 981-2364.

16 Acadiana Park Nature Trail A
East Alexander St.

A 21-mile azalea trail displays thousands of bushes which bloom from mid-February to mid-March; there are nice woodlands.

Daily; (318) 232-3737.

ST. MARTINVILLE

17 Longfellow-Evangeline State Commemorative Area H
Route 31

A museum of Acadian life lies on these 157-acre grounds which contain kitchen gardens and flower beds typical of the period.

9-5 Mon-Sat; 1-5 Sun; adults, under $3; students half; (318) 394-3754.

NEW IBERIA

18 Shadows-on-the-Teche ☆ A-BX-CA-HA-HH
117 E. Main St. (Rt. 182)

A classic revival mansion built in 1834 on the banks of the Bayou Teche. It is set in the midst of lovely period gardens restored in the 1920's by Weeks Hall, the planter's great-grandson. There are fine specimens of Live-Oaks covered with Spanish moss, cedars, very old hedges, boxwoods, aspidistras, and camellias. There is a gazebo which overlooks the Teche River.

Daily 9:30-4:30; closed Jan 1, Thanksgiving, Christmas; adults, under $3; 6-18, over 65, students with I.D., two-thirds; partial handicapped access; (318) 369-6446.

JEFFERSON ISLAND

19 Live Oaks Gardens ☆☆☆ A-CA-G-J-O-R-S
7 mi. south of New Iberia on Rts. 675 and 14

These 25 acres of gardens were begun in the 1870's and developed further in the middle of this century. Recently additional restoration work has been done and the garden reopened in 1984. The gardens have been planted so that a section is at its height during each season. There is a formal English garden, an Alhambra garden with fountains, an Oriental garden, old and new camellia gardens, a rose garden, a magnolia garden, a tropical glen, and a woodland garden. Large areas have been planted with perennials and annuals. Woodland paths connect the gardens. Excellent collections of camellias and Louisiana Iris are found here along with specimen trees of Camphor-Oak, Southern Live-Oak, with some more than 300 years old. The greenhouses contain orchids, camellias, and tropical plants.

Daily 9-6; closed holidays; adults, under $6; 4-16 half; tours; (318) 367-3485.

AVERY ISLAND

20 Jungle Gardens ☆☆☆☆ A-CA-J-S-W-WF
Avery Island Rd., off Rt. 329

300 acres of natural gardens display large plantings of azaleas, 1,000 varieties of camellias, and water lilies. There are sunken gardens. Fine collections of Louisiana Lilies, wildflowers, Wasi Oranges, *Xanthosoma*, and aralias have been planted. There is a huge thicket of Chinese timber bamboo and Chinese wisteria. A Chinese garden surrounds a lagoon. A bird sanctuary lies on the grounds.

Daily 9-5; adults, under $6; 6-12 half; (318) 365-8173.

BATON ROUGE

21 Zemurray Gardens ☆☆☆ A-CA-G-HA-P-WF
8313 O'Hara Court

This 150-acre garden established in 1936 presents more than 25,000 plants with special emphasis on camellias, azaleas, dogwoods, wildflowers, Louisiana Iris, and bulbs. Woodland trails lead through plantings of oak, gum, dogwood, and mountain laurel. The greenhouses contain a tropical collection.

10-6 March 1-July 1; adults, under $3; children, senior citizens, nominal; handicapped access; (504) 927-3500.

22 Mountain Hope Plantation HH
8151 Highland Rd.

This home, built in 1817, has been restored along with the garden. It contains many old Live-Oaks and a boxwood garden.

Daily 9-5; closed Christmas; adults, under $3; under 13 half; (504) 766-8600.

23 Laurens H. Cohn Arboretum ☆ HA-S-W
12056 Foster Rd.

These 16 acres contain more than 300 species of trees and shrubs with an especially fine collection of Japanese Maples. There is a water-lily pond. The display of spring flowers and flowering shrubs is best seen in February and March.

8-5 weekdays; 9-5 weekends; no admission charge; handicapped access; (504) 775-1006.

24   The Burden Gardens   R
Louisiana State University
Essen Lane and I-10

Numerous sculptures have been placed in 5 acres of semi-formal gardens. There is an All-American Rose Display garden as well as test gardens.

8-4 Mon-Fri; no admission charge; (504) 766-3471.

25   Hilltop Arboretum
Louisiana State University
11800 Highland Rd.

140 species of plants native to Louisiana have been planted on the 12-acre grounds of this arboretum. Eventually all native plants will be represented. The plants are labelled.

8-4 weekdays; (504) 924-0684.

BURNSIDE

26   Houmas House   HH
River Rd. (Rt. 942)

A Greek revival mansion built in 1840 has been restored along with a portion of its formal gardens. There are many Live-Oaks.

Daily 10-5, Feb 1-Oct 31; 10-4 rest of year; closed Jan 1, Thanksgiving, Christmas; adults, under $6; 13-18 half; 6-12 less; partial handicapped access; tours; (504) 473-7841.

GARYVILLE

27   San Francisco Plantation House   HH
River Rd. (Rt. 44)

A mid-19th century Creole mansion has been restored here along with its gardens. Old trees and shrubs may be found on the estate.

Daily 10-4; closed Jan 1, Mardi Gras Day, Easter, Thanksgiving, Christmas, adults, under $6; 12-17 two-thirds; 6-11 half; partial handicapped access; (504) 535-2341.

VACHERIE

28   Oak Valley Plantation   HH
3 mi. north on Rt. 18

2 rows of ancient Live-Oaks lead to this Greek Revival mansion which stands on an estate with gardens.

Daily 9-5:30, March 1-Oct 31; 9-5 rest of year; closed Jan 1, Thanksgiving, Christmas; adults, under $6; 13-18 two-thirds; 6-12 half; (504) 265-2151.

Long Vue Gardens

NEW ORLEANS

29 Long Vue House and Gardens ☆☆☆ G-CA-HA-O-R-S-W
7 Bamboo Rd.; Metairie Rd. exit from I-10

A fine home stands in 8 acres of well-landscaped gardens. The Spanish water garden
is unique in the United States and has been patterned after the Generalife in
Granada. There is an English country-house garden. The walled garden contains
fragrant plants. We also find a 'yellow' garden, a lily pond and a woodland area.
Native plants have been emphasized and the collection of camellias, magnolias,
roses, and native plants is good. The greenhouses have an orchid collection. There
are test gardens for roses, annuals, and vegetables.

10-4:30 Tues-Fri; 1-5 Sat, Sun; adults, under $6; students, children, half; gardens
only, under $3; students and children, half; partial handicapped access; (504) 488-
5488.

30 Audubon Park and Zoological Garden ☆☆ G-FE-P-S-W-WF
6500 Magazine St. and St. Charles Ave.

Animals are exhibited in their natural habitat in this large zoo. Each section has been
planted with appropriate plant materal. The Louisiana Swamp Exhibit is especially
interesting. The park contains good specimen of Live-Oak and fine gardens lie along
the lagoons. More than 800 species of wildflowers are displayed. The Heymann
Memorial Conservatory built in 1962 replaced the conservatory built for the World
Cotton Exposition of 1885 which was destroyed by a hurricane in 1915. 700 species
and cultivars of tropical plants are exhibited in the conservatory.

9:30-4:30 Mon-Fri; 9:30-5:30 Sat, Sun, May-Aug; daily 9-4:30 rest of year; closed Jan 1; Shrove Tues, Thanksgiving, Christmas; adults, under $3; 3-15 half; senior citizens free; (504) 861-2537.

31   Rose Gardens   ☆   A-CA-R
City Park Esplanade

This 1,500-acre park was once a plantation. A good rose garden has been created here along with a floral clock and plantings of azaleas, camellias and gardenias.

Daily, dawn-dusk.

32   Hermann-Grima Historic House   HA-HH
820 St. Louis St.

The courtyard garden of this house built in 1831 has been restored with plants typical of the period.

Daily 10:30-4; Sun 1-5; closed Wed; adults, under $3; handicapped access; (504) 525-5661.

33   Washington Artillery Park
Between Jackson Square and the levee

This small park contains fountains and a garden.

Daily, dawn-dusk.

34   Beauregard-Keyes House   HH
1113 Chartres St.

This home built in 1826 has been restored and furnished with period pieces. There is a small garden and a courtyard.

10-3 Mon-Sat; donation; (504) 529-2001 or 523-7257.

35   Sun Oak Faubourg Marigny   HH
2020 Burgundy St.

This fine home has been completely restored; it is surrounded by landscaped sub-tropical gardens.

By appointment only; (504) 945-0322.

36   Gallier House   HH
1118-32 Royal St.

The home of the famous architect James Gallier Jr. which was built in 1857 has now been restored. The courtyard contains a fountain and flowers placed according to early photographs.

10-5 Tues-Sat; 10-5 Sun; closed holidays; adults, under $3; over 61, students over 12, two-thirds; 5-12 half; (504) 523-6722.

MAINE

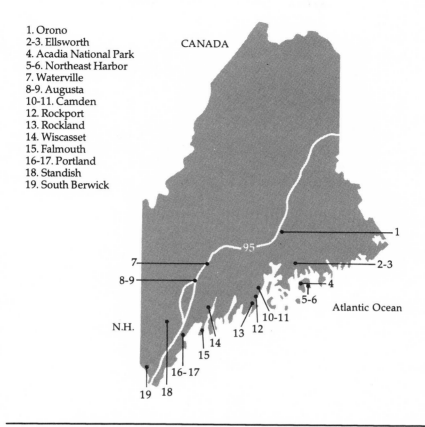

1. Orono
2-3. Ellsworth
4. Acadia National Park
5-6. Northeast Harbor
7. Waterville
8-9. Augusta
10-11. Camden
12. Rockport
13. Rockland
14. Wiscasset
15. Falmouth
16-17. Portland
18. Standish
19. South Berwick

CANADA

95

Atlantic Ocean

N.H.

ORONO

1 Fay Hyland Botanical Plantation   HA
University of Maine

Over 200 species of native plants may be seen on this 10-acre site established in 1865.
Fay Hyland helped to popularize the plants found in this area.

Daily, dawn-dusk; no admission charge; handicapped access; (207) 581-7461.

ELLSWORTH

2 Stanwood Homestead Museum and Bird Sanctuary   HH-W
Junction U.S. 1 and Route 3

The home of Maine's pioneer ornithologist, Cordelia Stanwood, has been turned
into a museum and preserve covering 50 acres. Nature trails lead through a
woodland; a bog area has many native trees and shrubs labelled.

Tues-Sun 10-4, June 15-Oct 15; donation requested; (207) 667-8460.

3 **Black House** HH
Surry Rd., Rt. 172

The formal gardens which surround this early 19th century mansion were laid out in 1903; they have been restored. The gardens are at their height in late July or early August.

10-5 weekdays, June 1-Oct 15; adults, under $3; under 12, half; (207) 667-8671.

ACADIA NATIONAL PARK

4 **Wild Gardens of Acadia** HA
Sieur de Monts Spring

This is a small garden of native plants found in the park; the botanical garden is built in 12 sections around the nature center. These include a beach area, a bog, a roadside plant area, and a meadow. Plants are well labelled and described. Late spring and early summer are best times.

Daily, May-Oct; no admission charge; handicapped access; (207) 228-3338.

NORTHEAST HARBOR

5 **Asticou Azalea Garden** ☆☆ A-HA-J-S

This 2-acre garden was designed by Charles K. Savage with the financial assistance of John D. Rockefeller Jr. Many of the plants were taken from Beatrix Farrand's Reef Point Gardens in Bar Harbor.It contains a Japanese sand garden; there is a fine collection of exotic azaleas and rhododendrons.

Spring to mid-Oct; no admission charge; handicapped access; call for times (207) 276-5456.

6 **Thuya Garden** A-S
Seal Harbor Rd.

A formal English garden which contains annuals and perennials in a 2 acre area. Exotic evergreens, rhododendron, kalmia, as well as native trees make up the special collections of plants. There is a library.

Daily 7-7, June-Oct; donation suggested; (207) 276-5130.

WATERVILLE

7 **Perkins Arboretum and Bird Sanctuary**
Colby College
Mayflower Hill Drive

This 128-acre arboretum has steadily expanded during the last decades; it emphasized flora and fauna of central Maine. Mature forest covers 20 acres; the remainder is 40 years old. There are marked trails.

Daily, dawn-dusk; no admission charge; (207) 873-1131 ext. 246.

AUGUSTA

8 **Augusta State Park**
State House to Kennebec River

A small state park with 22 species of native trees as well as many exotic trees is found here; the grounds are nicely landscaped.

Daily, dawn-dusk.

9   **Blaine House**   HH
State and Capitol Sts.

The governor's mansion was built in the 1830's and is set in a garden of perennials and annuals. Old elms and maples stand on the grounds.

Daily 10-4; no admission charge; (207) 289-2121.

CAMDEN

10   **Amphitheatre and Marine Park**
Atlantic Ave.

A park and garden center are part of this cultural complex.

Daily, dawn-dusk.

11   **Old Conway House and Museum**   HH
Conway Rd.; 1 mi. south on U.S. 1

This 18th century house is surrounded by gardens of the period; there are some formal plantings.

1-5 Mon-Sat, July 1-Aug 31; Sept by appointment; adults, under $3; under 16 half; (207) 236-2257.

ROCKPORT

12   **Vesper Hill Chapel**   B
Calderwood Lane

The well-landscaped grounds of this chapel have been planted in part with Biblical plants.

Daily, dawn-dusk.

ROCKLAND

13   **Ureneff Begonia Gardens**   WF
169 Camden St., 1½ mi. north on U.S. 1

This sunken garden watered by a small brook emphasizes tuberous begonias, some of which are hung from trees. Numerous wildflowers bloom early in the season.

Daily 8-5, July 1-Sept 21; no admission charge.

WISCASSET

14   **Sunken Garden**
Main St.

The burned out site of a hotel was utilized to create a sunken garden here in 1912 by the Sortwell family. It has been restored in accordance with a design of W. Andrews. There are many spring flowers, magnolias and a variety of shrubs, perennials and annuals.

Daily, dawn-dusk; no admission charge.

FALMOUTH

15 Gilsland Farm
Maine Audubon Society
118 U.S. 1

75 acres form a refuge for thousands of birds during their migration. A large perennial garden lies on the grounds.

10-4 weekdays; no admission charge; (207) 781-2330.

PORTLAND

16 Henry Wadsworth Longfellow Home H-HH
487 Congress St.

The original garden has been partly restored; it is a long narrow garden. There is a herb garden as well as plantings of shrubs, perennials, and annuals.

9:30-4:30 Mon-Wed, June 1-Oct 1; closed holidays; adults, under $3; under 12, nominal; (207) 772-1807.

17 The Rose Circle R
Derring Oaks Park
State St.

70 varieties of roses planted in 18 beds in 2 large circles; altogether there are more than 800 plants. Hedges and annuals complete this garden which is part of a larger park.

Daily, dawn-dusk.

STANDISH

18 Marrett House HH
Rt. 25; exit 8 from I-95

A late Georgian home built in 1789 which has been frequently modified stands in a small garden of perennials and annuals.

Tues, Thurs, Sun 1-5, June 15-Sept 4; adults, under $3; (617) 227-3956.

SOUTH BERWICK

19 Hamilton House and Garden HH
Vaughn's Lane; off Rt. 263 at junction Rt. 91

This late 18th century home overlooks the Piscatagua River; it is surrounded by a garden in the Colonial style with terraces which were designed early in this century by E. D. Tyson filled with flowering shrubs, perennials and annuals.

12-5 Tues, Thurs, Sat, Sun, June 1-Oct 15; closed holidays; adults, under $3; under 12, half; (207) 384-5269.

MARYLAND

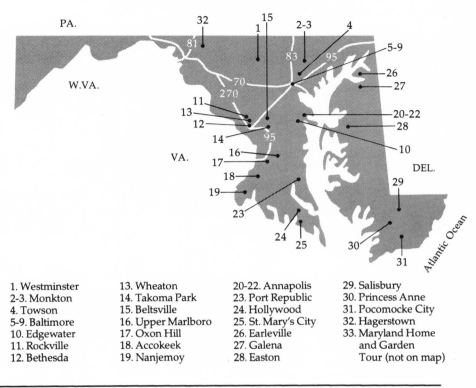

1. Westminster
2-3. Monkton
4. Towson
5-9. Baltimore
10. Edgewater
11. Rockville
12. Bethesda

13. Wheaton
14. Takoma Park
15. Beltsville
16. Upper Marlboro
17. Oxon Hill
18. Accokeek
19. Nanjemoy

20-22. Annapolis
23. Port Republic
24. Hollywood
25. St. Mary's City
26. Earleville
27. Galena
28. Easton

29. Salisbury
30. Princess Anne
31. Pocomocke City
32. Hagerstown
33. Maryland Home
and Garden
Tour (not on map)

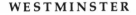

WESTMINSTER

1 Shellman House HH
Carroll Country Historical Society
206 E. Main

This home stands in a small 19th century garden with a gazebo.

9:30-3:30, Tues-Sun; closed major holidays; no admission charge; (301) 848-6494.

MONKTON

2 Ladew Topiary Gardens ☆☆☆☆ H-HA-HH-J-L-R-S-T-W
3535 Jarrettsville Pike (Rt. 146)

This is one of the few topiary gardens in the United States. It was developed by Harvey S. Ladew between 1929 and 1971 into 15 garden areas with grand allees, beautifully cut traditional forms and many whimsical figures of animals, all finely sculptured. Grand hedges surround the central and side gardens. There is a wild garden, a Victorian garden, a berry garden, a pink garden, a rose garden, a water lily garden, a tea house garden, a golden chain tunnel, an iris garden, a terrace garden, a cottage garden, a herb garden, a Japanese garden as well as gardens which emphasize a single color. These 22 acres are beautifully landscaped and maintained. There is a library.

Ladew Topiary Gardens

10-4 Tues-Sat and holidays; 12-5 Sun, mid-April to Oct 31; house open Wed and Sun Garden only; adults, under $3; over 62 and students, half; under 12, nominal; handicapped access; (301) 557-9466.

3   Breezewood Japanese Garden and Museum   J
3722 Hess Rd., 1 mi. west of Jarrettsville Pike

The museum has a small Japanese garden.

2-6, 1st Sunday of month from May to Oct; adults, under $3; children half.

TOWSON

4   Hampton National Historic Site   ☆   BX-G-H-HH-S
535 Hampton Lane, off Rt. 146

A Georgian home begun in 1783 and now restored; the 48-acre grounds contain an early 19th century garden with formal parterre terraces and boxwood hedges. There is a herb garden in the form of a wheel near the kitchen. Greenhouses and a restored orangery stand on the grounds.

Daily 9-5; closed Jan 1, Christmas; house has different days and hours; no admission charge; (301) 823-7054.

BALTIMORE

5   Sherwood Gardens   ☆   A-BX
204 E. Highfield Rd.

This 7-acre garden founded in 1927 is beautifully landscaped and planted with more than 100,000 tulips and other bulbs. The flowering cherries, dogwoods, and 5,000 azaleas produce a grand spring display. English boxwood marks the formal gardens.

Daily, dawn-dusk; April 15-May 15; no admission charge; handicapped access; (301) 467-6855.

6   Cylburn Wildflower Preserve and Garden Center ☆☆   .-BX-H-HA-S-WF
Cylburn Park
4915 Greenspring Ave.

176-acre preserve with large wildflower gardens established in 1954. Aside from the nature preserve with its trails there are formal gardens, a herb garden, an All-American garden, a garden of the senses for the blind, an ornamental grass section, and an arboretum with systematic plantings. The gardens possess good collections of magnolias, Japanese maples, boxwoods. There are demonstration and display gardens as well as a library.

Daily 7:30-3:30; no admission charge; handicapped access; (301) 396-0180.

7   City of Baltimore Conservatory ☆   G-HA-P-SU
Druid Hill Park
4915 Greenspring Ave.

This is one of the oldest American conservatories, established in 1888. It contains a fine collection of tropical plants. Three seasonal flower shows are held each year. There are oudoor gardens of bulbs and annuals.

Daily 10-4; no admission charge; handicapped access; (301) 396-0180.

8   Mount Clare HH
Carroll Park
Monroe St.

This 1754 home has been restored with a portion of its garden. The original terraces remain.

Weekdays 11-4; Sun 1-4; closed Jan 1, Good Friday, Easter, July 4, Thanksgiving, Christmas; adults, under $3; under 12, nominal; (301) 837-3262.

9   National Aquarium ☆   FE-HA-P
Pier 3, 501 Pratt St.

This major aquarium contains a tropical rain forest with an excellent display of foliage plants.

10-6 Sat-Thurs; 10-9 Fri; closed Jan 1, Christmas; adults, under $6; over 64 two-thirds; 3-12 half; handicapped access; (301) 727-6900.

EDGEWATER

10   London Town Publik House and Gardens ☆☆☆   A-CA-G-H-HH-L-W-WF
839 London Town Road

A mid-18th century inn which has been restored to reflect the life of that period. The beautifully landscaped area overlooks the South River. 8 acres of gardens contain a wildflower walk, a herb garden, a winter garden, a woodland, and plantings of azaleas, rhododendrons, camellias, magnolias, viburnums, and hollies. A garden of marsh plants has been added recently. A tobacco barn and greenhouses lie on the grounds.

10-4 Tues-Sat; 12-4 Sun, March 1-Dec 31; closed Easter, Thanksgiving, Christmas; adults, under $3; 6-12 nominal; partial handicapped access; (301) 956-4900.

ROCKVILLE

11 Civic Center
Edmonston Dr. and Baltimore Rd.

This 100-acre park contains an art gallery, a theater, and small formal gardens.

Daily 8-dusk; (301) 424-6867.

BETHESDA

12 Perkins Garden ☆ A-WF
Landon School
6101 Wilson Lane

A well-landscaped garden with a fine azalea collection; extensive hosta and wildflower plantings are found on this 4-acre garden established in 1937.

First weekend of May; other times by appointment only; no admission charge; (301) 320-3200

WHEATON

13 Brookside Gardens ☆☆☆ .-A-FE-G-HA-J-R-W
1500 Glenallen Ave.

A 50-acre garden established in 1969 with numerous smaller fine gardens including a Japanese garden, a rose garden, a winter garden, an azalea garden, a fragrance garden for the blind, a formal garden with clipped hedges, and an aquatic garden. There are good collections of azaleas, rhododendrons, dogwoods, crab-apples, flowering cherries, and ornamental grasses. Many rare trees and shrubs have been planted on these grounds. The greenhouses feature tropical plants, gesneriads and ferns. 3 seasonal flower shows are held. The gardens maintain demonstration and test gardens for roses and annuals.

Daily 9-5; closed Christmas; no admission charge; handicapped access; (301) 949-8230.

TAKOMA PARK

14 House and Garden Tour HH

Each May a series of homes and their gardens are open to the public.

For information call (301) 270-4048.

BELTSVILLE

15 U.S. Department of Agriculture Experimental Gardens ☆ CH-G-HA-R
Powder Mill Rd., off U.S. 1

Large experimental plantings of grain crops, vegetables, fruit as well as flowering plants may be seen here. There are fine beds of roses, chrysanthemums, lilies, gladiolas, and 6 acres of greenhouses.

8-4:30 Mon-Fri; closed holidays; self-guided tours; handicapped access; (301) 344-2483.

UPPER MARLBORO

16   Melwood Horticultural School   G-HA
5606 Dower House Rd.

A horticultural training center for retarded children and adults. It presents a model program for rehabilitation through its greenhouse and ground programs.

By appointment only; (301) 599-8000.

OXON HILL

17   Oxon Hill Farm   H-HH
Oxon Hill Rd., off I-95

A late 19th century exhibition farm along with its farm gardens of flowers and herbs.

Daily 8:30-5; closed Jan 1, Thanksgiving, Christmas; no admission charge; partial handicapped access; (301) 839-1177.

ACCOKEEK

18   National Colonial Farm   H
Bryan Point Rd.; exit 37 from I-495; Rt. 210 south;
Also by ferry service from Mt. Vernon.

This demonstration farm utilizes Colonial farming methods. There is a herb garden, a kitchen garden, a woodland trail, and a grove of 500 chestnut trees. Demonstration and test gardens for vegetables are maintained.

10-5 Tues-Sun, June 1-Labor Day; Fri, Sat, Sun only rest of year; adults, under $3; children half; (301) 283-2113.

NANJEMOY

19   Melwood Farm   G-H-HA

An outdoor training and nature center for retarded children and adults. There is a herb garden, a large greenhouse complex as well as nature trails.

By appointment only; (301) 599-8000.

ANNAPOLIS

20   William Paca House and Garden   ☆☆   BX-H-HH-R
186 Prince George St.

This mansion built in 1763 stands in a restored 18th century garden which uses only plants known at that time. There are parterre terraces, a gazebo, a rose garden, and a wilderness garden. The house contains a library.

10-4 Tues-Sat; 12-4 Sun; closed Thanksgiving, Christmas; garden only adults, under $3; 6-18 .75¢; partial handicapped access; (301) 267-8149.

21   The Helen Avalynne Tawes Garden   .-W
Rowe Blvd. and Taylor Ave.

6 acres of a new botanic garden are nestled among state office buildings. The gardens emphasize the preservation of Maryland's natural resources; a section reproduces

each type of the state's flora. There are ponds and a sensory garden for the handicapped.

Daily 8-dusk; no admission charge; (301) 269-2609.

22 **Home and Garden Tour**   HH

A tour of homes and gardens is held each spring.

For information call (301) 269-1714.

PORT REPUBLIC

23 **Biblical Gardens**   B
Christ P.E. Church
Broome Island Rd.

The Biblical gardens utilize plants indigenous to the area.

Daily; call for hours; (301) 568-0565.

HOLLYWOOD

24 **Sotterley on the Patuxent**   HH
Off Rt. 245.

A 1717 mansion stands in an English style country garden.

Daily 11-4, June-Sept; rest of year by appointment; adults, under $3; children half; (301) 373-2280.

ST. MARY'S CITY

25 **Margaret Brent Memorial Garden**
State House.

A garden in the Colonial style is being created here in memory of this early suffragette.

The garden is not open yet; (301) 685-3750.

EARLEVILLE

26 **Mt. Harmon Plantation**   BX-HH

This plantation house lies on the banks of the Sassafras River amidst formal boxwood gardens.

10-3 Tues, Thurs; 1-4 Sun; adults, under $3; children half; (301) 275-2721.

GALENA

27 **Shorewood Gardens**   HH
Willow Landing Rd., off Rt. 290 east

This estate on the Sassafras River contains formal gardens, pools, and fine shrubbery.

Open during the summer months; (301) 398-0200 ex 235.

EASTON

28 Historical Society of Talbot County
25 Washington St.

A museum stands in the midst of this historic town; there is a Federal period garden.

10-4 Tues-Sat; 1-4 Sun; adults, under $3; children half; (301) 822-0773.

SALISBURY

29 Historic Homes and Garden Tour   HH

A tour of homes and gardens is held each April.

For information call (301) 749-0144.

PRINCESS ANNE

30 Boxwood Garden   BX-HH

A mansion built in 1842 stands in a boxwood garden. This is part of a larger historic district

For hours call (301) 651-2968.

POCOMOCKE CITY

31 Hall-Walton Garden   HH
Costen House
206 Market St.

A small period garden with brick walks, a Victorian gazebo, and many fragrant annuals and perennials surrounds this old house

For hours call (301) 957-1919.

HAGERSTOWN

32 Miller House   HH
135 W. Washington St.

This Federal townhouse has been restored along with its 19th century garden.

1-4 Wed-Sat; 2-5 Sat, Sun, April 1-Dec 31; adults nominal; under 21 free; (301) 797-8782.

33 Maryland Home and Garden Tours   HH

There are annual spring tours in various parts of the state.

For information call (301) 685-3750.

MASSACHUSETTS

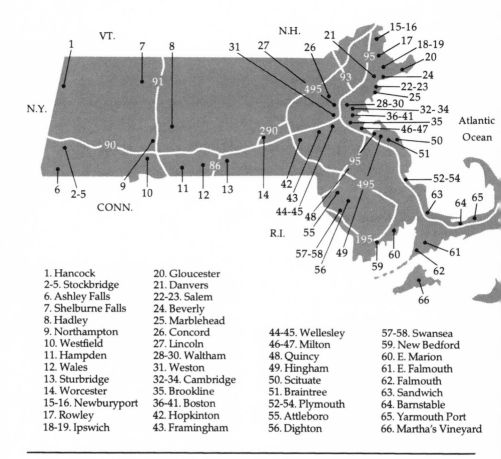

1. Hancock
2-5. Stockbridge
6. Ashley Falls
7. Shelburne Falls
8. Hadley
9. Northampton
10. Westfield
11. Hampden
12. Wales
13. Sturbridge
14. Worcester
15-16. Newburyport
17. Rowley
18-19. Ipswich

20. Gloucester
21. Danvers
22-23. Salem
24. Beverly
25. Marblehead
26. Concord
27. Lincoln
28-30. Waltham
31. Weston
32-34. Cambridge
35. Brookline
36-41. Boston
42. Hopkinton
43. Framingham

44-45. Wellesley
46-47. Milton
48. Quincy
49. Hingham
50. Scituate
51. Braintree
52-54. Plymouth
55. Attleboro
56. Dighton

57-58. Swansea
59. New Bedford
60. E. Marion
61. E. Falmouth
62. Falmouth
63. Sandwich
64. Barnstable
65. Yarmouth Port
66. Martha's Vineyard

HANCOCK

1 Shaker Village   ☆ H-HH
Rt. 20, 5 mi. west of Pittsfield

This village was originally settled in 1780 as the third of 18 Shaker communities; it is now a National Historic Landmark. There is a herb garden with culinary and medicinal plants; many are labelled. The garden design is akin to that of New Lebanon, N. Y.

Daily 9:30-5, June 1 - Oct 1; adults, under $6; over 64, 13-college, two-thirds; 6-12 half; partial handicapped access; (413) 443-0188.

STOCKBRIDGE

2 Berkshire Garden Center   ☆☆   .-A-F-G-H-HD-R
Junction Rts. 102 and 183

This educational center was established in 1934. The 15-acre grounds contain a rose garden, a rock garden, a herb garden with 90 kinds of culinary and medicinal plants, a perennial garden, an orchard, a vegetable garden, a pond, and a vineyard. There are good collections of hostas, azaleas, day lilies, dwarf conifers, bog, and water plants. A garden for the handicapped is marked in braille and demonstrates gardening possibilities for those in a wheelchair. The facility also has greenhouses, a lath house, demonstration and test gardens along with a library.

Daily 10-5, mid-May to mid-Oct; greenhouses open all year; admission under $3; partial handicapped access; (413) 298-3926.

3 **Chesterwood** HA-HH
Williamsville Rd., 2 mi. west

This estate was the summer home of the sculptor Daniel Chester French (1850-1931). The Georgian revival house was built in 1898 and has a neo-classic garden. There are a variety of perennials and annuals along the paths; they accent the open spaces which are emphasized in this garden. A forest surrounds it.

Daily 10-5, May 1-Oct 31; adults, under $3; senior citizens two-thirds; children half; partial handicapped access; (413) 298-3579.

4 **Naumkeag** ☆ BX-FE-HH-J-L-R-T-WF
Prospect St.

A series of terrace gardens surround this 1886 Victorian summer residence of the Choate family. There is an evergreen garden, a rose garden, a cutting garden, a fern and wildflower garden. Linden, pollarded locusts, boxwood, a variety of arbors, fountains and pools enhance the fine vistas of distant hills. The Chinese garden contains numerous figures and lanterns and leads to a Chinese summer cottage.

10-5 Tues-Sat; 11-4 Sun, holidays, late June-Labor Day; Sat 10-5; Sun, holidays 11-4 Memorial Day-late June and Labor Day-Columbus Day; garden only, under $3; 6-16 half; no handicapped access; (413) 298-3383.

5 **Mission House** F-H-HH
Main St.

This 1739 house was the home of John Sergeant, a missionary to the local Indians. There are three small gardens of modern design with numerous perennials and annuals. The side garden contains fruit trees, herbs, and vegetables.

10-5 Tues-Sat; 11-4 Sun, holidays, May 30-Columbus Day; adults, under $3; 6-16 half; (413) 298-3383.

ASHLEY FALLS

6 **Bartholomew's Cobble** RG-WF
Cooper Hill Rd. - 7A

This is a nature preserve with a natural rock garden. More than 700 species of plants have been catalogued; they include 500 species of wildflowers and 50 species of ferns. The plants are labelled along a self-guiding trail.

Wed-Sun 9-5, April 15-Oct 15; adults, under $3; under 17 half; (413) 229-8600.

SHELBURNE FALLS

7 **Bridge of Flowers** HA
Deerfield River

An unusual garden of perennials, annuals and shrubs has been built on a former trolley bridge; the view is enchanting. It is lighted during summer nights.

Daily, dawn-10:30; donation requested; handicapped access.

HADLEY

8 Porter-Phelps-Huntington House HH
130 River Drive

This Dutch Colonial house, built in 1782, stands in a transitional garden in which the landscaping and plant material represents styles from the Colonial to the Victorian period. There is a sunken garden.

1-4:30 Sat-Wed, May 15-Oct 15; no admission charge to the gardens; (413) 584-4699.

NORTHAMPTON

9 Botanic Garden of Smith College and Lyman Plant House ☆☆ A-C-CH-FE -G-H-HA-P-R-RG-S-SU-W-WF
West and Elm Sts. - Rt. 9

The entire 160-acre college campus has been developed into an arboretum and botanic garden. Initially designed by Olmsted and Eliot in 1891, it has been continually expanded and now contains more than 3,600 species of plants. 1,100 species of trees and shrubs are found here along with the best rock garden in New England with 800 labelled species and a herbaceous garden with 600 varieties. The rock garden is at its height in May. There is a pond for water plants, an azalea and rhododendron area, and a woodland wildflower area. The Capens Gardens acquired in 1921 include a herb garden, a turn-of-the-century annual garden, and a rose garden. Fine specimens of American Elm, White Willow, London Plane, Pond Cypress, and Dawn Redwood may be seen here. There are extensive greenhouses with 1,200 labelled varieties of tropical plants, ferns, cacti, succulents, and begonias. A spring bulb show and an autumn chrysanthemum show are held annually. There is a library.

Daily, dawn-dusk; greenhouses daily 8-4:15; no admission charge; handicapped access to greenhouses; (413) 584-2700 ex 2742.

WESTFIELD

10 Stanley Park ☆ A-FE-R
400 Western Ave.

This 180-acre estate of Frank Stanley Beveridge was founded in 1949. The grounds contain a formal rose garden of 2,500 bushes representing 50 varieties, an arboretum, an old-fashioned perennial garden, a rhododendron display, and a woodland wild-life sanctuary with ferns and forest plants. Concerts are held in the summer.

Daily, 8-dusk, Mother's Day-Columbus Day; no admission charge; Carillon concerts during summer months; (413) 568-9312.

HAMPDEN

11 Laughing Brook Education Center and Wildlife Sanctuary
789 Main St.

This Environmental Center is located on 259-acre grounds with numerous nature trails with many plants labelled. There are solar greenhouses.

10-5 Tues-Sun, holidays; closed Jan 1, Thanksgiving, Dec 24, 25; adults, under $3; under 16 and over 65, half; picnic facilities; (413) 566-8034.

WALES

12 Norcross Wildlife Sanctuary WF
Monson-Wales Rd., off Rt. 19

This 3,000-acre reservation displays many rare wildflowers and New England shrubs and trees. There are trails and two museums.

9-4 Mon-Sat; closed holidays; no admission charge; reservation for tours required; (413) 267-9654.

STURBRIDGE

13 Old Sturbridge Village ☆☆ F-H-HH
Exit 9, junction I-86 and I-90

These 200-acre grounds contain a restored early 19th century New England village with 40 buildings and 3 gardens along with various planted areas. The General Salem Towne House has a formal garden with a gazebo and a grape arbor; the Richardson house has a raised vegetable garden; on a hillside in the village there is an extensive terraced herb garden. The herb, vegetable and flower gardens display more than 500 species . The plants reflect gardens of the 1830's. There are extensive farm displays. An orchard is open by appointment. An annual garden week is held in late June.

Daily 9-5, April 1-Oct 31; 10-4 Tues-Sun, and holidays, rest of year; closed Jan 1, Christmas; adults, under $9; 6-15 half; (617) 347-3362.

WORCESTER

14 Worcester County Horticultural Society
30 Elm St.

The Society presents extensive exhibits in March, November, and December. There is a library.

9-4 Mon-Fri; adults, under $3; over 64 half; under 13 nominal; (617) 752-4274

NEWBURYPORT

15 Cushing House BX-HH-R
98 High St.

This 1808 Federal mansion stands in a restored small formal French garden with boxwood, roses, and a garden house.

10-4 Tues-Sat; 2-5 Sun, May 1-Oct 31; other times by appointment; adults, under $3; under 13 nominal; (617) 462-2681.

16 Spring Garden Tours

The Historical Society of Newburyport sponsors a garden tour of 12 area gardens during the 2nd week in June annually.

For information call (617) 462-2681.

ROWLEY

17 Nor'East Miniature Rose Inc. G-R
58 Hammond St.

There are display gardens and 10 greenhouses on the grounds of this miniature rose nursery.

8-4 Daily; (617) 948-2408.

IPSWICH

18 John Whipple House F-H-HA-HH-R
53 S. Main St.

This small two-story house built in 1640 has been restored along with its 2½-acre garden. There is a rose garden with old roses, formal flower beds, and an excellent herb garden with raised beds. 17th century plants have been used throughout the garden. There is an orchard and a pond.

10-5 Tues-Sat; 1-5 Sun; April 15-Oct 31; no admission charge to the gardens; handicapped access; (617) 356-2811.

19 Castle Hill, The Crane Estate R

Arthur Shurtleff designed a grand allee and rose garden to accompany this Charles II mansion built in 1927. The Olmsted Brothers firm designed the Italian garden which was planted with perennials and annuals. There is a maze. The grounds are principally used for a summer music and cultural events.

On scheduled days; for information call (617) 356-4070.

GLOUCESTER

20 Hammond Museum
80 Hesperus Ave.

An interior court around a pool has been designed to look like a 15th century French village square. The plant material, however, is tropical.

10-3 Tues-Fri; 10-4 Sat, Sun; adults, under $3; under 13 half; (617) 283-2080.

DANVERS

21 Glen Magna Farm HH
57 Forest St.

Behind this summer home of the Endicott-Peabody families lie formal gardens, a brick-walled garden, and a fine Colonial two-story tea-house.

1-4 Tues-Fri, June 1-Sept 30; other times by appointment; adults, under $3; under 16 nominal; (617) 774-9165.

SALEM

22 Ropes Mansion Gardens HA-HH-RG-W
318 Essex St.

This 1719 house is surrounded by a 1-acre formal geometric garden designed at the turn of this century. It is entered through an arbor; high brick walls surround much of it. There is a rock garden and a pool with water plants. The gardens contain a wide variety of annuals.

10-4 Tues-Sat; 1-4:30 Sun, June 1-Oct 15; 2-4:30 Tues-Sat, rest of year; no admission charge to gardens; handicapped access; (617) 744-0718.

23   House of Seven Gables   HH-S-T
54 Turner St.

This 1668 house made famous by Hawthorne has a modern knot garden with boards and raised beds. It follows the Jacobean pattern and contains plants in keeping with Hawthorne's period. There are espaliered yews and a good specimen of American Linden and a Horse Chestnut.

Daily 9:30-6:30, July 1-Labor Day; 10-4:30 Sept 6-June 30; closed Jan 1, Thanksgiving, Christmas; adults, under $6; 6-17 nominal; these are summer fees; lower in winter; (617) 744-0991.

BEVERLY

24   Long Hill   ☆   A-HH-R-S
572 Essex St.; Rt. 22, 3¼ mi. north. Exit 18 from Rt. 128

The Charleston style house, built in 1918, stands in extensive gardens, both formal and informal, with plants representing 400 species. There are azaleas, mountain laurels, tree peonies, lilacs, roses, a large collection of bulbs, as well as flowering trees. The remaining 114 acres are forest and wetland.

Daily, 8-dusk; adults, under $3; children free; (617) 922-1536

MARBLEHEAD

25   King Hooper Mansion   HH
81 Hooper St.

A formal garden patterned on 18th century English design lies behind this mansion.

1-4 Tues-Sun; closed Jan, Feb; no admission charge; (617) 631-2608.

CONCORD

26   Concord Art Association   HH
37 Lexington Rd. - Rt. 2A

This 1720 house turned into a museum stands in a small garden with a waterfall.

11-4:30 Tues-Sat; 2-4:30 Sun, mid-Feb to mid Dec; closed holidays; adults, nominal; under 14, over 62 free; (617) 369-2578.

LINCOLN

27   Codman House   HH-S
Codman Rd.

This Georgian mansion built in 1730 and enlarged at the end of that century stands in the midst of landscaped grounds now partially restored. The original gardens were placed on 5 levels with terrace walls and arbors. There is an Italian garden with some ornaments; many unusual trees may be found here.

12-5 Wed-Sun, June 1-Oct 15; adults, under $3; (617) 259-8843.

WALTHAM

28 Gore Place BX-H-HA-HH-R-T
52 Gore St.

This brick Federal mansion, built in 1806, is surrounded by several gardens. The small formal garden was laid out in 1972. There are boxwood hedges, roses, perennials, and a grape arbor. The herb garden is designed in a knot pattern.

10-5 Tues-Sat; Sun 2-5, April 15-Nov 15; closed holidays; handicapped access; adults, under $3; under 12 nominal; (617) 894-2798.

29 The Lyman Estate, "The Vale" Greenhouses ☆ CA-G-HH-S
185 Lyman St.

This Federal home built in 1793 originally stood in a large garden designed by William Bell, a follower of Repton. The modern diminished grounds are beautifully landscaped and contain specimen trees including a Copper Beech and White Pines. There is a kitchen garden. The greenhouses are the oldest in New England and house a collection of 19th and 20th century plants including a good collection of camellias, some more than a century old, "Black Hamburg" and "Muscat of Alexandria" grapes.

10-4 Thurs-Sun; no handicapped access; adults, under $3; under 12 free; house open by appointment for groups of 10 or more; (617) 893-7232.

30 Suburban Experiment Station G
240 Beaver St.
University of Massachusetts.

This series of demonstration and test gardens was established in 1925; it consists of 23 different areas, each dedicated to a specific study or series of plants. There is an Oriental vegetable garden as well as greenhouses.

Daily 9-dusk; late spring, summer, fall; (413) 545-2243.

WESTON

31 Case Estates of the Arnold Arboretum A-HD
135 Wellesley St.

These 112 acres once were a school for horticulture; now they are experimental nurseries for the Arnold Arboretum. There are a number of excellent collections including rhododendron, holly, hosta, and street trees. The ground cover display, mulch display, and herbaceous perennials are of special interest.

Daily 9-6, mid-April-Sept; no admission charge; (617) 524-1718.

CAMBRIDGE

32 Harvard University Botanical Museum ☆☆
Oxford St.
Harvard University

The Ware collection of hand-blown glass flowers created by Leopold and Rudolph Blaschka illustrates 847 species of plants. This is a unique display. The grounds of the university contain several small gardens and courtyard gardens; Lowell House and Leverett House should be noted.

9-4:30 Mon-Sat; 1:30-4:30 Sun; no admission charge; (617) 868-7600.

33 Longfellow House BX-HH
105 Brattle St.
Harvard University

This Georgian style house built in 1759 became the home of the great poet. Its garden has been restored with clipped boxwood, perennials, annuals, and lilacs.

Daily 10-4:30; closed Jan 1, Thanksgiving, Christmas; adults nominal; under 12 with an adult and over 62 free; (617) 876-4491.

34 Mount Auburn Cemetery ☆☆ S
580 Mount Auburn St.

This is the oldest garden cemetery in the United States; it was established in 1831 on 170 acres and now contains more than 1,000 labelled trees. Among the specimen trees are dogwood, crab-apple, 58 varieties of Japanese flowering cherries, sugar and Schwedler Norway Maples, weeping beech, Copper and Cut-leaf Beech. There are stands of Kentucky Coffee trees and Bald Cypress. Unusual trees include Japanese Umbrella Pines, cork trees, Turkish Hazelnuts, and Saw-Tooth Oaks. There are special gardens and paths of perennials and annuals.

Daily 8-7, May 1-Oct 1; 8-5 rest of year; (617) 547-7105.

BROOKLINE

35 Mary Baker Eddy Museum HH-R-S
120 Seaver St.

An 8-acre enclosed garden surrounds this mansion of the founder of Christian Science. There is a rose garden, a woodland garden, a formal sunken garden, and many specimen trees.

10-4:15 Tues-Sat; 1-4:15 Sun, April 1-Oct 31; closed holidays and Feb 1-28; adults, under $3; 12-20 nominal; (617) 277-8943.

BOSTON

36 Arnold Arboretum ☆☆☆☆ A-BO-G-HA-S
Arborway
Jamaica Plains

Founded in 1872 and leased to Harvard University, this 265-acre arboretum, designed by Frederick Law Olmsted, contains more than 6,000 species and varieties of trees and shrubs. Its founding director C. S. Sargent and the plant explorer E. H. Wilson introduced more than 500 plants to the United States. There is a Chinese Path which displays plants brought by Wilson from the Orient. The arboretum includes many special areas and collections including a dwarf conifer area, bonsai collection, rhododendron, azalea, flowering crab-apple, lilac, honeysuckle, mock orange, viburnum collections, and a rose garden. Specimen trees are numerous, among them are Sargent Weeping Hemlock, Golden Larch, Katsura, Carolina Hemlock, and Bald-Cypress. A large number of plants are labelled. There are greenhouses and a large library.

Daily, dawn-dusk; no admission charge; handicapped access; (617) 524-1718.

37 James P. Kelleher Rose Garden HA-R
Fenway Park
Park Drive

This park developed by Olmsted contains a well-maintained rose garden with several hundred varieties which are labelled.

Daily, dawn-dusk; handicapped access; (617) 323-2700.

38 **Public Garden** HA
Boston Common

This landscaped park contains a formal section; there are some rare trees as well as plantings of perennials and annuals.

Daily, dawn-dusk, Memorial Day-last Sun in Sept; adults nominal; under 12 nominal; handicapped access; (617) 323-2700.

39 **Isabella Stewart Gardner Museum** ☆ A-HA-HH-O-RG
280 The Fenway

The courtyard of this Venetian palace-like museum contains three small gardens with jasmines, orchids, azaleas, and rare plants in the interior garden and perennials and annuals outside. The Renaissance garden has statuary and a fountain, the woodland rock garden is densely planted, and there is a new formal garden.

1-9:30 Tues; 1-5:30 Wed-Sun; donation; handicapped access; (617) 566-1401.

40 **Spring Garden Tour**
Beacon Hill Garden Club
39 Beacon St.

Each May this garden club conducts a tour of the courtyard gardens of Beacon Hill.

For additional information call (617) 227-3550.

41 **Spring Flower Show**
Massachusetts Horticultural Society

A flower show is held in March annually.

For information call (617) 536-9280.

HOPKINTON

42 **Weston Nurseries**
E. Main St.; Rt. 135

This 500-acre nursery provides a display and educational garden in well-landscaped grounds.

8-4:30 Mon-Sat; longer hours April 2-Dec 22; closed national holidays; no admission charge; (617) 435-3414.

FRAMINGHAM

43 **Garden in the Woods** ☆☆☆ A-RG-S-WF
Hemenway St.

This 45-acre garden was established in 1901 and developed by W. C. Curtis and H. O. Stiles; it is now maintained by the New England Wildflower Society. The garden contains the largest landscaped collection of native Northeastern plants with more than 4,000 different species and cultivars. A field of 10,000 Cardinal Flowers presents a spectacular sight. All plants are labelled. Among the many areas are a bog, a pond, a woodland, a pine barren, a western rock garden, and a shady rock garden.

9-4 Mon-Sat; April-Oct; adults, under $3; senior citizens, children half; partial handicapped access; (617) 237-4924.

WELLESLEY

44 Alexandria Botanical Gardens and Hunnewell Arboretum ☆ A-FE-G-HA-W-WF
Wellesley College

This 21-acre botanical garden was established in 1876. It contains good collections of rhododendron, azalea, viburnum, cotoneaster, crab-apple, hawthorn, and ever-greens, dogwood, etc. There are several ponds, a marsh, and a wildflower garden with 85 families, 300 genera, and 600 species is being developed. The extensive greenhouses contain more than 1,000 different varieties of plants with good collections of cycads and ferns. Spring and fall exhibits are held here. There is a library.

Daily 8-4:30; no admission charge; handicapped access; (617) 235-0320.

45 Walter Hunnewell Pinetum A-HA-S-T
845 Washington St.

This 35-acre pinetum was established in 1852 and contains many mature specimens. There are 8 acres of conifers including good specimens of False Cypress, weeping hemlock, Alberta Spruce, White Fir, and Hatfield Yew. The 5 acres of rhododendron are a notable collection. An Italian topiary garden stands on the grounds.

By appointment only; no admission charge; handicapped access; (617) 235-0422.

MILTON

46 Trailside Museum WF
1904 Canton Ave., Rt. 138

This park displays flora and fauna of the Blue Hills Reservation. There are nature trails and wildflower gardens.

10-5 Tues-Sun; closed Jan 1, Thanksgiving, Christmas; adults, under $3; 3-13 half; (617) 333-0690.

47 The Suffolk Resolves House HH
1370 Canton Ave.

This 18th century home has a circular garden planted with perennials and annuals.

Most holidays and by appointment; (617) 333-0644.

QUINCY

48 Adams National Historic Site F-HH
135 Adams St.

This house, built in 1731, was used by 4 generations of the Adams family. The informal garden was developed in the mid-19th century with a variety of perennials, hedges, climbing plants, and a small orchard.

Daily 9-5, April 19-Nov 10; adults, nominal; under 16 free; (617) 773-1177.

HINGHAM

49 The Old Ordinary HH
21 Lincoln St.

This 17th century house is now a museum. The garden feature old Tulip trees as well as perennials and annuals.

1-4 Tues-Sat, early June-Labor Day; adults, under $3; under 12 half; (617) 749-0013.

SCITUATE

50 Mann Historical Museum
Stockbridge Rd. and Greenfield La.

This restored 18th century farm has a farm garden as well as field displays typical of the period.

2-5 Wed-Sat, mid-June to mid-Sept; adults, under $3; 5-12 nominal; (617) 545-0474.

BRAINTREE

51 General Sylvanus Thayer Birthplace   H-HH
786 Washington St.

This restored house built in 1720 has a herb garden planted with specimens typical of the period.

1:30-4 Tues, Thurs, Fri, Sun; 10:30-4 Sat, April 19-Oct 12; 1:30-4 Tues and Sat, rest of year; adults, under $3; under 12 nominal; (617) 848-1640.

PLYMOUTH

52 Cranberry World Visitor Center   HA
Water St.

3 demonstration bogs as well as a model of a Cranberry farm and a museum which deals with the history of the cranberry form this center.

Daily 9:30-5, April 1-Nov 30; no admission charge; handicapped access; (617) 747-2350.

53 Plimouth Plantation   HH
Rt. 3A at Plimouth Plantation Highway

A living museum of 17th century Plymouth has been created here. The garden plots are typical of the early colonists and the neighboring Indians.

Daily 9-5, April 1-Nov 30; adults, under $6; 5-13 half; (617) 746-1622.

54 Mayflower Society House   HA-HH-R
4 Winslow St.

This 18th century house has a formal garden designed at the end of the 19th century. There are roses, perennials, and annuals.

Daily 10-5, Memorial Day to mid-Sept; no admission charge to garden; handicapped access; (617) 746-2590.

ATTLEBORO

55 Capron Park
Rt. 123

This park contains a zoo with a rain forest and tropical plants.

Daily 10-3:30; no admission charge; (617) 222-2644.

DIGHTON

56 Bristol County Agricultural School
Center St. Segregansett

The grounds contain formal and informal gardens; an annual flower show is presented in late October.

Daily 9-4; no admission charge; (617) 669-6744.

NORTH SWANSEA

57 Martin House Farm HH-R
22 Stoney Hill Rd.

An early 18th century farmhouse has a garden with many shrub roses and a summer house.

10-4 Wed-Sun, May 1-Oct 31; adults, under $3; 6-12 nominal; (617) 379-0066.

58 Municipal Rose Garden R

The garden contains a collection of 18th century roses.

Daily 8-dusk.

NEW BEDFORD

59 The William Rotch Jr. House HH
396 County St.

This Greek Revival house built in 1834 is set in a flower garden which has been restored.

9-5 Mon-Sat; 1-5 Sun, July-Labor Day; adults, under $3; under 12 half; (617) 991-1776.

EAST MARION

60 Great Hill Farm ☆ A-G-HH-O
Delano Rd.

This large estate contains formal gardens, an arboretum, and a salt marsh as well as greenhouses with a large orchid collection and thirty kinds of accacias which provide a spectacular spring show. Azalea, rhododendron, mountain laurel as well as perennials may be found here.

8-4 Mon-Fri; closed holidays; no admission charge; (617) 748-1052.

EAST FALMOUTH

61 Ashumet Holly Reservation ☆ HA-S
Ashumet Rd.

This 45-acre reservation is maintained by the Massachusetts Audubon Society. There are good collections of American, Chinese, and English holly. Seasonal flower displays are held.

Daily, dawn-dusk; adults, under $3; children half; handicapped access; (617) 563-6390.

FALMOUTH

62 Historical Society Museum and Garden BX-FE-HH
Wood Rd., off Rt. 28

This house built in 1790 has been turned into a ship museum. The gardens have been restored with box hedges, a summer house surrounded by perennials and annuals as well as ferns near large chestnut trees.

Daily 2-5, June 15-Sept 15; adults, under $3; children half; (617) 548-4857.

SANDWICH

63 Heritage Plantation of Sandwich ☆☆☆ A-H-HA-HH-S-WF
Grove and Pine Sts.

This museum of Americana is spread over 76 landscaped acres which contain a variety of buildings and gardens. There is a holly dell, a day-lily garden, a herb garden, a wildflower garden, and a "dried" garden for plants which dry well. More than 1,000 labelled trees, shrubs, and flowers may be found here. The collection of Dexter rhododendron consists of thousands of plants. 500 kinds of day-lillies and holly are cultivated.

Daily 10-5, mid-May to mid-Oct; adults $3; 6-11 nominal; handicapped access; (617) 888-3300.

BARNSTABLE

64 St. Mary's Church
Rt. 6A

A charming 1½-acre garden created in 1946; it contains flowering fruit trees, narcissi, perennials, and annuals. There are fountains and pools and a small summer house.

Daily, dawn-dusk; no admission charge; (617) 362-3977.

YARMOUTH PORT

65 Botanic Trails Historical Society A-H
Gatehouse on Kingshighway

This 53 acre reservation contains extensive plantings of rhododendron, azalea, and heather as well as large areas of typical Cape Cod flora. There is a small herb garden.

Daily, dawn-dusk; adults and children nominal; (617) 362-3021.

MARTHA'S VINEYARD

66 Barnard's Inn Farm A-CA
Vineyard Haven

A private arboretum has been developed on 20 acres of this farm. More than 3,000 different kinds of plants are currently grown with special emphasis on rhododendron, crab-apple, dogwood, magnolia, and camellia.

By appointment only; R.F.D. 538, Vineyard Haven, 02568.

MICHIGAN

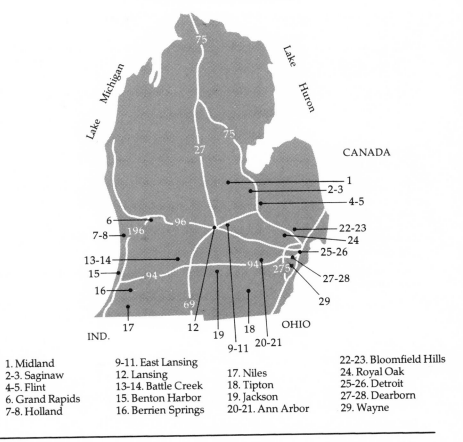

MIDLAND

1 Dow Gardens ☆☆ A-HA-S
1018 W. Main St.

This 60-acre estate established in 1899 contains formal and informal gardens. They represent a variety of styles. More than 600 species of shrubs and flowers have been planted on the grounds. Fine specimens of oak, maple, dogwood, magnolia, crabapple, pine, rhododendron, witch hazel, and viburnum may be found here. There are test and demonstration gardens and a library.

Daily 10-5; closed Jan 1, Thanksgiving, Christmas; no admission charge; handicapped access; (517) 631-2677.

SAGINAW

2 Tokushima Saginaw Friendship Garden J
Washington Ave. and Ezra Rust Drive

Yataro Suzue of Tokushima designed this Japanese garden in 1970 with bridges, a waterfall, a traditional gate and plant material adapted to local conditions. A tea house is being constructed.

Daily, dawn-dusk; no admission charge; (517) 776-1480.

3 **Saginaw Rose Gardens** R
Rust and S. Washington Aves.

Hundreds of rose bushes representing many varieties have been planted in this park which covers the city's reservoir.

Daily, dawn-dusk; (517) 776-1480.

FLINT

4 **For-Mar Nature Preserve and Arboretum** WF
5360 E. Potter Rd.

An arboretum of native trees, shrubs, and wildflowers has been created on this 400-acre site. Numerous trails cross the area.

Daily, 8-dusk; no admission charge; tours; (313) 736-7100.

5 **Riverbank Park**
Downtown along the Flint River

Fountains, flower gardens, and flowering water walls are part of this 4 1/2-block river front park. The beds are planted with perennials and annuals.

Daily, dawn-dusk; (313) 766-7169.

GRAND RAPIDS

6 **John Ball Park Zoo** HA-P
I-196 and Rt. 45

A fine zoo with animals displayed in natural settings. The zoo has established a good collection of tropical plants.

Daily 10-7:30, Apri 15-Oct 15; 10-4:30 rest of year; adults, under $3; under 16, nominal; handicapped access; (616) 456-3800.

HOLLAND

7 **Windmill Island** HA
8th and Lincoln Sts.

A miniature Dutch village complete with windmill and medieval post-house is surrounded by large tulip gardens which present a dazzling display in spring. Annuals provide color later in the season.

9-6 Mon-Sat; 11:30-6 Sun, May 1-31 and July l-Labor Day 10-5 Mon-Sat; 11:30-5 Sun, June 1-30; limited hours Labor Day-Oct 31; adults, under $3; 6-12, half; handicapped access; (616) 396-5433.

8 **Tulip Time Festival** ☆

Each May a special festival is held as millions of bulbs bloom. This is a tulip growing center with large commercial nurseries.

For additional information call (616) 392-9084.

EAST LANSING

9 Beal Botanical Garden ☆☆ HA-S
Michigan State University

A 5-acre collection established in 1873 now contains more than 5,000 species and cultivars of plants. They have has been arranged into four gardens: systematic, economic, landscape, and ecological. Many plants are labelled. There are test and demonstration gardens.

Daily, dawn-dusk; no admission charge; handicapped access; (517) 355-9582.

10 Michigan State University Campus ☆☆☆ A-HA-R

These gardens began on a hundred acres in 1855 and now extend along 60 miles of walks on this 5,200-acre campus. More than 7,000 species are represented. Fine collections of trees, shrubs, evergreens, rhododendrons, azaleas, and annuals have been established. A botanical garden has been planted along the Red Cedar River; there is an All-American rose selection garden as well as test and demonstration gardens and an excellent library.

Daily; no admission charge; handicapped access; (517) 355-5191.

11 Francis Park Memorial Gardens R
2600 Moores River Drive

A rose garden is part of this park; many varieties have been planted.

Daily, dawn-dusk.

LANSING

12 Carl G. Fenner Arboretum HA
2020 E. Mount Hope

This nature center has created an Indian garden which contains many prairie and woodland plants.

8-5 Mon-Fri; 12-5 Sat, Sun; no admission charge; handicapped access; (517) 483-4224.

BATTLE CREEK

13 Leila Arboretum
West Michigan Ave and 20th St.

The Kingsman Museum of Natural History is surrounded by a 72-acre arboretum of native trees and shrubs.

9-5 Tues-Sat; 1-5 Sun; adults, children, nominal; partial handicapped access; (616) 965-5117.

14 Irving Park
North Ave.

A beautifully landscaped park which also contains a zoo.

Daily, dawn-dusk.

BENTON HARBOR

15 Blossom Time Festival F

A weeklong festival with numerous orchard tours and a floral parade.

Usually held during the first week of May; call (616) 983-5478 or 926-7397.

BERRIEN SPRINGS

16 Botanical Gardens
Andrews University
¼ mi. north on US 31

This 1500-acre campus contains a small botanical garden with trees, flowering shrubs, perennials and annuals.

Daily, dawn-dusk; (616) 471-7771 or 471-3243.

NILES

17 Fernwood Botanic Garden and Nature Center   ☆☆   A-BX-FE-H-J-R-RG-S-WF
1720 Range Line Rd.; 3 mi. north of Niles

A 100-acre nature center was established in 1964 with several distinct areas. There is a large woodland area, tall grass prairie, wilderness, and marsh - all with trails. Good herb, perennial, rock, lilac, rose, boxwood, groundcover, blue and silver foliage, and wildflower gardens have been planted. There are collections of crab-apples, irises, hostas, peonies, day-lilies, French and species lilacs, boxwoods and ferns as well as shade and street trees. A waterfall, and a waterwheel are part of the landscaped areas. A Japanese garden and a pioneer garden are of special interest. There are test and demonstration gardens for flowers and vegetables and a library.

9-5 weekdays; 10-5 Sat; 12-5 Sun, March-Nov; adults, under $3; under 12, free; partial handicapped access; (616) 695-6491.

TIPTON

18 Hidden Lake Gardens   ☆   A-BX-FE-HA-P-R-S-W-WF
4 mi. west on Rt. 50.

This fine garden has been planted in a hilly section of the state; more than 1,800 species are represented. The grounds contain a deciduous shrub garden, ornamental shrub garden, shrub rose garden, and an ornamental evergreen garden. Fine collections of maple, birch, boxwood, hawthorn, ash, juniper, magnolia, crab-apple, cherry, rhododendron, and azalea are displayed. A large area has been set aside for native trees, wildflowers, ferns and marsh plants. There is a conservatory with a good tropical collection; demonstration and test gardens are maintained.

Daily 8-sunset, April-Oct; 8-4:30, Nov-March; per person or per vehicle, nominal; tours; handicapped access; (517) 431-2060.

JACKSON

19 Rose Festival Garden Tours R

More than a dozen homes with large rose gardens are opened during one Sunday in mid-June.

For information call (517) 782-8221.

ANN ARBOR

20 **Matthaei Botanical Gardens**   ☆☆☆   BR-C-FE-G-H-HA-O-P-R-S-SU-T-WF
University of Michigan
1800 Dixboro Rd.

250 acres of beautifully landscaped grounds and wild area make ups this garden. This major university botanical garden contains more than 3,000 species. There is a rose garden and a medicinal plant garden, an excellent fern collections, a herb garden in knot design, a grass collection, an *Ericaceae* and minor bulb collection, and a perennial garden.

3 miles of nature trails lead to a pine plantation, an old hickory forest, a lowland forest, a reconstructed tall-grass prairie, a flood plain, a wildflower collection, and a marsh. There are greenhouses with tropical plants, cacti, succulents, bromeliads, ferns, orchids. February through early May find the conservatories at their height. The library is good. Nearby the university maintains the Radrick Bog and Forest Preserve and the Horner Woods.

Daily, 8-sunset; conservatory 10-4:30; closed New Year, Thanksgiving, Christmas; adults, under $3; senior citizens, three-quarters; children, half; handicapped access; (313) 764-1168.

21 **Nichols Arboretum**
Geddes Ave.

This is a natural park with a collection of indigenous trees and magnolias.

Daily, dawn-dusk.

BLOOMFIELD HILLS

22 **Cranbrook House and Gardens**   ☆☆   H-HH-L-R-S-WF
380 Lone Pines Rd.

40 acres of well-landscaped formal gardens with fountains, sculpture, hedges, and flowering ornamentals. There is a sunken garden, a herb garden, a rose garden, an English garden, and a wildflower collection. The gardens are planted with annuals appropriate for the season. The evergreen collection is good.

1-5 weekends, May-Oct; 1-5 weekdays, Memorial Day-Labor Day; adults, under $3; students and senior citizens, nominal; (313) 645-3149.

23 **Schjolin Wildflower Garden**   WF
3 mi. southeast of Cranbrook Gardens

The Schjolin house overlooks the Rouge River and is surrounded by many kinds of wildflowers. The garden was established in the 1950's and is crossed by numerous trails.

By appointment only; (313) 645-3147.

ROYAL OAK

24 **Detroit Zoological Park**   HA-P-RG
8450 W. 10 Mile Road

This large modern zoo spreads over 122 acres with fine plantings suitable for each habitat. The zoo contains a rock garden and a dahlia garden as well as a good collection of trees and shrubs.

10-5 Mon-Sat; Sun, holidays 9-6, April 15-Sept 13; 10-4 Wed-Sun rest of year; closed Jan 1, Thanksgiving, Christmas; adults, under $6; 6-12, half; senior citizens free all year; handicapped access; parking $2; (313) 398-0900.

DETROIT

25   Anna Scripps Whitcomb Conservatory ☆☆☆☆   C-FE-HA-G-O-P-SU-W
Belle Isle

10 acres of gardens surround this conservatory. The formal gardens contain perennials, dahlias, and water-lily ponds. The conservatory built in 1904 has a fine permanent collection of palms, ferns, orchids, and cacti. Five annual flower shows emphasize seasonal plants and present grand displays.

Daily 9-6; no admission charge; handicapped access; (313) 224-1097.

26   Fisher Mansion and Bhaktivedanta Cultural Center ☆   HH
383 Lenox Ave.

This mansion is surrounded by 4 acres of formal landscaped gardens with perennials and annuals overlooking the Grayhaven Canal.

Noon-9 Fri, Sat, Sun; tours (313) 331-6740.

DEARBORN

27   Greenfield Village   HH
Village Rd. and Oakwood Blvd.

Historical homes, shops, and other buildings have been moved to this 240-acre setting which treats 300 years of American industrial and rural history. The vegetable and flower gardens which have been planted here typify the early 1900's.

Daily 9-5; closed Jan 1, Christmas; adults, under $9; 6-12, half; handicapped access; (313) 271-1620.

28   Fair Lane   HH
University of Michigan at Dearborn

The former mansion of Henry Ford, built in 1915, is surrounded by 70 acres of gardens and woods. The original garden with flowering shrubs, perennials and annuals has been replanted.

Sun 1-4:30; other times when not used for conferences; adults under $3; senior citizens, under 12, two-thirds; (313) 593-5590.

WAYNE

29   Wayne County Extension Education Center   CH-F-G-R
5454 Venoy Rd.

An outdoor garden with ponds and beds of roses, chrysanthemums, dahlias, and annuals have been built on this 15-acre site. More than 1,000 rose bushes representing many varieties have been planted. There is a small orchard, vegetable gardens, and grass displays. A herb garden is planned. The greenhouses contain a selection of tropical plants.

Weekdays 10-4; no admission charge; (313) 721-6550.

MINNESOTA

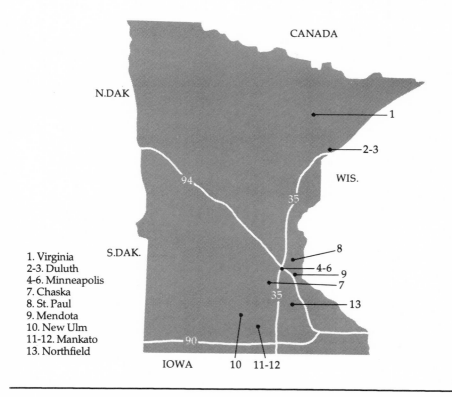

CANADA

N.DAK

——— 1

——— 2-3

WIS.

S.DAK.

——— 8

——— 4-6
———— 9
——— 7

——— 13

1. Virginia
2-3. Duluth
4-6. Minneapolis
7. Chaska
8. St. Paul
9. Mendota
10. New Ulm
11-12. Mankato
13. Northfield

IOWA   10   11-12

VIRGINIA

1   Olcott Park   G-HA
9th St. and 9th Ave.

A greenhouse with seasonal floral displays is part of this large park.

Daily 8-dusk; no admission charge; handicapped access.

DULUTH

2   Glensheen   HA-HH
University of Minnesota
3300 London Rd.

This Jacobean revival style mansion, built in 1908 on the western shore of Lake Superior, stands in a formal garden with geometric flower beds. Charles Leavitt designed it. Shrubs, perennials, and annuals are featured. Best visited in July and August.

Daily 9-5, June-Sept; closed Wed; tours of house only remainder of year; adults, under $3; senior citizens three-quarters; under 16 half; handicapped access; (218) 724-8864.

PARK RAPIDS

3 **Itaska State Park** S
U.S. 71, 28 mi. north

A large state park which contains the headwaters of the Mississippi in Lake Itaska. The State Biological Station with specimens of many native plants lies nearby. There are stands of virgin Norway Pine; some more than 200 years old.

Daily; under $6 per car; (218) 266-3656.

MINNEAPOLIS

4 **Eloise Butler Wildflower and Bird Sanctuary** ☆☆ A-FE-S-W-WF
3800 Bryant Ave. South

This wildflower garden was established in 1907; it covers 20 acres and contains more than 1,000 different species of plants. Emphasis has been placed on indigenous plants. There is a violet path, a bog, and a prairie garden. Collections of azaleas, rhododendrons, lady-slippers, ferns, triliums, hepaticas, wild callas, and ginger may be found here.

Daily 10-6; no admission charge; (612) 374-4305

5 **Lake Harriet Rose Garden** R
Lyndale Park and Garden Center
Dupont Ave. South and 42nd St.

This park contains a rose garden.

Daily, dawn-dusk.

6 **Minnesota Zoo** ☆ P-S-W
12101 Johnny Cake Ridge Rd.; 15 mi. south on I-35W

A large modern zoo with more than 1,700 kinds of animals. Special attention has been given to the plants which provide a natural setting. More than 2,000 species and cultivars of plants have been used. There is a tropical trail with 15,000 trees, shrubs, and flowers. Fine bog, tall-grass and short-grass prairie areas have been developed.

Daily 9:30-6 Memorial Day-Labor Day; 9:30-5 April 1-Memorial Day and Labor Day-Oct 31; 9:30-4:30 rest of year; adults, under $3; 12-16 and over 62 half; 6-11 one-third; handicapped access; (612) 432-9010.

CHASKA

7 **Minnesota Landscape Arobretum** ☆☆ A-R-S
3675 Arboretum Drive
Rt. 5 between Chanhassen and Victoria

A varied terrain of rolling hills, open fields, lakes, and marshlands make up this 560-acre arboretum. Its collection of hardy plants has grown to more than 4,000 species and cultivars. There are collections of azaleas, crab-apples, forsythias, hedges, magnolias, roses, dahlias, hostas, irises, ground covers, day-lilies, as well as annuals. Some good specimen of Burr Oak, White Oak, Sugar Maple, Basswood. Trails lead through the arboretum.

Daily 8-sunset; adults, under $3; partial handicapped access; (612) 443-2460.

ST. PAUL

8   **Como Park Conservatory**   ☆☆☆   BR-C-FE-G-HA-P-SU-W
Midway Park and Kaufman Drive

This 3-acre conservatory established in 1915 has a fine fern collection, lily ponds, palms, economic garden, sunken garden as well as a display of more than 150 kinds of tropical plants. "Gates Ajar", a special winter floral display. Seasonal flower shows. There are good collections of bromeliads, cacti, and ferns.

Daily 10-6 summer; 10-4 winter; no admission charge; handicapped access; (612) 489-1740.

MENDOTA

9   **Sibley House Associates**   HH
Water St.

This is the first stone house built in Minnesota in 1835 by a man destined to become the first governor. This house and a neighboring one have been restored along with their gardens.

10-5 Tues-Sat; Sun, holidays 1-6, May 1-Oct 31; adults, under $3; 6-15 nominal; (612) 452-1596.

NEW ULM

10   **The August Schell Gardens**   HA-HH
Jefferson St. South

These gardens are located on the bluffs of the Cottonwood River and surround the mansion which continues to be used as a home. The formal Victorian gardens with their waterfalls and walks complement the house.

Daily 1-5; no admission charge; handicapped access; (507) 354-4217.

MANKATO

11   **Blue Earth County Historical Society Museum**   HH
606 S. Broad St.

The mansion built in 1881 is surrounded by a Victorian garden, done in the formal manner. It is planted with perennials and annuals.

1-5 Tues-Sun; closed holidays; no admission charge; (507) 345-4154.

12   **Sibley Park**

Park Lane and Given St.

A beautiful 100-acre park contains a small botanical garden as well as some fine plantings of annuals and perennials.

Daily; no admission charge; picnic area.

NORTHFIELD

13   **All-American Selection Trials**
Northrup King Co.
3 mi. east toward Stanton.

A portion of the trial area of this large seed company is open to the public. The plants are labelled.

Weekdays 9-4; no admission charge; (612) 781-8011.

MISSISSIPPI

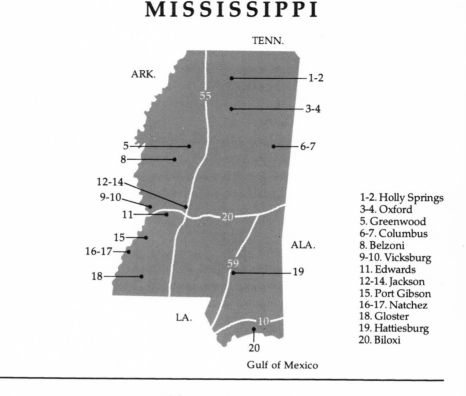

TENN.

ARK.

1-2

3-4

6-7

5

8

12-14

9-10

11

15

16-17

18

20

59

ALA.

19

LA.

10

20

Gulf of Mexico

1-2. Holly Springs
3-4. Oxford
5. Greenwood
6-7. Columbus
8. Belzoni
9-10. Vicksburg
11. Edwards
12-14. Jackson
15. Port Gibson
16-17. Natchez
18. Gloster
19. Hattiesburg
20. Biloxi

HOLLY SPRINGS

1 Antebellum homes HH
Annual spring home and garden week

A fine series of homes and surrounding gardens reflecting the 1850's are open each April; the gardens are beautifully planted.

P.O. Box 12 Holly Springs MS 38635; adults, under $12; 13-18 half; (601) 252-5602.

2 Montrose Arboretum HH-S

A classical revival home built in 1858 is set in restored gardens which extend over 5 acres. 40 labeled specimen trees native to the area are displayed.

By appointment; adults, under $3; (601) 252-2838 or 252-1914.

OXFORD

3 Rowan Oak HH
University of Mississippi

Set in a secluded cedar grove near the university, this home of Nobel Prize winner William Faulkner has been restored. The 31 acres of surrounding grounds contain a formal garden designed by the author.

10-12 and 2-4 Mon-Fri; 10-12 Sat when university is in session, closed during exam periods; no admission charge; (601) 234-3284.

4 Annual Spring Festival HH

A large number of homes and gardens are open during this period.

For information call (601) 232-7073.

GREENWOOD

5 Cottonlandia Museum WF
U.S. 49 and 82 Bypass, 2½ mi. west

The museum mainly deals with the history and development of cotton. A small wildflower garden with a selection of native plants lies adjacent to the museum.

9-5 Tues-Fri; 2-5 Sat, Sun; closed major holidays; no admission charge; partial handicapped access; (601) 453-0925.

COLUMBUS

6 Columbus Pilgrimage A-CA-HH

A springtime pilgrimage held in late March; a few of the more than 100 antebellum homes and garden are open each year. Rosewood Manor contains an English formal garden along with azaleas and camellias. The Colonnade has a formal garden.

Some homes are open by appointment throughout the year. For further information call (601) 328-4491.

7 Waverley BX-HH-S
Rt. 50 north of Columbus

This mansion on a knoll near the Tombigbee River has been restored along with some of the gardens. There are 150-year-old boxwoods as well as some fine old trees.

Daily, dawn-dusk; adults, under $3; children under 6 free; (601) 328-4491

BELZONI

8 Wister Henry Garden ☆☆ A-CH-F-G-HH-R
Rt. 7 north of the city

A fine colonial house lies in the center of 14 acres of gardens. The gardens were begun in 1937 and have been developed over a forty year period. 8,000 azaleas bloom in April along with tulips, spring bulbs and fruit trees. There are 2 rose gardens with more than a 1,000 bushes. An Italian fountain, a small lake and a gazebo add to the charm of this garden. Chrysanthemums both outdoors and in greenhouses bloom in fall. A walk through the town streets will pass many small gardens.

Daily 8-5; no admission charge; (601) 247-3025.

VICKSBURG

9 Vicksburg Pilgrimage HH

A series of antebellum homes are open for the annual spring and fall pilgrimage held in March and October. Only a few of the homes have gardens. Planter's Hall has a small patio garden; Anchuca's garden reflects a mixture of antebellum and contemporary styles.

For further information call (601) 638-6514 or 636-9421.

10 Grey Oaks H-HH-R-S
Rifle Range Rd.

A 5-acre garden surrounds this old home. There is a rose garden, a kitchen garden as well as nature trails which lead to some specimen trees.

Daily during pilgrimage; adults, under $6; (601) 683-3690.

EDWARDS

11 Cactus Plantation ☆ C-SU
Champion Hill Rd.

More than 3,500 kinds of succulents and cacti are planted here in an attractive setting.

Daily 9-5; no admission charge.

JACKSON

12 Mynelle Gardens ☆☆ A-CA-J-R-W
4736 Clinton Blvd.

This 6-acre informal garden was begun in 1920 and now contains thousands of azaleas, magnolias, gardenias and camellias as well as a fine rose garden with an excellent and broad selection. Many bulbs bloom in spring; irises, hydrangeas, and day-lilies grace the grounds later. Hybridizing day-lilies is a specialty. A lake and lagoon contain water lilies. One section is done in Japanese style. More than 1,000 species and cultivars of plants may be found here.

Daily, sunrise-sunset; adults, under $3; under 12 free; (601) 960-1894.

13 Botanical Garden ☆ G-R
Jackson State University

5 acres at the West end of the campus are devoted to a botanical garden with a wooded area, a rose garden, ponds, an All-American-Selection garden, and greenhouses. The nearby Presidential Garden contains formal beds of perennials and annuals. Test gardens are maintained. The gardens are best visited in May, June, or July.

Weekdays 7-3; (601) 968-2121.

14 Josh Halbet Garden HH
City Hall

The antebellum city hall built in 1854 is surrounded by a garden which contains hedges, magnolias, and plantings of spring bulbs and annuals.

Daily, dawn-dusk.

PORT GIBSON

15 Annual Pilgrimage HH

A 2-day pilgrimage held in this town of 3,000 each spring opens many of its homes. Englesing, a Federal style cottage built in 1817 has the state's oldest formal garden.

For further information call (601) 437-4351.

NATCHEZ

16 Rosalie A-HH-S
South Broadway

This 1820's brick mansion stands in a beautiful garden which is laid out informally. There are fine old trees; azaleas bloom in spring.

Daily 9-5; closed on major holidays; admission charge; (601) 445-4555.

17 Spring and Fall Pilgrimage HH

An opportunity to visit thirty historic antebellum homes and gardens through 2 daily tours is provided each spring and fall. Half a dozen homes possess notable gardens.

For further information call (601) 446-6631 or (800) 647-6742.

GLOSTER

18 Gladney Arboretum ☆ A-HA-L
Frank Schutz Rd., off Rt. 24

A 327-acre arboretum established in 1962 with an excellent collection of magnolias and numerous types of azaleas, crab-apples, dogwoods, maples, and red-buds. Many varieties of hollies, lilies, day-lilies and narcissuses form a special collections. Another is devoted to rare native plants. The gardens are used extensively by the Louisiana State University landscape school.

Daily by appointment; no admission charge; handicapped access; (504) 225-4216.

HATTIESBURG

19 The Crosby Arboretum WF
3702 Hardy St.

A new arboretum established in 1980 on 58 acres; it specializes in plants of the Pearl River basin. More than 300 species of trees, shrubs, wildflowers and grasses have been planted.

Will open in mid-summer 1984; (601) 264-5249.

BILOXI

20 Beauvoir, the Jefferson Davis Shrine A-CA-R
U.S. 90

74 acres of woodland and gardens with good collections of azaleas, camellias, magnolias, roses, and neriums. All landscaped in an informal manner.

Daily 8:30-5, closed Christmas; adults, under $3; 8-17 half; (601) 388-1313.

MISSOURI

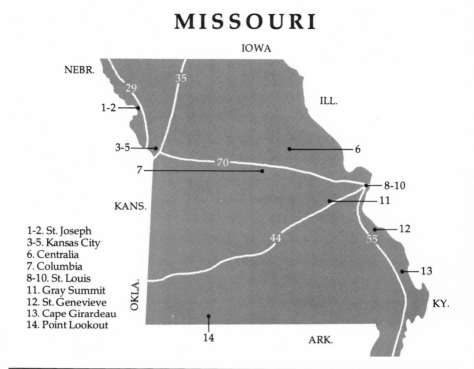

IOWA

NEBR.

ILL.

1-2

3-5

7

KANS.

29

35

70

44

55

6

8-10

11

12

13

KY.

OKLA.

14

ARK.

1-2. St. Joseph
3-5. Kansas City
6. Centralia
7. Columbia
8-10. St. Louis
11. Gray Summit
12. St. Genevieve
13. Cape Girardeau
14. Point Lookout

ST. JOSEPH

1 Albrecht Art Museum R
2818 Frederick St.

This Georgian style mansion is now an art museum; there is a formal rose garden which lies behind the building.

10-4 Tues-Fri; 1-4 Sat, Sun; closed Jan 1, Thanksgiving, Christmas; adults, under $3; children free if with an adult; (816) 223-7003.

2 Krug Park W
11th St. and King's Park Rd.

This well-landscaped park has a water lily pond; there are extensive beds of annuals and perennials.

Daily, dawn-dusk.

KANSAS CITY

3 Country Club Plaza HA
Ward Parkway

This 50-year-old Spanish-Moorish shopping plaza contains many small gardens on its 55 acres. They are adorned with sculpture, wrought iron, and fountains. The area is beautifully planted.

Daily; handicapped access.

4 **Laura Cenyers Smith Rose Garden** R
5200 Pennsylvania Ave.

A rose garden with numerous varieties.

Daily 8-dusk.

KANSAS CITY, KANSAS

5 There are some small gardens in this neighboring city

CENTRALIA

6 **The Chance Gardens** J-R
319 Sneed St.

A small Oriental garden was established here in 1936 with a brook meandering through the valley. There is also a formal garden with a good selection of roses, perennials, and annuals.

Daily May-Oct; illuminated at night; partial handicapped access.

COLUMBIA

7 **University Woodland and Floral Gardens** A-RG
University of Missouri

These gardens, created since 1978 by a group of students feature a rhododendron area, a native woodland display of Ozark trees and shrubs, an oak grove, a rock garden, and a floral garden of bulbs and annuals. The university research greenhouses are open by appointment only.

Daily 8-dusk; no admission charge; (314) 882-2745.

ST. LOUIS

8 **Missouri Botanical Gardens** ☆☆☆☆ .-BR-C-CA-G-HA-J-O-R-P-S-T-W
2101 Tower Grove Ave.

This major botanical garden displays more than 5,000 species of plants on 75 acres. It was founded in what was then a frontier community in 1859 by Henry Shaw who retired from business at age 40. Its Climatron geodesic-dome greenhouse contains four different climates under its ½-acre. There are more than 1,000 exotic plants along with a waterfall, lily pond, hibiscus garden, economic plants, and rain forest; fine orchid collection; trees of Africa and South America. Seasonal flower shows. The Mediterranean House contains a large specialized collection. The Linnean house is the oldest greenhouse west of the Mississippi and is filled with camellias.

Outside there is a water lily garden, Italian garden, English woodland garden, herb garden, scented garden for the blind, Seiwa-en Japanese garden which cover 14 acres and is the largest in the United States, rose gardens. Specimen trees include Copper Beech, Osage Orange, Ginkgo, Bald-Cypress; there are demonstration and test gardens; the library contains a fine rare book collection. Illustrated guide booklets available. The new Ridgway Center provides a dramatic area for floral displays and educational programs.

Daily 9-6 May 1-Oct 31; 9-5 rest of year; closed Christmas; adults, under $3; 6-16 half; family rate; handicapped access; (314) 577-5100.

9   Jewel Box   ☆☆   G-HA-R-W
1501 Oakland Ave.

A conservatory with step-like tiers of sparkling glass which contain seasonal displays. Exterior gardens contain a lily pond; numerous rose beds with many varieties; also a floral clock formed from 25,000 perennials.

Daily 9-5; admission nominal; free 9-noon Mon and Tues.; handicapped access; (314) 535-0400 or 543-9433.

10   Laumeier International Sculpture Park   S

A 96-acre garden very well landscaped with displays of contemporary sculpture; fine specimen trees.

Daily 8-dusk.

GRAY SUMMIT

11   Shaw Arboretum of the Missouri Botanical Gardens
35 mi. west on I-44

A 2,400-acre preserve of plants of the Ozark region; founded in 1925. Trails lead through the area.

Daily 8-5; adults, under $3; children half; partial handicapped access; (314) 742-3512 or 772-7600.

Missouri Botanical Gardens

ST. GENEVIEVE

12 Bolduc House HH

This house begun in 1770 is surrounded by an 18th century garden; it is well maintained. Some old plantings are found here.

Daily 10-4; 11-5 Sun; April 1-Nov 1; winter by appointment; adults, under $3; children half; partial handicapped access; (314) 883-3359.

CAPE GIRARDEAU

13 Rose Display Garden R
Parkview Drive and Perry Ave.

A garden which contains a selection of old classical roses as well as the latest All-American selections. 188 varieties are found here. There are test gardens.

Daily April-Nov.

POINT LOOKOUT

14 Greenhouses and Arboretum G-O
School of the Ozarks

This college overlooking Lake Taneycomo is developing an arboretum with emphasis on the woody plants of Missouri. The greenhouses contain a 6,000 plant orchid collection.

Weekday 8-5; 1-5 weekends for greenhouses; dawn-dusk for arboretum; no admission charge; (417) 334-6411.

MONTANA

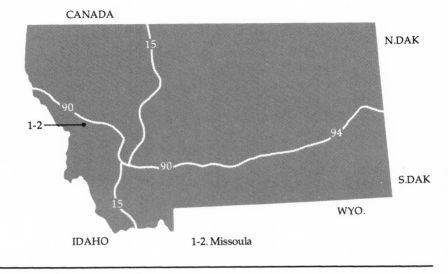

CANADA

N.DAK

90

1-2 ——————

94

S.DAK

15

WYO.

IDAHO   1-2. Missoula

MISSOULA

1 University of Montana
University and Arthur Aves.

The University Center contains a mall with some fine small gardens of perennials and annuals. The University also maintains an experimental forest for native and new trees at another location.

Daily, dawn-dusk; (406) 243-0211.

2 Memorial Rose Garden   R
700 Brook St.; U.S. 93 South

The American Rose Society established this garden in 1947; its beds contain more than 2,500 bushes of many varieties.

Daily, dawn-dusk.

NEBRASKA

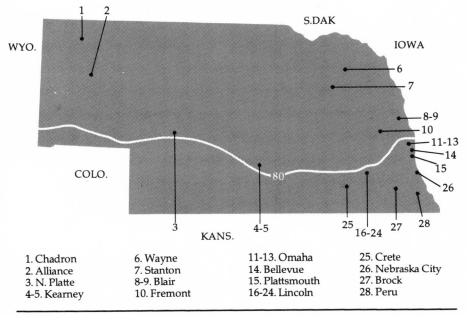

1. Chadron	6. Wayne	11-13. Omaha	25. Crete
2. Alliance	7. Stanton	14. Bellevue	26. Nebraska City
3. N. Platte	8-9. Blair	15. Plattsmouth	27. Brock
4-5. Kearney	10. Fremont	16-24. Lincoln	28. Peru

A statewide system of arboreta was established in 1978; each arboretum has been developed since then in accordance with local priorities. It is not possible to gauge their current condition or to provide an accurate description of the plant material used. Almost every site, however, has been listed.

CHADRON

1 Museum of the Fur Trade HA
Rt. 2, off U.S. 20

A garden of Indian crops has been planted as part of this museum. There is a collection of vegetables and herbs obtained from native sources; they include early beans, pumpkins, and squash as well as midget corn. Mandan Tobacco has also been planted.

Daily 8-6 June 1-Labor Day; by appointment only rest of year; adults, under $3; under 18 nominal; handicapped access; (308) 432-3843.

ALLIANCE

2 Sallows Arboretum and Conservatory C-O-SU

This 55-acre arboretum contains a small conservatory with succulents and orchids as well as tropical plants. There is an annual Christmas show.

Call about hours; (308) 762-5400.

NORTH PLATTE

3 North Platte Experimental Station
University of Nebraska

A field-testing site with large plantings of 600 species and cultivars of shrubs, ornamentals, and fruit trees as well as chrysanthemums, roses, cotoneasters, mock oranges, lilacs, and other plants. All are being bred for hardiness.

Daily 8-5; (308) 532-3611.

KEARNEY

4 **Kearney State College Arboretum**
Kearney State College

The college campus is part of a 195-acre arboretum now placed into the statewide system. Approximately 100 different species of trees have been planted and more are added each year. A guide map of the campus has been prepared.

8-dusk when college is in session; (308) 236-8441.

5 **Cottonmill Park**

This 99-acre park and arboretum is part of the state-wide system. Further development is being undertaken.

Call about hours; (402) 472-2971.

WAYNE

6 **Wayne State College Arboretum**

This well-planted campus is being developed into a 130-acre arboretum of native trees and shrubs as part of the statewide system.

Daily 9-5; (402) 472-2971.

STANTON

7 **Maskenthine State Recreation Area**
1½ mi. north on gravel road

A 400-acre state park with a wide variety of native trees, shrubs, and grasses. This park is now included in the statewide system of arboreta.

Daily, dawn-dusk spring and summer months; (402) 371-7313.

BLAIR

8 **Dana College Arboretum**   R
Dana College
2848 College Drive

This 250-acre arboretum forms the college campus; the grounds contain a rose garden established in honor of Danish royalty's visit to the campus in 1939.

Daily, dawn-dusk; (402) 426-4101.

9 **Blair City Parks Arboretum**

18-acre arboretum displays plants suitable for the plains; it is part of the statewide system.

Daily, dawn-dusk.

FREMONT

10 Luther Hormel Memorial Park   S-WF
Rt. 77 near Platte River

This 167-acre arboretum is part of the statewide system. The area is divided into forest, pond, marsh, and prairie segments. There are some fine specimens of cottonwood, basswood, and other native trees.

Daily, dawn-dusk.

OMAHA

11 Elmwood Arboretum

365-acre arboretum which is part of the statewide system. There is a small display of perennials and annuals.

Daily, dawn-dusk; (402) 472-2971 or 444-5900.

12 Gerald Ford Birth Place   R
32nd St. and Woolworth Ave.

This site has a rose garden with a gazebo.

Daily 8-11.

13 Memorial Rose Garden   R
57th and Underwood Aves.

A municipal rose garden.

Daily, dawn-dusk.

BELLEVUE

14 Bellevue College Arboretum
Bellevue College

The campus of this college has been added to the statewide system of arboreta. Plants will be catalogued and classified; a brochure is being prepared.

Daily, dawn-dusk; (402) 731-3140.

PLATTSMOUTH

15 Horning Farm

240-acre arboretum which is part of the statewide system.

Daily 9-5; (402) 472-2971.

LINCOLN

16 Earl Maxwell Arboretum   WF
University of Nebraska, Lincoln East Campus
38th and Holdpege St.

4½-acre arboretum was established here in 1969. A section has been planted with small groves of trees representing more than 60 species, including Red Oak, Green Ash, a variety of pines, Douglas Fir, juniper; some are labelled. 45 species of wildflowers and 16 types of native grasses are displayed. This is primarily a research facility dedicated to tree improvement.

By appointment only; (402) 472-6627.

17 Chet Ager Nature Center H
Van Dorn and S.W. 40th Streets

This 55-acre arboretum contains a collection of native grasses. There are trails through a woodland and a prairie area around ponds and streams. A herb garden has been planted.

Daily 9-5; (402) 471-7895.

18 Centennial Mall
15th and K Sts.

Floral displays and lighted fountains provide a pleasant setting.

Daily, dawn-dusk.

19 Sunken Gardens
27th and Capitol Parkway

Beautiful plantings of perennials and annuals.

Daily, dawn-dusk.

20 Nebraska State Fairgrounds

280-acre arboretum which is part of a state-wide system.

Call about hours (402) 472-2971.

21 Alice Abel Arboretum
Nebraska Wesleyan University

40-acre arboretum which is part of a statewide system. There are extensive plantings of flowering crab-apples. A native plant garden includes many shrubs as well as prairie grasses. A wildflower garden has been begun and there are plans for a dwarf conifer collection.

Daily, dawn-dusk; (402) 466-2371.

22 Joshua Turner Arboretum
Union College

21-acre arboretum which is part of a statewide system. It contains 75 species of trees; many are labelled. New species are planted each year.

Daily, dawn-dusk; (402) 488-2331 ext. 214.

23 Antelope Park R
23rd and N Sts.

A small garden of perennials and annuals.

Daily, sunrise-sunset.

24 Folson Children's Zoo and Botanical Garden R
2800 A St.

A pleasant small rose garden as well as plantings of trees and shrubs enhance this zoo.

Daily 10-4, Sunday 12-4; no admission charge; (402) 471-7847.

CRETE

25   Doane College   A-R-S
1014 Boswell St. Exit 388 from I-80

The 50-acre campus has become an arboretum which is part of a statewide system. There is an All-American-Rose Selection garden, a collection of 30 Exbury Azaleas, a garden of forbs and native grasses. A restored prairie, fountains, waterfalls and 2 small lakes along with nature trails . The small greenhouse is used for educational purposes. Mid-April to July is the best time.

Daily 8-dusk; (402) 826-2161.

NEBRASKA CITY

26   Arbor Lodge State Park   ☆☆   L-S-WF

This 65-acre arboretum is part of the statewide system; it is the former estate of J. Sterling Morton, the founder of Arbor Day. The original plantings were undertaken in 1891. It contains an Italian terraced garden. The formal gardens around the mansion are being restored. There is a 2-acre stand of pines; good specimens of tulip trees, chestnuts, ginkgos. The prairie plants garden contains a large collection of grasses and wildflowers.

Daily 8-sunset; (402) 873-3221.

BROCK

27   Coryell Memorial Park

24-acre arboretum which is part of a statewide system.

Daily, dawn-dusk; (402) 472-2971.

PERU

28   Thousand Oaks Arboretum
Peru State College

85-acre arboretum is part of a statewide system. There are oaks, trees native to southeast Nebraska, and a greenhouse.

Daily 8-dusk; (402) 872-3815.

NEVADA

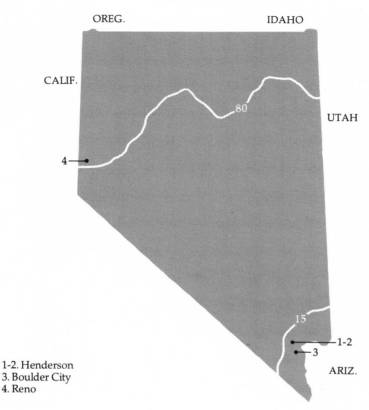

OREG.

IDAHO

CALIF.

80

UTAH

4

15

1-2

3

1-2. Henderson
3. Boulder City
4. Reno

ARIZ.

HENDERSON

1 Southern Nevada Museum C-HA
1850 S. Boulder Highway

The outdoor exhibits at this museum include a small cactus garden with some fine specimens.

Daily 8-5; closed Christmas; adults, under $3; 6-16 and over 59, half; handicapped access; (702) 565-0907.

2 Botanical Garden C-SU
Ethel M. Chocolate Factory
2 Cactus Garden Drive

A new botanical garden with emphasis upon desert plants. There is a good collection of cacti and succulents which has been created in a few years. The garden covers 2 acres.

Daily 9:30-4:30; no admission charge; (702) 458-8864.

BOULDER CITY

3 **Botanical Garden** HA
Alan Bible Visitor Center; Lake Mead National Recreation Area
Jnct. U.S. 93 and Lake Shore Rd.; 4 mi. east

Numerous examples of desert plants are to be found in the small botanical garden
which surrounds the Visitor Center. A loop trail runs through the area.

Daily 8:30-4:30; closed Jan 1, Christmas; no admission charge; handicapped access;
(702) 293-4041.

RENO

4 **Municipal Rose Garden** R
2055 Idlewild Drive

A small rose garden with numerous varieties.

Daily, dawn-dusk.

NEW HAMPSHIRE

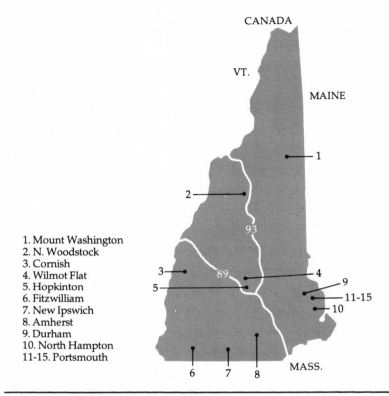

1. Mount Washington
2. N. Woodstock
3. Cornish
4. Wilmot Flat
5. Hopkinton
6. Fitzwilliam
7. New Ipswich
8. Amherst
9. Durham
10. North Hampton
11-15. Portsmouth

MOUNT WASHINGTON

1 Sherman Adams Summit Building   WF
Mount Washington
Via toll road or cog railroad

More than 100 species of Alpine flowers may be found along the trails above the timberline in numerous different micro-climates. There is no formal botanical garden; geological specimens as well as specimens of plant and animals life, of the area, may be viewed in the museum.

Daily 9-6, Memorial Day-Columbus Day, depending on the weather; no admission charge; (603) 466-3388.

NORTH WOODSTOCK

2 Lost River Reservation   WF
Rt. 112, Kinsman's Notch

This gorge with the Paradise Falls, giant potholes, and caves also features a natural garden with more than 300 species of wildflowers as well as moss and ferns. Many of the plants are labelled.

9-5:30 Daily, May 15-Oct 15 weather permitting; adults, under $6; children half; (603) 745-8031.

CORNISH

3   Saint-Gaudens National Historic Site   ☆   HH
Off Rt. 12A

The former home of the artist has been turned into a museum. It is surrounded by formal gardens now restored to its 1907 appearance. There are conifer hedges, a beech allee, shrubs, and numerous perennials. Some of the artist's sculpture is displayed in the garden. A nature area with trails through a fern area, wetlands, and woodlands forms part of the site. In summer modern sculpture exhibits are held.

8:30-4:30 daily, May 20-Oct 31; adults nominal; children free; (603) 675-2175.

WILMOT FLAT

4   Freedom Acres

8 acres with a grand view of the Sunapee Range have been planted with more than 500 tuberous begonias, annuals, and perennials. There is a woodland.

Daily 9-dusk; (603) 526-6080.

HOPKINTON

5   The Fragrance Shop   H
College Hill Rd.

A pleasant exhibition garden featuring herbs, perennials, and annuals has been created here.

Daily 10-5, May 1-Nov 1; no admission charge; (603) 746-4431.

FITZWILLIAM

6   Rhododendron State Park   A-WF
2½ mi. northwest

15 acres of this 300-acre state park are filled with fine growth of 5 wild native rhododendron species; they are in bloom early July. There are foot trails with a good view of Grand Monadnock and wildflower walks. This area has been designated as a National Natural Landmark.

Daily dawn-dusk; (603) 271-2155.

NEW IPSWICH

7   Barrett House   HH
Main St.

A Federal mansion set on large grounds has been restored along with a portion of the garden. There is a latticed summer house, a vegetable garden and an annual garden.

12-5 Tues, Thurs, Sat, Sun, June 1-Oct 15; closed holidays; adults, under $3; (603) 227-3956.

AMHERST

8   Ponemah Bog
Stearns Rd. off Rts. 101A and 122

This 100-acre bog has been turned into a botanical preserve by the Audubon Society. A boardwalk leads through the bog; many of the plants are labelled.

Weekdays 9-5; reservations necessary; adults, under $3; (603) 224-9909.

DURHAM

9 Lilac Arboretum
University of New Hampshire

A large number of lilacs have recently been planted in this new arboretum.
Weekdays 9-dusk; (603) 862-2190.

NORTH HAMPTON

10 Fuller Gardens ☆☆ A-CH-G-HA-J-R
Off Rt. 1A at 10 Willow Ave.

A 2-acre garden established in 1939 on this seaside estate. There are several formal
gardens including a rose garden which contains 1,500 bushes, a Japanese garden and
a demonstration garden. Fine collections of azaleas, rhododendrons, wisterias,
spring bulbs. In autumn there is a large display of chrysanthmums among fountains
and statuary. There are greenhouses with tropical and desert plants.

Daily 10-6, early May to mid-Oct; adults, under $3; seniors nominal; groups,
nominal; handicapped access; (603) 964-5414.

PORTSMOUTH

11 Moffatt-Ladd House ☆ H-HH-R
154 Market St.

A colonial garden built around the home of William Wipple, a signer of the
Declaration of Independence. The design and plants are typical of the period in this
2½-acre garden established in 1862. Formal flower beds, terraces, peonies, herbs,
roses, and perennials are found here.

10-4 Mon-Sat; 2-5 Sun; June 11-Oct 15; adults, under $3; children half; group rates;
(603) 436-8221.

12 Governor Langdon Mansion Memorial HH
143 Pleasant St.

An 18th century Georgian Mansion with a formal garden behind the house has been
partially restored.

12-5 Tues-Sun, June 1-Oct 15; closed holidays; adults, under $3; (603) 431-1800.

13 Prescott Park HA
Marcy St. between Strawbery Banke and the waterfront.

A formal garden with fountains and a great variety of flowers which are displayed in
a series of beds is part of this park.

Daily, dawn-dusk; no admission charge; handicapped access; (603) 436-8010.

14 Strawbery Banke H-HA-HH
Old South End

This is a 10-acre restoration site on the spot upon which the city began in 1630; 35
buildings as well as landscaping and gardens have been restored. This work is
continuing and several gardens and a fine herb garden may be viewed now.

9:30-5 April 15-Nov 15; adults, under $6; senior citizens three-quarters; children
half; handicapped access; (603) 436-8010.

15 Rundlet-May House HH
364 Middle St.

A house surrounded by a simple garden; a landscape and architectural plan which
exists shows how little the garden has changed since 1807.

12-5 Sat, Sun, June 1-Oct 15; adults, under $3; (603) 431-1800.

NEW JERSEY

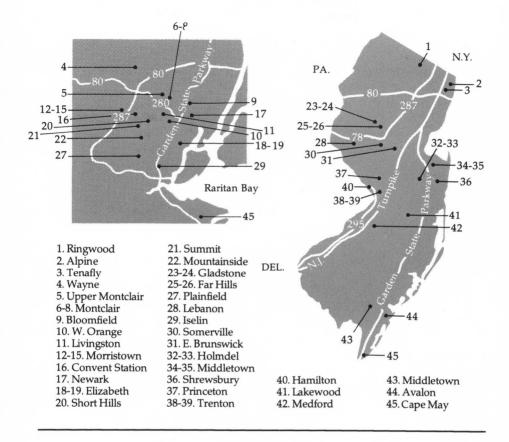

1. Ringwood
2. Alpine
3. Tenafly
4. Wayne
5. Upper Montclair
6-8. Montclair
9. Bloomfield
10. W. Orange
11. Livingston
12-15. Morristown
16. Convent Station
17. Newark
18-19. Elizabeth
20. Short Hills

21. Summit
22. Mountainside
23-24. Gladstone
25-26. Far Hills
27. Plainfield
28. Lebanon
29. Iselin
30. Somerville
31. E. Brunswick
32-33. Holmdel
34-35. Middletown
36. Shrewsbury
37. Princeton
38-39. Trenton

40. Hamilton
41. Lakewood
42. Medford

43. Middletown
44. Avalon
45. Cape May

RINGWOOD

1 Skylands Gardens of Ringwood State Park ☆☆ A-G-HA-HH-WF
Skylands Rd.

This state park aside from other interesting sights contains formal gardens which were established in 1880 and developed by C.M. Lewis between 1920 and 1950. They are being restored. The 300-acre park contains many different informal and formal areas, including an octagonal garden, a magnolia walk, an azalea garden, a peony garden, a pinetum, a wildflower garden, a heather and heath garden, a bog garden, and a rhododendron garden. There are good collections of horse chestnuts, and berberries. Demonstration and test gardens are maintained along with greenhouses. 900 additional wooded acres feature walking trails.

Daily, sunrise-sunset; parking fee during summer months, weekdays, under $3; weekends slightly higher; handicapped access; (201) 962-7031.

ALPINE

2 Greenbrook Sanctuary HA-WF
Rt. 9 W., off Palisades Interstate Parkway

A 165-acre site planted with native trees, shrubs and wildflowers of lower New York and central New Jersey

Daily, dawn-dusk; to members only; handicapped access; (201) 768-1360.

TENAFLY

3   **Davis Johnson Park and Jack D. Lissemore Rose Garden**   A-R
137 Engle St. and Westevelt Ave.

This 5½-acre park contains the Van Vorst Azalea collection, an iris collection, as well as an AARS rose garden. Some plants are in bloom throughout the growing season. A greenhouse is being constructed.

Daily 10-dusk.

WAYNE

4   **Dey Mansion**   H-HH
199 Tottowa Rd.

This was George Washington's headquarters in 1780; the house stands on a ¾-acre garden. The 18th century display farm contains a herb garden.

1-5 Tues, Wed, Fri; 10-12 and 1-5 Sat; 10-5 Sun and holidays; closed Jan 1, Thanksgiving, Christmas; adults, nominal; under 16 free; (201) 696-1776.

UPPER MONTCLAIR

5   **Presby Memorial Iris Garden**   ☆☆   S
Upper Mountain Ave.

This garden contains a complete collection of iris including new varieties and hybrids. There are numerous Siberian and Japanese iris along a stream. Beds historically arranged show types from ancient times to the present. The plants are labelled. The height of the blooming season is from late May to mid-June.

Daily, dawn-dusk; no admission charge.

MONTCLAIR

6   **Montclair Art Museum**
Bloomfield and S. Mountain Aves.

This museum of American Indian art has grounds which form a small arboretum.

10-5 Tues-Sat, 2-5 Sun Sept-June; no admission charge; (201) 746-5555.

7   **Israel Crane House**   B-H-HH
110 Orange Rd.

This 18th century Federal style house has been restored after being moved to a new location; a herb, kitchen, and vegetable garden bordered by boxwood lie behind the house. A gazebo stands at the end of the lawn.

2-5 Sundays, July and Aug; by written appointment rest of year; P.O.Box 322, Montclair, NJ 07042; no admission charge.

8   **Avis Campbell Gardens**   H
60 S Fullerton Ave.

This small garden displays bulbs, herbs, perennials, and annuals. There is a floral

'Wheel of Life'.

Daily 10-4; no admission charge; (201) 746-9614.

BLOOMFIELD

9   Brookdale Park Rose Garden   R
Division St. and Wildwood Ave.

This rose garden with 1,200 bushes is the largest in the state. The larger park in which it lies was designed by the Olmsted brothers. The rose garden was planted in 1959.

Daily 8-dusk; (201) 482-0967.

WEST ORANGE

10   Glenmont   G-S
Edison National Historic Site
Main St. and Lakeside Ave.

A 15½-acre estate surrounds Edison's home with small flower gardens, a conservatory, and some specimen Sargent Hemlocks. The 19th century landscaping was done by Calvert, Vaux, and Olmsted.

12-4 Wed-Sun; closed legal holidays; tours by reservation only; adults, nominal; under 16, over 62 free; (201) 736-0550.

LIVINGSTON

11   Force Home   H-HH
Livingston Ave.

This historic house, which is on the register of National Historic Landmarks, has a small herb garden.

Daily, dawn-dusk.

MORRISTOWN

12   The George Griswold Frelinghuysen Arboretum   ☆☆☆   .-A-B-HA-S
53 E. Hanover Ave.

A 127-acre arboretum with formal gardens and informal plantings. Many of the plants are labelled and there is a braille trail. There is a pinetum as well as many trees and shrubs from the 19th century including some old Atlas Cedars, maples, oaks, and boxwood. There are collections of flowering cherries, crab-apples, maples, lindens, Bald Cypresses, Silver Bells, poplars, cedars, magnolias, Japanese maples, sour gums, sweet gums, horse chestnuts, dwarf conifers as well as rhododendrons, azaleas, lilacs, and ferns. Demonstration and test gardens for annuals and turf grass are maintained along with a fine library.

9-5 Mon-Fri; 9-6 Sat, Sun; mid-March to early Dec; 9-5 Mon-Fri rest of year; closed Feb 12 and 22, Thanksgiving, Christmas; no admission charge; handicapped access; (201) 285-6166.

13   Acorn Hall   HH
68 Morris Ave.

This house stands on 3 acres of gardens. The shrubs and flowers are typical of those used in the 19th century.

11-3 Thurs; 1:30-4 Sun; except Jan and Feb; adults nominal; (201) 267-3465.

14 Wicks House HH
Morristown National Historical Park

This 18th century farmhouse has been restored along with the surrounding garden. Plants typical of the period have been used.

9-5 Daily; closed Jan 1, Thanksgiving, Christmas; no admission charge.

15 Schuyler-Hamilton House H-HH
5 Olyphant Place

This 18th century house has been restored along with the medicinal herb garden of its original owner, Dr. Jabez Campbell. There is also small garden of annuals.

For hours call (201) 267-4039.

CONVENT STATION

16 Shakespeare Garden SH
College of St. Elizabeth

A small Shakespearean garden was begun on this 400-acre campus in 1925. The plants are arranged according to the plays or poems in which they appear. The garden is best visited in spring and summer.

Daily 9-dusk; no admission charge; (201) 539-1600.

NEWARK

17 Cherry Blossom Festival
Branch Brook Park

An annual festival is celebrated each April, when 3,000 cherry trees bloom.

Daily, dawn-dusk.

ELIZABETH

18 Chatfield Memorial Garden A
Warinanco Park

A garden of perennials and annuals as well as large plantings of azaleas and cherry trees are found here.

Daily, dawn-dusk.

19 Boudinot Mansion State Historic Site HH
1073 E. Jersey St.

This house built in the 1750's has a small garden; it has been reconstructed along 18th century lines.

9-12, 1-6 Wed-Fri; 10-12, 1-6 Sat; 1-6 Sun; closed Jan 1, Thanksgiving, Christmas; (201) 648-4540.

SHORT HILLS

20 Cora Hartshorn Arboretum and Bird Sanctuary A-S-WF
324 Forest Drive South

This 17-acre arboretum established in 1961 has some 55 species of trees with several fine specimens. There are also numerous azaleas, rhododendrons, and mountain laurels. The arboretum possesses an excellent collection of wildflowers and ferns representing several hundred species.

Daily, dawn-dusk; no admission charge; handicapped access; (201) 376-3587.

SUMMIT

21   Reeves-Reed Arboretum   A-C-H-HA-R
165 Hobart Ave.

A rose garden and a herb garden are the main features of this arboretum established in 1974; it is spread over 12 acres and contains woodland trails. There is an azalea collection as well as greenhouses and a library.

Daily, dawn-dusk; no admission charge; handicapped access; (201) 273-8787.

MOUNTAINSIDE

22   Trailside Nature and Science Center   A
Wachtung Reservation
Coles Ave. and New Providence Rd.

A 5-acre rhododendron garden is located on this 2,200-acre reservation. More than 314 species are represented. There are trails through the woods; plans for an arboretum have been made. A large tree nursery lies on the reservation.

Daily, dawn-dusk; Visitor Center 1-5; no admission charge; handicapped access; (201) 232-5930.

GLADSTONE

23   Willowwood Arboretum   ☆☆   HH-L-S-WF
Hacklebarney Rd., off Rt. 512 and Union Grove Rd.

This 130-acre arboretum established in 1908 contains a collection of 3,500 different species of native and exotic plants. There are 35 kinds of oak, 50 types of maple, 110 varieties of willow, a fine specimen of Dawn Redwood as well as good collections of lilacs, magnolias, hollies, cherries, conifers, and wildflowers of both field and forest. The 1792 home has two small formal gardens, but the informal plant collection established during this century by the Tubbs brothers is of primary interest.

9-5 Weekdays; check for weekend and winter hours; no admission charge; (201) 234-1246.

24   Bamboo Brook Outdoor Education Center   S
Hacklebarney Rd. near Willowwood Arboretum

A formal garden designed along English and Italian lines by Martha Hutcheson who graduated from MIT with a landscape architect degree in 1901, the second American woman to do so. Brooks, small waterfalls, fountains, statuary, fine specimen trees and shrubs may be found in this garden. A trail guide is available.

9-5 weekdays; check for weekend and winter hours; no admission charge; (201) 285-6166.

FAR HILLS

25   Leonard J. Buck Gardens   ☆   RG-S
Far Hills and Layton Rds., off I-287

The intriguing rock outcroppings on this estate have been used to form a beautiful informal garden with a wide variety of plants; many are labelled. The garden was begun in the 1930's and contains mature trees.

Visits currently limited to groups of ten or more, by appointment only; (201) 873-2459.

26   **Rudolf van der Groot Rose Garden of the Colonial Park Arboretum** ☆☆   .-A-HA-R-S
Mettlers Rd.

The rose garden established in 1971 contains 275 different varieties among its 4,000 bushes which is the largest collection in the state. All plants are labelled. There is also a fragrance and sensory garden with more than 80 species of plants; they are labelled in script as well as braille. The arboretum which covers 100 acres has good collections of azaleas, rhododendrons, lilacs, flowering shrubs, and cherry trees, as well as dwarf conifers.

Daily 8-dusk; rose garden 10-5 June 1-Oct 1; handicapped access; no admission charge; (201) 873-2459.

PLAINFIELD

27   **Shakespeare Garden**   SH
Cedar Brook Park
Park Ave.

Most of Shakespeare's plants may be found in this garden; there is also a collection of peonies and an iris garden in this park.

Daily, dawn-dusk.

LEBANON

28   **Hunterton County Arboretum**   G-W
Rt. 31, Clinton Township

Trails lead through this small arboretum; there is an All-American Selection garden, a solar greenhouse, and a boardwalk through a swamp. The display of perennials and annuals is large.

Daily, dawn-dusk.

ISELIN

29   **Garden for the Blind**
Iselin Library
Green St.

Every plant in this small garden is marked in braille and appeals to the sense of touch, taste or smell. All planters are waist high and are filled with herbs, perennials, and annuals. The sensory garden is framed by a 200 ft. botanic garden.

Daily, dawn-dusk; (201) 283-1200.

SOMERVILLE

30   **Duke Gardens Foundation**   ☆☆☆☆   C-CA-G-J-O-P
1½ mi. south, off U.S. 206 South

11 glass enclosed gardens are displayed in this conservatory established in 1959 on a

large estate. There are Italian, Colonial, Edwardian, French, English, Chinese, Japanese, Indo-Persian, desert, tropical, and semi-tropical gardens. Orchids, camellias, gardenias, jacarandas, tree ferns, and cacti are especially good. Seasonal displays are presented in Oct, Dec, Jan and April.

12-4 Daily but reservations are necessary; 8:30-10:30 Wed, Thurs evenings Oct 1-June 1; closed Jan 1, Thanksgiving, Christmas; adults, under $3; 6-12 half; (201) 722-3700.

EAST BRUNSWICK

31 Rutgers Research and Display Gardens ☆☆   A-S
U.S. 1 at Ryders Lane

Founded in 1935, this 50-acre arboretum contains an excellent collection of 125 kinds of hollies, including more than 100 Japanese hollies. They are at their best in November. There are good collections of small trees, azaleas, rhododendrons, dogwoods, and shade trees, as well as hedge and vine displays. Trails lead through virgin stands of timber. An annual garden along with a demonstration and test garden are found here also.

Daily 8-dusk; closed Dec 15-Jan 1; no admission charge; (201) 932-9639.

HOLMDEL

32 Holmdel Park Arboretum ☆☆   HA-S
2 mi. north on Longstreet Rd.

More than 260 species of trees and shrubs are displayed in this 20-acre arboretum established in 1963. There is a dwarf evergreen garden and a synoptic garden. Good collections of crab-apples, flowering cherries, magnolias, cedars, hollies, dogwoods, and fragrant shrubs may be found here.

Daily 8-dusk; no admission charge; handicapped access; (201) 431-7906.

33 Holmes-Hendrickson House   HH
Longstreet and Roberts Rds.

This mid-18th century Dutch style house has been restored along with a period kitchen and herb garden which has been carefully researched.

1-4 Tues, Thurs; 10-4 Sat; 1-4 Sun; June-Oct; closed July 4; adults, under $3; 6-18 and senior citizens, half; (201) 462-1466.

MIDDLETOWN

34 Deep Cut Park Horticultural Center ☆   A-C-F-H-R-RG
Newman Springs Rd. off Red Hill Rd.
Parkway exit 114

This 40-acre site is intended as a demonstration area for the home gardener. It includes an orchard, a vinyard, a vegetable garden, a herb garden, a rockery, an azalea garden, a perennial garden, a shade garden, an All-American rose selection garden, and greenhouses.

8-4:30 Daily; closed Jan 1, Thanksgiving, Christmas; no admission charge; (201) 671-6050.

35 **Lambertus C. Babbink Memorial Rose Garden**   R
Thompson Park

A municipal rose garden with a good selection.

Daily, dawn-dusk.

SHREWSBURY

36 **Allen House**   H-HH

This mid-18th century home served as a tavern and has been restored along with a small herb garden.

1-4 Tues, Thurs; 10-4 Sat; 1-4 Sun; April-Dec; closed July 4, Thanksgiving, Dec 24, Christmas; adults, under $3; children half; senior citizens three-quarters; (201) 462-1466.

PRINCETON

37 **Princeton University Campus**   ☆   HA-S

The 215-acre campus founded in 1746 contains more than 2,000 trees representing 140 exotic and native species. 38 species are found in Prospect Garden, a small arboretum on the campus which contains flower beds. They follow an old English 'half-wheel' design. Fine specimen elms are displayed.

Daily; no admission charge; handicapped access; tree tours available; (609) 452-3600.

TRENTON

38 **Trent House**   HH-T
539 S. Warren St.

This home, built in 1719 has been restored along with its small gardens which are laid out like English knot gardens.

10-4 Mon-Sat; 10-5 Sun, holidays; closed Jan 1, Thanksgiving, Christmas; adults nominal; children less; (609) 695-9621.

39 **Pack Memorial Arboretum**
Washington Crossing State Park
8 mi. northwest on Rt. 29

This arboretum has a good collection of native trees and shrubs. A state forest nursery lies nearby.

8-8 Mon-Fri; 9-8 Sat, Sun, holidays, summer; 8-4:30 Mon-Fri; 9-4:30 Sat, Sun, holidays, winter; parking, under $3 Memorial day to Labor Day; free on Tues; picnicking; (609) 737-0623.

HAMILTON

40 **Kuser Farm Mansion**   HH
¾ mi. from I-295

This mansion of a film magnate built in 1892 has a formal garden planted with flowering shrubs, perennials and annuals. There is a gazebo.

11-3 Thurs-Sun; April 3-Dec 5; no admission charge; picnicking; free concerts during summer; (609) 890-3782.

LAKEWOOD

41 Georgian Court College ☆☆ BX-J
Lakewood Ave.

Bruce Price designed the gardens of 'Georgian Court' for George Jay Gould between 1897-1902. They continue to be maintained by the college now located here. There is an Italian garden with a fountain and statues; the sunken garden contains a lagoon. The formal garden has 16 flower beds bordered by boxwood. The Japanese garden completed in 1915 contains wooden bridges, a tea house, and mature trees and shrubbery.

Daily, dawn-dusk; no admission charge; (201) 364-2200.

MEDFORD

42 Medford Leas A-WF
Rt. 70

A continuing care retirement community is located in this 120-acre arboretum. There are collections of rhododendrons, magnolias, hollies, and daffodils. The wooded area contains flora indigenous to the area.

Visitors must sign at the reception desk; 9-5 daily; (609) 654-3000.

MIDDLETOWN

43 Marlpit Hall H-HH

This house was built around a Dutch cottage constructed in 1685. It has been carefully restored along with a small herb garden.

1-4 Tues, Thurs; 10-4 Sat; 1-4 Sun; April-Dec; closed July 4, Thanksgiving, Dec 24, Christmas; adults, under $3; children half; senior citizens three-quarters; (201) 462-1466.

AVALON

44 Leaming's Run Botanical Garden ☆☆ HA
Rt. 9 near Avalon exit, Garden State Parkway

27 gardens are located along a mile of trail on these 20-acre grounds. The gardens were established in 1977; they contain collections of magnolia, oak, holly, and ferns.

Daily 9:30-5; July 1-Oct 31; adults, under $3; handicapped access; (609) 465-5871.

CAPE MAY

45 Gus Yearick's Hedge Garden T
158 Fishing Creek Rd.

A topiary garden has been created on 2 acres by this enthusiastic couple. Privet has been extensively used to create some unusual forms.

Daily 9-5; donation; (609) 886-5148.

NEW MEXICO

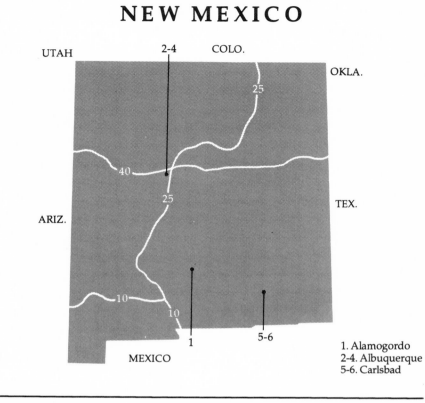

UTAH · 2-4 · COLO. · OKLA. · 25 · 40 · 25 · ARIZ. · TEX. · 10 · 10 · 1 · 5-6 · MEXICO

1. Alamogordo
2-4. Albuquerque
5-6. Carlsbad

ALAMOGORDO

1 Alamogordo Garden Center R
10th and Orange Streets

This experimental garden contains plants and shrubs which will thrive in this area. It is designed to help the local gardener. There is a memorial rose garden.

Daily 9-5; no admission charge.

ALBUQUERQUE

2 Rio Grande Zoo ☆ P
Rio Grande Park, 903 10th Street S.W.

This zoo with more than 800 mammals, birds, and reptiles contains a large rain forest with a good selection of sub-tropical plants.

Daily 10-7 Memorial Day to Labor Day; 10-5 remainder of year; closed Jan 1, Thanksgiving, Christmas; adults, under $3; children half; must be accompanied by an adult; senior citizens free; (505) 766-7823.

3 Physical Plants Department ☆ C-HA-SU
University of New Mexico
Central Ave. and Yale Blvd.

These 416 acres present an unusually attractive landscaped site. This arboretum which was established in 1889 combines desert plants with semi-tropical plants. There are 270 species on campus and 333 species in an atrium.

Daily all hours; atrium 8-4:30 weekdays; herbarium by appointment; handicapped access; (505) 277-2421.

4 **Rose Garden** R
Prospect Park
8205 Apache Ave. NE

A rose garden with numerous varieties is planted in this municipal park.

Daily, dawn-dusk.

CARLSBAD

5 **Living Desert State Park** ☆☆ C-G-HA-SU
On mesa 4 mi. northwest, U.S. 285

This botanical and zoological state park covers 1,100 acres; more than 2,000 varieties of cacti and 3,000 species and cultivars of southwestern plants, many native to the Chihuahuan Desert may be found here. The entire area has been beautifully landscaped. The greenhouse contains 1,000 species. There are trails and a library.

8-8 summer; 9-5 winter; adults, under $3; group rate half; tours; (505) 887-5516.

6 **Carlsbad Cavern National Park** O-SU
20 miles southwest on U.S. 62 and 180
(near Living Desert State Park)

These 46,000 acres which surround the famous caverns contain more than 600 species of plants; many are marked on the nature trails. There are many kinds of agaves, yuccas, native crotons, and stream helleborines (orchids).

7:30-6 mid-May; 7:30-8 early June to Labor Day; 7:30-5 remainder of year; Under $3 per car; (505) 785-2233.

NEW YORK

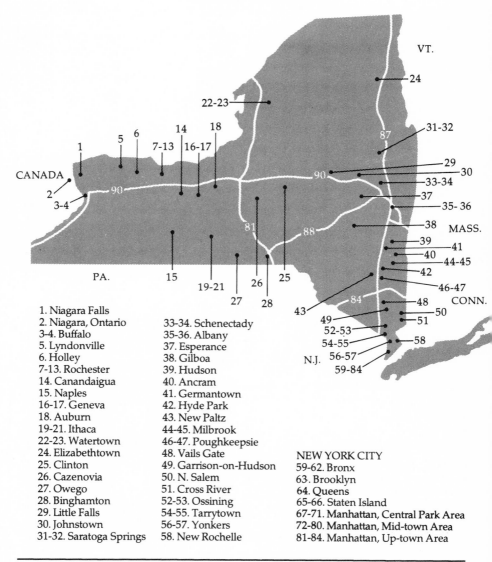

VT.

24

22-23

31-32

14 18

5 6

7-13 16-17

1

CANADA

2

3-4

29
30

33-34

37

35- 36

38 MASS.

39
41
40
44-45

42

46-47

CONN.

PA.

15

19-21

26 25

27 28

43

84 48
50

49 51

52-53

54-55 58

N.J. 56-57

59-84

1. Niagara Falls
2. Niagara, Ontario
3-4. Buffalo
5. Lyndonville
6. Holley
7-13. Rochester
14. Canandaigua
15. Naples
16-17. Geneva
18. Auburn
19-21. Ithaca
22-23. Watertown
24. Elizabethtown
25. Clinton
26. Cazenovia
27. Owego
28. Binghamton
29. Little Falls
30. Johnstown
31-32. Saratoga Springs

33-34. Schenectady
35-36. Albany
37. Esperance
38. Gilboa
39. Hudson
40. Ancram
41. Germantown
42. Hyde Park
43. New Paltz
44-45. Milbrook
46-47. Poughkeepsie
48. Vails Gate
49. Garrison-on-Hudson
50. N. Salem
51. Cross River
52-53. Ossining
54-55. Tarrytown
56-57. Yonkers
58. New Rochelle

NEW YORK CITY
59-62. Bronx
63. Brooklyn
64. Queens
65-66. Staten Island
67-71. Manhattan, Central Park Area
72-80. Manhattan, Mid-town Area
81-84. Manhattan, Up-town Area

NIAGARA FALLS

1 Winter Gardens ☆☆ C-HA-P-SU
Rainbow Blvd.

A modern glass-enclosed garden covers an entire city block with walkways on the
ground and upper level. It contains more than 7,000 tropical and semi-tropical plants
in a secluded, restful area with waterfalls, small streams, and pools. There is a good
selection of palms, bamboos, cacti, agaves, ficuses, philodendrons, and crotons.

Daily 10-10; no admission charge; handicapped access; illuminated at night; (716)
278-8112.

NIAGARA, ONTARIO

2   See Ontario   ☆☆☆☆

A series of splendid gardens which present a vivid contrast to the park on the United States side.

BUFFALO

3   Buffalo and Erie County Botanical Gardens   ☆   C-CH-FE-G-HA-P
U.S. 62 and McKinley Parkway

Beautiful floral and plant displays have been arranged in 12 greenhouses with special collections of cacti, ferns, and palms. The Conservatory was founded in 1899. The Spring Flower show begins on Palm Sunday; the Autumn chrysanthemum show begins second week of November.

Daily 9-4; no admission charge; handicapped access; (716) 825-9816

4   Martin Luther King Jr. Rose Garden   R
Fillmore and Best Sts.

A small rose garden with a selection of roses has been planted here, but now suffers from neglect.

Daily, dawn-dusk.

LYNDONVILLE

5   Robin Hill Arboretum   ☆   HA-L
Platten Rd.

A 43-acre family arboretum founded in 1935 now has more than 400 species of trees planted in a beautiful site. There are many winding woodland paths.

Daily; no admission charge; handicapped access; (716) 765-2614.

HOLLEY

6   Fancher Arboretum   S
State University College
5 miles west on Rt. 31; Lynch Rd.

A 50-acre arboretum established in 1967 to display the trees native to the state. Fine specimens of Shagbark hickory, Hop-Hornbeam. Especially beautiful in autumn.

Daily; some guided tours; (716) 638-6922.

ROCHESTER

7   Durand-Eastman Park   ☆☆   HA-S
Kings Highway north of city

540 acres of parkland contain more than 4,000 species and cultivars of plants. Emphasis has been placed on flowering trees crab-apples, magnolias, dogwoods, and flowering cherries. The park contains old specimens of Snowbells and a good conifer collection.

Daily, dawn-10 summer, sunrise-4 winter ; no admission charge; handicapped access; (716) 244-4640.

8 **Highland Park** ☆☆ A-R-S
Mt. Hope Ave. and S. Goodman St. at Reservoir and Highland Aves

A 130-acre arboretum founded in 1888. It now contains numerous mature specimen trees including European Hornbeam, Asiatic Maples, hawthorn, holly, Turkish Hazelnut, ash, and oaks. This was a test site for many plants introduced from China at the turn of the century. The lilac collection is among the largest in the United States with more than 600 varieties, some dating to colonial times; there are 2,000 plants. Fine areas of rhododenrons, azaleas, tulips, roses, peonies, annuals, and chrysanthemums have been planted.

Daily 7-10; no admission charge; lilac gardens illuminated in mid-May; concerts in summer; (716) 244-4640 or (716) 546-3070.

9 **Lamberton Conservatory** ☆☆ C-FE-G-HA-P-SU
Highland Park

A large conservatory with more than 40,000 plants and fine seasonal displays. Emphasis has been placed on tropical and sub-tropicals; they include palms, ferns, cycads, cacti, succulents, agaves, and others. Special collections are maintained. There is a library.

Daily 10-5; no admission charge; handicapped access; (716) 244-4640 or (716) 546-3070.

10 **Maplewood Park** HA-R
Lake Avenue

A 40-acre park whose main feature is a rose garden. hawthorns and flowering crabs are also displayed.

Daily; handicapped access.

11 **Gardens of Fragrance** H-R
Museum of Arts and Science
687 East Ave.

This museum presents a herb garden arranged in 8 beds with displays of medicinal, culinary and aromatic herbs. There is also a fine display illustrating the history of the rose beginning with 1,000 B.C.; special beds of Chinese and Victorian roses have been planted.

Daily 8-11; adults, under $3; senior citizens, students through grade 12, half; free Sat 9-12; height of blooming season June-Sept; (716) 271-4320

12 **Mount Hope Cemetery** ☆ L-S
Mt. Hope Ave.

This is one of the oldest Victorian cemeteries in the country; it contains numerous good specimens of mature trees. Plantings of perennials and annuals are well maintained. Spectacular views of the Genesee River have been created. There is interesting sculpture and wrought iron work.

Daily 9-4.

13 **Moreton Farm** ☆ HD
Harris Seed Co.
3670 Buffalo Rd.

Large trial grounds with 10 acres of over 1,000 experimental varieties of perennials and annuals are planted here each year. A model home garden has been created on these grounds.

9-4 weekdays June-Sept; no admission charge; (716) 594-9411.

CANANDAIGUA

14   Sonnenberg Gardens   ☆☆☆   G-HA-HH-J-L-R-RG-S
Thruway Exits 43/44 on Rt. 21, 1½ mi. northeast

A 47-acre estate surrounds this late-19th century mansion, filled with period rooms. Opened to the public a decade ago, the beautifully arranged gardens include a Japanese garden, rose garden, colonial garden, Italian garden, pansy garden, blue, rock garden and white garden. Excellent specimen trees stand on the grounds. There is a conservatory near the mansion.

Daily 9:30-6 mid-May to mid-October; adults, under $6; senior citizens half; 6-18 quarter; handicapped access; (716) 394-4922.

NAPLES

15   Wild Winds Farm

Flower beds of perennials and annuals, vegetable gardens as well as nature trails lie on these grounds.

For hours call (716) 374-5523.

GENEVA

16   Legg Dahlia Gardens   ☆
Hastings Road

More than 500 varieties of dahlias planted in beautifully designed beds which cover 3 acres of this commercial nursery. The best floral display may be seen from August through October.

Daily, sunrise-sunset.

17   Geneva-on-the-Lake   HH-L

An Italian Renaissance villa has been turned into a resort. It has formal gardens of perennials and annuals as well as paths through the woodlands.

Call about hours; (315) 789-7190.

AUBURN

18   Hoopes Memorial Park   HA-R
1¼ mi. east on U.S. 20 at E. Genesee St.

This park contains rose gardens as well as fine plantings of trees and shrubs around a lake. Concerts are given during the summer months.

Daily; no admission charge; handicapped access.

ITHACA

19   Liberty Hyde Bailey Hortorium   ☆   G-HA-P-SU
467 Mann Library
Cornell University

An excellent collection of tropical plants including palms, succulents, and many others is housed in this large greenhouse. The large herbarium is the partial resource for the numerous books on tropical plants published by this organization. The

Hortorium was established in 1935. Library.

Daily 8-5; no admission charge; handicapped access; (607) 256-2131.

20   The Cornell Plantations   ☆☆   A-H-HA-R-RG-S-WF
Cornell University
100 Judd Falls Road

This 1,500-acre arboretum contains collections of azaleas, rhododendrons, roses, ground covers, nut trees, vines, herbs, lilacs, viburnums, peonies, and tree peonies, magnolias, and native wild flowers. Special areas include the Mary Rockwell Azalea Garden, a wildflower garden, a shrub and hedge garden, a rock garden, test gardens, a pinetum, a synoptic garden, a floriculture garden, a poplar grove, and a meadow. The W.C. Muenscher Poisonous Plant Garden is located at the Veterinary College. There is a library.

Daily, sunrise-sunset; no admission charge; handicapped access; (607) 256-3020.

21   Stewart Park   HA-R
Cayuga Lake

A large well-designed rose garden is part of this municipal park.

Daily, dawn-dusk; handicapped access.

WATERTOWN

22   Garden Village   HA-HH
Black River Garden Center
4½ mi. east on Rt. 3

A number of local historic buildings have been reconstructed on this site. The grounds are landscaped in mid-19th century style.

9-5 Mon-Sat; 12-5 Sun; closed Jan and holidays; no admission charge; handicapped access.

23   Victorian Garden
Jefferson County Historical Society Museum
220 Washington St.

This small Victorian garden is a recent addition to the museum.

For times call (315) 788-4400.

ELIZABETHTOWN

24   Colonial Garden
Church Street

A reproduction of an early American garden of the Colonial period has been planted by the Essex County Historical Society. Beds of annuals and perennials have been laid out in authentic fashion.

Daily; June-Sept; adults, under $3; under 16 half; (518) 873-6466.

CLINTON

25   Root Glen   A-FE-RG-S
College Hill Road

The 7½ acres of gardens here were established in 1849 and opened to the public in

1964. Special collections include Saunders peonies, azaleas, hemlocks, and all New York State ferns. Specimen Black Walnut and hemlock.

Daily, sunrise-sunset; no admission charge; partial handicapped access; (315) 859-7193.

CAZENOVIA

26 Lorenzo HH
Rt. 13, south of jnct. Rts. 13 and 20

This 1807 mansion lies on extensive grounds. There is a formal garden of perennials and annuals and an arboretum.

9-5 Wed-Sat, Mon, holidays; 1-5 Sun, mid-April to mid-Oct; no admission charge; (518) 474-0456

OWEGO

27 Tioga Gardens G

This small conservatory is devoted to tropical and sub-tropical plants.

10-4 weekdays; (607) 772-8860.

BINGHAMTON

28 Cutler Gardens A-H-RG-S-WF
Exit 5 from I-81 at 840 Front St.

This 3½-acre garden is part of a Master Gardener training program. Special sections include a rock garden, a herb garden a wildflower walk, perennials, annuals, vegetables, and a rhododendron grove. Some specimen trees.

9-5 weekdays April 15-Oct 15; no admission charge; guided tours; (607) 772-8953.

LITTLE FALLS

29 General Herkimer Home State Historical Site H-HH
3 mi east off Rt. 55; south side of the Mohawk River and Barge Canal

This mid-18th century site includes a fine home along with colonial vegetable and herb gardens. Guided tours are provided.

9-5 Wed-Sat; 1-5 Sun; closed Jan l, Easter, Thanksgiving, Christmas; no admission charge; (315) 823-0398.

JOHNSTOWN

30 Johnson Hall H-HH
Hall Ave.

This Mohawk Valley plantation home was built in 1763; it has been restored along with its garden of 18th century herbs.

9-5 Wed-Sun; (518) 762-8712.

SARATOGA SPRINGS

31 Casino and Congress Park ☆ L
U.S. 9 off Broadway

A well-landscaped park contains an Italian garden along with beautifully displayed outdoor sculpture including works by D.C. French and B. Thorvaldsen. A museum stands on the grounds.

Daily 9:30-4:30, July 1-Aug 31; 10-4 Mon-Sat; 1-4 Sun, May 30-June 30; 1-4 Wed-Sat rest of year; adults, under $3; seniors and students, half; under 12 nominal; (518) 584-3255.

32 Yaddo R
Union Ave. at Exit 14 from Northway

Artists now use this private estate which has a rose garden.

Daily during summer; call for hours; (518) 584-3255.

SCHENECTADY

33 Jackson Garden and Robison Herb Garden ☆☆ H-O
Union College Campus
Nott St.

A 19-acre garden established in 1834 contains the Robison Herb Garden and a fine tree peony collection with specimens a hundred years old. There are Orchid Society test gardens which demonstrate winter hardiness; more than 175 different species of trees on the campus are labelled; a tree guide is available. There is a library.

Daily spring, summer, fall; closed winter; no admission charge; handicapped access; (518) 370-6262.

34 Rose Garden R
Central Park

A formal rose garden has been planted in this park.

Daily, dawn-dusk.

ALBANY

35 St. Michael's Episcopal Church Gardens and Arboretum ☆ BR-C-G-FE-H-HA-RG-SU
49 Killean Park, north of Rt. 5

A 3-acre garden with a solar greenhouse lies on the church grounds. Emphasis has been placed on native, alpine, and bog plants. There is a herb garden. Special collections include more than 60 species of fern, 30 aloe, 60 agave, 40 species of cycad, 40 varieties of nepenthe, carniverous plants as well as many unusual specimen are found here among the 2,000 species grown in the greenhouses.

Daily 9-5; no admission charge; handicapped access; (518) 869-6417.

36 Schuyler Mansion State Historic Site H-HA-HH
27 Clinton St.

A ½-acre garden surrounds this historic home; it contains many fruit trees, an herb garden as well as an 18th-century parterre garden.

9-5 Wed-Sun; no admission charge; handicapped access; (518) 474-3953.

ESPERANCE

37   **George Landis Arboretum and Van Loveland Gardens**   ☆☆   A-FE-R-RG-S
2 miles north

100-acre arboretum established in 1951 contains more than 2,500 kinds of plants including special collections of rhododenrons, lilacs, and southern Apalachian plants. This site tests shrubs and trees for hardiness in the northern climate. Special gardens include a rose garden, an iris garden, a spring bulb garden, a woodland plant garden, a fern garden, and a garden of perennials and annuals. The Beal Peony Garden and the Quarry Rock Garden also lie on the grounds. There are good specimens of the Bristlecone Pine and a 400-year-old White Oak. A library is associated with the arboretum.

Daily, sunrise-sunset; no admission charge; (518) 875-6935.

GILBOA

38   **Schoharie Creek Bridge**
West of bridge

Fossil tree stumps of *Eospermatoperis*, a seed-bearing tree fern, which is the oldest known species of tree in the world may be seen here.

Daily, dawn-dusk.

HUDSON

39   **Olana State Historic Site**   HH-L

The mansion and its grounds were designed by Frederic Edwin Church, the famous 19th century painter. The spectacular views have been carefully planned and landscaped with trees and shrubs.

All year 8-dusk, grounds only; mansion has different hours; adults, under $3; under 12 free; (518) 828-0135.

ANCRAM

40   **Crailo Gardens**
Rt. 82

This collection of evergreens includes more than 100 species of trees and shrubs.

2-dusk, Sun, May-Sept; also by appointment; no admission charge; (518) 329-0601.

GERMANTOWN

41   **Clermont State Historic Park**   ☆   HH-L-S-WF
Rt. 9G, 6 mi. north of Kingston-Rhinecliff Bridge

The Livingstone family lived in this mansion continuously from 1777 to 1962 and developed both the house and the 463-acre park which surrounds it. Fine specimen trees may be seen from various trails. There is a lilac grove, a 20th century walled garden, a 'long view' walk through locust trees, a wilderness garden, and a spring garden which is being restored. Many fine views of the Hudson River and the Catskill Mountains appear along the trails.

Daily 8-sunset, grounds only; house, Memorial Day to Oct; call about hours; (518) 537-4240.

HYDE PARK

42   Vanderbilt Mansion National Historic Site   HH-L-S
north on U.S. 9

A large mansion built in 1898 is set in grounds with a commanding view of the Hudson. The arboretum on this estate was begun in 1828 by Dr. David Hosack who engaged the Belgian landscape designer Andre Parmentier. Dr. Hosack was the founder of the Elgin Botanic Gardens which stood on the site of the Rockefeller Center. Some interesting old Sugar Maples, ginkgos, White Pines, and Kentucky Coffee Trees have survived. An Italian garden also remains.

Daily 9-5; closed Jan 1 and Christmas; adults, under $3; under 16, over 61 free; (914) 229-8114.

NEW PALTZ

43   Mohonk Mountain House   ☆☆☆   FE-H-HH-L-R-S-WF
Mohonk Lake

A hotel set in magnificent grounds of more than 7,500 acres filled with trails which wind around a lake, and through woodlands. The gardens were begun by Albert Smiley in 1869 and reflect the influence of Andrew Downing; the Victorian style predominates. There are 15 acres of garden with plantings of annuals and perennials, a herb garden, a rock garden, fern and wildflower garden, and a cutting garden. Good specimens of flowering crab-apples, Japanese Maples, beeches, and tree lilacs may be seen here; new varieties of trees are added annually.

Daily 7-dusk; adults, under $6; under 12 half; (914) 255-1000.

MILBROOK

44   Innisfree Garden   ☆   A-FE-J-S-W
Tyrrel Road; 1¾ mi. from Taconic Parkway

A series of terraced natural gardens surround a lake in the midst of a forest; the plantings and rocks create an unusual bowl-like setting. All of this was designed by Walter Beck in 1930. The 200 acres of garden contain streams and fine walkways. There are good collections of rhododenrons, azaleas, as well as specimen trees, some ferns, and water lilies.

10-4 Wed-Fri; 11-5 Sat-Sun; May-Oct; open on Mondays which are legal holidays; no admission charge; (914) 677-8000.

45   Cary Arboretum, New York Botanical Garden   ☆   S

This 2,000-acre arboretum was established in 1971 with emphasis on woody plants of North America and Asia. There are strong collections of native trees as well as plants from Japan, Korea, and the Soviet Union. A perennial garden lies near the headquarters building. This is primarily an ecological research station. There is a library.

9-4 weekdays; 1-4 Sunday; visitor permit must be obtained at Gifford House; some tours; no admission charge; (914) 677-5343.

POUGHKEEPSIE

46   Vassar College Arboretum   G-HA-S-SH
Vassar College, Raymond Ave.

This arboretum founded in 1861 is spread over 450 acres which surrounds the campus. Special areas include a Shakespearean garden and a perennial garden. There are greenhouses. Fine specimen of old trees may be seen here as well as good display beds of bulbs and annuals.

Daily, dawn-dusk; no admission charge; handicapped access; (914) 542-7000.

47 Locust Grove HH
Young Morse Historic Site

This 17th century estate with its mid-19th century house has gardens designed by Samuel S.B. Morse in the style of Andrew Jackson Downing. They are currently being restored. A wildlife sanctuary lies on the grounds.

10-4 Wed-Sun, Memorial Day through Sept; open on holidays; adults, under $3; 7-16 half; under 7 free; tours; ((914) 454-4500.

VAILS GATE

48 Knox Headquarters H-HH
Forge Hill Rd., off Rt. 94

A herb garden lies on the grounds of this 18th century Georgian-style home.

9-5 Wed-Sun; (914) 561-5498.

GARRISON-ON-HUDSON

49 Boscobel Restoration ☆☆ BX-F-G-H-HA-O-R
Route 9D, north of town

The early 19th century Federal style Morris Dyckman mansion and grounds have been restored. The estate cover 36 acres and includes fine English gardens, a rose garden, a herb garden, a boxwood garden, an apple orchard, and an excellent orangery. An orchid collection may be viewed in the greenhouses.

9:30-5 April-Oct; 9:30-4 Nov, Dec, March; closed Tues, Thanksgiving, Christmas, Jan, Feb; grounds only, under $3; handicapped access; (914) 265-3638.

NORTH SALEM

50 Hammond Museum Stroll Garden ☆ A-HA-J-S
Deveau Rd. off Rt. 128 ¼ mi. north of Rt. 116

Oriental gardens have been arranged according to the style of 17th century Edo Japanese design. There are 14 loosely connected gardens spread over 4 acres; they include a Zen garden, a dry landscape garden, a lake garden, an autumn garden, and a reflecting pool garden. Fine specimen of pines and azaleas are grown here. There is a museum.

11-5 Wed-Sun mid-May to Oct 31; adults, under $3; senior citizens half; under 12 quarter; handicapped access; (914) 669-5033.

CROSS RIVER

51 Meyer Arboretum, Ward Pound Ridge Restoration WF
Rt. 121 south of junction Rt. 35

This 175-acre arboretum founded in 1961 emphasizes native plants and trees. It contains the Luquer-Marble Memorial Wildflower Garden with more than a hundred species of wild flowers. There are labelled nature trails.

Daily 9-sunset; guided tours; picnic area; (914) 763-3493.

OSSINING

52   Teatown Lake Reservation   WF
Spring Valley Road

306-acre nature and arboretum site. This is an outreach station of the Brooklyn Botanical Gardens with numerous nature trails and a labelled area of summer flora.

9-5 Tues-Sat; 1-5 Sun; (914) 762-2912.

53   Kitchawan Research Laboratories
712 Kitchawan Road

A research plant site on 223 acres established by the Brooklyn Botanical Gardens; there are some nature trails.

Call for hours; (914) 941-8886.

TARRYTOWN

54   Lyndhurst   G-HH-L-R-RG-S
635 S. Broadway; U.S. 9

This 19th century Gothic revival mansion overlooks the Hudson and is surrounded by 67 acres of gardens and an arboretum begun under the influence of A. J. Downing in the 1840's. Successive generations have added to the gardens. Fine old specimen of larch, linden, weeping beech, ginkgo, Star Magnolia, Japanese Cut-Leaf Maple as well as other native and exotic trees may be seen here. There is a rockery and a rose garden with 127 varieties. The greenhouse, once the largest private conservatory in the country, is now being restored.

10-5 Tues-Sun, May 1-Oct 31; 10-4 rest of year; closed Jan 1, Easter, Thanksgiving, Christmas; adults, under $3; senior citizens half; (914) 631-0046.

55   Sunnyside   HH
W. Sunnyside Lane, off U.S. 9

This former home of Washington Irving was built according to the author's design. It is set in landscaped grounds.

Daily 10-5; closed Jan 1, Easter, Thanksgiving, Christmas; adults, under $6; over 60, 6-14 half; (914) 631-8200.

YONKERS

56   Untermeyer Park and Gardens   ☆

This estate provides a grand view of the Hudson River; its Beaux Arts design provides a landscape filled with formal shrubbery, mosaics, Grecian pillars, and more than 40 fountains. It has been recently restored.

Call for hours; (914) 965-4027.

57   Philips Manor Hall   BX
Warburton Ave. and Dock St.

This 18th century Georgian stone house is surrounded by boxwood hedges and terraced gardens with flowering shrubs.

12-5 Wed-Sat; 1-5 Sun; May 18-Nov 2; no admission charge; (914) 965-4027.

NEW ROCHELLE

58 Wildcliff Museum and Greenhouse ☆ C-FE-G-H-HA-R-RG-S-SU
Wildcliff Road

This 3-acre site contains a rock garden, a herb garden, a rose garden as well as good annual, perennial, and vegetable beds. There is a collection of dwarf conifers; cacti, ferns, succulents, carnivorous plants, and epiphytic plants may be found in the greenhouses.

1-4:30 daily except Friday; adults, under $3; handicapped access; (914) 636-2108.

NEW YORK CITY

BRONX

59 New York Botanical Garden ☆☆☆☆ A-C-FE-H-J-O-P-R-S-SU
Bronx Park

A 250-acre botanical garden established in 1891 with one of the largest botanical collections in the world; more than 15,000 kinds of plants are displayed. It includes a large research station, 40 acres of hemlock forest, 3½-acre rock gardens with 1,200 varieties of plants, a herb garden, a Japanese garden, a rose garden, a native plant garden, a chemurgic garden. There are large azalea, rhododenron, and magnolia collections and more than 200 species of conifer, numerous native trees as well as annual and perennial beds. The Enid Haupt Conservatory has recently been restored and features 2,000 kinds of tropical, sub-tropical and desert plants, ferns, palms, and orchids under 2 acres of glass. Research library.

Daily 9-dusk; conservatory 10-4 Tues-Sun; no admission charge for grounds; conservatory adults, under $3; senior citizens, students half; (212) 220-8728.

60 Wave Hill ☆☆ C-G-H-R-SU-W
675 West 252 St.

28 acres of gardens, established in 1965, contain an English style wild-garden, a rose garden, a herb garden, an aquatic garden as well as many annuals and perennials. 3 greenhouses display a good cacti collection along with succulents and tropical plants.

Daily 10-4:30; greenhouse 10-12, 2-4; no admission charge weekdays; Sat, Sun $1; senior citizens .50¢; under 14 free; handicapped access; (212) 549-2055.

61 Van Cortland Mansion Museum H
Van Cortland Park
Broadway and 246th St.

The mansion built in 1748 is furnished with period pieces and stands in an 18th century garden. A herb garden with appropriate plants has also been established.

10-4:45 Tues-Sat; 12-4:45 Sun; closed Jan 1, Feb 1-28; adults, under $3; under 12 free, but must be with an adult; (212) 543-3344.

62 Bartlow-Pell Mansion and Museum H
Pelham Bay Park

A herb garden has been placed in a meadow setting on these grounds.

1-5 Tue-Fri, Sun; no admission charge to the grounds; (212) 885-1461.

BROOKLYN

63 **Brooklyn Botanic Garden** ☆☆☆☆ .-A-BO-BR-C-FE-G-H-HA-J-O-P-R-RG-S-SH-SU-W-WF

1000 Washington Ave.; entrances Flatbush Ave. and Empire Blvd.; Washington Ave. and Eastern Parkway.

A magnificent 50-acre botanic garden with more than 12,000 kinds of plants. It was founded in 1910. The grounds contain large formal gardens, a rose garden, a herb garden, a rock garden, a fragrance garden for the blind, a Shakespearean garden, a Japanese garden, a Ryoanji Temple Stone Garden, water lily pools, along with annuals and perennials. The mature arboretum has special collections of Kwanzan cherries, Japanese cherries, crab-apples, maples, and rhododendrons. There are fine specimens of Monarch Birch, Chinese Tree Quince, Daimyo Oak, and Chinese Zelkova. Many systematic collections of trees stand in this park. There is a wisteria arbor and a hedge wheel. The greenhouses display cacti, succulents, cycads, bromeliads, ferns, and a bonsai collection. Reference library.

8-4:30 Tues-Fri; 10-4:30 Sat, Sun, holidays; greenhouses 10-4 Tues-Fri; 11-4 Sat, Sun, holidays Sept-April; longer hours during summer; no admission charge except nominal fee for Ryoanji garden and greenhouses; handicapped access; (212) 622-4433.

QUEENS

64 **Queens Botanical Garden** ☆☆ .-A-G-H-HA-R
42-50 Main St. Flushing

39 acres of gardens were established in 1963. A fine tulip and bulb display is mounted each spring and chrysanthemum follow in autumn. There is a rose garden, an Elizabethan herb garden, a bee garden, a heath garden, a fragrance garden for the blind, a backyard garden, a bird garden. A section is devoted to dwarf conifers. Good collection of azaleas and rhododendrons is maintained. The greenhouse contains tropical plants.

Daily 9-dusk; no admission charge; handicapped access; (212) 886-3800.

STATEN ISLAND

65 **Staten Island Botanical Garden** BO-H-R-S-W
914 Richmond Terrace

A 28-acre site which includes a rose garden, a herb garden, a bonsai collection. There are specimen trees, a saltwater marsh, and lakes.

Daily 9-5; no admission charge; (212) 273-8200.

66 **Jacques Marchais Center of Tibetan Art** W
338 Lighthouse Ave.

This fine museum of Tibetan art is housed in buildings which resemble a Tibetan Monastery. A small garden, and a lotus pond lie near them.

1-5 Sat, Sun; April through Nov; 1-5 Thurs, Fri; June, July, Aug; adults, under $3; under 12 half; (212) 987-3478.

MANHATTAN, CENTRAL PARK AREA

67 Conservatory Gardens
106th St. and 5th Ave.

Seasonal displays of flowers in large beds are arranged on this site which formerly housed a conservatory.

Daily, dawn-dusk.

68 Pinetum S
80th St. near reservoir in Central Park

A large collection of pine trees, labelled and spaced to produce good specimens has been planted here. A guide book is available.

Daily, dawn-dusk.

69 Shakespeare Garden SH
near Delacorte Theater

A small garden of plants mentioned by Shakespeare is being restored.

Daily, dawn-dusk.

70 Astor Chinese Garden Court ☆ HA-J
Metropolitan Museum of Art
5th Ave. at 82nd St.

The Chinese wing of this grand museum has established an interior garden which reproduces a Ming dynasty scholar's garden. Great care has been exercised to use authentic building and plant material as far as that is possible. The garden court was opened in 1981. The special plantings in the American Wing of the museum should be noted also.

10-8:45 Tues; 10-4:45 Wed-Sat; 11-4:45 Sun; adults, under $6; senior citizens, students half; handicapped access; (212) 535-7710.

71 Courtyard Gardens—Frick Museum ☆ HH
1 East 70th St.

This museum housed in a grand mansion contains a courtyard with a central fountain surrounded by a wide variety of flowering plants and shrubs. Seasonal displays add to its beauty.

10-6 Wed-Sat; 1-6 Sun, June 1-Aut 31; 10-6 Tues-Sat; 1-6 Sun, rest of year; closed Jan 1, July 4, Thanksgiving, Dec 24, 25; adults, under $3; senior citizens, students half; Sunday, under $3; children restricted; (212) 288-0700.

MANHATTAN, MID-TOWN AREA

72 The Abigail Adams Smith Museum HH
421 East 61 St.

An 18th century garden established was restored here in 1939 and continues to be maintained. It contains native shrubs, old-fashioned flower beds, lilac, and ivy.

Mon-Fri 10-4; adults under $3; senior citizens half; children free; (212) 838-6878.

73 United Nations Rose Garden
First Ave. and 45th St.

A formal rose garden which overlooks the East River beneath the General Assembly Building. The planting has been restricted to hybrid tea, grandiflora, and floribunda which have won the All-American Rose designation.

Daily 9-4:45; closed Jan 1 and Dec 24, 25; adults, under $3; students half; under 5 not permitted; (212) 754-7710.

74 Japan House J
  333 E. 47th St.

Fine exhibits of Japanese art are housed in this museum which contains a small courtyard reminiscent of a Japanese garden. An indoor court is built around a pool.

Daily 11-5 during exhibits; donation; (212) 832-1155.

75 Ford Foundation Indoor Garden ☆ HA
  320 East 43rd St.

An 11 story atrium which contains large plantings of magnolias, ficuses, ferns, azaleas, camellias, crotons, ivies, baby tears, Korean grasses, as well as seasonal plants.

Daily; no admission charge; handicapped access.

76 Chemical Bank Building
  Park Avenue at 43rd St.

A 6 story atrium filled with tropical and semi-tropical plants; seasonal displays add to its beauty.

Weekdays during office hours.

77 IBM Building
  Madison Ave.

The high atrium of this building contains a small forest of bamboo which provide a tropical setting.

Weekdays during office hours.

78 Fisher Building
  55 East 52nd St.

The open plaza contains 4 large beds with a variety of semi-tropical and flowering plants.

Weekdays during office hours.

79 Rockefeller Center Pool Garden
  5th Ave. at 50th St.

Interesting floral displays are maintained here and changed seasonally. This is a small setting maintained with much care.

Daily, all hours.

80 Atriums and Vest Pocket Parks

Mid-town Manhattan provides an increasing number of atriums which are planted with a variety of tropical and sub-tropical plants. Both office and apartment buildings house them. In addition there are dozens of small parklets on the sites of office buildings and churches which are planted with annuals during spring, summer, and autumn.

MANHATTAN, UP-TOWN AREA

81 Biblical Garden of the Cathedral of St. John the Divine   B-HA
1047 Amsterdam Ave.

The cathedral has established a small garden of plants mentioned in the Bible which will grow in this climate. It was founded in 1973.

Daily 7-sunset; no admission charge; handicapped access; (212) 678-6886.

82 The Cloisters—Metropolitan Museum   ☆ H-HA-HH
Fort Tryon Park
North Ave and Cabrini Circle

This superb medieval museum housed in cloisters moved from Europe includes several medieval courtyard gardens which feature plants grown in Europe before 1520. Irises are found in the Cuxa Cloister, Christmas plants in the Saint-Guilhem Cloister, and herbs in the Bonnefont Cloister. 70 of the 150 herbs are taken from a list of Charlemagne and the rest from other medieval lists.

10-4:45 Tues-Sat; 1-4:45 Sun; adults, under $3; senior citizens and students half; handicapped access; (212) 923-3700.

83 Morris-Jumel Mansion
W. 160th St. and Edgecombe Ave.

A colonial herb garden and a rose garden lie behind this historic house. There are good views of the Harlem River.

9-4 Tues-Sun; adults, under $3; senior citizens and students half; (212) 923-8008.

84 Flower Shows

A number of special flower shows are offered seasonally by the various botanical gardens, the New York Horticultural Society, Gramercy Park, and other organizations.

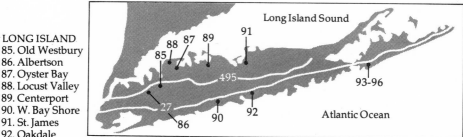

LONG ISLAND
85. Old Westbury
86. Albertson
87. Oyster Bay
88. Locust Valley
89. Centerport
90. W. Bay Shore
91. St. James
92. Oakdale
93-96. Southhampton

LONG ISLAND

OLD WESTBURY

85 Old Westbury Gardens   ☆☆☆☆   A-BX-H-HA-HD-J-R-S-WF
71 Old Westbury Rd. Between Rt. 495 (Long Island Expressway) and Rt. 25 (Jericho Turnpike).

This 100-acre estate of John S. Phipps has gardens which were first established in 1905. The Georgian Mansion is set in an 18th century style park with broad avenues of linden and beech trees which lead to the house. A number of grand gardens lie on the estate; among them are a 2-acre Italian garden with floral borders, a boxwood garden, a cottage garden, a rose garden, and a wild garden. Several demonstration gardens are intended to provide ideas useful to a modern visitor; among them are a rose test garden, a herb garden, and a Japanese style garden. The pinetum is extensive. A large variety of rhododendrons and azaleas are displayed throughout the grounds. There are fine specimens of Crack Willow, White and Korean Pines, Cucumber Magnolia, Atlas Cedar, and Silver Maple. A library is available.

10-5 Wed-Sun, May-Oct; adults, under $3 garden only; under $6 house and garden; children half; handicapped access; (516) 333-0048.

ALBERTSON

86 Fanny Dwight Clark Memorial Garden ☆☆   A-H-HA-R-RG-WF
Brooklyn Botanical Garden
193 I.U. Willets Rd.

A 12-acre garden founded in 1966 with special collections of roses, rhododendrons, herbs, wildflowers, and ferns as well as hundreds of trees grouped around 3 lakes. Special areas include a herb garden, a rose garden, a wildflower garden, a dried flower garden, a children's garden, a rock garden, a day-lily garden, and a marsh garden.

8-4:30 weekdays; 10-4:30 weekends and holidays; spring to fall; adults, under $3; children half; handicapped access; (516) 621-7568.

OYSTER BAY

87 Planting Field Arboretum ☆☆☆☆   A-C-CA-G-HA-O-R-S-SU
West via Mill River Rd. and Glen Cove Rd.

409 acres of magnificent gardens with an arboretum established in 1916 and planted with well-established trees. There are now more than 5,500 kinds of plants. The Synoptic Garden contains ornamental shrubs and small trees arranged alphabetically and identified by their botanical and common names along with the country of origin. More than 600 varieties of rhododendrons and azaleas have been planted on this estate. There are also good collections of holly, and dwarf conifer. Fine specimens of Silver Linden, Golden English Elm, European Beech, Cedar of Lebanon, and Sargent Weeping Hemlock may be seen here. The conservatory contains one of the largest collections of camellias, cacti, succulents, begonias, orchids, and other tropical plants. There is a library.

Daily 10-5 May 1-Sept 1; weekends and holidays only Sept 1-April 30; adults, under $3; under 12 free; handicapped access; (516) 922-9200.

LOCUST VALLEY

88 Bailey Arboretum ☆☆   HA-R-S
194 Bayville Rd.

A 43-acre arboretum with a fine collection of unusual trees; among them are junipers, pines, Dawn Redwoods, maples, and beeches as well as dwarf conifers. There are good tree peonies as well as large beds of perennials and annuals. Special areas include a rock garden, a rose garden, a lilac walk, an iris garden, a bulb garden and a bog.

9-4 Tues-Thurs; adults nominal; handicapped access; guided tours; (516) 676-4497.

CENTERPORT

89 Vanderbilt Museum and Mansion A
Little Neck Rd. 1½ mi. north of Rt. 25A

The estate with its Spanish-Moroccan style mansion includes small gardens of azaleas, perennials, and annuals.

10-4 Tues-Sat; 12-5 Sun and holidays May 1-Oct 31; adults, under $3; 8-12 and over 65 three-quarters; (516) 261-5656.

WEST BAY SHORE

90 Sagtikos Manor
Montauk Highway

This 17th century manor stands in a walled garden planted with shrubs and perennials. There is a herb garden.

1-4 Sun, June and Sept, Thurs and Sun in July and Aug; no admission charge; (516) 665-0093.

ST. JAMES

91 Holly-by-Golly
76 Long Beach Rd.

A 3-acre garden which specializes in holly with many new cultivars developed by Ms. Meserve has been created here.

By appointment only; (516) 584-5410.

OAKDALE

92 Bayard Cutting Arboretum ☆☆ A-HA-R-S
Montauk Highway

This 690-acre arboretum was designed in 1886 by Frederick Law Olmsted; it contains more than 400 species of trees and shrubs with a fine Pinetum. 75 acres are landscaped with azalea, laurel, dogwood, rhododendron, holly, and lilac. There is a rose garden as well as perennial and annual beds. Good specimens of Cilician Fir, Blue Atlas Cedar, Sargent Weeping Hemlock, Sawara-Cypress may be viewed along the trails. A walk leads to a grove of Swamp Cypress.

10-5 Wed-Sun, legal holidays; 10-4 winter and spring; adults, under $3; children under 12 free; handicapped access; (516) 581-1002.

SOUTHAMPTON

93 Parish Art Museum HA-S
25 Job's Lane

A 3-acre arboretum founded in 1897 is connected with this museum. Some 250 kinds of trees and shrubs are represented here with some good specimen trees.

10-5 Tues-Sat; 1-5 Sun; no admission charge; handicapped access; (516) 283-2118.

94 Old Halsey Homestead   H-F
South Main St.

Built in 1648 with later additions, this house has been restored along with a colonial herb garden and a small orchard.

11-4:30 Tues-Sat and holidays; 2-4:30 Sun June 12-Sept 12; adults, under $3; under 12 nominal; (516) 283-0605.

95 Thompson Greenhouse   ☆☆   G
Near Southampton College Campus
Exit 7 from Sunrise Highway

These greenhouses contain a collection of more than 1,400 different varieties of begonias, one of the largest in the world. Some are in bloom thoughout the year. An extensive perennial garden surrounds the conservatory.

9-12 Mon, Wed, Thurs, Sat; 2-5 Fri; closed Tues, Sun; also by appointment (516) 283-3237 or 283-1633.

96 Commercial nurseries

Some interesting commercial nurseries are located in the Southampton area; several have extensive landscaped displays.

NORTH CAROLINA

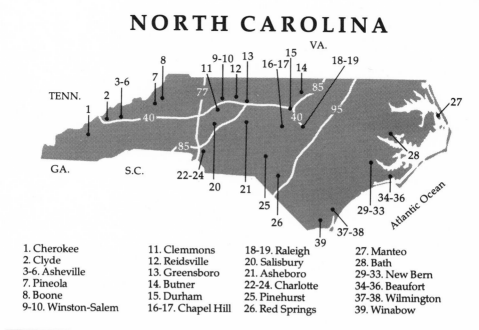

VA.

TENN.

GA.   S.C.

Atlantic Ocean

1. Cherokee
2. Clyde
3-6. Asheville
7. Pineola
8. Boone
9-10. Winston-Salem

11. Clemmons
12. Reidsville
13. Greensboro
14. Butner
15. Durham
16-17. Chapel Hill

18-19. Raleigh
20. Salisbury
21. Asheboro
22-24. Charlotte
25. Pinehurst
26. Red Springs

27. Manteo
28. Bath
29-33. New Bern
34-36. Beaufort
37-38. Wilmington
39. Winabow

CHEROKEE

1 Cherokee Botanical Garden HH-WF
Oconaluftee Indian Village
Off U.S. 441

The palisaded Indian village lies adjacent to a garden with 150 species of trees, shrubs, and wildflowers native to the Smoky Mountains. Plants are labelled. Nature trails run through the grounds.

Daily 9-5:30, mid-May-late Oct; no admission charge; (704) 497-2111.

CLYDE

2 Haywood Horticultural Gardens ☆ A-H-R
Haywood Technical College
Freedlander Drive

A botanical garden and arboretum is being developed on this campus as part of the instructional program. Begun in 1978, a herb garden, a rose garden, a rhododendron grove, a native plant garden, a dahlia garden, and a pond area have been completed. Future plans call for a pinetum, shrub garden, Appalachia collection, and greenhouses. Nature trails run through a woodland area.

Daily 9-4; no admission charge; (704) 627-2821.

ASHEVILLE

3 Biltmore House and Gardens ☆☆ A-BX-HA-L-P-R
Exits 50 or 50B from I-40

A French renaissance chateau built in the 1890's on an 8,000-acre estate by George

W. Vanderbilt. There are 35 acres of formal gardens based on Vaux-le-Vicomte and an arboretum designed by Frederick Law Olmsted. The Italian garden contains 3 formal pools. There is a 4-acre walled espaliered English garden, an azalea garden with a most extensive collection of native species, a rose garden of more than 5,000 bushes, and a shrub garden. Fine boxwoods, ivies, wisterias, hollies, kalmias, rhododendrons, azaleas, and magnolias may be found here. A palm court lies in the house.

Daily 9-6; closed Jan 1, Thanksgiving, Christmas; tours of upstairs or downstairs, under $9; 12-17 slightly less; handicapped access; (704) 274-1776.

4　**University Botanical Gardens at Asheville**　☆　.-H-HA-WF
University of North Carolina
Weaver Blvd.

10 acres devoted to indigenous trees, shrubs, and flowers; the arboretum was established in 1960 and now contains more than 2,000 species of plants. It is well landscaped; there is a fragrance garden, herb garden, wildflower garden and a large collection of native flora.

Daily, sunrise-sunset; Botany Center Display Area closed Dec, Jan, Feb; no admission charge; handicapped access; (704) 252-5190.

5　**Biltmore Country Market**　G-H-WF
1000 Henderson Rd.

A series of small gardens including a herb garden, wildflower garden, and vegetable garden. There is a small greenhouse.

Daily 9-5; no admission charge.

6　**Craggy Gardens**　A
Blue Ridge Parkway, mile 364

This park is actually in Virginia; it contains 600 acres of Catawba Rhododendrons which bloom in mid-June at an elevation of 6,000 ft. They present a magnificent sight.

9-5 Visitor Center, April 1-Nov 30.

PINEOLA

7　**Gardens of the Blue Ridge**　FE-RG-W-WF
2 mi. south of Linville on U.S. 221

This large commercial nursery features display gardens with emphasis on wildflowers, bog plants, ferns, and rock garden plants.

Daily 9-5; no admission charge; (704) 756-4339.

BOONE

8　**Daniel Boone Native Gardens**　☆　A-HA-RG-WF
Horn in the West Drive

8 acres of informally landscaped gardens which emphasize indigenous plants. Established in 1961, the garden has pools, a sunken garden, a rock garden, and a meadow area. There are numerous varieties of azaleas, dogwoods, and wildflowers, with special emphasis on North Carolina native plants.

Daily 9-5, May-Oct; 9-7 July, Aug; admission nominal; theater performances in the evening; handicapped access; (704) 264-2120.

WINSTON-SALEM

9 Reynolda Gardens of Wake Forest University ☆☆ BX-C-G-HA-O-R-S
100 Reynolda Village

115 acres of gardens surround the house which is now a museum. There are 4 acres of formal gardens with boxwoods, flowering cherries, dogwoods, magnolias and lily-turf. Good collections of junipers and hollies. The garden contains fine specimens of weeping cherry, Bald Cypress and Cryptomeria. Special emphasis has been placed upon native plants of North Carolina. More than 1,000 species of plants are found here. Demonstration and test gardens for vegetables and berries are maintained along with an All-American Rose Selection area. There are greenhouses with bromeliads, orchids, and cacti.

Daily 9-3; greenhouses, Mon-Fri, 9-3; no admission charge; admission for museum; trails; handicapped access; (919) 761-5593.

10 Old Salem Inc. HA-HH
Salem Station

This is a restored Moravian congregation town which was founded in 1766. There are a number of gardens on these 40 acres of grounds. Flower and vegetable beds have been accurately restored to reflect the period between 1759-1764. The grounds contain a good collection of indigenous shrubs and trees.

Always open; no admission charge except for houses; handicapped access; (919) 723-3688.

CLEMMONS

11 Tanglewood Park HA-R
U.S. 158 off I-40

A very large park and recreation area which also contains an arboretum, a rose garden, and some formal plantings.

Daily 7-11; each car, under $3; or each person nominal; handicapped access; (919) 725-6421.

REIDSVILLE

12 Chinqua-Penn Plantation House R
Off U.S. 29 By-pass; 3 mi. northwest

An English country house now a museum for Chinese and Nepalese objects. There are formal gardens which include a pagoda as well as a rose garden.

10-4 Wed-Sat; 1:30-4:30 Sun; March 1 to mid-Dec; closed July 4, Thanksgiving; adults, under $3; over 64, 6-12 half; partial handicapped access; (919) 349-4576.

GREENSBORO

13 Bicentennial Garden ☆ A-CA-R-RG-WF
Between Hobbs and Holden Rds. north of Friendly Ave.

A new garden is being developed on this 7½-acre area. In addition to massed plantings of spring bulbs and annuals, there is a fragrance garden for the blind, a camellia and azalea garden, a wildflower garden, a rock garden, and a small rose garden.

Daily, dawn-dusk; (919) 373-2558.

BUTNER

14 Fragrance Garden
Rehabilitation Center for the Blind

A small fragrance garden for the blind has been built by this rehabilitation center.

Weekdays 10-4; (919) 575-7972.

DURHAM

15 Sarah P. Duke Gardens ☆☆☆☆ A-CH-FE-R-RG-S-W
Duke University, West Campus

20 acres of formal and informal gardens are surrounded by groves of pines, magnolias, and other trees which spread over 35 additional acres. There is a fine rose garden, rock garden, iris garden, water garden, formal terraces, woodland garden, azalea court garden, grass garden, and a fern glade. Good collection of flowering crab-apples, cherries, redbuds, and dogwoods are displayed. There is a chrysanthemum show in autumn. The gardens are designed for continuous year-round blooming.

Daily 8-5; no admission charge; partial handicapped access; ((919) 684-3698.

CHAPEL HILL

16 North Carolina Botanical Garden ☆☆☆ H-S-WF
University of North Carolina
Totten Center
Laurel Hill Rd.

This 307-acre arboretum contains a woodland of mature pines, some virgin forest as well as a fine collection of indigenous trees, shrubs, and flowers of the Southeastern states. Plants are displayed according to geographic habitat regions. A good display of wildflowers has grown since the garden's founding in 1952. Emphasis of this garden has been placed upon conservation of native plants. A plant-family garden and a well labelled herb garden are also found here. Test and demonstration gardens for perennial wildflowers, woody trees and shrubs have been established. There is a library.

8-5 weekdays; 10-4 Sat; 2-5 Sun; closed weekends mid-Nov to mid March; no admission charge; partial handicapped access; (919) 967-2246.

17 Coker Arboretum ☆ C-HA-S
University of North Carolina Laurel Hill Rd.

This arboretum established on a former swamp in 1903 has a fine collection of dwarf and mature conifers numbering more than 350 varieties. There is a good display of narcissuses and cacti and demonstration and test gardens. There is a library.

All hours; no admission charge; handicapped access; (919) 933-3776.

RALEIGH

18 North Carolina State University Arboretum ☆☆ H-HA-J-S-WF
Beryl Rd.

This new arboretum established in 1976 has a rapidly growing collection which already contains more than 3,500 species. There are specimen Cut-Leaf Japanese

Maples, *Lagerstroemia fauriei,* and the only Dwarf Loblolly Pines in the United States. More than 1,000 unusual species are displayed in a lath house. A good collection of herbs of the southeastern states is found here. The garden has a French parterre and a Japanese Garden. The demonstration and test gardens emphasize woody trees, shrubs, and perennial wildflowers.

Daily dawn-dusk; no admission charge; handicapped access; (919) 737-3133.

19   Raleigh Little Theater and Rose Garden   R
301 Pogue St.

A small rose garden with a good selection.

Daily 9-5; (919) 821-4579.

SALISBURY

20   Poet's and Dreamer's Garden   B-SH
Livingston College

Special plantings honor poets and dreamers in this garden. There is a Biblical garden and a Shakespearean garden.

Daily, dawn-dusk; no admission charge; (704) 633-7960.

ASHEBORO

21   North Carolina Zoological Park   HA
Off U.S. 64, 6, mi. southeast

A 30-acre zoo with animals in their natural habitat; the aviary contains a collection of tropical plants.

9-5 Mon-Fri; 10-6 Sat Sun, April 1-Sept 30; daily 9-5 rest of year; closed Jan 1, Christmas; adults, under $3; 2-15, over 62 half; handicapped access and no admission charge; (919) 879-5606.

CHARLOTTE

22   The Gardens of the University of North Carolina at Charlotte   ☆☆   A-C-G-O-SU
University of North Carolina

A number of special collections have been beautifully displayed in this 9-acre garden established in 1965. A collection of hardy ornamentals, rhododendron hybrids, and plants native to the Carolinas has been assembled. The greenhouses contain good orchid and succulent collections. There are trial and test gardens for rhododendrons. The library contains a special collection on succulents.

9-4 weekdays; outdoor gardens always open; no admission charge; partial handicapped access; (704) 597-2315.

23   Wing Haven Foundation Inc.   HA-WF
248 Ridgewood Ave.

A collection of native plants and wildflowers along with other trees and shrubs has been established on this 3-acre site since 1971.

3-5 Mon, Tues, Wed; no admission charge; handicapped access; (704) 332-5770.

24   Hezekiah Alexander Homestead   H
3500 Shamrock Drive

This site administered by the Mint Museum has a small herb garden and flower walk which reflects the mid-19th century period.

1-4 Tues-Fri; 2-4 Sat, Sun; closed on holidays; adults, under $3; children nominal; tours; (704) 332-5770.

PINEHURST

25   Clarendon Gardens   A-CA
Linden Rd.

These gardens contain large collections of azaleas, camellias, and hollies. Perennials as well as blooming ornamentals are also found here.

Weekdays 10-4; Sun 2-4; adults, under $3; children half; (919) 295-6651.

RED SPRINGS

26   Flora Macdonald Gardens   WF
Adjacent to Flora Macdonald College

13 acres of swampland have been reclaimed as an informal garden with hundreds of species of trees, shrubs, and wildflowers native to the Southeast. Some areas have recently become overgrown through neglect. Many varieties of rhododendron and azalea bloom in spring. The garden has been placed on the National Register of Historic Places.

Daily 8-dusk; (919) 843-5441.

MANTEO

27   Elizabethan Gardens   ☆☆   A-CA-F-H-L-R-T
Fort Raleigh National Historic Site

This 10½-acre garden which lies along Roanoke Sound has been planted in part to remind the visitor of an Elizabethan pleasure garden with formal terraces, a sunken garden with parterres, and winding paths. There is a knot garden, a wildflower garden and a herb garden. Surrounding this area are large plantings of azaleas, dogwoods, flowering ornamentals, fruit trees, roses, gardenias, magnolias, *Lagerstroemia*, hydrangeas, hibiscus, camellias and impatiens. Some are planted along the President's walk and others on the Overlook Terrace. Old Live Oaks grace the garden.

Daily 9-5; 9-8 during summer months; adults, under $3; under 12 free with adult; partial handicapped access; (919) 473-3234.

BATH

28   Ruth McCloud Smith Memorial Garden   A
Bonner house, Rt. 92.

This home built in 1830 is surrounded by a garden planted with azalea, crape-myrtle, wisteria, gardenia as well as annuals.

Tours 9-5 Tues-Sat; 1-5 Sun; closed Thanksgiving, Dec 24, 25; adults, under $3; under 12 half; (919) 923-3971.

NEW BERN

29 Tyron Palace Restoration ☆☆☆☆ A-F-H-HA-L-S-T-WF
George and Pollock Sts.

The Colonial capitol and royal palace built in 1770 has been restored with 18th century English landscape gardens. Only plants known before 1770 have been used. The Maude Moore Latham Garden is geometrical in design with clipped yaupon hedges and annuals; paths of special brick designs. The Kellenberger Garden is surrounded by brick walls covered with pyracantha, jasmine and various vines. Green Garden contains beautifully clipped hedges; Hawks Allee has low flowering plants and a pleached allee of yaupon. There are topiary hedges, a kitchen garden, espaliered fruit trees, and a wilderness garden. Fine specimen Darlington Oaks, rhododendrons, and azaleas are found here. There is a library.

Guided tours 9:30-4 Tues-Sat, also Easter Mon, Memorial Day, Labor Day; 1:30-4 Sun; closed Jan 1, Thanksgiving, Dec 24-26; adults, under $6; students through high school, quarter; handicapped access; (919) 638-5109.

30 Jones Wright Stanley House A-CA
Tyron Palace Restoration
George and Pollock Sts.

This 1780 house lies in an 18th century period garden with azaleas, gardenias, and raised beds of camellias.

Same hours as Tyron Palace; combination tickets available.

31 Stevenson House
Tyron Palace Restoration
George and Pollock Sts.

An early 19th century home with a small nicely planned gardens, which mainly feature annuals.

Same hours as Tyron Palace; combination tickets available.

32 Stanley House
Tyron Palace Restoration
George and Pollock Sts.

An 18th century townhouse with a small garden; the brick walls support old fashioned plantings.

Same hours as Tyron Palace; combination tickets available.

33 Samuel Smallwood House and Garden (Cypress Tree)
520 East Front St.

This house was built in 1884 and contains a small garden. The cypress tree at the rear of the house is one of 20 trees in the Hall of Fame of American Trees.

Check for hours; no admission charge; (919) 637-3111.

BEAUFORT

34 Joseph Bell House
Beaufort Restoration
Turner St.

This was the townhouse of a wealthy plantation owner, built in 1767. It stands in a period garden of perennial shrubs and annuals.

9-4 Mon-Sat; 2-4 Sun; adults, under $3; 8-12 half; (919) 728-5225.

35   Josiah Bell House . BX
Beaufort Restoration
Turner St.

This home was built in 1825. There is a small garden with old boxwood adjacent to it.

Same hours as Joseph Bell House; combination tickets available.

36   Apothecary Shop   H
Beaufort Restoration
Turner St.

This mid-18th century shop has a herb garden of medicinal herbs.

Same hours as Joseph Bell House; combination tickets available.

WILMINGTON

37   Greenfield Gardens   ☆   A-CA-HA-R-S
South 3rd St.

A pubic park surrounding a large lake with magnificent plantings of azaleas, flowering crab-apples, dogwoods, camellias, roses, and hawthorns. Good collections of kalmia, cherry, Judas tree, Bald Cypress and wisteria. An azalea festival is held here annually. February through April is best time for seeing this garden in bloom.

Daily 8-11; no admission charge; handicapped access; (919) 763-9871.

38   The Airlie Azalea Gardens   ☆   A-CA-HA-S
2 mi. west U.S. 76

A large estate of more than 100 acres with natural plantings of azaleas, camellias as well as other flowering plants. There are fine specimens of Virginia Oaks, magnolias, and rare evergreens.

8-5 daily; April 1-May 1; adults, under $3; under 12 free; handicapped access; (919) 763-9991.

WINABOW

39   Orton Plantation   ☆☆☆   A-CA-F-HA-L-S-T
Rt. 133

A Greek Revival mansion built in 1735 surrounded by a grand garden of more than 20 acres. There is a scroll garden with beautifully cut hedges. Further along there is a sun garden, white garden, and water garden. Good collections of azaleas, camellias, dogwoods, fruit trees, and wisterias. Woody ornamentals are displayed. Live Oaks border the majority of the garden walks. The garden contains old specimen Virginia Oak, Loblolly Pine, and camphor trees. Plants are in bloom from January through September. A refuge for waterfowl has been created in the former rice fields.

Daily 8-5 March-Aug; 8-6 Sept, Nov; adults, under $3; 6-12 half; handicapped access; (919) 371-6851.

NORTH DAKOTA

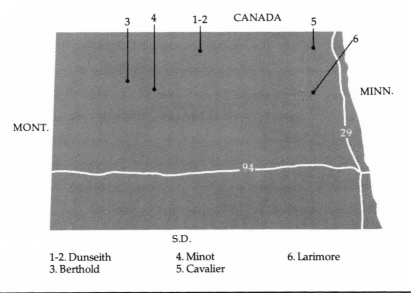

1-2. Dunseith   4. Minot   6. Larimore
3. Berthold   5. Cavalier

DUNSEITH

1 International Peace Garden ☆☆ L-JR
12 mi. north

These beautifully landscaped formal gardens are part of a 2,300-acre preserve established in 1932 on both sides of the American and Canadian border. There are terrace gardens and sunken rose gardens with more than 2,000 bushes. Fine beds of annuals and perennials are spread throughout the garden along with a floral clock. There is an arboretum.

Daily all hours; per car, under $2; partial handicapped access; (701) 263-4390.

2 Manitoba Horticultural Society Arboretum
Canadian Loop Rd.

This small arboretum on the Canadian side of the Peace Garden provides a well-labelled, small collection of native trees and shrubs. One must watch for the sign along the road.

Daily all hours; no admission charge; (701) 263-4390.

BERTHOLD

3 Berthold Public School Arboretum

This arboretum established in 1932 on 2 acres is devoted to ornamentals which are hardy in the north. 125 species are represented.

Daily all hours; handicapped access; (701) 453-3484.

MINOT

4 Roosevelt Park and Zoo   HA
1051 Burdick Parkway

These 10 acres contain formal gardens with a collection of annuals and perennials; there is a sunken garden.

8-5 Daily; no admission charge; handicapped access.

CAVALIER

5 Gunslong Arboretum
Rt. 5, 6 mi. west; adjacent to Icelandic State Park

This 200-acre arboretum is a preserve of undisturbed land; it contains a collection of native plants and wildlife. Ecological studies are conducted here.

9-5 daily; no admission charge.

LARIMORE

6 Myra Arboretum
off Rt. 18, 2 mi. east and 1 mi. north

This small arboretum lies on the south branch of the Turtle River and contains a new woody plant collection.

9-5 daily; no admission charge; picnicking.

OHIO

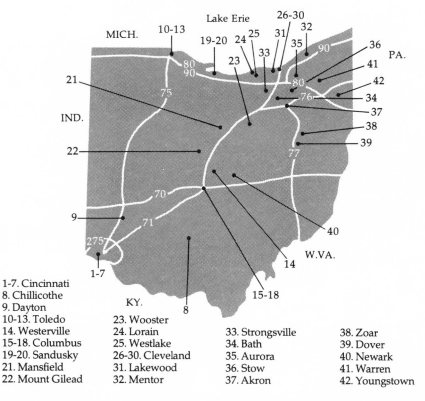

1-7. Cincinnati
8. Chillicothe
9. Dayton
10-13. Toledo
14. Westerville
15-18. Columbus
19-20. Sandusky
21. Mansfield
22. Mount Gilead

23. Wooster
24. Lorain
25. Westlake
26-30. Cleveland
31. Lakewood
32. Mentor

33. Strongsville
34. Bath
35. Aurora
36. Stow
37. Akron

38. Zoar
39. Dover
40. Newark
41. Warren
42. Youngstown

CINCINNATI

1 Irwin M. Krohn Conservatory ☆☆☆ C-FE-HA-G-O-P-SU
950 Eden Park Drive

This conservatory established in 1902 and rebuilt in 1933 contains a good collection of tropical plants, tree ferns, orchids, and palms as well as desert plants. About 700 species are represented. Six annual seasonal flower shows are presented.

10-5 Mon-Sat; 10-6 Sun; evening hours during Christmas and Easter weeks; no admission charge; handicapped access; (513) 352-4090.

2 Mount Airy Forest Arboretum ☆ A-HA-S
5083 Colerain Ave.

120 acres of the 1,500-acre park have been set aside as an arboretum which displays more than 1,700 species of trees, shrubs, and flowers. Green Garden features ground covers, Daisy Jones Gardens of perennials, Braam Gardens of azaleas and rhododendrons, Garden of the States of official trees, shrubs, and flowers. Good collections of flowering quince, azalea, rhododendron, lilac, dwarf conifers; fine specimens of maple, oaks, and beeches. Nearby lies the the nation's first major municipal reforestation project carried out in 1911.

Daily 6-10; no admission charge; handicapped access; (513) 352-4080.

3   **Sooty Acres, the Cornelius J. Hauck Botanical Garden and Civic Garden Center**   ☆   HA-R-S
    950 Eden Park Drive

This estate developed since 1924 lies adjacent to the Cincinnati Garden Center; it contains a selection of dwarf evergreens, azaleas, Japanese maples, *Styrax, fagus.* Specimens of Manchurian Sawtooth Oak, Lea Oak. There is a small rose garden and a garden for the blind; library.

Daily 10-4:30; handicapped access; (513) 221-0981.

4   **The Stanley M. Rowe Arboretum**
    4500 Muchmore Rd.

A 140-acre garden and arboretum established in 1935 with a collection of dwarf evergreens as well as crab-apples, magnolias, beeches, oaks and viburnums. The park is well landscaped.

Daily 9-4; no admission charge; (513) 561-7340.

5   **Ault Park**   FE-H-HD-R-SU

A dahlia test garden lies in this park. Various plant societies have adopted plots in a special area in which sample herb, fern, begonia, succulent, and rose gardens have been planted.

Daily, dawn-dusk; (513) 352-4080.

6   **Spring Grove Cemetery**   ☆☆   L-R-S
    4521 Spring Grove Ave., Mitchell Ave. Exit from I-75

This old cemetery established in 1845 contains a fine rose garden as well as a good collection of English Ivy and American Holly. Many specimen trees not found in arboreta are located here including Bald-Cypress, European and American Beech, Burr and White Oaks. More than 400 species of plants are represented and many are labelled. This cemetery under the guidance of Adoph Strauch played a major role in the 19th century cemetery beautification movement. Fine stone work and wrought iron.

Daily 8-5; tours for groups; (513) 681-6680.

7   **Cincinnati Zoological Garden**   ☆   G-HA-P
    3400 Vine St.

Excellent plantings of hardy plants and tropical plants are used to duplicate natural habitats. More than 1,000 species are used with good representations of dwarf conifers, palms, hardy bamboos, and others.

Daily 9-6 summer; 9-5 rest of year; adults, under $6; senior citizens and under 12, half; handicapped access; (513) 281-4701.

CHILLICOTHE

8   **Adena**
    Adena Rd. off Orange St.

This Georgian style mansion was built in 1807 by Benjamin Latrobe who also built the nation's capitol. Every effort has been made to restore the grounds to their original conditions with plants of the early 19th century.

9:30-5 Wed-Sat and holidays; 12-5 Sun, May 26-Sept 6; Sat, Sun only Sept 7-Oct 31; adults, under $3; 6-12 half; (614) 772-1500.

DAYTON

9 James M. Cox Arboretum ☆☆ C-G-H-S-SU
6733 Springboro Pike

These 153 acres of trees and shrubs have rapidly developed since their founding in 1962. Good collections of crab-apples, synoptic shrub garden, herb garden, shade and native trees, ivies, and endangered species are maintained. The greenhouses have a collection of cacti and succulents. There are demonstration and test gardens for ground covers, shrubs, and woody ornamentals. There is a library.

Daily 8-dusk; greenhouses 8-4:30; partial handicapped access; (513) 434-9005.

TOLEDO

10 George P. Crosby Gardens ☆☆☆ A-FE-G-H-HA-R-WF
5403 Elmer Drive

These 40 acres established in 1970 emphasize indigenous plants. There is a good collection of rhododendrons, azaleas, and ferns. Special areas include a rose garden, herb garden, fragrance garden, wildflower garden, and a children's garden. There are greenhouses and an 1837 pioneer homestead with its plantings stands on the grounds.

Daily, dawn-dusk; no admission charge; handicapped access; (419) 536-8365.

11 The Stranahan Arboretum ☆
University of Toledo
33 Birckhead Place

Indigenous plants are featured in this 50-acre arboretum established in 1965. There are 400 species of hardy woody ornamentals, crab-apples, small lakes, and a natural woods.

Weekdays 8:30-4; Sat, Sun, open house in afternoon from May to Oct; partial handicapped access; (419) 537-2065.

12 Toledo Zoological Gardens ☆ C-CH-G-R-W
2700 Broadway

Along with the zoological collection there is a rose garden with 400 varieties planted, a lily pond as well as greenhouses with cacti and tropical plants. There is an annual chrysanthemum display.

Daily 10-5, April 1-Sept 30; 10-4 Oct 1-March 31; adults, under $3; 2-11 half; (419) 385-4040.

13 Secor Metropark
Oak Openings Preserve
Oaks Opening Parkway

A 200-acre arboretum of native trees and shrubs has been created in the midst of 400 acres of woodland and meadow.

Daily, dawn-dusk; (419) 829-2761.

WESTERVILLE

14 Inniswood Botanical Garden and Nature Preserve HA-H-R-RG
940 Hempstead Rd.

This estate has been augmented to become a 91-acre park with formal and informal gardens. There is a rose garden, a rock garden, a day-lily garden, a herb garden as well as peony and iris collections. The wildflower and nature preserve extends over 54 acres.

8-4:30 Mon-Fri; some weekends and evenings during blooming seasons; no admission charge; handicapped access; (614) 895-6216.

COLUMBUS

15 **Chadwick Arboretum** HA
Dept. of Horticulture
Ohio State University
2001 Fyffe Court

This arboretum consists of 15 acres of plantings scattered around the university campus; the work was begun in 1970. There is a collection of mature woody ornamentals, as well as tulips, perennials, and annuals.

Daily 8-5; handicapped access; (614) 422-9775.

16 **Columbus Park of Roses** ☆ A-H-HA-R-WF
4105 Olentangy Blvd.

A 13-acre rose garden established in 1951 with more than 7,000 bushes representing 200 varieties along with a rose test garden. The roses begin to bloom in June. There is also a display of rhododendron, narcissus, wildflowers, and herbs.

Daily 9-dusk; no admission charge; handicapped access; (614) 222-7520.

17 **Franklin Park Conservatory** ☆☆ C-G-HA-O-P-SU
E. Broad St. and Nelson Rd.

The conservatory opened in 1895 is a copy of one constructed at the Chicago World's Fair in 1893. 1,500 different tropical and sub-tropical species are displayed. There is a good collection of orchids, *Gesneriacaea*, palms, tropical and subtropical plants, carnivorous plants, cacti, and succulents. 3 annual seasonal flower shows are presented. There is a library.

Daily 10-4; closed holidays; no admission charge; handicapped access; (614) 222-7447.

18 **Annual Haus and Garten Tour**
German Village

German settlers built this village between 1840 and 1860. The homes have been restored along with some gardens.

An annual tour is held on the last Sunday in June; for information call (614) 221-8888.

SANDUSKY

19 **Cedar Point** ☆
Ohio Turnpike exit 7

This 365-acre lakefront amusement park contains fine plantings of shrubs, perennials, and annuals.

Daily 9-10, May 15-Sept 6, except closes at 8 Mon-Fri, May 17-June 4 and Aug 30-Sept 3; 12-8 Sat, Sun Sept 7-30; adults and children, under $15; over 65 three-quarters; (419) 626-0830.

20 Sunken Garden
Washington Park

Some unusual trees as well as plantings of perennials and annuals are found in this garden. It has been designed in the Victorian style.

Daily, dawn-dusk.

MANSFIELD

21 Kingwood Center ☆☆☆ C-CH-G-H-HH-R-S-WF
900 Park Ave. West

An old garden beautifully landscaped on 47 acres with more than 6,000 species surround this French Provincial house. The garden has a very large display of tulips, 400 kinds of peonies, 400 varieties of day-lilies, 1,000 of irises, 150 of dahlias, 50 of lilies. There is a large rose garden, herb garden as well as major displays of wildflowers, and chrysanthemums. A good collection of ornamental trees and shrubs is found here. The greenhouses contain columneas and cacti; there are test and demonstration gardens. There is a library.

8-5 Tues-Sat; 1:30-4:30 Sun, Easter-Oct 31; closed Sun rest of year; closed holidays; no admission charge; partial handicapped access; (419) 522-0211.

MOUNT GILEAD

22 Annual Show
American Gourd Society
Morrow County Fairgrounds

The Gourd Society with headquarters here has an annual show on the first Saturday and Sunday of October.

For further information write Box 274, Mt. Gilead, 43338.

WOOSTER

23 Secrest Arboretum ☆☆ A-HA-R-S
Ohio Agricultural Research and Development Center
U.S. 250

This old arboretum founded in 1906 on 85 acres is part of a 2,000-acre experimental station. More than 1,500 species are represented. There is a rhododendron garden, holly garden, 3 acre "Garden of Roses of Legend and Romance" with 500 varieties of roses. The excellent collections consist of yews with 100 varieties, 135 crab-apples cultivars , 93 kinds of hollies, also junipers, ivies, redwoods, dwarf evergreens, chestnuts, Cedars of Lebanon, pines, firs, and spruces. There is a library.

Daily, dawn-dusk; no admission charge; handicapped access; (216) 264-1021.

LORAIN

24 Rose Garden R
Lakeview Park
W. Erie Avenue

40 varieties of roses are represented in this circular garden which has 3,000 bushes.

Daily, dawn-dusk.

WESTLAKE

25   **Clague Park**   J
Clague and Hilliard Rds.

A Japanese style garden with numerous flowering cherry trees.

Daily, dawn-dusk.

CLEVELAND

26   **The Garden Center of Greater Cleveland**   ☆☆   H-HA-J-R-W
Western Reserve Herb Garden
11030 East Blvd.

This 4-acre center was established in 1930. The herb garden is arranged according to the use of the herb—fragrant herbs, dye plants, medicinal plants, culinary herbs. There is a Japanese garden, and a rose garden with historical and modern roses. The Whitney Evans Memorial Reading Garden is devoted to perennials, shrubs, ground covers and vines, aquatic pool. The Center presents flower shows and maintains a library.

9-5 Mon-Fri; 2-5 Sun; closed holidays; no admission charge; handicapped access; (216) 721-1600.

27   **Kent H. Smith Courtyard**   WF
Cleveland Museum of Natural History
Wade Oval
University Circle

300 species of wildflowers from every section of northeast Ohio are planted.

10-5 Mon-Sat; 1-5:30 Sun; adults, under $3; seniors, 6-18 half; (216) 231-4600.

28   **Rockefeller Park Greenhouses**   ☆☆   A-C-FE-G-J-O-P-R-SU
750 E. 88th St.

Good displays of tropical plants, economic plants, ferns, palms, cacti, succulents, orchids are presented by these greenhouses. The 'talking garden' contains textured and scented plants; braille signs are also provided. Seasonal flower shows are held each year. Adjoining the greenhouses is a Japanese style garden with large plantings of azaleas and rhododendrons.

Daily 9:30-4:30; no admission charge; partial handicapped access; (216) 664-3103.

29   **Cleveland Cultural Gardens**   SH
Rockefeller Park

35 acres are devoted to 20 nationality gardens as well as a Shakespearean Garden. The gardens represent plants of Poland, Greece, Germany, Italy, Hungary, Israel, and other lands.

Daily, dawn-dusk.

30   **Cleveland Metro Parks Zoo**   G
Denison at West 25th

Greenhouses, an animal garden, and a perpetual garden calendar are part of this large zoo.

9-5 Mon-Sat; 9-7 Sun in summer; 9-5 rest of year; closed Jan 1 and Christmas; adults, under $3; 2-11 half; (216) 661-6500.

LAKEWOOD

31   Oldest Stone House   H
14710 Lake Ave.

An 1830 pioneer house has been restored along with a herb garden for culinary, scented, and dye plants. An old-fashioned flower garden has been planted alongside.

Daily, dawn-dusk; no admission charge; (216) 221-7343.

MENTOR

32   Holden Arboretum   ☆☆☆   A-HA-L-R-S-WF
9500 Sperry Rd.

This 2,200-acre woodland and field arboretum was established in 1932 and displays more than 5,000 species. There are wildflower gardens, a nut tree collection, and 200 kinds of ornamental fruit trees which flower in May. Special collections consist of maples, horse-chestnuts, conifers, magnolias, crab-apples, lilacs, hollies, rhododendrons, and azaleas. The rose garden is extensive. The Stebbins Gulch sub-station contains sub-arctic plants in its gorges. There is a library. A new Visitor Center has been built.

9-5 Tues-Sun; adults, under $3; 6-16 and over 65, half; handicapped access; (216) 946-4400.

STRONGSVILLE

33   Gardenview Horticultural Park   ☆☆   A-HA-R-W
16711 Pearl Rd. Rt. 42

Founded in 1949 by H.A. Rose on a barren, clay 16-acre area. It has been developed single-handedly into a beautifully landscaped garden. The gardens contains good collections of azaleas, flowering crab-apples, maples, hostas, and uncommon bulbs. There are annual and perennial gardens as well as fine areas of spring plantings and lily ponds, and rose gardens along with an arboretum. There is a library.

12-6 Sat, Sun; adults, under $3; children half; open all hours to members; March 1-Nov 1; handicapped access; (216) 238-6653.

BATH

34   Jonathan Hale Homestead and Western Reserve Village   H
Richfield exit from I-77

A restored village around an 1826 home displays a herb garden and an old-fashioned vegetable garden.

10-5 Tues-Sat;12-5 Sun, holidays, May 1-Oct 31; 10-2 Tues-Sat; 12-5 Sun, holidays Dec 1-31; closed Dec 24, 25; adults, under $3; 6-16, over 60 half; (216) 861-4573.

AURORA

35   Seaworld
3 mi. northwest on Rt. 43

This 80-acre marine life park has been beautifully landscaped with a number of special gardens of perennials and annuals.

Daily 9-7 May 22-Sept 7; adults, under $12; 3-11, over 60 three-quarters; (216) 562-8101.

STOW

36 Adell Durban Park and Arboretum WF
3300 Darrow St.

Self-guiding nature trails lead through this 36-acre arboretum. More than 200 trees and shrubs have been marked. There are numerous wildflowers.

Daily, dawn-dusk; (216) 688-8238.

AKRON

37 Stan Hywet Hall Foundation ☆☆☆ A-CH-HH-J-L-R-S
714 N. Portage Path

A 65 room Tudor Revival mansion was built in 1915 by Frank A. Seiberling. The 70-acre gardens contain an English walled garden, a rose garden, a Japanese garden, birch allee, rhododendron allee, English landscape garden, pools, terraces, statuary. Grand floral display in spring when 20,000 tulips, 50,000 daffodils, crab-apples, rhododendrons, azaleas, 3,500 irises, and 400 varieties of peonies bloom. Massed flower displays for other seasons are presented. There are fine flowering fruit trees, a test and demonstration gardens for roses, chrysanthemums, and vegetables. There are greenhouses.

10-4 Tues-Sat; 1-4 Sun; closed holidays first 2 weeks of Jan; adults, under $3; 6-12 half; for gardens only. Seasonal events; Shakespearean plays; partial handicapped access; (216) 836-5535.

ZOAR

38 Zoar Village State Memorial B
Rt. 212

Founded as a communal settlement in 1817, it was dissolved in 1898, but has been restored along with its gardens. The community garden is laid out in a geometrical pattern as a symbol of the New Jerusalem based on the Book of Revelations.

9:30-5 Wed-Sat; 12-5 Sun May 26-Sept 6; Sat, Sun only Sept 7-Oct 31; adults, under $3; 6-12 half; partial handicapped access; (216) 874-3211.

DOVER

39 Warther's
331 Karl Ave.

A museum devoted to the evolution of steam power with a Swiss style garden.

Daily 9-5; closed Jan 1, Thanksgiving, Christmas; adults, under $3; 6-17 half; partial handicapped access; (216) 343-7531.

NEWARK

40 Dawes Arboretum ☆☆ A-FE-J-S
7770 Jacksontown Rd.

325 developed acres make up this arboretum established in 1929. One area remains

as a virgin forest and has marked trails. 2,000 species are represented. There is a Japanese garden utilizing hardy plants, a children's garden, and a Bald-cypress swamp. Good collections of rhododendrons, azaleas; crab-apples, magnolias, American hollies, hawthorns, and ferns are found here. Fine specimens of White Pines, beeches, oaks, and maples stand in this arboretum. The small greenhouse contains tropical plants. The demonstration and test gardens specialize in woody ornamentals, annuals, and vegetables.

8:30-4:30 Mon-Fri; 12-5 Sat, Sun; closed Jan 1, Thanksgiving, Christmas; no admission charge; partial handicapped access; (614) 323-2355.

WARREN

41 Rose Garden R
Packard Park

A small formal rose garden is part of this municipal park. A garden of annuals and perennials lies nearby.

Daily, dawn-dusk.

YOUNGSTOWN

42 Fellows Riverside Gardens ☆ R
Mill Creek Park
816 Glenwood Ave.

15 acres of this large park are planted as formal gardens. The rose garden is especially good as are collections of iris, day-lily, and heath. There are fine plantings of annuals and perennials.

Daily 7:30-dark; no admission charge; (216) 744-4171.

OKLAHOMA

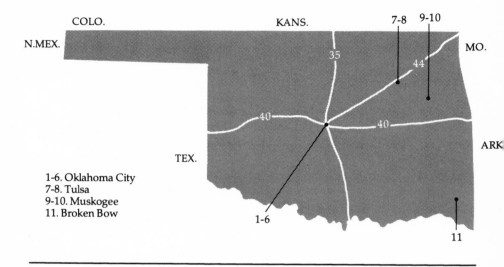

COLO.

KANS.

7-8   9-10

N.MEX.

35

MO.

44

40

40

ARK

TEX.

1-6. Oklahoma City
7-8. Tulsa
9-10. Muskogee
11. Broken Bow

1-6

11

OKLAHOMA CITY

1   Will Rogers Park and Horticultural Garden   ☆☆☆   A-C-G-HA-L-P-R-S-SU
3500 N.W. 36th St.

30 acres of gardens and arboreta with more than 1,000 kinds of plants. It contains a fine formal rose garden with 5,000 bushes representing 340 varieties, many of them old-fashioned roses. There is a large perennial garden with 68 varieties of peonies, 45 of cannas, 350 of irises. The arboretum features an azalea trail with hundreds of plants, 250 kinds of junipers, 17 varieties of redbuds, a native tree area, as well as fine collections of holly, crape myrtle, and hibiscus. The garden is beautifully landscaped. The conservatory displays tropical plants, succulents, and cacti. Test gardens are maintained. April to November are the best months.

Daily 7-sunset; no admission charge; handicapped access; (405) 943-3977.

2   Hambrick Botanical Gardens   ☆   RG
National Cowboy Hall of Fame and Western Heritage Center
1700 N.E. 63rd St.

This garden is part of the complex at the Cowboy Hall of Fame. A variety of hollies and other ornamentals are grown alongside numerous trees. There is a rock garden. 200 species are labelled.

Daily 8:30-6 May 30-Sept 6; 9:30-5:30 rest of year; closeed Jan 1, Thanksgiving, Christmas; adults, under $3; 6-12 half; (405) 478-5266.

3   Oklahoma City Zoo   BR-C-WF
2101 N. E. 50th St.

This medium-sized zoo has a special survival center for rare hoofed animals. The collections of native perennial wildflowers, cacti, and bromeliads add to the zoo's attractiveness.

9-6 Mon-Sat; 9-7 Sat, Sun, holidays; May 30-Sept 6; 9-5 rest of year; adults under $3; 3-11 nominal; (405) 424-3344.

4 1889'er Harn Museum and Gardens HH
313 N.E. 16th St.

These 10 acres commemorate the Oklahoma land rush of 1889. The Victorian style mansion is surrounded by the original garden with plantings of the period.

10-4 Tues-Sat; no admission charge; (405) 235-4058.

5 Robert A. Hefner Jr. Conservatory HH
Anthony Oklahoma Heritage Gardens
Oklahoma Heritage Center
201 N.W. 14th St.

The family mansion of Judge R.A. Hefner lies in a garden of fountains, statuary, trees, and flowering shrubs. The small conservatory contains sub-tropical plants.

9-5 Mon-Sat; 1-5 Sun and holidays; closed Jan 1, Thanksgiving, Christmas; adults, under $3; 2-12 half; (405) 235-4458.

6 Omniplex
2100 N.E. 52nd St.

A small greenhouse with tropical plants and a ½-acre outdoor garden of perennials and annuals has been recently installed.

Weekdays 9-5; no admission charge; (405) 424-5545.

TULSA

7 Philbrook Art Center ☆☆ L-T
2727 S. Rockford

A fine estate with 23 acres of formal gardens. The large Italian gardens are marked by terraced waterways, fountains, and some topiary. A small botanical gardens lies on the grounds. There are annual and perennial gardens as well as a test garden. There is a library.

10-5 Tues-Sat; 1-5 Sun; closed holidays; no admission charge to gardens; partial handicapped access; (918) 749-7941.

8 Municipal Rose Garden R

A well-laid-out rose garden with more than 1,000 bushes has been attractively landscaped. Many varieties are represented.

Daily, dawn-dusk.

MUSKOGEE

9 Honor Heights Park ☆ A-W
40th St. and Park Blvd.

Gardens and a lily pond are part of this prize-winning park which contains a collection of 35,000 azaleas of 625 varieties. Many of the bushes are more than 25 years old. An annual azalea festival is held for 3 weeks during April.

Daily 8-dusk; no admission charge; picnic area; (405) 682-6602.

10 Spring Garden Tour

A tour of local gardens is held each April; for information call (405) 682-2401.

BROKEN BOW

11 **Forest Heritage Center** HA
Beavers Bend State Park

This museum deals with the forest from ancient times to the present. There is a well-labelled nature trail of indigenous plants. The 7-sided museum is built around a courtyard of representative native trees and shrubs.

9-4:30 Tues-Sat, holidays; 1-4:30 Sun; March 1-Nov 30; closed Thanksgiving; adults, under $3; 6-15 nominal; handicapped access; (405) 494-6497.

OREGON

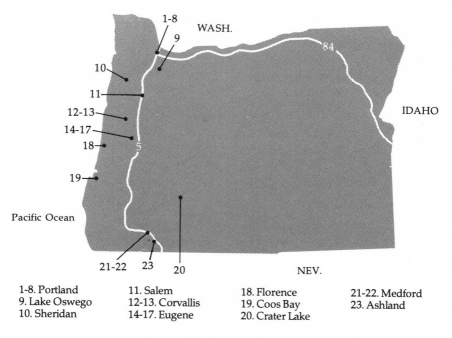

WASH.

1-8
9
84
10
11
IDAHO
12-13
14-17
18
5
19
Pacific Ocean

21-22   23   20   NEV.

1-8. Portland	11. Salem	18. Florence	21-22. Medford
9. Lake Oswego	12-13. Corvallis	19. Coos Bay	23. Ashland
10. Sheridan	14-17. Eugene	20. Crater Lake	

PORTLAND

1   Berry Garden   ☆   A-G-S
11505 S.W. Summerville Ave.

This 5-acre garden was begun in 1932 and became public in 1978. The founder, Mrs. A.C.U. Berry subscribed to major plant-hunting expeditions of 1930's in China and Tibet and so established a special collection of rare plants from the Pacific Rim, including 70 threatened species; there are 5 major plant collections including a fine lily collection, rhododendrons, primulas, and alpines. There is a greenhouse and a library.

March through Oct by appointment only; members have visiting privileges; (503) 636-4112.

2   Hoyt Arboretum   ☆☆   HA-L-S
4000 S.W. Fairview Blvd (Washington Park)

This garden of 214 acres contain one of the largest collections of gymnosperms in the United States; it is located on a rugged hillside above the city. More than 650 species of trees including California Nutmeg, Western Yew, Sitka Yew, and Sitka Spruce are planted here. Some plants are labelled. There is a library.

Daily, sunrise-sunset; guided tours Sat-Sun 2:30, April 1-Oct 31; Wed 6:30 May 1-Sept 30; no admission charge; handicapped access; (503) 228-8732.

3   Crystal Springs Rhododendron Garden   ☆☆   A-S-RG
28th Ave. S.E. near Woodstock/bordering Eastmoreland Golf Course near Crystal Springs Lake

Founded in 1950, this 6-acre garden is planted on an island and a peninsula; it contains 2,500 azaleas and rhododendrons, representing 600 species and making this one of the finest collections in the world. They are planted in beautiful woodland and lakeside settings. Smaller species and hybrids planted in rock gardens. Some R. Cynthia more than 25 feet in height, also Douglas Firs, Dawn Redwoods, Franklinias, oaks, maples, magnolias, dove trees, dogwoods, and flowering cherries. Best seen in April and May.

Daily 8-dark; no admission charge except Mother's Day under $3; partial handicapped access.

4   **Leach Botanical Garden**   WF-

6704 S.E. 122nd St.

This 5-acre garden is developing a collection of Pacific Northwest native plants; the founders, John and Lilla Leach, spent two decades searching for such plants. Spring and fall are the best times for visiting.

Daily, dawn-dusk, garden only; house 10-2 Tues-Sat; (503) 761-9503.

5   **International Rose Test Garden**   ☆☆☆   A-CA-HA-L-R
400 S.W. Kingston St.

In this beautifully landscaped 4-acre garden, we find more than 10,000 roses representing 520 varieties; well labelled. There are also large plantings of azaleas, rhododendrons, camellias, and tulips. Special collections of All-American Rose Selections; Portland award winning roses since 1919. Roses bloom late May to autumn; best time, June.

Daily 6-noon; no admission charge; handicapped access. (503) 227-1911.

6   **Japanese Gardens**   ☆☆☆☆   BO-HA-J-L
Kingston Ave to Washington Park
(above Rose Test Garden)

Among the very finest Japanese Gardens in the United States; 5 traditional gardens and a pavilion capture the mood of ancient Japan. Designed by Prof. P. Takuma in 1962; many plants imported from Japan provide additional authenticity. Includes Flat Garden (Hiraniwa), Strolling Pond Garden (Chisen-Kaiyu-Shiki), Tea Garden (Rojiniwa), Natural Garden (Shukeiyen), Sand and Stone Garden (Seki-tei). Gardens provide a fine view of Portland and Mt. Hood. Annual bonsai display.

10-6 May 15-Sept 15; 10-4 rest of year; adults, under $3; children 6-11, senior citizens half; handicapped access; (503) 223-1321

7   **Sunken Rose Garden**   ☆☆☆   HA-R
N. Ainsworth and N. Albina Streets in Peninsula Park

Large formal beds of roses form one of the finest rose gardens in the United States with 15,000 roses representing 700 varieties. Bloom from May to autumn.

Daily; no admission charge; handicapped access.

8   **The Sanctuary of Our Sorrowful Mother**   ☆   FE-HA-L-R
N.E. Sandy Blvd. at 85th St.

This garden was built by the Servite order; monastery and garden are located at the top of a cliff. The grotto in ten story cliff serves as outdoor cathedral. Rose garden, ferns, flower beds.

9-6 May 1-Sept 30; 10-4:30 Mon-Fri; 9-5 Sat-Sun, rest of year; elevator fee, nominal; handicapped access; (503) 254-7371.

Japanese Gardens

LAKE OSWEGO

9 Bishops Close
11800 Military Lane

A 13-acre garden surrounds the Manor House of the old Peter Kerr estate. It was designed by Olmsted. There are fine magnolias, native trees, rhododendrons, and azaleas.

Weekdays 10-4; some weekend hours; no admission charge; (503) 636-5613.

SHERIDAN

10 Western Deer Park and Arboretum
#18 northwest of Salem; near   22;
half way between Portland and the coast

This park contains 80 different species of native trees in addition to a private collection of birds and animals.

May 1-Oct 31; adults, under $3; Sr. citizens, children half; (503) 843-2152.

SALEM

11 Bush Pasture Park   A-R
600 Mission St.

This is an 80-acre city park planted with varieties of rare trees and shrubs; there are

also many azaleas, rhododendrons, peonies, roses, flowering cherries, and crab-
apples.

Daily; no admission charge; picnic area.

CORVALLIS

12 Peavy Arboretum ☆ HA-S
5 miles north of Corvallis Rt. 99W

This 80-acre arboretum is part of Oregon State University School of Forestry which
also manages 11,000 acres of forests nearby. There are several hundred species of
native trees and shrubs as well as woody plants from other parts of world which have
been planted since its establishment in 1925. A Tree Museum lies on the grounds.
Maps, a plant list, and a self-guiding brochure are available. Many trees labelled.

Daily 8-sunset; no admission charge; handicapped access; picnic area.

13 Corvalis Rose Garden R
Avery Park
2245 N.W. 11th St.

This rose garden presents many varieties of roses among its hundreds of bushes.

Daily, dawn-dusk.

EUGENE

14 Greer Gardens ☆ A-HA
1280 Goodpasture Island Rd., off Delta Highway

This is an azalea and rhododendron display garden and nursery; it maintains one of
the largest collections of rhododendrons in the United States in a natural setting.
More than 4,000 hybrids have been developed here, among them R. 'Trude
Webster'; dwarf conifers and Japanese Maples may also be seen here.

9-5:30 Mon-Sat; 11-5:30 Sun, April and May; no admission charge; handicapped
access; (503) 686-8266.

15 Mount Pisgah Arboretum H-WF
Mount Pisgah Rd.

This 118-acre arboretum established in 1973 emphasizes native trees; there is a good
collection of herbs. An annual wildflower show is provided in late spring. There is a
library.

Daily, sunrise-sunset, no admission charge; (503) 747-3817.

16 Hendricks Park Rhododendron Garden ☆☆ A
Skyline Blvd.

This 20-acre garden is part of a larger park, which is the oldest in the city. There are
more than 6,000 rhododendrons and azaleas; many rare hybrids are represented.
Some 300-year-old specimen trees stand in the park. An annual rhododendron
show is held.

Daily 6-dusk; no admission charge; (503) 687-5334.

17 Owens Rose Garden ☆☆ R
North Jefferson Ave at the river

This 5-acre rose garden has been charmingly designed along the river. There are

2,900 bushes representing 160 varities of modern roses. 100 old-fashioned varieties and wild species, 50 miniature varieties, as well as single roses. New bushes are added each year. An old Tartar Black Cherry remains from a riverfront orchard established in 1847.

Daily 6-dusk; no admission charge; (503) 687-5333.

FLORENCE

18 **Darlingtonia Botanical Wayside**
84505 U.S. 101 S. 5 mi. north of city

This park contains unique plantings of the Darlingtonia, a carnivorous plant.

Daily, dawn-dusk; no admission charge.

COOS BAY

19 **Simpson Gardens** ☆ A-BX-R-S-W
Shore Acres State Park
Cape Arago Hwy.

13 mi southwest of city

A formal garden originally built by the lumber tycoon, L.J. Simpson has been restored. There is a rose garden with 30 types of roses, a boxwood hedged garden of perennials and annuals include hydrangeas and dahlias, and a lily pond. A Japanese garden lies nearby. A wooded area of Sitka Spruce, Wax Myrtle, and rhododendron stands on the cliffs.

Daily 8-dusk; no admission charge; weekends, holidays, under $3 per car; (503) 888-4902.

CRATER LAKE

20 **Castle Crest Wildflower Garden** WF
¼ mile from Park Headquarters

There are fine displays of wildflowers during short summer season which are spectacular from July 1 to early August; they include Lewis Monkey Flowers, Anderson's Lupine, Skyrocket Gilia and Elephant Head. 570 species of plants are found in park.

Daily; per car, under $3; Rim Village Visitor Center open summer and autumn; guided tours; (503) 594-2211.

MEDFORD

21 **Claire Hanley Arboretum** H-HD-J-RG
Southern Oregon Experiment Station
Oregon State University
569 Hanley Rd.

This arboretum was established to display plants which could be of landscape value for southern Oregon. New plants are tested. There is a miniature Japanese Rock garden, a herb garden and a lawn test area.

Weekdays 10-4; some weekend hours; no admission charge; (503) 772-5165.

22 Jackson and Perkins Co. R
1 mi. south on Rt. 99

This large rose grower maintains a test and display garden here for All-American Rose Selections. Their growing area is near Bakersfield, California. Flowers are in bloom from mid-May to mid-October.

9-5:30 Mon-Sat; 12-5 Sun; no admission charge; (503) 776-2277.

ASHLAND

23 Lithia Park H-J-R

This park contains a herb garden, a small Japanese garden and a rose garden as well as a sycamore grove.

Daily 8-dusk.

PENNSYLVANIA

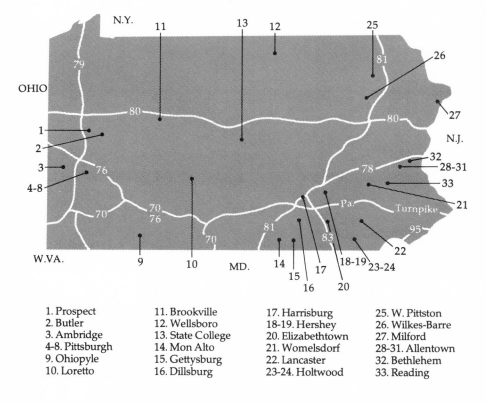

1. Prospect	11. Brookville	17. Harrisburg	25. W. Pittston
2. Butler	12. Wellsboro	18-19. Hershey	26. Wilkes-Barre
3. Ambridge	13. State College	20. Elizabethtown	27. Milford
4-8. Pittsburgh	14. Mon Alto	21. Womelsdorf	28-31. Allentown
9. Ohiopyle	15. Gettysburg	22. Lancaster	32. Bethlehem
10. Loretto	16. Dillsburg	23-24. Holtwood	33. Reading

PROSPECT

1 Agway Inc Vegetable Seed Farm
Monroe St.

The vegetable and flower trial gardens of this 60-acre commercial seed producer may be visited. Mid-summer is the best time for viewing this seed farm.

8-4 weekdays; no admission charge; (412) 865-2096.

BUTLER

2 Jenning Blazing Star Nature Reserve   WF
U.S. 8, 12 mi. north of Butler

A 20-acre site with great areas of the prairie flower, the Blazing Star, may be seen in the midst of this 280-acre reserve. Several hundred species of native wildflowers, grasses, and shrubs are grown.

Daily 10-sunset; closed Mon; no admission charge; call for information on height of blooming of Blazing Star; (412) 794-7503.

AMBRIDGE

3 Old Economy ☆ H
14th and Church Sts.

The German Harmony Society established a settlement here in 1824; it was maintained until 1905. 18 original structures and the gardens remain; they have been restored. There are vegetable and herb gardens as well as flower gardens with reflecting pools, pavilions and grottos. Most plants are those of the early 19th century.

9-5 Tues-Sat; 12-5 Sun, late April to late Oct; 10-4:30 Tues-Sat; 12-4:30 Sun, rest of year; closed holidays, election days; 12-64, under $3; (412) 266-4500.

PITTSBURGH

4 Phipps Conservatory ☆☆☆ BO-BR-C-CH-FE-G-H-HA-J-O-R-SU-W
Schenley Park

Founded in 1893 and so among the older American conservatories, this series of 13 showhouses has 2½ acres under glass. There is an Oriental garden, a cacti and succulent display, a formal garden, a palm court, a fern and orchid section, and an economic garden. Good collections of orchids, bromeliads, ferns and cacti are maintained. 3 annual seasonal flower shows follow special themes each year and are among the best in the country. Hundreds of varieties of chrysanthemums are displayed in fall. Outside the conservatory there are lily ponds, a herb garden, a rose garden, and a garden of perennials and annuals. The trees nearby form a small arboretum; they are labelled. Portions of the conservatory will be reconstructed over a number of summers and may be closed for several months each year. The *Hunt Institute for Botanical Documentation,* which contains a large collection of rare books and has continuous botanical exhibits, is nearby, as is the Biblical Botanical Garden of the *Rodef Shalom Congregation* which will open in the summer 1986.

Daily 9-5; during flower shows also 7-9; adults, under $3; under 12 nominal; handicapped access; guided tours; (412) 255-2376; Hunt Institute, 8:30-5 Mon-Fri; closed holidays; (412) 578-2434. Rodef Shalom (412) 621-6566.

5 Pittsburgh Plate Glass Building ☆ G-HA-P
Market Square

This stunning complex of glass Gothic towers contains a large atrium winter garden with palms, bamboos, semi-tropical plants, and seasonal annuals.

Daily 9-5; no admission charge; (412) 434-3131.

6 Pittsburgh Civic Garden Center H-HD
Mellon Park
1059 Shady Ave.

This garden center maintains a series of small demonstration gardens and a miniature herb garden. There is a library.

9-4 Mon-Fri; no admission charge; (412) 441-4442.

7 Hartwood Acres HH-R-RG
215 Saxonburg Blvd.

This former estate and its grounds of 629 acres have been turned into a cultural center extensively used for concerts and theater during the summer. There is a rose garden, a formal vegetable and cutting garden, a rock garden, and an oak forest. Maintenance has diminished during the last years.

Daily 9-5; no admission charge; (412) 767-9200.

8   **Racoon Creek Wildflower Reserve**   WF
U.S. 30, 25 mi. west of Pittsburgh

Good displays of western Pennsylvania wildflowers are part of the this Western Pennsylvania Conservancy reserve. It is best visited in spring.

Daily 10-6; no admission charge; (412) 391-4100 ext. 1539.

OHIOPYLE

9   **Bear Run Nature Reserve**   A-S-WF
Rt. 381, 3½ mi. northeast

This reservation is best known for Fallingwater, a home designed by Frank Lloyd Wright. The home is surrounded by stands of rhododendrons and azaleas. The reservation contains numerous species of wildflowers and good specimens of hickory, sour gum, oak, and hornbeam. It is part of the Western Pennsylvania Conservancy.

Daily 10-4; Fallingwater 10-4 Tues-Sun April 1-mid Nov; reservations necessary; adults, under $3; no children admitted; (412) 239-8501.

LORETTO

10   **Schwab Estate**   ☆☆   HA-L-S
Franciscian Monastery
Mt. Assissi

A grand former estate garden is part of a larger park with old specimen trees. This is the best formal garden in Western Pennsylvania with its water cascades, lily ponds, and large fountain. The 3-acre garden is partially enclosed by stone trellissed walkways covered with wisterias, roses, and other climbing plants. An old weeping beech, a variety of conifers, flowering shrubs, perennials and annuals have been beautifully planted.

Daily, dawn-dusk; no admission charge; handicapped access; small parking area immediately on left after entering grounds leads to garden path; (814) 472-7870.

BROOKVILLE

11   **Western Pennsylvania Laurel Festival**

An annual laurel festival is held here during the 2nd or 3rd week of June.

For information call (814) 849-3477.

WELLSBORO

12   **Pennsylvania State Laurel Festival**

An annual laurel festival is held here during the 2nd week of June.

For information call (717) 724-2352.

STATE COLLEGE

13 College of Agriculture
Pennsylvania State University

The college maintains a large agricultural research center which includes vegetable and flower gardens.

Daily 9-5; closed in winter; no admission charge; (814) 865-7517.

MON ALTO

14 Mon Alto Arboretum   HA
Mon Alto Campus
Pennsylvania State University

This arboretum was established in 1903 on 10 acres; it specializes in trees of the north temperate zone. Some oaks are more than 300 years old. There are collections of native and Asian trees along with demonstration and test gardens.

Daily, dawn-dusk; no admission charge; handicapped access; (717) 749-3111.

GETTYSBURG

15 Apple Blossom Festival

This festival is held throughout Adams County annually, usually during the first weekend of May. More than 20,000 acres of fruit trees are in bloom.

For information call (717) 334-8151.

DILLSBURG

16 The Coover Arboretum   BX
Rt. 3

A 10-acre arboretum established in 1948. It maintains collections of boxwood, holly, magnolia, conifer, and dwarf conifer.

By appointment only; no admission charge; partial handicapped access; (717) 766-6681.

HARRISBURG

17 Governor's Mansion Gardens   HA-R
2035 N. Front St.

This Georgian style mansion stands in a recently renovated garden. It is planted in keeping with the style of the mansion with flowering shrubs, perennials, and annuals. There is a rose garden.

10-2 Tues and Thurs; no admission charge; handicapped access; (717) 787-1192.

HERSHEY

18 Hershey Rose Garden and Arboretum   ☆☆☆   CH-HA-J-L-R-RG-S
Hotel Rd.

Established in 1936, this 23-acre garden continues to develop and expand its planted area. There are 6 gardens including a Japanese garden, a rose garden, an old-fashioned rose garden, a rock garden, an English formal garden, an Italian garden, an annual garden and a grass collection, along with other special areas. The 42,000 rose bushes represent 1,200 varieties; in autumn more than 14,000 chrysanthemums representing 175 cultivars. The collection consists of 100 varieties of hollies, 500 of tulips, 150 of daffodils, 40 of hyacinths, 200 of day-lilies, 200 species and cultivars of annuals. There are large plantings of dogwood, magnolia, spirea, False Cypress, viburnum, juniper, and cedar. The pinetum and evergreen collections are good.

Daily 9-7, June 1-Aug 31; 9-5 April 11-May 31, Sept 1-Oct 31; adults, under $3; 5-18 half; handicapped access; (717) 534-3060.

19 ZooAmerica at Hershey Park
300 Park Blvd.

The zoo is part of a larger theme park. The zoo maintains a collection of native animals and plants which represent 5 areas of North America.

Daily, 10-closing hours vary, mid-May-Labor Day; theme park, adults and children, under $15; over 62 half; under 4 free; (717) 534-3916.

ELIZABETHTOWN

20 Masonic Homes Arboretum   HA

A formal Renaissance garden has been created on 6 acres since 1920. Emphasis has been placed on a green garden with collections of hollies, oaks, evergreens, and weeping evergreens.

Daily, dawn-dusk; no admission charge; handicapped access; (717) 367-1121.

WOMELSDORF

21 Farr Nursery
Conrad Weiser Park
U.S. 422, ½ mi. east

128 acres are devoted to plant displays of perennials and annuals as well as ornamentals. There is a Garden Center and a Christmas cottage.

Daily 9-6 April 1-June 30, Sept 1-Nov 16; Mon-Sat 9-6 July 1-Aug 31; Mon-Fri 8-5 Jan 1-March 31; 9-9 rest of year; no admission charge; (215) 589-2934.

LANCASTER

22 Dutch Wonderland
U.S. 30, 4 mi. east

This theme park with numerous rides contains large plantings of evergreens and trees, as well as special gardens of perennials and annuals.

Daily 10-7, Memorial Day-Labor Day; Sat-Sun 11-6, Easter-Memorial Day, Labor Day-Oct 31; adults and children, under $6; under 4 free; (717) 291-1888.

HOLTWOOD

23 Holtwood Arboretum
Holtwood Rd. off Rt 372

A small arboretum stands on the Lake Alfred (Susquehanna River) preserve of the

Pennsylvania Power and Light Company. 43 native species of trees are marked; there is a guide book.

Daily, dawn-dusk; no admission charge; picnic facilities; (717) 284-2278.

24 Shenks Ferry Glen Wildflower Preserve WF
Shenks Ferry Rd. off Rt. 324

A wide variety of spring wildflowers may be seen in late April and May.

Daily, dawn-dusk; no admission charge; picnic facilities; (717) 284-2278.

WEST PITTSTON

25 Cherry Blossom Festival
River Common

An annual cherry blossom festival is held early in May.

For information call (717) 655-3470.

WILKES—BARRE

26 Cherry Blossom Time
River Common

An annual cherry blossom festival is held here for 1 week at the end of April.

For information call (717) 823-2101.

MILFORD

27 Pinchot Institute for Conservation Studies BX-S
Grey Towers
U.S. 6, exit 10 I-84

The father of American conservation, Gifford Pinchot, twice governor of Pennsylvania and first chief of the Forest Service, built this French style chateau in 1886. The site is a National Historic Landmark and contains a formal garden and patio area, largely planted with evergreens, a boxwood hedge and specimen trees. Trails lead through the 100-acre preserve; there is a trail guide.

1-4 Mon-Fri, winter; 10-4 summer; no admission charge; tours through the house; (717) 296-6401.

ALLENTOWN

28 Trexler Park ☆ CH-G-O
Cedar Crest and Parkway Blvds.

Aside from plantings of perennials and annuals, this 142-acre park contains greenhouses with tropical and sub-tropical plants. A chrysanthemum show is held in mid-November and an orchid show in January.

Daily 10-4; no admission charge; (215) 437-7628.

29 Cedar Creek Parkway R-W
19th and Linden Sts.

An old-fashioned rose garden along with lagoons filled with water lilies stands in this 124-acre park. There is a dogwood arboretum and a Memorial Arboretum.

Daily, dawn-dusk; no admission charge; (215) 437-7628.

30 **West Park** ☆ S
Fulton and 16th Sts.

An 8-acre park contains a miniature arboretum with hundreds of exotic trees and shrubs. Most are marked and a guide book is available. There is a tulip show in spring followed by annuals in summer and fall.

Daily, dawn-dusk; no admission charge; (215) 437-7628.

31 **Malcolm W. Gross Memorial Garden** R
16th and Linden Sts.

A small rose garden has been planted.

BETHLEHEM

32 **Rose Garden** R
8th St. and West Union Blvd.

A small rose garden stands in this historic district.

Daily, dawn-dusk; no admission charge; (215) 868-1513.

READING

33 **Reading Public Museum and Art Gallery** HA-WF
500 Museum Rd.

This 25-acre botanical garden, established in 1904, lies along the edge of a stream. There is a Sculpture garden, a Friendship garden, and a garden of perennials and annuals. Special collections include exotic trees as well as Pennsylvania wildflowers.

Weekdays 9-5; Sat 9-12; Sun 2-5; no admission charge; handicapped access; (215) 371-5850.

METROPOLITAN PHILADELPHIA

DOYLESTOWN

34 **Delaware Valley College** A-G-H-O-S
Rt. 202 and New Britain Rd.

This 725-acre preserve with its 45-acre main campus contains a number of gardens. There is a woodland garden with azaleas and rhododendrons, a hedge demonstration garden, a herb garden, an arboretum, and a dwarf conifer collection with more than 100 species. Many mature specimen tree may be found here including 200-year-old Sassafras, a 300-year-old American Sycamore, as well as oaks. The Kerr orchid collection is displayed in the greenhouses. A commercial crop production area is used for student projects.

Daily, dawn-dusk; no admission charge; (215) 345-1500.

WARMINSTER

35 **Burpee Seed Display Gardens**

A display garden will be opened here by this well known seed company. The garden is scheduled to open in the summer of 1985.

For information call (215) 674-4900.

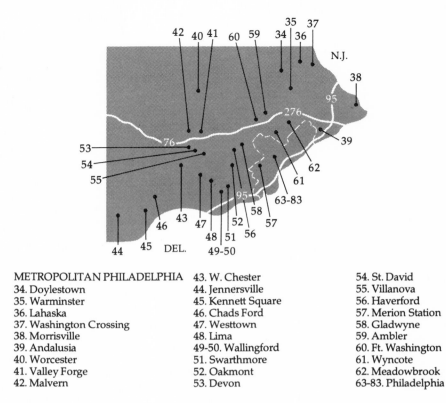

METROPOLITAN PHILADELPHIA
34. Doylestown
35. Warminster
36. Lahaska
37. Washington Crossing
38. Morrisville
39. Andalusia
40. Worcester
41. Valley Forge
42. Malvern

43. W. Chester
44. Jennersville
45. Kennett Square
46. Chads Ford
47. Westtown
48. Lima
49-50. Wallingford
51. Swarthmore
52. Oakmont
53. Devon

54. St. David
55. Villanova
56. Haverford
57. Merion Station
58. Gladwyne
59. Ambler
60. Ft. Washington
61. Wyncote
62. Meadowbrook
63-83. Philadelphia

LAHASKA

36 Peddler's Village
Rts 202 and 263

This outdoor shopping center has a garden; 25,000 bulbs bloom in spring; flowering shrubs, perennials, and annuals have been planted.

Daily 8-5; (215) 345-4552.

WASHINGTON CROSSING

37 Bowman's Hill Wildflower Preserve ☆ A-FE-S-W
Washington Crossing Historic State Park
Off Rt. 32

Established in 1934, this 100-acre nature preserve displays more than 1,000 different kinds of trees, shrubs, and wildflowers native to Pennsylvania. Trails lead through special collections; among them are the violet, gentian, marshmarigold, azalea, bluebell, fern, and medicinal plant walks. There is a lily pond and a bog. Among the specimen trees is a Canadian Hemlock more than 240 years old. Many flowers are in bloom during the summer; the height of the season is mid-April to June.

9-5 Mon-Sat; 12-5 Sun late April to late Oct; 10-4:30 Mon-Sat; 12-5 Sun; no admission charge; (215) 862-2924.

MORRISVILLE

38 Pennsbury Manor F-HA-HH
Bordentown Rd., exit 29 off Turnpike

William Penn's country home built in 1683 has been reconstructed along with 23 other buildings and the gardens. There is a formal parterre garden, a kitchen garden, orchards, a vineyard, and agricultural displays. 17th and 18th century plant material has been used to a large extent.

9-5 Tues-Sat; 12-5 Sun late April to late Oct; 10-4:30 Tues-Sat; 12-4:30 Sun rest of year; closed Mon, holidays; adults, under $3; handicapped access; (215) 946-0400.

ANDALUSIA

39   Andalusia   ☆☆   HA-L-R-T
State Rd. near Station Ave.

This estate on the Delaware River contains a fine 19th century Greek Revival home designed by Benjamin H. Latrobe; a rose garden, a perennial garden, a maze, and a collection of ornamental dwarf evergreens surround it. There are beautiful views of the river.

By appointment only for groups of 4 or more; four people $15; handicapped access; (215) 848-1777.

WORCESTER

40   Peter Wentz Farmstead   H-HH-Schultz and Shearer Rds.
Rt. 363, King of Prussia Exit from Turnpike

This farm established in the 1750's has a traditional Pennsylvania German garden. The raised beds contain 18th century perennial flowers, herbs, and vegetables.

10-4 Tues-Sat; 1-4 Sun; no admission charge; (215) 584-5104.

VALLEY FORGE

41   Valley Forge National Historical Park   ☆   A-S
Exit 24 off Turnpike

This 2,500-acre historic park contains one of the best stands of dogwood in the country with more than 50,000 trees in bloom during late April and early May. Rhododendron, azalea, and mountain laurel are grown.

Daily 8:30-5; closed Christmas; no admission charge; (215) 783-7700.

MALVERN

42   Swiss Pines   ☆☆☆☆   A-H-J-L-S
Charlestown Rd. off Rt. 29

The main feature of this 19-acre series of gardens is a large Japanese garden created since 1957 by Arnold Bartschi and several Japanese landscape architects, including Hiroshi Makita since 1970. There is a tea-house garden, a bamboo grove, a stone garden, more than 100 lanterns, streams, waterfalls, a pond, and a spectacular display of azaleas in May. Old Swiss Pines and other specimen trees and bushes are scattered through the gardens. There is also a rhododendron and azalea garden, a heather garden, a herb garden with 62 culinary and 52 aromatic herbs, and a pinetum.

Mon-Fri 10-4; Sat 9-12; closed Dec 15-March 15 and holidays; no admission charge; (215) 933-6916.

WEST CHESTER

43 David Townsend House
225 N. Matlack St.

David Townsend, a botanist, surrounded this house with a late 19th century garden.
Many of his original plantings remain.

By appointment only; (215) 431-6365.

JENNERSVILLE

44 Star Rose Gardens R
U.S. 1 and Rt. 796

A rose garden which displays a wide variety of roses; several thousand bushes
bloom throughout the summer months. This formerly was a rose production area.

Daily, dawn-dusk; (215) 869-2426.

KENNETT SQUARE

45 Longwood Gardens ☆☆☆☆ A-BR-BO-C-CH-FE-G-H-HA-HD-J-L-O-P-R-RG -
S-SU-T-W-WF
U.S. 1 at Rt. 52

This is one of the greatest gardens in North America with more than 12,000 species
of plants on 700 acres. The gardens were begun by Pierre S. du Pont in 1906 and
included an arboretum established in 1800 by Joshua and George Peirce. There are
grand fountain displays in the main fountain garden with fine stone work and the
Italian water garden of 5 acres. Beautiful vistas are found everywhere. The gardens
include a topiary garden, a maze, a dwarf conifer garden, a rose garden, a rock
garden, a heather garden, a herb garden, a vegetable garden, a wildflower garden, an
annual garden, a lily pond, in addition to example gardens. There are excellent
collections of dozens of species of trees, shrubs, and flowers.

The arboretum contains outstanding specimens of numerous trees including
ginkgo, Bald-Cypress, Kentucky Coffee, paulownia, California Incense-Cedars,
larch, magnolia, and others. The conservatories housed in 16 display greenhouses
which extend over 4 acres, display collections of palms, ferns, orchids, cycads,
bromeliads, camellias, acacias, nepenthes, an azalea house with a lawn and pools,
cacti, succulents, and vines. There are seasonal flower displays. An extensive
educational program is maintained; concerts, ballets, plays are presented during the
summer months. There is a school of horticulture and a library.

Daily 9-6; 9-5 Nov-March; conservatories 10-4; adults, under $6; 6-14 half;
handicapped access; (215) 388-6741.

CHADS FORD

46 Brandywine Conservancy Museum HA-L-WF
U.S. 1 at Rt. 100

An art museum housed in a restored grist mill is surrounded by a wildflower garden.
Nature trails overlook the river.

Daily, dawn-dusk; museum 9:30-4:30 except Christmas; no admission charge for
garden; handicapped access; (215) 459-1900.

WESTTOWN

47 **Westtown School Arboretum** S
Westtown Rd.

The 12-acre grounds of this Quaker school contains 400 trees including 43 species of pines, 32 of firs, and 27 of spruces. There are some excellent old specimens including a Mexican White Pine, an Umbrella Pine, a ginkgo, a Lobb's Temple Cedar, a Copper Beech and others. Many trees are labelled; the collection is currently being rebuilt.

By appointment only; no admission charge; (215) 339-3915.

LIMA

48 **John J. Tyler Arboretum** ☆☆☆ .-A-S
515 Painter Rd. off Rt. 352

Founded in 1830, this 700-acre preserve adjoins a large state park. It contains more than 4,000 different kinds of plants. There are extensive collections of rhododendrons, azaleas, dogwoods, dwarf conifers, cherries, crab-apples, magnolias, lilacs, hollies, and shade trees, along with a 25 acre pinetum. A fragrance garden for the blind is maintained. Specimen trees planted in the 1850's include Giant Sequoia, ginkgo, Cedar of Lebanon, and Parry Pinyon Pine. Many trees are labelled; 20 miles of trails run through the grounds. There are demonstration and test gardens and a library.

Daily 8-dusk; library Sun 2-5, April-July, Sept-Oct; no admission charge; (215) 566-5431.

WALLINGFORD

49 **Taylor Memorial Arboretum** ☆ A-BX-HA
10 Ridley Drive

This 35-acre arboretum was founded in 1931 and contains more than 1,500 species and cultivars. There are good collections of azalea, cotoneaster, magnolia, holly, and boxwood.

Daily, dawn-dusk; no admission charge; handicapped access; (215) 874-5700.

50 **Wallingford Rose Gardens** ☆ A-G-R-S
Brookhaven Rd.

These 4 acres are planted with rhododendrons, azaleas, hollies, and roses. The special collections include holly, 80 varieties of climbing roses, tea roses. The roses are at their best in June. Specimen trees include Dawn Redwood, Dove Tree, katsura trees, and cedars. There is a greenhouse.

By appointment only; no admission charge; handicapped access; (215) 566-2110.

SWARTHMORE

51 **Arthur Hoyt Scott Horticultural Foundation** ☆☆ A-L-RG-S
Swarthmore College
Rt. 320; Chester Rd.

The 350-acre campus of this college forms an arboretum with more than 5,000 species. Among them are 2,000 varieties of rhododendrons, 600 of daffodils, 300 of azaleas, 200 of hollies, as well as large collections of flowering cherries, crab-apples, magnolias, tree peonies, lilacs, and conifers. The spring display of blooms is spectacular. There is a rock garden, a woodland garden as well as a contemporary courtyard garden, and a library. The American Association of Botanical Gardens and Arboreta maintains its headquarters here.

Daily, dawn-dusk; no admission charge; (215) 447-7025.

OAKMONT

52 The Grange Estate
Near jnct. Darby and Manoa Rds.

An English Gothic style mansion built in the 19th century is surrounded by terraced gardens and a woodland.

By appointment only; (215) 446-4958.

DEVON

53 Jenkins Arboretum   A-WF
631 Berwyn Rd.

Established in 1974, this 46-acre preserve contains good collections of azaleas, rhododendrons, 100 varieties of day-lilies, and 250 marked species of wildflowers. There are shrub demonstration gardens, test gardens for day-lilies, and woody ornamentals. Best visited in May and June. There is a library.

Daily 8-dusk; no admission charge; partial handicapped access; (215) 647-8870.

ST. DAVID

54 Chanticleer   ☆☆   L-WF

This 30-acre private estate with 2 homes has been developed by a single family for 70 years. There is a French style formal garden and a more recent pleasure garden as well as a vegetable garden, a stream, pond, and wooded area with wildflowers.

By appointment only for groups of 20 or less; no admission charge; (215) 688-5020.

VILLANOVA

55 Parsons—Banks Arboretum   ☆☆   A-BX-FE-R-WF
Appleford
770 Mnt. Moro Rd.

A 22-acre site is divided into 2 distinct areas; small formal gardens designed by Sears in 1920 lead into each other. They feature roses, lantanas, wisterias, fruit trees, hedges, and perennials. The informal section contains large plantings of rhododendrons, ferns, and wildflowers.

Daily, dawn-dusk; no admission charge; (215) 525-9430.

HAVERFORD

56 Campus Arboretum   ☆   A-HA
Lancaster Ave. at College Lane
Haverford College

The original design which Carvill established in 1835 along the lines of Repton has largely disappeared in this expanded 216-acre arboretum with 400 species of trees and shrubs. There are good collections of rhododendrons, azaleas, ornamental fruit trees, pines, and native trees. There is a library.

Daily, dawn-dusk; no admission charge; handicapped access; (215) 896-1101.

MERION STATION

57 Arboretum of the Barnes Foundation ☆☆ R-S-WF
300 Latches Lane

2,500 species of plants are found on these 12 acres with the oldest trees planted in the 1880's. Many small gardens display roses, shrubs, alpines, perennials, and annuals along with a woodland area. Special collections include magnolias, viburnums, cotoneasters, peonies and dwarf conifers. There are fine specimens of cedar, ginkgo, magnolia, oak, holly, pine, and others. The school of horticulture was founded in 1922. There is a library and an excellent art museum.

9:30-4 Mon-Thurs (visitors must register); 9:30-4 Fri, Sat; 1:30-4 Sun with passes for which a reservation is required; no admission charge; (215) 664-8880.

GLADWYNE

58 The Henry Foundation for Botanical Research ☆ A-S-WF
801 Stony Lane

This foundation is dedicated to the preservation of American plants. A task Mary C. Henry began through her research in the 1920's. 40 acres are maintained in their natural form without paths. Among the hundreds of species of trees, shrubs, and flowers found here are many rare and endangered species as well as varieties of rhododendron, magnolia, holly, and others.

10-4 Tues and Thurs April-Oct; also by appointment; guides available; no admission charge; (215) 525-2037.

AMBLER

59 Ambler Campus ☆ BX-F-G-S
Temple University

The entire 180-acre campus is an arboretum and outdoor laboratory for the school of horticulture and landscape design. There are more than 800 varieties of woody plants and dwarf shrubs, 3-acre orchards of peach, apple, and small fruit trees, and a collection of dwarf conifers. 10 acres of formal gardens contain boxwood, an allee of Japanese cherries, herbaceous borders of perennials and annuals. The greenhouses feature tropicals and seasonal flowers. There are test and demonstration gardens and a large library.

Daily, dawn-dusk; produce gardens and greenhouses 8:30-4:30 Mon-Fri; closed holidays; no admission charge; (215) 643-1200.

FORT WASHINGTON

60 The Highlands H-HH-S
7001 Sheaf Lane

This 18th century country estate and its English walled garden have been partially restored. There is a herb garden. Some old specimen oaks.

Daily, dawn-dusk; house 9-5 Mon-Fri, May-Oct; no admission charge; partial handicapped access; (215) 641-2687.

WYNCOTE

61 Curtis Arboretum
Church Rd. and Greenwood Ave.

Founded in 1937 on 49 acres, this arboretum has become part of the Cheltenham Township Park system. Many of the shrubs, perennials, and annuals are labelled.

Daily 8-9:30 mid-April to mid-Oct; 8-6:30 rest of year; no admission charge; partial handicapped access; (215) 884-7675.

MEADOWBROOK

62 Meadowbrook Farm ☆☆ A-G-H-HH-T
1633 Washington Lane

These gardens have been developed over a period of 40 years. They form a series of garden rooms with espaliered plants and topiary on terraced grounds. There is a 19th century gazebo, several pools, a small herb garden, and many stone containers used in an interesting fashion. A good selection of shrubs, small trees, annuals and perennials may be found in this ½-acre garden. The greenhouses contain tropical plants.

By appointment only; only one group accomodated per day; greenhouses 10-5; closed Sun, holidays; no admission charge; (215) 887-5900.

PHILADELPHIA

63 Morris Arboretum ☆☆☆ A-FE-G-H-HA-J-L-R-RG-S
Germantown Ave. and Stanton Ave.
Chestnut Hill

This arboretum, started in the 1880's on 175 acres, has been part of the University of Pennsylvania since 1933. More than 3,500 species of plants are represented; the mature arboretum contains collections of azaleas, hollies, witch-hazels, magnolias, viburnums, small Asian maples, redwoods, cherries, and stewartias. Special gardens include a rose garden, a heather garden, a rock garden, a fern area and a fernery in the conservatory, a medicinal garden, and several Oriental gardens.

Among its rare specimen trees there are Henry and Trident Maples, Lace-Bark Pine, Tartar-Wing Celtis, Bender Oak, Siberian and Chinese Elms, Blue Atlas Cedar, European Weeping Beech, Katsura, and a grand oak allee. There is a library and a horticultural training program.

Daily 9-5 April 1-Oct 31; Wed eve to 8, June 1-Aug 31; 9-4 Nov 1-March 31; closed Christmas; adults, under $3; children and senior citizens, half; under 6 free; handicapped access; (215) 247-5777.

64 The Awbury Arboretum ☆ FE-HA-S-WF
Chew Ave. at Washington Lane
Germantown

This 57-acre arboretum is now used as a general park. The arboretum was developed in 1917 following English landscape design of long vistas. There is a woodland section with wildflowers and ferns as well as a pond. Among specimen trees is a 250-year-old Black Oak, and a 100-year-old River Birch.

Daily, dawn-dusk; no admission charge; handicapped access; (215) 843-5592.

65 Stenton HH
18th and Windrim Sts.

This home built between 1723-30 by William Pennn's aide, James Logan, has a small garden typical of the period.

1-5 Tues-Sat; closed holidays; adults, under $3; children nominal; (215) 329-7312.

66 Cliveden HH
6401 Germantown Avenue

A Georgian country house begun in 1763 which has been restored along with its garden. The house is surrounded by 6 acres of old trees.

10-4 Tues-Sat, 1-5 Sun April-Dec; also by appointment; adults, under $3; senior citizens, students half; (215) 848-1777.

67 Wyck ☆ BX-F-HH-R-WF
6026 Germantown Ave.

2 acres of lawn and gardens surround this house which is one of the oldest in Philadelphia, built in the 17th century. The records left by 6 generations of gardeners form an important botanical collection. There is a rose garden with some descendents of 18th century roses. Some rare shrubs, wildflowers, boxwoods, and fruit trees should be noted.

1-4 Tues, Thurs, Sat May-Oct; by appointment, Tues, Sat rest of year; adults, under $3; children half; (215) 848-1690.

68 Grumblethorpe HH
5267 Germantown Ave.

An 18th century mansion which has been restored along with its gardens; they are best visited in summer.

By appointment only; (215) 925-2251.

69 Horticultural Center ☆☆ CH-G-HA-P-S
Fairmount Park
Horticulture Ave. near Belmont Ave.

Located on the site of the 1876 Centennial Horticultural Hall, this new center was built in 1976. The greenhouses present seasonal flower shows and a continuous exhibit of tropical plants. The 22-acre arboretum contains economic woody plants as well as ornamentals. There are some fine old specimen trees.

Daily 10-4; closed some holidays; adults and children, nominal admission charge; handicapped access; (215) 686-1776.

70 Japanese House and Garden HA-J
West Fairmount Park

This reconstruction of an early Japanese house stands in a ½-acre garden with pools, waterfalls, and authentic plantings.

10-5 Wed-Sun April 1-Oct 31; adults, under $3; children half; handicapped access; (215) 686-1776.

71 Philadelphia Zoological Garden A-HA-HH
Fairmount Park
34th St. and Girard Ave.

This zoo has an appropriate selection of plants for the natural habitats of the animals. In addition the 42 acres contain large beds of perennials and annuals and plantings of

Japanese cherries, crab-apples, azaleas and other blooming shrubs. The beautiful mansion 'Solitude' stands on these grounds.

Daily 9:30-6; closed Jan 1, Thanksgiving, Dec 24, 25, and 31; handicapped access; adults, under $6; 2-11 half; (215) 243-1100.

72 Cedar Grove H-HH
Fairmount Park
Landsdowne Drive

This 18th century Quaker farmhouse has a small herb garden.

Daily 10-5; closed Tues and legal holidays; adults, under $3; under 12 half; (215) 763-8100.

73 Laurel Hill Cemetery ☆ L
3822 Ridge Ave.

Designed in 1836 on a site adjoining Fairmont Park, this cemetery overlooks the Schuylkill River. It was the first of the rural park cemeteries and was influential in 19th century park, garden, and cemetery design. The central landscaped area is being restored. Victorian architecture and landscape design may be viewed here.

Daily 8-dusk.

74 Ebenezer Maxwell Mansion HH
200 W. Tulpehocken St.

The grounds of this Victorian mid-19th century mansion were partially designed by Downing as a naturalistic woodland with irregular flowerbeds. The side and back gardens are by Scott and are more formal.

Daily, dawn-dusk; no admission charge; house has other hours and an admission charge; (215) 438-1816.

75 Philadelphia Flower and Garden Show
Civic Center

A spring flower show is held annually in March; it is sponsored by the Philadelphia Horticultural Society.

For information call (215) 625-8250.

76 Herb Garden H
Mutter Museum
College of Physicians
19 S. 22nd St.

A small medicinal herb garden.

10-4 Tues-Fri; closed Federal holidays; no admission charge; (215) 561-6050, ex 41.

77 Independence National Historical Park H-HA-R
Third and Chestnut Sts.

More than 40 historic buildings and their small gardens are located in this area. Some gardens have been restored; others have been replaced by modern urban gardens. There is a rose garden, a magnolia garden, the 18th century Norris and Pemberton Gardens as well as other smaller gardens.

Daily 9-5; no admission charge; handicapped access; (215) 597-8974.

78 Pennsylvania Horticultural Society H-HA-F
325 Walnut St.

A small 18th century garden has been planted here; there is a formal section with parterres, a vegetable and herb area, and and a miniature orchard. Modern varieties of species grown 200 years ago have been used.

Daily 9-5; July-Aug 8:30-4:30; no admission charge; handicapped access; (215) 625-8250.

79   **The Physic Garden**   H-WF
The Pennsylvania Hospital
8th and Pine Sts.

An 18th century garden of medicinal plants, recreated in 1976, contains herbs, wildflowers, and some shrubs.

Daily, dawn-dusk; no admission charge; (215) 829-3971.

80   **The Hill—Physick—Keith House**   HH
321 S. 4th St.

This was once the home of Dr. P.S. Physick, the father of American surgery. The 18th century house has a 19th century-style garden.

10-4 Tues-Sat; 1-4 Sun; closed holidays; adults, under $3; students, children half; (215) 925-7866.

81   **The Samuel Powel House**   HH
244 S. 3rd St.

This 1765 house stands in a restored garden.

10-4 Tues-Sat; 1-4 Sun; closed holidays; adults, under $3; students half; children nominal with an adult; (215) 627-0364.

82   **Efreth's Alley**   HH
2nd St. between Arch and Race Sts.

Several 18th century homes and gardens may be toured from time to time.

By appointment only; (215) 574-0560.

83   **Bartram's Garden**   ☆   HH
54th St. and Lindbergh Blvd.

This was the site of one of America's first botanic gardens, begun in 1730. The house of John Bartram, America's best known plant explorer and naturalist, has been restored. Some plants from the days of his sons who continued his work remain. They include a yellow-wood and ginkgo. The garden has been replanted with plants known to the Bartram family.

Daily, dawn-dusk; house open Tues-Sun 10-4, April-Oct; Nov-March by appointment; no admission charge; house, adults, under $3; (215) 729-5281.

84   **Historic Garden Tours**

Some homes and their gardens are open each May.

For information call (215) 625-8250.

RHODE ISLAND

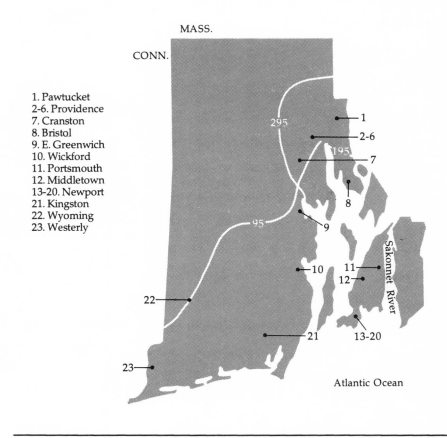

MASS.

CONN.

1. Pawtucket
2-6. Providence
7. Cranston
8. Bristol
9. E. Greenwich
10. Wickford
11. Portsmouth
12. Middletown
13-20. Newport
21. Kingston
22. Wyoming
23. Westerly

Atlantic Ocean

PAWTUCKET

1 Slater Mill Historic Site   HH
Roosevelt Ave.; exits 28 or 29 off I-95

The first textile mill in the United States was established here in 1793, making the transition from handcraft to machine production. The small adjacent textile garden contains mainly plants and flowers related to natural dyes and the production of hard fiber.

10-5 Tues-Sat, 1-5 Sun June 1-Sept 5; 1-5 Sat, Sun March 1-May 31; Sept 6-Dec 22; other days groups by reservation; closed Jan, Feb; adults, under $3; 6-14 half; (401) 725-8638.

PROVIDENCE

2 Roger Williams Park Greenhouses and Gardens   ☆☆   A-CH-G-HA-J-R
Elmwood exit off I-95

This 450-acre park contains 10 small lakes with formal gardens, a rose garden, rhododendron and azalea walks, a 1¼-acre Japanese garden and 4 greenhouses. 3

seasonal flower shows, including a tulip and chrysanthemum show are held each year.

Daily sunrise-9; greenhouses 11-4; no admission charge; handicapped access to most sections; (401) 785-7450.

3 The Museum of Rhode Island History at Aldrich House
110 Benevolent St.

A small garden lies across the street from the museum; its fountain is surrounded by raised beds in this formal garden filled with perennial bushes and annuals.

11-4 Tues-Sat; 1-4 Sun; closed holidays adults, under $3; 12-18 and over 65 half; under 12 nominal; (401) 331-8575.

4 Governor Stephen Hopkins House   HH
Hopkins and Benefit Sts.

An 18th century parterre garden is situated next to this 1707 mansion. Above it lies a terraced garden.

1-4 Wed and Sat, April 1-Dec 15; no admission charge; (401) 861-2935.

5 Swann Point Cemetery   ☆   CH-S
585 Blackstone Blvd.

The 200-acre cemetery grounds contain more than 300 species of trees. There is an annual tulip show in spring and a chrysanthemum show in autumn; both are held in the chapel gardens.

Daily 8-dusk; no admission charge.

6 Shakespeare's Head   BX-H
21 Meeting St.

The Rhode Island Federation of Garden Clubs headquarters maintains a walled Colonial garden here. It contains boxwood, quince trees, and a herb garden, along with seasonal flowers.

9-5 Mon-Fri; no admission charge.

CRANSTON

7 Winsor Azalea Garden   ☆   A
44 Marden St.

This private garden on the shores of Fenner's Pond is open for several weeks in late May and early June each year. Numerous varieties of azaleas and rhododendrons are displayed here.

Daily 10-7; donation; (401) 277-2601.

BRISTOL

8 Blithewold Gardens and Arboretum   ☆☆   HA-HH-R-RG-S-W-WF
Ferry Rd.

Located on a 33-acre site overlooking Narragansett Bay, the mansion is surrounded by a variety of gardens including a rock garden, a rose garden, a water garden, a woodland garden, and 10 acres of meadow with wildflowers. There are mature specimens of Japanese and Chinese plants among them Chinese Toon trees, ginkgos, and Japanese lilacs. The gardens have the largest sequioa east of the Rockies. There is a library.

Daily 10-4; closed Mon and holidays; mansion May-Oct 12-4; adults, under $3; children half; handicapped access; (401) 253-8714.

EAST GREENWICH

9   **General James Mitchell Varnum House Museum**   HH
57 Pierce St.

A fine, small Colonial garden lies behind this frame house built in 1773.

1-4 Tues-Sat Memorial Day-Labor Day; also by appointment; adults, under $3; under 12 half; (401) 884-4622.

WICKFORD

10   **Smith's Castle**   H-HH
Cocumscussoc
1½ mi. north on U.S. 1

This home was originally built in 1683 as a fortified blockhouse. It has been restored along with an 18th century flower and herb garden.

10-5 Thurs-Sat; 1-5 Sun; adults, under $3; under 12 half; (401) 294-3521.

PORTSMOUTH

11   **Green Animals**   ☆☆☆☆   BX-H-HA-R-T
Cory's Lane, off Rt. 114

This unique topiary garden was begun in 1880. There are more than 100 pieces of topiary in the gardens including ornamental designs, geometric figures, and 18 animals. Golden Boxwood, American Boxwood, and California Privet have been used. In addition there are formal gardens, a herb garden, a dahlia garden as well as perennial and annual beds. Espaliered fruit trees, a rose arbor and a magnolia arbor are unusual. A museum of Victorian toys stands on the grounds.

Daily 10-5 May 1-Sept 30; Oct, 10-5 weekends and holidays; adults, under $3; 6-11 half; handicapped access; (401) 847-1000.

MIDDLETOWN

12   **Whitehall**   HH
Berkeley Ave.

George Berkeley, the philosopher lived here while in America; the house was built in 1729. Adjacent there is a small 18th century garden.

Daily 10-5 July 1-Labor Day; closed Mon; weekends 2-5 June and Sept; adults, under $3; children half; (401) 846-9896.

NEWPORT

13   **Beechwood Mansion**   HH-R
580 Belleview Ave

The Astor family built this Italian style mansion in 1855. The grounds contain a formal garden, a rose garden, and a cliff walk.

Daily 9:30-7; adults, under $6; under 12 free; (401) 846-3774.

14   The Breakers HH-S
Ochre Point and Ruggles Aves.

This is the grandest of the turn-of-the-century mansions. It was built in 1895 for Cornelius Vanderbilt and has extensive grounds overlooking the ocean. There are some fine specimens of Copper Beech, Japanese Maples, and Pin Oaks.

Daily 10-5 April 1-Nov 13; eves during summer; adults, under $6; 6-11 quarter; (401) 847-1000.

15   The Elms HH-S
Bellevue Ave.

Formal gardens with terraces, sunken gardens, fountains, gazebos, and statuary surround this French neo-classic mansion. The gardens have been designed in the 18th century French style. There are many rare trees and shrubs which are labelled.

Daily, 10-5 May 1-Nov 13; 5-8 Sat, July 1-Sept 15; 10-5 Sat, Sun only rest of year; adults, under $6; 6-11, quarter; (401) 847-1000.

16   Hammersmith Farm ☆ HH
Ocean Drive

This 28-room mansion which served as the summer White house for President Kennedy is surrounded by garden designed by Frederick Law Olmsted. The cutting garden contains more than 100 varieties of perennials and annuals. It remains a working farm.

Daily 10-7, Memorial Day-Labor Day; 10-5 April 1-May 30 and Labor Day-Oct 31; 10-5 Sat, Sun March 13-31 and Nov 1-30; adults, under $6; 6-12 half; (401) 847-0420.

17   Marble House HH
Belleview Ave.

The Louis XIV period dominates this 1892 mansion. The grounds contain a Chinese Tea House built in 1913.

Daily 10-5 April 1-Nov 13; 5-8 Tues, July 1-Sept 15; 10-4 Sat, Sun, rest of year; adults $6; 6-11 quarter; (401) 847-1000.

18   Rosecliff ☆ HH
Belleview Ave.

The Grand Trianon at Versailles was used as a model for this mansion built in 1902. The formal gardens contain statuary and ornaments by Saint-Gaudens.

Daily 10-5, April 1-Nov 13; 5-8 Mon, July 1-Sept 15; adults $6; 6-11 quarter; (401) 847-1000.

19   Samuel Whitehorne House HH
416 Thames St.

This Federal period home built in 1811 has been restored along with its garden.

10-5 Sun, Mon, holidays April-Oct; Tues-Fri by appointment only; adults, under $6; students, children quarter; (401) 847-2448.

20   Wanton—Lyman—Hazard House HH
Broadway near Washington Square

Built in 1675, this is now the oldest restored house in Newport. The furnishings and the Colonial garden reflect 18th century styles.

10:30-5 Mon-Sat, June 1-Labor Day; adults, under $3; children free; (401) 846-0813.

KINGSTON

21   **University of Rhode Island**   G

The university campus contains some fine plantings of spring and fall flowers. There are greenhouses which provide 3 flower shows annually.

9-5 Mon-Fri; no admission charge; (401) 792-1000.

WYOMING

22   **Meadowbrook Herb Garden**   G-H
Rt 138, 1 mile east of I-95

This formal herb garden and the adjacent greenhouses display more than 200 species of herbs. There are medicinal, culinary, and ornamental herbs.

10-12, 1-4 Tues-Sat; closed holidays; (401) 539-7603.

WESTERLY

23   **Wilcox Park**   ☆☆   G-H-HA-RG-S-T-W
High St.

During the last decades portions of this 18-acre park, established in 1908, have been turned into an arboretum of unusual trees, including 130 dwarf conifers from the Gotelli Collection of the National Arboretum. The herb garden consists of two 16th century knot gardens surrounded by 4 perennial culinary gardens and 2 annual herb beds. A garden for the blind and handicapped contains elevated beds, many with scented plants and signs in braille and raised letters. There is a perennial garden, a rock garden, and a lily pond. Many of the plants in the gardens are labelled. Greenhouses and a library also lie on the grounds.

Daily 9-5; handicapped access; tours by appointment; (401) 348-8362.

SOUTH CAROLINA

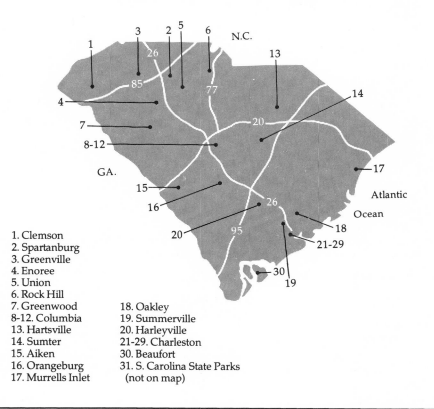

N.C.

GA.

Atlantic
Ocean

1. Clemson
2. Spartanburg
3. Greenville
4. Enoree
5. Union
6. Rock Hill
7. Greenwood
8-12. Columbia
13. Hartsville
14. Sumter
15. Aiken
16. Orangeburg
17. Murrells Inlet

18. Oakley
19. Summerville
20. Harleyville
21-29. Charleston
30. Beaufort
31. S. Carolina State Parks
   (not on map)

CLEMSON

1 Clemson University Horticultural Gardens ☆☆☆ A-CA-FE-H-HA-J-S-WF
Clemson University

More than 2,200 species are to be found in this 70-acre garden established in 1963. There is a pioneer complex with an authentic log cabin, a grist mill, spring houses, and a kitchen garden. A tea house is set in an Oriental garden. The gardens include a wildflower garden, fern garden, bog garden, an 80-station braille trail, a horticultural therapy garden, a garden for the physically handicapped. There is one of the largest shrub collections in the East as well as good collections of woody ornamentals, camellias, rhododendrons, azaleas. The big demonstration and trial gardens present 300 varieties of daffodils, numerous perennials, and annuals in 2½ acres of beds.

Daily, 8-sunset; no admission charge; handicapped access; (803) 565-3403.

SPARTANBURG

2 Walnut Grove Plantation BX-H-HH
Near junction I-26 and U.S. 221

This 18th century plantation is surrounded by fine boxwood gardens along with many old trees and shrubs. There is a herb garden and a flower garden around a dipping well.

11-5 Tues-Sat, April 1-Oct 3l; 2-5 Sun, June-Aug; adults $6; over 65, 6-18 half; (803) 576-6546.

GREENVILLE

3   Japanese Garden   ☆   J-R
Furman University
Poinsett Highway, 5 mi. north on U.S. 25

A Japanese garden, designed by Umberto, Innocenti, and Webel, has been built on this university campus in the foothills of the Blue Ridge Mountains. There is a rose garden with 800 floribunda and tea roses.

Daily, 8-dusk; no admission charge; (803) 294-2179.

ENOREE

4   Longview   HH
U.S. 221 north 3.6 mi., then left onto Rt. 42-116 for 2 mi.

A handsome plantation house built in 1847 overlooks the Enoree River. The house has been restored along with well-landscaped gardens.

By appointment only; (803) 576-6546.

UNION

5   Rose Hill State Park   BX-HH
Rt. 16 west of U.S. 176

This home of South Carolina's secessionist governor was built in 1828 and named for its rose garden. A boxwood garden in the shape of a Confederate flag may be found here.

Daily, dawn-dusk; mansion tours, Sat, Sun 1-4; no admission charge; (803) 427-5966.

ROCK HILL

6   Glencairn Gardens   ☆☆   A-S
Charlotte Ave. and Crest St.

A grand display of azaleas and dogwoods is found in these formal, terraced gardens in late April. They were established in 1928 and are being expanded. There are reflecting pools, old trees, fine beds of perennials and annuals.

Daily, dawn-dusk.

GREENWOOD

7   George W. Park Seed Co.   ☆   HA
6 mi. north on Rt. 254

Well-landscaped grounds surround the headquarters of this large seed company founded in 1868. There are good beds of perennials and annuals and 10 acres of experimental gardens. The South Carolina Festival of Flowers is held here during the 3rd weekend of July.

Tours by appointment 9, 10:30, 1, 2:30 Mon-Fri; grounds 8-4:30 Mon-Fri; no admission charge; handicapped access; (803) 374-3341.

COLUMBIA

8   Boyleston House and Gardens   A-BX-HH
Richland and Lincoln Sts.

A formal boxwood garden with major plantings of azaleas has been restored.

By appointment only; (803) 779-5350.

9   Woodrow Wilson Boyhood Home   HH
1705 Hampton St.

This home built in 1872 was occupied by the president during his teenage years. The century-old garden was originally planted by Mrs. Wilson.

10-4 Tues-Sat; 2-5 Sun; adults, under $3; children half; (803) 779-5350.

10   Robert Mills Historical House and Garden   HH
1616 Blanding St.

This house designed by Robert Mills in 1823 is of national architectural significance. The mansion along with the gardens have been carefully restored.

10-4 Tues-Sat; 2-5 Sun; adults, under $3; children half; (803) 779-5358.

11   Riverbanks Zoological Gardens   P
I-126 and Greystone Blvd.

A large collection of animals and birds displayed in their natural habitat. There is also a botanical garden with a collection of palms, tropical, and exotic plants.

9-5 Mon-Fri; 9-6 Sat, Sun, May-Sept; 9-5 daily, rest of year; adults, under $3; 6-12 quarter; students over 12, over 65 half; partial handicapped access;(803) 779-8717.

12   Columbia Museum of Science and Art
Bull and Senate Sts.

This good regional museum has a small garden which portrays the 3 different sections of South Carolina's vegetation.

10-5 Tues-Sat; 2-6 Sun; closed Jan 1, July 4, Thanksgiving, Christmas; no admission charge; (803) 253-4021.

HARTSVILLE

13   Kalmia Gardens   ☆   A-CA-W
Coker College
W. Carolina Ave.

This 24-acre arboretum located on the site of an early 19th century plantation contains more than 700 species of trees and shrubs native to the area. The kalmia is the dominant plant of the garden which surrounds 3 small lakes. There are blackwater swamps, laurel thickets, Pin-Oaks, holly uplands, and a beech bluff as well as azaleas and camellias.

Daily, dawn-dusk; no admission charge; partial handicapped access; (803) 332-1381.

SUMTER

14   Swan Lake Iris Garden   ☆☆   A-CA-S
36 Artillery Drive

Gardens, lawns, lakes, and pinewoods spread over more than 160 acres and create a natural setting for a display of azaleas, camellias, native plants, and *Kaempferi*. The iris collection is unique with more than 6 million Japanese iris as well as Dutch varieties. The entire garden is beautifully landscaped.

Daily 8-dark; no admission charge; partial handicapped access; (803) 773-9363.

AIKEN

15   Hopeland Gardens ☆☆   .- A-CA-HA-S
Dupree Place, off Rt. 19

The 15-acre estate of C. Oliver Iselin has been turned into a public garden with reflecting pools, gazebos, and brick-lined walkways. It is planted with Live-Oak, magnolia, azalea, camellia, Japanese lilies, crape myrtle, dogwood, wisteria as well as perennials and annuals. There is a touch and scent trail marked in braille. Concerts and theater performances are given here. The Thoroughbred Racing Hall of Fame lies on the grounds.

Daily, dawn-dusk; Thoroughbred Hall of Fame, Tues-Sun 2-5; (803) 649-7700.

ORANGEBURG

16   Edisto Memorial Gardens   ☆   A-CA-HA-R
U.S. 301 South

This 90-acre garden lies along the Edisto River and was created from a swamp in 1927. A fine rose garden with 6,000 bushes representing 110 varieties is found here. There are excellent plantings of azaleas, dogwoods, crape-myrtles, wisterias, and camellias. The garden maintains an All-American rose selection test garden.

Daily, dawn-dusk; no admission charge; handicapped access; (803) 534-6376.

MURRELLS INLET

17   Brookgreen Gardens   ☆☆☆☆   A-HA-L-R-S-W-WF
U.S. 17 4 mi. south

This garden was founded in 1931 mainly for the display of more than 400 pieces of 19th and 20th century sculpture and the preservation of the flora and fauna of the area. Earlier this had been a plantation. The combination of nature and sculpture has worked out beautifully and makes this one of the grand gardens of the South with more than 700 species of plants with excellent collections of hollies and specimens of Live Oaks which form a grand avenue. There is a dogwood garden, a palmetto garden, and a rose garden. Special collections of magnolias, crape-myrtles, jasmines and azaleas may be found here. The garden emphasizes indigenous plants; its wildflower area has the best display of blooms during the first 2 weeks of April. There is also a wildlife sanctuary as well as an aviary in a cypress swamp.

Daily 9:30-5:45; closed Christmas; adults, under $3; 6-12 half; tape tours; nature trails; picnic area; handicapped access; (803) 237- 4218.

OAKLEY

18   Cypress Gardens   ☆☆☆   A-CA-HA-S
Off U.S. 52; 24 mi. north of Charleston

A fine garden created in a cypress swamp which stands on 250 acres of the former Dean Hall Plantation on the Cooper River. It was created in 1927 and specializes in azaleas and camellias; more than 40 hybrids of Indian azaleas are represented along with 300 varieties of camellias. Many spring bulbs have been planted with an especially beautiful daffodil collection. There are huge old Bald-Cypress. The garden also serves as a bird sanctuary.

Daily 8-6 Feb 15-May 1; adults, under $6; children over 12 with an adult half; children under 12 with an adult free; boat rides; handicapped access; (803) 577-6970.

SUMMERVILLE

19 Azalea Park A
Main St.

Informal azalea gardens lie along reflecting pools and gazebos. They have been planted in this City of Pines, which prohibits cutting trees by ordinance.

Daily; dawn-dusk; Flowertown festival during the 1st weekend in April; for further information call (803) 873-2931.

HARLEYVILLE

20 Francis Beidler Forest ☆ WF
Off Rt. 28, 11 mi. south

Boardwalks lead through a portion of this 3,600-acre cypress and tupelo swamp of the Audubon Society. Trees, shrubs, and wildflowers are marked. A trail guide booklet is available.

9-5 Tues-Sun; closed major holidays; adults, under $3; children half; seasonal canoe trips, Feb-July by reservation; (803) 462-2150.

CHARLESTON

21 Magnolia Plantations and Gardens ☆☆☆ A-B-CA-H-HA-HH-S-T-W-WF
Ashley River Rd. (Rt. 61)

This estate and plantation have been in the Drayton family since 1676. Originally formal gardens surrounded this rice plantation's mansion. Rev. John Grimke-Drayton changed it to a naturalistic garden in the 1840's. He planted numerous camellias in 1843 and the main collection of azaleas in 1851. There are now 950 varieties of camellias and 250 kinds of azaleas. The original great avenues of magnolias are gone, but many fine specimens remain; among them are Live-Oaks with Spanish Moss, Bald Cypress, old redwood. There is a garden of native plants, streams and ponds with a water garden, an 18th century herb garden, and a 16th century maze, a small garden of Biblical plants. In total there are 50 acres of superb plantings. Camellias bloom October through April; azaleas in March and April.

Daily 8-6; house 10-4:30; closed Christmas; adults, under $6; 13-19, over 65 three-quarter; 4-12 half; add $1 to all admissions March 15-April 15; trails; canoeing; handicapped access; (803) 571-1266.

22 Middleton Place ☆☆☆☆ A-CA-HH-L-R-S
Rt. 61, 4 miles beyond Magnolia Gardens

Established in 1741 by Henry Middleton, President of the First Continental Congress; this is the oldest landscaped garden in the United States. There are magnificent camellia allees, terraces and artificial lakes in the style of French and English gardens. It took a decade to finish this 65-acre garden which lies on an estate of 6,000 acres.

The naturalist André Michaux planted the first camellias in the United States here and some of those bushes survive. There is a formal series of gardens which contain a moon garden, octagonal garden, terraced gardens, secret garden, sundial garden, bamboo grove, rare camellia garden, and a rose garden. The gardens contain more than 35,000 azaleas as well as fine specimens of magnolias, Bald-Cypress, crape-myrtle, a thousand-year-old Live-Oak, kalmias, and *Lagerstroemia*.

Daily 9-5; house has different hours; adults, under $6; 4-12, half; trails; museum; (803) 556-6020.

23 Boone Hall Plantation A-CA-HA-HH
9 mi. north on U.S. 17

An 18th century plantation mansion reached by a ¾-mile avenue of Spanish-moss draped Live-Oaks. There is a formal garden area with serpentine walks and patterned brick walks. Plantings of azaleas and camellias are the garden's chief attraction.

8:30-6:30 Mon-Sat, 1-6:30 Sun April 1-Labor Day; 9-5 Mon-Sat, 1-6 Sun rest of year; closed Thanksgiving, Christmas; adults, under $6; 6-12 nominal; partial handi-capped access; (803) 884-4371.

24 Charlestown Landing A-CA-HA
1500 Old Towne Rd., off I-26

The first English settlers built their town here in 1670. This park is of interest only for its azaleas and camellias during their brief blooming season.

Daily 9-6, June-Aug; 9-5 rest of year; adults, under $6; senior citizens, 6-14 half; picnic area; boating; tram tours; handicapped access; (803) 556-4450.

25 Nathaniel Russel House HH
51 Meeting St.

An Adam-style house built in 1809. It is set in a spacious garden which is well maintained.

10-5 Mon-Sat; 2-5 Sun; closed Dec 25; adults, under $3; partial handicapped access; (803) 723-1623.

26 The Joseph Manigault House HH
350 Meeting St.

An Adams-style home built in 1803 with a fine garden which has been recently restored along its original lines.

Daily 10-5; closed holidays; adults, under $6; 6-18 half; partial handicapped access; (803) 722-2996.

27 Hampton Park
Rutledge Ave. and Moultrie St.

This public park contains a sunken garden with a good display of annuals and perennials.

Daily, dawn-dusk.

28 Heyward Washington House HH
87 Church St.

Built in 1772, this home of a signer of the United States Declaration of Independence stands in an old garden. It has been restored.

Daily 10-5; closed holidays; adults, under $3; 6-18 half; partial handicapped access; (803) 722-2996.

29 Festival of Houses HH

Walking tours of homes and gardens built from 1712 to 1850; held annually mid-March to mid-April.

For reservations call (803) 722-3405.

BEAUFORT

30 Spring Tour of Homes and Gardens HH

A tour of old homes and gardens is held each March and April.

For reservations call (803) 524-6334.

SOUTH CAROLINA STATE PARKS

31 Annual Spring Wildflower Weekends WF

2 April weekends each in the lowland and highland area provide tours with naturalists of outstanding wildflower areas. Every major type of South Carolina plant habitat is included.

Advance reservations must be made; limited to those over 13; registration $3; (803) 758-3622; South Carolina State Parks, 1205 Pendleton St, Columbia, SC 29201.

264

SOUTH DAKOTA

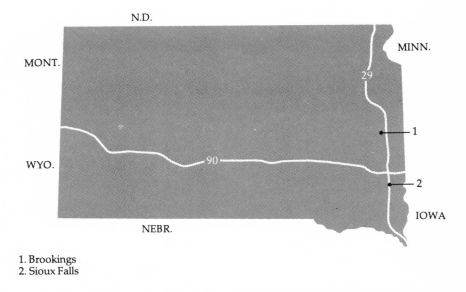

1. Brookings
2. Sioux Falls

BROOKINGS

1 McCory Gardens ☆ H-HA-HD-S
South Dakota State University
6th St.

50 acres of the campus are devoted to gardens and an arboretum with emphasis on hardy plants. 350 species of flowering annuals and 100 perennials are found here; many plants are labelled. The garden has a fine display of junipers. 90 different grasses are found in a special section. There are good collections of peonies, irises, day-lilies, sedums, and delphiniums. All-American Selection trial and display gardens are maintained. The Pharmaceutical Garden specializes in plants used in prescriptions and patent medicines.

Daily, dawn-dusk; no admission charge; handicapped access; (605) 688-5136.

SOUIX FALLS

2 McKennon Place
21st St. and 2nd Ave.

This park contains some formal gardens which cover several acres and contain a large variety of annuals and perennials. It is well-landscaped.

Daily 8-dusk.

TENNESSEE

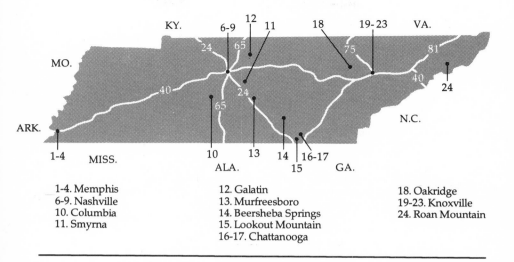

1-4. Memphis
6-9. Nashville
10. Columbia
11. Smyrna

12. Galatin
13. Murfreesboro
14. Beersheba Springs
15. Lookout Mountain
16-17. Chattanooga

18. Oakridge
19-23. Knoxville
24. Roan Mountain

MEMPHIS

1 Memphis Botanic Garden ☆☆☆ A-BR-CA-G-HA-J-R-S-WF
750 Cherry Rd.

Established in 1947, this major garden covers 88 acres and contains many specialized areas. There is a fine Japanese garden, the Ketchum Iris garden. The Michie magnolia garden has more than 80 varieties; the rose garden contains more than 3,500 bushes of many varieties. Also found here is a daffodil garden, dahlia garden, wildflower garden, dogwood and azalea trail. The garden is known for its excellent specimens of holly, Japanese cherry trees, crab-apple, trees and shrubs of the South. The conservatory contains a large display of crotons, the Charles Deere orchid collection, a bromeliad display as well as acanthus and arrow-root. There is a library.

9-4:30 Mon-Fri; 1-4:30 Sat, Sun; no admission charge; (901) 685-1566.

2 Dixon Gallery and Gardens ☆ A-FE-HA-L
43339 Park Ave.

An art museum set in 17 acres of beautifully landscaped grounds. It was opened to the public in 1976 with a fine collection of dogwoods, oaks, azaleas, ferns, shade trees, and ground covers. There is a library.

11-5 Tues-Sat; 1-5 Sun; adults, under $3; Tues free; handicapped access; (901) 761-5250.

3 Southwestern Arboretum L-S
Southwestern College of Memphis
200 N. Parkway

A collection of trees and shrubs of the South spread over 100 acres. This arboretum is well-landscaped and has been continually expanded since its founding in 1955. There is a library.

Daily 9-dusk; no admission charge.

4 Magevney House H-HA-HH
198 Adams Ave.

This home built in 1836 has a small, but well arranged garden of medicinal plants and herbs found in Memphis before 1850.

10-4 Tues-Sat; 12-3 Sun; no admission charge; handicapped access; (901) 526-4464.

NASHVILLE

6 Cheekwood ☆☆☆ BR-BX-CA-G-H A-HH-J-L-O-S-WF
Tennessee Botanical Gardens and Fine Arts Center
Forrest Park Drive

A Georgian mansion used as an art museum lies in the midst of this 55-acre garden which was established in 1959. The formal gardens with their boxwood borders are built around streams, fountains, pools, and statuary. There are wildflower gardens, a Japanese garden, evergreen plantings, good collections of day-lilies, daffodils, hollies, crab-apples, irises, and magnolias. The greenhouses contain the Bainbridge camellia collection, bromeliads, orchids, and tropical plants. There is a library. Nature trails lead through a woodland.

9-sundown Tues-Sat; 12-sundown Sun; museum has different hours; closed major holidays; adults, under $3; 7-17 half; handicapped access; (615) 352-5310.

7 The Hermitage ☆ HH-R-S
I-40, Hermitage Exit

The home of President Jackson built in 1819 contains a fine garden laid out according to a design of William Frost. Brick walks meander through magnolias, hickories, and other plants available during his lifetime; more than 50 species are planted and include irises, peonies, roses, hyacinths, pinks, jonquils, crape-myrtles, Smoke Trees, and other plants. All plants have been documented in letters or journals. Nearby lies another mansion built for his nephew which is placed in a grove of tulip trees.

Daily 9-5; closed Thanksgiving, Christmas; adults, under $6; 6-13 one-third; partial handicapped access; (615) 889-2941.

8 Tennessee Game Farm Zoo HA
I-24, New Hope Rd. Exit

The trees and plants on this preserve which features animals, have been carefully labelled. The plants recreate the natural habitat of the animals.

9-5 Tues-Sun, holidays, March 1-Nov 30; 9-5 Sat, Sun, holidays Dec 1-Feb 28; closed Mon except Memorial Day and Labor Day; adults, under $3; over 60 slightly less; 5-12 half; handicapped access; (615) 746-5667.

9 Opryland Hotel ☆☆ F-G-L-P
2800 Opryland Drive

The recent addition to this hotel included a 2-acre conservatory with 8,000 tropical plants representing 212 species. They include large specimens of 15 types of palms and 4 kinds of banana trees, as well as 6 kinds of ficuses. The winding walkways lead through ravines, terraces, rocky coves, and past waterfalls.

Daily; (615) 889-6600.

COLUMBIA

10 **James Knox Polk Home** BX-HH-S
303 W. 7th St.

The home of this president lies amidst four gardens and a wild area. A formal garden with the family's favorite flowers is surrounded by boxwood. There is a natural garden with statues and tulips and a Court garden with a fountain. The cutting garden primarily features peonies and lilies of the valley. The garden contains some fine old trees.

9-5 Mon-Sat, April-Oct; 10-4 Mon-Sat, rest of year; 1-5 Sun all year; closed Christmas; adults, under $3; 6-18 half; partial handicapped access; (615) 388-2354.

SMYRNA

11 **Sam Davis Home** BX-HH-R-S
Rt. 102

The home of the Confederate hero built in 1810 has been restored along with its outbuildings and gardens. It contains a fine boxwood period garden as well as good specimen trees. Some roses antedate the Civil War. Dogwoods, redbuds, thousands of jonquils, and irises bloom in the spring, in the wild section of the garden.

9-5 Mon-Sat, 1-5 Sun, March 1-Oct 31, 10-4 Mon-Sat, 1-4 Sun rest of year; closed Thanksgiving and Christmas; adults, under $3; under 12 half; partial handicapped access; (615) 459-2341.

GALATIN

12 **Cragfront** HH
Rt. 25, 5 mi. east

This late Georgian period home was built on a rocky bluff in 1802. The old garden has been restored along with its gazebo.

Weekdays 10-5; Sun 1-5; closed Mon; April 15-Nov 1; adults, under $3; 6-12 nominal; under 6 free; (615) 452-7070.

MURFREESBORO

13 **Oaklands Mansion** HH
North Maney Ave., off U.S. 70, east

This Romanesque revival mansion stands in a restored 19th century garden surrounded by a woodland.

10-4:30 Tues-Sat; 1-4:30 Sun; closed major holidays; adults, under $3; 6-16 half; (615) 893-0022.

BEERSHEBA SPRINGS

14 **Beersheba Wildflower Gardens** ☆ WF

This nursery lies in the midst of a display garden for native perennial wildflowers.

Hundreds of species are displayed. Mid-April to mid-June is the best time to visit. Weekdays 9-4:30; (615) 692-3575.

LOOKOUT MOUNTAIN

15 Rock City Gardens ☆ L-WF
1400 Patten Rd.

400 species of native plants may be found in this 10-acre arboretum established in 1932. It is located in a spectacular site among lichen covered sandstone formations, chasms, and crevices.

Daily 8-sunset, June 21-Labor Day; 8:30-sunset rest of year; adults, under $6; 6-12 half; (404) 820-2531.

CHATTANOOGA

16 Warner Park Rose Garden R
1101 McCallie Ave.

A rose garden has been planted in this park.

Daily 8-dusk; (615) 698-8923.

17 Chattanooga Nature Center WF
Garden Rd.

A 300-acre preserve of trees, shrubs, and wildflowers along with a nature center. Some plants are labelled.

9-5 Mon-Sat; 2-5 Sun; closed holidays; adults, under $3; 3-16 half; (615) 821-1160.

OAKRIDGE

18 University of Tennessee Arboretum ☆ S
901 Kerr Hollow Rd.

A 250-acre arboretum established in 1964 displays more than 600 species. It contains a shrub garden, holly garden, heath garden and more than 37 kinds of dogwood. Fine specimens of weeping hemlock, magnolia, dwarf conifer, pine, juniper, and willow are grown. It is best viewed in spring. There are demonstration and test gardens for endangered plants, woody ornamentals, shade trees. There is a library.

Daily 8-sunset; no admission charge; partial handicapped access; (615) 483-3571.

KNOXVILLE

19 Governor Blount Home H-HH-WF
Gay St. and W. Hill Ave.

This home built in 1792 stands in the midst of an 18th century garden. There is a herb garden; wildflowers are grown.

9:30-5 Tues-Sat, March 1-Oct 31; 9:30-4:30 rest of year; 2-5 Sun; closed Mon Dec 15-Jan 1; adults, under $3; 6-12 half; (615) 525-2375.

20 Craighead—Jackson House BX-HH
200 W. Hill Ave.

This 19th century mansion stands in a formal boxwood garden. It now serves as the

Visitor Center for the Blount Mansion.

Same conditions as Governor Blount Home.

21 Armstrong—Lockett House HH
2728 Kingston Pike

The garden of this house is in the process of being restored. It should open in 1985.

22 Dogwood Arts Festival

This festival is celebrated through more than 300 activities in mid-April. 6 Dogwood trails and 4 garden paths lead visitors through thousands of blooming trees and shrubs. Dozens of gardens are open to the public.

For information call (615) 522-8733 or 523-7263.

23 Trial Gardens H
University of Tennessee
Neyland Drive

This All-American Trial Garden is managed by the department of horticulture. A perennial garden lies nearby. A herb garden is being planted.

Daily, dawn-dusk; no admission charge; (615) 974-1000.

ROAN MOUNTAIN

24 Roan Mountain Rhododendron Garden ☆ A
Roan Mountain State Park

600 acres of purple rhododendrons provide a spectacular display in mid-June. The wild garden lies on top of the 6,3000 ft. mountain in a large park.

Daily, dawn-dusk; no admission charge.

TEXAS

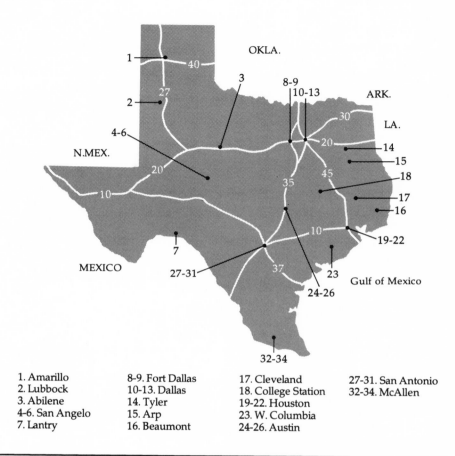

1. Amarillo	8-9. Fort Dallas	17. Cleveland	27-31. San Antonio
2. Lubbock	10-13. Dallas	18. College Station	32-34. McAllen
3. Abilene	14. Tyler	19-22. Houston	
4-6. San Angelo	15. Arp	23. W. Columbia	
7. Lantry	16. Beaumont	24-26. Austin	

AMARILLO

1 Amarillo Garden Center HA
1400 Street Drive; exit 65 from I-40W

This garden center has a fragrance garden; there are fine seasonal flower displays of perennials and annuals with the main blooming season May-Oct. Flower shows are presented annually.

9-5 Mon-Fri; no admission charge; handicapped access; (806) 352-6513.

LUBBOCK

2 Ranching Heritage Center G-HA-HH
Texas Tech University
4th and Indiana Aves.

This 14-acre exhibit of early ranch life contains numerous rebuilt structures as well as the associated gardens of the early ranching period. The university greenhouses are located nearby.

9-4:30 Mon-Sat, 1-4:30 Sun; closed holidays; adults, under $3; students half; handicapped access; (806) 742-2442.

ABILENE

3 McMurry Garden ☆
McMurry College

This garden specializes in irises and displays more than 629 varieties in its symposium gardens. New varieties are added annually. The garden is at its height from April 9 to May 15.

Daily, dawn-dusk; (915) 692-3938.

SAN ANGELO

4 Municipal Rose Garden R-W
Civic League Park
W. Beauregard and Park Streets

950 rose bushes representing 75 cultivars have been planted. There is a lily pond as well as beds of perennials and annuals.

Daily 8-dusk.

5 Sunken Garden Park
Ave. D at Abe St. Bryant Blvd. U.S. 87 South

40 cultivars of cannas are grown and some have been developed here.

Daily 8-dusk.

6 Rio Concho Garden
Rio Concho Park
Section A, near Rio Concho Manor

This garden displays both native and cultivated plants. There are trees, shrubs, vines, perennials, and annuals.

Daily 8-dusk.

LANGTRY

7 Judge Roy Bean Visitor Center ☆ C-HA-SU
Loop 25

This botanical garden was founded in 1968. Its 6 acres contain a good cactus display on terraced beds. Many plants are labelled. There are more than 110 species of plants native to the Lower Pecos River area.

Daily 8-5; closed Jan 1 and Dec 24-26; no admission charge; handicapped access; (915) 291-3270.

FORT WORTH

8 Fort Worth Botanic Garden ☆☆☆☆ A-FE-G-J-O-R-W
3220 Botanic Garden Drive or Houston and 13th Sts.

This 115-acre park contains more than 2,500 species including 500 varieties of flowering trees. The large rose gardens built on a former swamp feature more than 14,000 bushes. There is an iris garden, water garden, perennial garden, fragrance garden for the blind, azalea grove, arboretum and test areas. The fine Japanese Tea garden with pools and a pagoda and tea house is a recent addition. The "Meditation garden" is designed like the Ryoan-ji temple garden in Kyoto. The greenhouses have a good collection of ferns and orchids. There is a library.

Daily 8-dark, grounds; 8-4 Mon-Fri, greenhouses; no admission; Japanese Garden 10-4 Tues-Sat, 1-5 Sun, May 1-Labor Day; 10-4 Tues-Fri, 10-5 Sat, 1-5 Sun rest of year; adults $1; under 12 free with adult; partial handicapped access; (817) 870-7686 or 737-3330.

9 **Fort Worth Water Gardens** ☆
   1501 Commerce St.

A spectacular water display built in 1974 which covers 4½ acres and includes fine specimens of ginkgos, junipers, Live-Oaks, Bald Cypresses, turpentine trees, and tamarisks.

Daily 12-midnight; no admission charge; partial handicapped access; (817) 870-7016.

DALLAS

10 **Dallas Garden Center** ☆☆☆ A-BR-FE-G-HA-O-P
    State Fair Grounds; U.S. 67 and 80

These gardens spread over 7 acres. They were established in 1936 and now display more than 5,000 species. There are a number of special gardens with fine plantings of azaleas, redbuds, bulbs, and roses as well as annuals and perennials. The atrium and greenhouses contain good collections of tropical and semi-tropical plants with exceptionally fine orchids, bromeliads, ferns, and *Pepperomia*. There is a library and a botanical museum.

10-5 Mon-Fri, 2-5 Sat, Sun; closed Dec 24, 25; no admission charge except to greenhouses; adults, under $3; children half; handicapped access; (214) 428-7476.

11 **Dallas Arboretun and Botanical Society** HH
    8617 Garland Road

These 66 acres are being developed into a botanical garden. The estate gardens around the DeGolyer home have been restored with shrubs, perennials, and annuals.

Daily 9-5; no admission charge except to mansion; (214) 327-8263.

12 **Winniford—Henson—Ferris Garden** HH
    7122 Hazel St.

A 1-acre garden which specializes in day-lilies. They are at their peak at the beginning of June.

For hours call (214) 428-7476.

13 **Samuel Grand Municipal Gardens** R
    6200 E. Grand Blvd.

A rose garden is maintained in this park.

TYLER

14   Municipal Rose Gardens ☆☆ BR-CA-FE-G-P-R
West Front St.

This is among the largest rose gardens in the country with more than 30,000 bushes on 22 acres representing more than 500 varieties. There are tall rose trees as well as miniature rose beds. The fine camellia garden and woodlands of oak and native pine should also be visited. The conservatory houses cycads, bromeliads, ferns, and anthuriums.

Daily 8-5; no admission charge; partial handicapped access; (214) 593-2131.

ARP

15   Arboretum Incorporated
Route 1

This arboretum, established in 1971, lies on 80 acres of land on Lake Tyler East. It is dedicated to the display of East Texas trees, shrubs, and vines. There is a collection of more than 200 species. Many are fine specimens. An illustrated self-guiding booklet is available.

Daily 9-5; no admission charge.

BEAUMONT

16   Beaumont Art Museum ☆ A-CA-HA-HH-L
1111 Ninth St.

A shaded, terraced garden, spread over 5 acres which was established in 1935 surrounds this Regency style mansion, which is now a museum. There is a good collection of azaleas, dogwoods, camellias, and gardenias. Very well-landscaped with sculpture set on the grounds.

10-5 Tues-Fri, 2-5 Sat, Sun; no admission charge; handicapped access; (713) 3432.

CLEVELAND

17   Hilltop Herb Farm H-HA
10 mi. north on Rt. 1725, between Rts. 105 and 150

This herb garden, begun in 1957, is located in the middle of the National Forest. More than 2,000 species and cultivars of herbs are grown and well displayed in various special sections. This is a commercial venture.

Daily 9-5; handicapped access; (713) 592-5859.

COLLEGE STATION

18   Brazos County Arboretum HA-S
Department of Horticulture
Texas A & M University

This garden concentrates upon native plants of central Texas. Its 5 acres, founded in 1978 are nicely landscaped. There is a pinetum and a graminetum with fine trails. Illustrated self-guiding pamphlet available.

Daily, all hours; no admission charge; handicapped access; (713) 845-2844.

HOUSTON

19 The Houston Arboretum and Botanical Society H-WF
4501 Woodway Drive

This is a mixed deciduous forest on 265 acres which was established in 1967 with 250 species. Some specimen trees and a collection of wildflowers are displayed. There is a small herb garden.

Daily 8:30-8, May 1-Oct 31; 8:30-6 rest of year; no admission charge; handicapped access; (713) 681-8433.

20 Bayou Bend Gardens ☆☆☆ A-CA-G-HH-RG-T
1 Westcott St.

The gardens which surround this mansion (now a museum with 24 period rooms) are approached over a wooden suspension foot bridge. 14 acres of Ima Hogg's gardens, begun in 1927, contains an Italian garden, a garden in the English style, a white garden, an azalea walk, a topiary garden, a rock garden, a butterfly garden, as well as greenhouses. Many varieties of azaleas, camellias, and magnolias are grown.

Tues-Sat by reservation only; closed during August; adults, under $3 for house and garden; (713) 529-8773.

21 Houston Garden Center ☆ P-R
1500 Hermann Drive

This garden center is surrounded by a series of gardens. There is a fine rose garden with many varieties as well as areas of tropicat plants, perennials, and annuals.

Weekdays 8-4; no admission charge; (713) 529-5371.

22 Houston Zoological Gardens
Hermann Park

Plants appropriate to the natural habitat of the animals exhibited may be found in this 43-acre zoo and its indoor aviary.

Daily 9:30-8, May 1-Sept 30; 9:30-6 rest of year; no admission charge; (713) 523-0149.

WEST COLUMBIA

23 Varner—Hogg Plantation HH
Rt. 35 northeast

This fine Greek revival plantation home was built in 1836 and is surrounded by 65 acres of estate and garden. Both formal and informal gardens appropriate for the antebellum period are displayed.

Daily 1-5, closed Mon, Memorial Day-Labor Day; 1-4:30 rest of year; no admission charge; different hours for house and admission charge; (512) 479-4890.

AUSTIN

24 Austin Area Garden Center HS-J
Zilker Park

This park contains a 3-acre Oriental garden and a fragrance garden for the blind.

8-4:30 Mon-Fri, 2-5 Sat, Sun; no admission charge; handicapped access; (512) 477-8672.

25 Governor's Mansion HH
Colorado Ave.

A recently restored garden surrounds this mid-19th century mansion.

Daily 10-4; (512) 475-4101.

26 National Wildflower Research Center WF
2600 FM 973 North

This research institute was founded in 1982 by Lady Bird Johnson. It specializes in wildflower research. There are 72 test plots on the grounds.

By appointment only; (512) 929-3600.

SAN ANTONIO

27 Brackenridge Park J-P-W
N. Saint Mary's St.

A sunken Oriental garden, terraces, and lagoons with water lilies are part of this park. Shrubs, trees, and a variety of tropical plants have been planted here.

Daily, dawn-dusk; miniature rail-rides; (512) 732-8481.

28 Paseo del Rio C-P

Footpaths run through several acres of parkland along the river banks. This downtown park has been planted with tropical foliage and cacti.

Daily.

29 Mission Conception Gardens
807 Mission Rd.

The garden area has been planted in the Spanish mission style: very simply and with few plants.

Daily 9:30-5:30; adults, under $3; 7-12 nominal; (512) 532-3155.

30 Zoological Gardens and Aquarium
3903 N. St. Mary's St.

This large zoo with 700 species of animals utilizes a good collection of tropical and native plants to create a suitable environment for the animals.

Daily 9:30-6:30, Apr 1-Sept 30; 9:30-5 rest of year; adults, under $3; over 62 nominal; 3-11 nominal; handicapped access; (512) 734-7183.

31 San Antonio Botanical Center ☆☆ B-G-H-HA-R
555 Funston Place

A new botanical garden is nestled adjacent to the San Antonio Garden Center. The series of gardens include a rose garden, a Biblical garden, a herb garden, a garden for the blind, an aquatic garden, a fountain garden, an old-fashioned garden, and a childrens garden. The native Texas area displays plants fron 3 of the 10 vegetative regions fo the state. There are greenhouses and demonstration gardens.

9-5 weekdays; 12-5 Sat, Sun; no admission charge; handicapped access; (512) 821-5115.

McALLEN

32 McAllen Nature Center C-SU
Bus. U.S. 83 in West McAllen

This 20-acre park contains a sunken garden with waterfalls and semi-tropical plants. There is a large cactus garden.

Daily, dawn-dusk; (512) 682-1517.

33 Sharyland Plantation F
Rt. 494, 4 mi. south of Rt. 107

This family was the first to grow citrus trees in the valley; the house is not open to the public, but the gardens may be viewed. They are planted with semi-tropical trees and shrubs.

Daily, dawn-dusk.

34 Cactus Garden C-SU
Rt. 281, 6 mi. north of Edinburg

A 20-acre cactus garden surrounds this restored home; many varieties are represented.

Daily; no admission charge; tours; (512) 383-2996.

UTAH

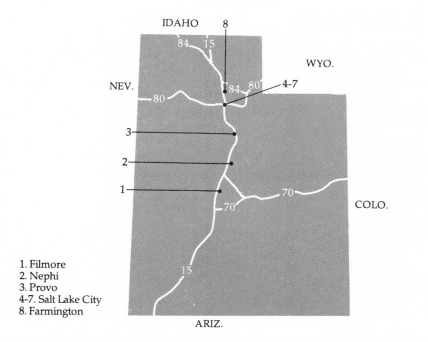

IDAHO

WYO.

NEV.

4-7

COLO.

ARIZ.

1. Filmore
2. Nephi
3. Provo
4-7. Salt Lake City
8. Farmington

FILMORE

1 American Rose Society Trial Garden R
U.S. 91 at Territorial State House Historical Site

A rose garden with 800 bushes of many varieties which surround the Territorial State House. The area is well landscaped.

Daily 8-5; 8-7 May-October; adults, nominal; picnic area; (801) 743-5316.

NEPHI

2 Memorial Rose Garden R
100 E. North St.

A small rose garden with many varieties has been planted in this park.

Daily, dawn-dusk.

PROVO

3 Brigham Young University Arboretum S
Benjamin Cuff Bldg., 8th North St.

This 3-acre, 40-year-old garden contains more than 100 species of trees and shrubs indigenous to North America; the giant sequoias and Bald Cypress are fine mature specimens and are of special interest. They are planted around a pond.

Daily; no admission charge; (801) 378-2582.

SALT LAKE CITY

4 **International Peace Garden** S
Jordan Park
9th West and 10 South Streets
These gardens were begun in 1939; they represent 18 nations and the continent of
Africa. Each garden follows a unique design and has been prepared by the specific
nationality group involved. There are some fine specimen trees as well as formal
plantings, streams, pools, fountains, and clipped hedges.

8-5 May 1-Sept 30; no admission charge; partial handicapped access.

5 **Liberty Park**
5th to 7th St. East; 9th to 13th St. South

This 80-acre park contains a conservatory and an aviary with a collection of plants
appropriate for the birds of each area.

Daily 9:30-8:30 summer; 9:30-4:30 winter; no admission charge; (801) 535-7994.

6 **State Arboretum, University of Utah** ☆☆ C-G-HA-L-O-P-R-S-SU
Follow signs along S. Campus Drive/ Wasatch Drive

The 1500-acre campus has been planted with more than 7,000 trees representing 300
species. There are special collections of hybrid oak, beech, and conifer. The cactus
and rose garden are beautifully designed. Fine specimens of Russian Olive and Giant
Sequoia are found here. The conservatory houses a good display of orchids,
succulents, cacti, and exotics. Self-guided tour pamphlet available. There is a library.

8-5 Mon-Fri; no admission charge; handicapped access; (801) 581-5888.

7 **Church of Jesus Christ of Latter Day Saints** HA
Temple Square

Beautiful gardens surround the Temple. There is a spectacular spring display, April
10-May 1 as well as fine summer and autumn displays.

Daily; guided tours; no admission charge; handicapped access; (801) 531-2534.

FARMINGTON

8 **Utah Botanical Gardens** ☆☆ CH-F-HD-R
1817 N. Main St.

These gardens, founded in 1954, contain 7 acres of formal displays and 5 acres of
experimental plots. There is a tea rose garden with more than 100 hybrids, an iris
walk, a day-lily garden, a perennial and annual garden, a vegetable and fruit display,
along with collections of chrysanthemums, peonies, and lilacs. The native landscape
garden and specialty gardens are intended as home demonstration gardens.

Daily, dawn-dusk; no admission charge; handicapped access; (801) 451-3204.

VERMONT

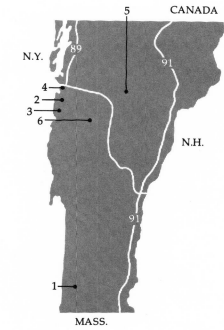

CANADA

N.Y.

N.H.

1. N. Bennington
2. Shelburne
3. Charlotte
4. S. Burlington
5. Plainfield
6. Waitsfield

MASS.

NORTH BENNINGTON

1 Park-McCullough House and Gardens   HH-S-W

This Victorian mansion is situated in a recently restored garden, not as elaborate as the original Victorian design. There is a lily pond, some old specimen trees including maple, locust, Yellow-Wood, horse-chestnut, and catalpa.

10-4 Mon-Fri, 12-4 Sun, May 10-Oct 31; adults, under $3; over 65 slightly less; 12-18 half; 6-12 less; (802) 442-2747.

SHELBURNE

2 Shelburne Museum   ☆   H-HA-HH-R-RG-S
U.S. 7

This outdoor museum of New England life contains 35 restored buildings on 45 acres and was established in 1947. Many of the buildings have been moved from other sites. All have been placed in well-landscaped grounds which reflect the gardening tradition of colonial times and the 19th century. There are old-fashioned rose gardens, a herb garden, and a rock garden; hollyhocks, apple trees, azaleas, and 400 varieties of lilacs make up interesting collections.

Daily 9-5, mid-May to mid-Oct; 1-4 Sun only in winter; adults, under $9; 6-15 half; handicapped access; (802) 985-3344.

CHARLOTTE

3   Vermont Wildflower Farm   WF
South of jnct. U.S. 7 and Rt. F5

Winding paths through fields and forest planted with many species of wildflowers. All plants are labelled in this commercial establishment.

Daily 10-5; (802) 425-3500.

SOUTH BURLINGTON

4   University of Vermont Agricultural Experiment Station   FE-HA
Adjacent to Hills Bldg.
Rt. 7

A wide variety of ornamentals, shrubs, and trees are tested here for hardiness. There is a collection of 250 kinds of day-lilies and large beds of annuals. The greenhouses display more than 30 species of ferns.

8-4:30 Mon-Fri; handicapped access; (802) 656-2630.

PLAINFIELD

5   Greatwood Gardens   R
Goddard College

These formal gardens were originally established in the 1920's with a fountain, a rose garden, as well as plantings of perennials and annuals. The garden depends upon students for maintenance and its quality has varied through the decades.

Daily, dawn-dusk; no admission charge; (802) 454-8311.

WAITSFIELD

6   Millhouse—Bundy Performing and Fine Arts Center   ☆
3¼ mi. south on Rt. 100

An outdoor sculpture garden with winding woodland trails, meadows and fine plantings of perennials and annuals has been created here. Everything has been arranged to provide an appropriate setting for the sculpture.

10-5 Thurs-Tues, June 15-Oct 15; Fri-Sun only, rest of year; closed July 4; no admission charge; (802) 496-3713.

VIRGINIA

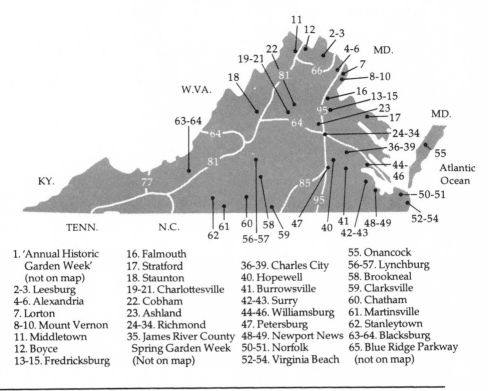

1. 'Annual Historic
   Garden Week'
   (not on map)
2-3. Leesburg
4-6. Alexandria
7. Lorton
8-10. Mount Vernon
11. Middletown
12. Boyce
13-15. Fredricksburg

16. Falmouth
17. Stratford
18. Staunton
19-21. Charlottesville
22. Cobham
23. Ashland
24-34. Richmond
35. James River County
    Spring Garden Week
    (Not on map)

36-39. Charles City
40. Hopewell
41. Burrowsville
42-43. Surry
44-46. Williamsburg
47. Petersburg
48-49. Newport News
50-51. Norfolk
52-54. Virginia Beach

55. Onancock
56-57. Lynchburg
58. Brookneal
59. Clarksville
60. Chatham
61. Martinsville
62. Stanleytown
63-64. Blacksburg
65. Blue Ridge Parkway
    (not on map)

A large number of private homes and gardens are open during the annual spring 'Historic Garden Week', but they have not been included as the list changes each year. Also omitted are estates and other sites which contain very small gardens or remnants of formal gardens.

1 Annual 'Historic Garden Week'

A series of different gardens are open to the public each year throughout the state during this period.

For information call (804) 295-3141.

LEESBURG

2 Oatlands ☆☆ BX-HH-S
U.S. 15, 6 mi. south

A grand Federal style mansion with a Greek Revival portico, built in 1800 and completely restored along with its formal gardens. Terraced gardens with 150-year-old boxwood, gazebo, reflecting pool have been developed on this 261-acre estate. There are fine plantings of tulips, daffodils, and perennials which bloom in spring and early summer. Specimen oaks planted by George Carter, the original owner, still stand along with magnolias, a boxwood allee, a bowling green, and 40 species of trees. This is primarily a green garden and so interesting at all seasons.

10-5 Mon-Sat, 1-5 Sun, April-end of Oct; adults, under $6; students, senior citizens two-thirds; partial handicapped access; (703) 777-3174.

3 **Morven Park** ☆ BX-HH-S-WF
Old Waterford Rd. and Morven Park Rd.

A fine old home with colonial gardens set in a 1,200-acre estate which continues to be farmed. There are boxwood gardens, and a reflecting pool surrounded by magnolias. Especially interesting are the parterre sundial garden, the boxwood allee, and the wildflower garden.

10-5 Tues-Sat, 1-5 Sun, Memorial Day-Labor Day; 10-5 Sat, 1-5 Sun, May 1-Memorial Day and Labor Day-Oct 17; adults, under $3; senior citizens slightly less; 6-12 half; partial handicapped access; (703) 777-2414.

ALEXANDRIA

4 **Carlyle House** HH
121 N. Fairfax

This small garden lies in the section of old Alexandria which has been partially restored or renewed in the colonial style. The neighboring streets lead past various nicely planted miniature gardens.

10-5 Tues-Sat; 12-5 Sun; closed January 1, Thanksgiving, Christmas; adults, under $3; over 59 and 6-17 half; (703) 549-8454.

5 **Lee—Fendall House** HH
429 N. Washington St.

This historic home of the Lee family was built in 1785. It stands in a small colonial style garden.

10-4 Tues-Sat; 12-4 Sun; closed Jan 1, Christmas; adults, under $3; 6-16 half; (703) 548-1789.

6 **River Farm** ☆☆ BX-F-HD-R-WF
American Horticultural Society
7931 E. Boulevard Drive

These 25 acres were once part of George Washington's Mt. Vernon farm. The headquarters of the Society, acquired in 1973, display boxwood hedge gardens and wildflower plantings. The Society maintains large demonstration gardens for perennial borders, roses, dahlias, a fruit orchard, and an idea garden. Official test gardens for numerous plant societies have been located here. There is a library.

8:30-5 weekdays; no admission charge; partial handicapped access; (703) 768-8882.

LORTON

7 **Gunston Hall** ☆ BX-H-HH-L-S
Rt. 242, east from U.S. 1

This Georgian colonial home, begun in 1755 by George Mason, stands in an 18th century garden. It presents excellent English boxwood parterres, some in an allee with 12 ft. high plants. There are 2 acres of formal gardens, a herb garden, a cutting garden as well as specimen trees and shrubs. The grounds provide a beautiful view of the Potomac.

Daily 9:30-5; closed Dec 25; adults, under $3; 6-15 half; partial handicapped access; (703) 550-9220.

MOUNT VERNON

8   **Mount Vernon** ☆☆ BX-F-G-H-HH-L
Mount Vernon Memorial Highway

George Washington's home sited high above the Potomac has been restored along with its out-buildings and gardens in accordance with Washington's design. The grounds contain an orchard with native and exotic trees, a kitchen garden, and a large flower garden with boxwood hedges. There is a bowling green and greenhouses Some of the original trees have survived. The gardens provide a good view of the Potomac.

Daily 9-5, March 1-Nov 1; 9-4 rest of year; adults, under $6; over 60 slightly less; 6-11 half; partial handicapped access; (703) 780-2000.

9   **Woodlawn** ☆☆ HA-HH-R-S
9000 Richmond Highway (U.S. 1)

This estate, originally a part of Mount Vernon, contains an 18th century mansion along with magnificently restored 20 acres of gardens. The parterre gardens of old-fashioned roses are best seen toward the end of May. Nature trails lead through a portion of the 2,000-acre estate. There are specimen of Camperdown Elms and magnolias.

Daily 9:30-4:30; closed Jan 1, Thanksgiving, Christmas; adults, under $3; over 62 nominal; 6-18 half; handicapped access; (703) 780-3118.

10   **Pope—Leighey House** ☆ HH-FE-WF
U.S. 1, 14 mi. south of Washington

This home was designed by Frank Lloyd Wright in 1940; the native shrubs, ferns, and wildflowers blend with the house. The grounds contain a wildflower and a fern garden.

9:30-4:30 Sat and Sun, March-Oct; also by appointment; adults, under $3; children half; (703) 780-3118.

MIDDLETOWN

11   **Belle Grove** H-HA-HH
Rt. 727 off U.S. 11

A colonial mansion built in 1787 with advice from Thomas Jefferson; the 4-acre garden of this working farm has been partially restored. There is a herb garden.

10-4 Mon-Sat 1-5 Sun, April 1-Oct 31; adults, under $3; over 65 three-quarters; 6-16 half; handicapped access; (703) 869-2028.

BOYCE

12   **Orland E. White Arboretum** ☆☆ BX-H-HA-R-S
University of Virginia
Rt. 50, 1½ mi. east of junction Rt. 50 and 340

There are 5,000 species on these 100 acres established in 1926. Emphasis has been placed on conifers, woody trees, and shrubs which are arranged according to 50 botanical families and other groupings. Many plants are labelled. There are collections of barberries, saxifrages, magnolias, roses, asters, and ginkgos. A demonstration boxwood garden and herb garden have been planted.

Daily, dawn-dusk; no admission charge; handicapped access; (703) 837-1758.

FREDERICKSBURG

13 Kenmore BX-H-HH-S
1201 Washington Ave.

The colonial Tidewater Georgian home of Washington's sister reflects the mid-18th century architecture and landscaping with boxwood, a herb garden, and old specimen trees and shrubs.

Daily 9-5 April 1-Oct 31; 9-4 rest of year; closed Jan 1, 2, Dec 25, 26; adults, under $3; 6-high school, half; partial handicapped access; (703) 373-3381.

14 Mary Washington House and Garden BX-H-HH
Charles and Lewis Sts.

The home of George Washington's mother has a small English garden with old boxwood, some planted by her. A herb garden, kitchen garden, and pleasant shrubbery have been planted.

Daily 9-5, April 1-Oct 31; 9-4 rest of year; closed Jan 1, Dec 24, 25, 31; adults, under $3; 6-18 half; (703) 373-1569.

15 James Monroe Museum and Memorial Library HH
908 Charles St.

This house was used by Monroe for his legal practice from 1786 to 1789. There is a quaint walled garden with plants and shrubs of the colonial period.

9-5 weekdays; adults, under $3; (703) 373-8426.

FALMOUTH

16 Belmont, the Gari Melchers Memorial Gallery A-BX-HH
224 Washington St.

The gardens of this 1761 home include informal plantings of azaleas and spring bulbs. There are boxwood-lined walks.

Daily 1-5; closed Thurs; adults, under $3; (703) 373-1776.

STRATFORD

17 Stratford Hall Plantation ☆☆ BX-H-HA-HD-R
Rt. 214

This colonial plantation home built in 1725 was the birthplace of Robert E. Lee. It is operated as a mid-19th century plantation with labelled crops in cultivated fields, woodlands, and meadows. There are excellent formal gardens with boxwood, a rose garden, a herb garden, a kitchen garden, and flowering shrubs. An exhibition vegetable garden has also been established.

Daily 9-4.30; closed Dec 25; adults, under $3; children half; handicapped access; (804) 493-8038.

STAUNTON

18 Woodrow Wilson Birthplace BX-HH
Coalter and Frederick Sts.

A small Victorian garden lies behind this home; it is well designed and typical of the period. Bow-knot flower beds with boxwood borders form part of this garden which leads to a gazebo.

Daily 9-5; summer 9-6; closed Sun, Thanksgiving, Dec 1-Feb 28; adults, under $3; over 62 two-thirds; 6-16 half; (703) 885-0897.

CHARLOTTESVILLE

19   Monticello   ☆☆☆☆   H-HA-HH-L-S
I-64, exit 24A on Rt. 53

The home and garden of Thomas Jefferson who designed and built it beginning in 1769. The house and grounds have been beautifully and accurately restored. The grand oval lawn leads to vistas surrounded by old trees. The grounds contain a flower garden, a large vegetable garden recently the site of a horticultural archeological excavation. Jefferson's interest in horticulture and gardening is evident everywhere.

Daily 8-5, March 1-Oct 31; 9-4:30 rest of year; closed Christmas; adults, under $3; 6-11 half; handicapped access; (804) 295-8181.

20   Ash Lawn   ☆   BX-H-S
Rt. 795 2 mi. from Monticello

The home of James Monroe designed by Thomas Jefferson. The house and garden have been restored. There is a beautiful old boxwood garden with specimen plants. A 300-year-old oak and old pines overshadow the garden. In addition there is a herb garden and a kitchen garden.

Daily 9-6, March 1-Oct 31; 10-5 rest of year; closed Jan 1, Thanksgiving, Christmas; adults, under $3; 6-11 half; partial handicapped access; (804) 293-9539.

21   University of Virginia   ☆   HA-L-S
U.S. 29 and Business U.S. 250

This 800-acre campus established in 1817 was designed by Thomas Jefferson. The campus is beautifully landscaped with many specimen oak and holly. A map locating various species of trees is available.

Daily; no admission charge; handicapped access; (804) 924-0311.

COBHAM

22   Castle Hill   BX-S
Rt. 231, 11 mi. east of Charlottesville

A mansion built in 1765 with boxwood gardens; there are terraces with 200-year-old specimens. The well-landscaped grounds also contain trees, shrubs, and beds of perennials and annuals.

Daily 10-5, March 1-Nov 30, house and grounds; grounds only rest of year; adults, under $3; 6-12 half; (804) 293-7297.

ASHLAND

23   Scotchtown   HH
Rt. 738 west

This was the home of Patrick Henry, the first governor of Virginia. The house built in 1719 has been restored as have the gardens.

Daily 10-4:30; 1:30-4:30 Sun; adults, under $3; (804) 798-5401.

RICHMOND

24 **Maymont Foundation** ☆☆ H-J-S-W-WF
1700 Hampton St.

105 acres of garden surround this Victorian mansion which is now a museum. There is an Italian garden with water cascades and statuary as well as a 7-acre Japanese garden planted along classical lines. The grounds contain a herb garden and a wildflower garden. More than 200 species of trees and shrubs are found here; many are excellent specimens. A lily pond lies in the garden.

Daily 10-7, March 31-Oct 31; 10-5 rest of year; other hours for museum and buildings; no admission charge; partial handicapped access; (804) 358-7166.

25 **Agecroft Hall** BX-H-HA-HH
4305 Sulgrave Rd.

A 15th century Tudor manor house was brought to this location overlooking the James River in 1926; formal period gardens covering 23 acres surround the house. There is ornamental boxwood, a shrub garden, a herb garden, and woodlands.

10-4 Tues-Fri, 2-5 Sat, Sun; closed holidays; adults, under $3; senior citizens two-thirds; students half; handicapped access; (804) 353-4241.

26 **Edgar Allan Poe Museum** HA-HH
1914 East Main St.

This oldest house of Richmond built of river stone in 1685 has a small old-fashioned garden. Specially featured are plants mentioned in Poe's writings.

10-4 Tues-Sat, 1:30-4 Sun, Mon; closed Christmas; adults, under $3; students half; handicapped access; (804) 648-5523.

27 **Valentine Museum** HA-HH
1015 E. Clay St.

A museum of local history in an 1812 mansion which is surrounded by a 19th century garden. Plants and designs of the period have been used.

10-5 Tues-Sat, 1:30-5 Sun; adults, under $3; senior citizens two-thirds; students half; family, under $6; handicapped access; (804) 649-0711.

28 **The Mews—St. John Church**
24 and Broad Sts.

A small community garden decorated with excellent cast iron work taken from homes and gardens which no longer exist has been created here.

10-4 Mon-Sat, 1-4 Sun, March 15-Dec 1; (804) 649-7938.

29 **Virginia House** HH
Wakefield and Sulgrave Rds.

This Tudor mansion partly assembled from original English material was built in 1928 and belongs to the Virginia Historical Society. A small handsome garden overlooks the James River.

By appointment; (804) 353-4251.

30 **Wilton House** HH
South Wilton Rd.

This Georgian mansion built in 1750 was moved to its present site in 1934. The grounds were appropriately landscaped 2 years later.

10-4 Tues-Sat, 2:30-4:30 Sun; closed Sun July 1-31; closed Sat and Sun Aug 1-31; closed 2nd Thurs, Oct 1-May 31; adults, under $3; 6-18 half; (804) 282-5936.

31   Windsor Garden   BX-HH
The Windsor Foundation
Sulgrave Rd.

Modern formal gardens surround this Georgian style house; boxwood and large specimen trees lie on the grounds.

For hours call (804) 644-7776.

32   Bryan Park Azalea Garden   ☆   A
Hermitage Rd. and Bellevue Ave.

45,000 azaleas and rhododendrons representing more than 50 varieties on 20 acres make a spectacular display in spring. There are also many fine dogwoods. This public park contains fountains stream, and a floral cross of white and red azaleas.

Daily, dawn-dusk; no admission charge.

33   Meadow Farms—Crump Museum   F
Mountain and Courenay Rds.

This is a living historical farm maintained around an 1810 farmhouse. There are gardens, an orchard, and nature trails.

10-4 Tues-Sun; adults, under $3; under 12 half; (804) 788-0391.

34   Philip Morris Plant

A set of modern gardens has been built around this tobacco plant which lies on 200 landscaped acres.

9-4 Mon-Fri; closed holidays and weeks of July 4 and Dec 25; no admission charge; (804) 274-3688.

JAMES RIVER COUNTRY

35   Spring Garden Week   HH

Many homes and gardens of the James River basin are open for tours in spring.

For information and reservations call (804) 644-7776 or 643-7141.

CHARLES CITY

36   Shirley Plantation   HH
20 southeast of Richmond on Rt. 5

The estate has been in the same family since 1613. The 1723 mansion is set in a small formal garden.

Daily 9-5; closed Christmas; adults, under $6; over 60 three-quarters; students half; 6-12 one-third; (804) 795-2385.

37   Berkeley Plantation   BX-HH-S
22 mi. southeast of Richmond on Rt. 5

This mansion built in 1726 was the ancestral home of President Benjamin Harrison. The house is surrounded by a terraced boxwood garden. Many old specimen trees are found here.

Daily 8-5; closed Christmas; adults, under $6; over 62 two-thirds; 6-12 half; (804) 795-2453.

38   Sherwood Forest HH-S
3 mi. east on Rt. 5

An early 18th century frame mansion set on 12 acres of grounds. More than 80 species of trees and some fine specimens stand on this estate.

Daily 9-5; adults, under $3; 6-12 half; (804) 829-5377.

39   Belle Air Plantation BX-H-HH
Rt. 5, ¼ mi. east

This frame house built in 1670 is unique in Virginia. The grounds include a herb garden, mature English boxwood, and a flowering border. There is also a 200-acre farm.

By appointment for tour groups only; (804) 644-7776.

HOPEWELL

40   Weston Manor BX-H-HH
Dirt road from 21 Ave.

A Georgian clapboard house built in 1735 is set in an old boxwood garden. There is a kitchen herb garden.

10-4 Wed-Sat; adults, under $3; (804) 866-8665.

BURROWSVILLE

41   Brandon BX-HH-S
5 mi. northeast on Rt. 611

This 18th century mansion was designed by Thomas Jefferson; the grounds extend from the river to the house. There are boxwood enclosures, tulip trees, exotic trees from West Indies brought 300 years ago. The grounds contain specimen cucumber trees and old mulberries which record the attempt to begin silk industry here. This remains a working farm of 1,800 acres.

Daily 9-5:30; adults, under $3; house during garden week only; (804) 866-8486.

SURRY

42   Chippokes Plantation State Park ☆ A-BX-H-HH-S-W
Rt. 10, 1½ mi. east, then Rt. 634

6 acres of gardens with an extensive collection of crape-myrtle lie behind the mansion. There are boxwood and magnolia. Massive plantings of azaleas make this garden spectacular in spring. The old mulberry trees are a reminder of the attempt to begin a silk industry here. A kitchen garden lies near the house. Trails lead through 1,400 acres of marsh, cypress swamp, woods, and fields.

Daily, sunrise-sunset; no admission charge; (804) 294-3625.

43   Smith's Fort Plantation   HH
Rt. 31 to Jamestown Ferry Landing

This early 18th century country house is surrounded by picturesque gardens of shrubs, perennials, and annuals.

10-5 Wed-Sat, 1-5 Sun, April 25-Nov 1; adults, under $3; students half; (804) 795-2453.

WILLIAMSBURG

44   Colonial Williamsburg   ☆☆☆☆   A-BX-F-H-HA-HH-L-RG-S

An 18th century Colonial town has been magnificently restored with great attention to accuracy and detail; dozens of gardens have been planted with the vegetation of 200 years ago. There is a grand boxwood allee. The 100 gardens vary from the simplest home garden to the Governor's Palace Garden. There is a fine display of ornamentals and bulbs in the spring.

The Governor's Palace   ☆☆☆   BX-F-HH-L-T

This is an elaborate formal English garden covering 10 acres. It is precisely geometrical in design and has been subdivided into 7 sub-gardens including diamond-shaped patterres, formal boxwood garden, bowling green, ballroom garden, fruit garden, holly maze, terraced garden, fish pond, and canal. There is some fine topiary of yaupons as well as a pleached beech allee. The garden was originally attached to a 350-acre hunting and fishing preserve.

George Wyeth House   BX-F-HH-T

The garden of the law professor who taught Jefferson contains boxwood hedges with topiary cones, geometrical flower beds, and a pleached allee of hornbeams. There is a small ballroom garden and an orchard.

Orlando Jones House   BX-HH-T

An oval lawn is surrounded by old boxwood with garden seats inset. There is also topiary boxwood, mulberry, and crape-myrtle. A small flower garden lies near the house.

Norton—Cole House   BX-HH-T

A curved boxwood hedge along with English ivy are found here. The topiary boxwood forms a helix.

Prentis House   BX-HH

This garden consists of 4 square boxwood parterres with a buckeye in the center of each. Espaliered apple trees run along the fence.

Alexander Craig House   BX-HH

This is a very formal garden with brick walks surrounding a round central flower bed with boxwood hedges.

Powell—Waller House   HH

Here we have a compact circular garden which is quite small with brick walls, dogwood trees.

There are also a number of kitchen gardens and herb gardens. Fine specimen trees are found throughout the restoration. The gardens are designed to be green during all seasons.

Visitor Center 9-5, longer hours in spring and summer. Admission according to number of buildings and gardens to be visited; 'Patriots Pass' for multiple entry, under $18; 6-12 half; handicapped access; (804) 229-1000 ext 2751.

45 Bassett Hall ☆ HH
Waller and Francis Sts.

This mid-18th century home was occupied by the Rockefellers when they began the Williamsburg restoration project. The 585-acre estate contains a formal garden.

Daily 10-5, March 15-Dec 31; 10-5 Fri-Mon rest of year; adults, under $6; 6-12 half; reservations may be necessary; partial handicapped access; (804) 229-1000.

46 Carter Grove ☆ BX-H-HH
6 mi. southeast

A magnificent mansion built in 1751 lies on this 400-acre estate which once consisted of 300,000 acres. There are huge lawns and boxwood hedges around flower gardens. A kitchen garden is located near the house.

Daily 9-5, March 1-Nov 30 and holiday season; adults, under $6; 6-12 half; grounds only, nominal; partial handicapped access; (804) 229-6883.

PETERSBURG

47 Center Hill Mansion HH
Center Hill Court, off Franklin St.

A great mansion built in 1823 with later restorations is now a museum of the antebellum period. The grounds have been restored in the style of the period.

9-6 Mon-Sat, 12:30-5 Sun, Memorial Day-Labor Day; 9-5 Mon-Sat rest of year; closed Jan 1, Thanksgiving, Dec 24, 25; donation; (804) 732-8081.

NEWPORT NEWS

48 Hampton Roads Garden Center
Museum Drive

A small shaded garden with old hemlock, dogwood, and crape-myrtle. There is a display of bulbs in spring.

Weekdays 9-5; no admission charge.

49 Temple Sinai Biblical Garden
11620 Warwick Blvd.

A Biblical garden is now being developed here. Mediterranean plants are used when possible; otherwise related plants appropriate to the region have been utilized.

By appointment; (804) 596-8352.

NORFOLK

50 Norfolk Botanical Gardens ☆☆☆☆ A-CA-G-H-HA-J-L-O-P-R-SU-RG-S-W
Airport Road

175 acres of gardens established in 1937 have collection of more than 7,000 species.

The enormous azalea collection of 250,000 plants representing 700 varieties is spectacular in spring. There are large collections of rhododendron, dogwood, laurel, crape-myrtle, and camellia. The grounds contain a 3½-acre rose garden, a Japanese garden, a holly garden, a colonial garden, a fragrant garden for the blind, a heather garden, and a heath garden. Stands of hemlocks, white pines, and junipers lie on the grounds. The garden is built near a large lake. The greenhouses display orchids and tropical plants. There is a demonstration garden for roses. There is a library.

Daily 8:30-dusk; adults, under $3; boat and train tours in spring and summer; handicapped access; (804) 855-0195.

51   Lafayette Zoological Park   ☆☆   C-G-R-SU
3500 Granby St.

A mid-sized zoo which also has 3 display greenhouses for tropical and desert plants. A rose garden, children's garden, perennial, and annual garden are on the grounds.

Daily 10-5; closed Jan 1, Christmas; adults, under $3; 2-12 nominal; handicapped access; (804) 441-2706.

VIRGINIA BEACH

52   Adam Thoroughgood House   HH
Near jnct. U.S. 13 and 60

A charming small 17th century brick home which has been restored along with its little "Gentlemen's Garden".

10-5 Tues-Sat, 12-5 Sun, April 1-Nov 30; daily 12-5 rest of year; closed Jan 1, Christmas; adults, under $3; military and 6-12 half; (804) 622-1211.

53   Lynnhaven House   H-HH
4405 Wishart Rd.

This is a small brick 17th century plantation house; it is now furnished as a yeoman's farm house with a herb garden.

10-5 Tues-Sat, 12-5 Sun; adults, under $3; children half; (804) 460-1688.

54   Tidewater Arboretum   ☆
1444 Diamond Springs Road, off Rt. 13

A small arboretum with more than 430 species of unusual trees and shrubs on 1-acre has been created here. It is best visited Between April and November.

Daily 9-dusk; no admission charge; (804) 464-3528.

ONANCOCK

55   Kerr Place   HH
Market St.

A Georgian brick house built in 1799 with unusually fine brick and wood work which has been restored. The grounds are landscaped in keeping with the period.

Weekdays 9-4; adults, under $3.

LYNCHBURG

56 Miller—Claytor House BX-HH
2200 Rivermont Ave.

This 18th century home has been moved and restored by the Lynchburg historical society. There is a boxwood garden. Jefferson introduced the tomato to Lynchburg here.

Weekdays 9-4; adults, under $3; (703) 750-6678.

57 Point of Honor HH
Daniel's Hill

This Federal style home built in 1815 overlooks the James River. The garden of shrubs, perennials, and annuals has been restored.

Weekdays 9-4; adults, under $3; (703) 750-6678.

BROOKNEAL

58 Red Hill BX-HH
Odd Rt. 40, 5 mi. east

A series of buildings including the last home of Partrick Henry and his legal office. The colonial gardens with their boxwood edging may be viewed along a winding walk.

Daily 9-5; adults, under $3; under 12 half; (703) 376-2044.

CLARKSVILLE

59 Prestwould House HH
2 mi. north on U.S. 15

This 18th century stone manor house has been carefully restored as has the garden house. The gardens have also been replanted according to the original design.

By appointment only; (804) 848-2505.

CHATHAM

60 Chatham Hall Gardens A-BX
Pruden St.

Azaleas, boxwoods, and a terraced walk are the main features of these campus gardens.

Daily 10-4; no admission charge; (703) 432-2941.

MARTINSVILLE

61 Piedmont Arts Association H-R
215 Starling Ave.

This early 20th century home lies amidst giant oaks and magnolias. There is a sunken garden with 200 rose bushes, and a herb garden.

Weekdays 9-4; (703) 632-3221.

STANLEYTOWN

62 Stoneleigh ☆ BX-HH-R
Edgewood Drive and Oak Level Rd.

A magnificent mansion now owned by Ferrum College lies in 56 acres of rolling hills. The gardens have been restored, including an Elizabethan formal garden, a rose garden, a boxwood garden, and a vegetable garden.

By appointment only; (703) 632-3119.

BLACKSBURG

63 Smithfield Plantation HH
Rt. 314; Virginia Tech Exit off U.S. 460

This 18th century frame house has been restored; the garden is now being replanted with shrubs, perennials, and annuals.

1-5 Wed-Sat, Sun; April 15-Nov 15; adults, under $3; 5-16 half; (703) 951-2060.

64 Horticultural Gardens
Virginia Polytechnical Institute and State University

These new gardens include an All-American Display Garden and a herbaceous perennial collection. The gardens will expand.

Daily 8-dusk; (703) 961-6301.

BLUE RIDGE PARKWAY

65 Craggy Gardens A
Mile 364, 17 mi. northeast of Ashville

A magnificent wild grove of rhododendron at 6,000 ft; plants bloom in mid-June; trails.

Visitor Center, daily 9-5; (704) 258-2850 ext. 779.

WASHINGTON

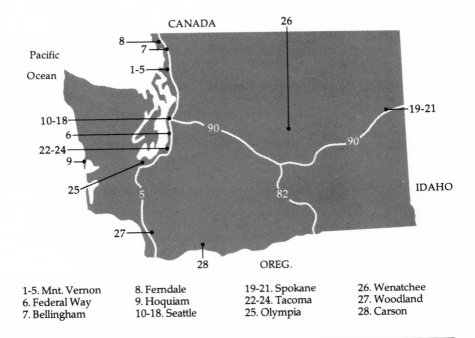

CANADA

Pacific

Ocean

IDAHO

OREG.

1-5. Mnt. Vernon	8. Ferndale	19-21. Spokane	26. Wenatchee
6. Federal Way	9. Hoquiam	22-24. Tacoma	27. Woodland
7. Bellingham	10-18. Seattle	25. Olympia	28. Carson

MT. VERNON

1 Hillcrest Park   J
13th and Blackburn Sts.

A small Oriental garden lies within this public park.

Daily, dawn-dusk.

2 Edgewater Park
Skagit River

A scented garden for the blind has been developed here.

Daily, dawn-dusk.

3 Washington Bulb Company
1599 Beaver Marsh Road

This is the largest grower of bulbs in the United States. There are numerous tulip fields.

Mon-Fri 9-5; (206) 424-5533.

4 West Shore Acres
956 Downey Road

A 1½-acre display garden surrounds the stately 1886 Victorian home. Hundreds of varieties of bulbs have been planted by this commercial nursery.

Weekdays 9-5, 10-6 Sun mid-March to Mother's Day; (206) 466-3158.

5 Flower Fields

Cutflowers and spring bulbs are a major agricultural product of this area. The Chamber of Commerce prints a flower field location map each year in early March. A tulip festival is held in mid-April.

Contact Chamber of Commerce (206) 336-9555.

FEDERAL WAY

6 Rhododendron Species Foundation   ☆☆☆   A-G-S
Exit 142 from I-5; near Weyerhaeuser Headquarters

These 23 acres are devoted entirely to rhododendron with more than 22,000 plants representing 475 species and therefore 90% of those now cultivated. This is the largest collection in the United States. A conservatory houses less hardy species. There is a good library. Self-guided walk booklet available.

Weds 10-3, April 3-May 29; Sun 1-5, March 20; 10-5 one weekend, mid-Oct; schedule varies slightly each year; also by appointment; adults, under $3; partial handicapped access; guided tours; park at Weyerhouse West parking area 2½ blocks away; (206) 927-6960.

BELLINGHAM

7 Sehome Hill Arboretum   L-S
Footpath from Western Washington University

The arboretum lies in a spectacular location overlooking Bellingham Bay, Mount Baker, and the San Juan Islands. It posseses a fine collection of trees and shrubs from the Olympic Peninsula and the Cascade Range.

Daily, dawn-dusk; (206) 733-2900.

FERNDALE

8 Hovander Homestead   HH
1 mile south on Hovander Rd.

This 1903 homestead has been restored and the garden replanted. Along with the house and farm there are display gardens which are authentically planted for the period.

Daily 8-dusk; home 10-6 Wed-Sun, May 31-Sept 6; adults, under $3; partial handicapped access; picnic area; (206) 384-3444.

HOQUIAM

9 Polson Park   R
1611 Riverside Ave.

The park contains a museum of local history. It is surrounded by plantings of exotic trees and a rose garden.

Daily 9-5; museum 12-4 Wed-Sun, June-Aug; 12-4 Sat, Sun rest of year; (206) 533-5862.

SEATTLE

10 Drug Plant Gardens and Laboratories ☆☆ G-H-HA
University of Washington
17th Avenue North

These 2 acres of formal gardens form one of the largest medicinal and culinary gardens in the world with 1,500 species represented. There are greenhouses and research facilities.

Daily 8-5; no admission charge; handicapped access; (206) 543-1942.

11 Carl S. English Jr. Gardens ☆ HA-L-S
Army Corps of Engineers
3015 N.W. 54th St.

7 acres of well-landscaped grounds have been planted with more than 500 species of a wide variety of plants. This arboretum founded in 1917 contains some fine old specimens.

Daily 7:30-9; no admission charge; handicapped access; (206) 783-7001.

12 Japanese Tea Garden ☆☆☆ HA-J-S
University of Washington Arboretum
East Madison and Lake Washington Blvd. East

A 3-acre Japanese garden designed in Japan by Juki Iida and built by Japanese landscape architects in the 1960's. All the plants are seen and may be grown in Japan. There are fine specimens of plum and cherry trees. The tea house, pagoda, and 10 ancient lanterns add beauty to the garden; self-guiding tour booklets are available.

Daily 10-6, Feb-Oct, longer hours in summer months; adults, under $3; children, Sr. citizens, handicapped nominal; handicapped access; tours by arrangement; (206) 625-2635.

13 Washington Park Arboretum ☆☆☆☆ A-CA-G-HA-P-S-W
University of Washington
East Madison and Lake Washington Blvd. East

This 156-acre arboretum contains more than 5,000 species of plants. Founded in 1934 it has an exceptional collection of azaleas, 700 kinds of rhododenrons, magnolias, hollies, California lilacs, camellias, flowering cherries, and crab-apples. There are unusual specimens of Nootka-Cypress and an Elm hybrid called 'Ice-cream Tree' as well as Southern Beech and Medlar-Hawthorn. The arboretum has many trails including one along a waterfront planted with semi-aquatic plants. The excellent Japanese garden listed has been described separately. There are some greenhouses. Some plants flower each season, but the height of the blooming season is from April through mid-June.

Daily, sunrise-sunset; greenhouses 8-4 Mon-Fri; no admission charge except Japanese Garden; handicapped access; (206) 543-8800.

14 The Seattle Conservatory ☆☆ G-O-P
Volunteer Park on Capitol Hill
15th Ave. E. and E. Galer St.

The conservatory, built in 1912, reflects the Victorian style of the London Crystal Palace. Palms, cycads, and tropical flowers are displayed along with the Anna Clise Orchid Collection, begun in 1919. There are seasonal displays.

Daily 9-5; no admission charge; (206) 625-4043.

15 The Rose Garden R
Woodland Park
Fremont Ave. N. and N. 50th St.

This formal garden, established in 1922, is an official test garden of the All-American Rose Selection Committee. There are 5,200 plants representing 190 varieties.

Daily 8-dusk; no admission charge.

16 Lake Washington Ship Canal and Locks HA-S
1519 Alaskan Way, South

7 acres of gardens accompany the Hiram M. Chittenden Locks as part of a program of developing gardens along the banks of the canal from Shilshole Bay to Union Bay. There are numerous kinds of flowers and shrubs as well as trees from China, Tibet, Burma, and India.

Daily 7-9; visitor center 11-8 daily, June 15-Sept 15; 11-5 Thurs-Mon, rest of year; handicapped access; (206) 783-7059.

17 Woodland Park Zoological Gardens ☆ HA-P
Pinney Ave between N. 50th and N. 59th St.

A 1,000 animal zoo set in a magnificent natural setting of temperate, tropical and semi-tropical plants. The aviary contains an entire tropical forest. Some plants are labelled.

Daily 8:30-6, May-Sept; 8:30-5 Oct-Dec; 8:30-4 rest of year; adults, under $3; children half; Sr. citizens and handicapped free; (206) 782-1265.

18 Rhododendron Show

An annual show of rhododendrons is held each May.

For details call (206) 543-8800.

SPOKANE

19 Manito Park ☆☆ G-HA-J-P-R
4 West 21st Ave.

12 acres of gardens include a classical Japanese garden as well as the formal 19th century style Duncan Gardens. They feature large symmetrically balanced beds of annuals. There is a rose garden with a good collection as well as informal gardens. The floral display is at its height from late August to frost. Fine planting of lilacs has led to a annual lilac festival in May. The conservatory houses a tropical plant collection. These gardens were established in 1907.

Daily, grounds; conservatory 8-dusk; closed Christmas and New Year; Japanese Garden daily 8-dusk, May-Nov; no admission charge; handicapped access; (509) 456-4331.

20 John A. Finch Arboretum ☆☆ A-HA-S
West 3404 Woodland Blvd, off Sunset Highway

A 65-acre arboretum which occupies a site along Garden Spring Creek. There are more than 600 species and varieties represented, with 2,000 trees and shrubs labelled. The arboretum contains fine flowering crab-apples, 75 varieties of lilacs as well as many ornamentals. There is a rhododendron glen and a braille garden. There is a library. Self guiding tour pamphlet available.

Daily, dawn-dusk; no admission charge; handicapped access; (509) 456-4331.

21   River Front Park   HA-J-L
Downtown along river

This park was left by the Expo '74 and contains a Japanese garden as well as some other formal gardens. It has been beautifully designed.

Daily 11-10, mid-May through Labor Day; shorter hours spring and fall; adults, under $3; children half; handicapped access; (509) 456-5511.

TACOMA

22   Wrights Park   ☆   CA-G-HA-O-P
South 3rd and G St.

This park contains the classically shaped Seymour Conservatory with a large collection of tropical plants and 2,000 orchids. There are seasonal special exhibits. The park is developing an arboretum with paulownias, ginkgos and katsuras as well as more than 100 other species. A large planting of camellias is found here.

Daily 8-4:20; no admission charge; handicapped access; (206) 272-5543.

23   W.W. Seymour Botanical Conservatory   ☆   G-O-P
South 4th and G Street

This Victorian style conservatory displays orchids, cacti, and tropical plants. Seasonal flower displays are held. There is also an All-American Display Garden.

Mon-Sun 8-4:20; no admission charge; (206) 591-5330.

24   Point Defiance Park and Zoo   ☆☆   A-CA-HA-J-R
5402 N. Shirley Ave.

This park contains 198 acres of gardens and zoo; there is a fine rose garden of 3,000 bushes featuring 180 varieties; large camellia, rhododenron, and azalea plantings, Japanese Tea garden, and 20 flower beds with thousands of annuals. The dahlia test gardens display 84 varieties.

Daily 10-8, Memorial Day-Labor Day; 10-5 rest of year; adults, under $3; Sr. citizens half; children less; handicapped access; (206) 759-0118.

OLYMPIA

25   State Capitol Campus and Conservatory   ☆   C-CH-G-HA-P-SU

A large conservatory and 3 greenhouses display tropical and sub-tropical plants as well as cacti and succulents. There is a chrysanthemum collection. The nearby sunken garden is planted with roses, perennials and annuals. Mt. Rainier as well as Puget Sound may be seen from the 160-acre landscaped grounds.

Daily 9-5; no admission charge; handicapped access; (206) 753-5686

WENATCHEE

26   Ohme Gardens   ☆☆   L-RG-S
3 miles north, off U.S. 97

An unusual 9-acre garden overlooking the Columbia River from a rocky bluff. These once arid slopes have been developed into an alpine garden. There are rock bordered pools, fine alpine plantings of shrubs and hundreds of evergreens. The garden has special summer plantings of flowering plants of the Northwest.

Daily 9-dusk, April 1-Oct 31; adults, under $3; children half; (509) 662-5785.

WOODLAND

27 Hulda Klager Lilac Gardens   S
1½ miles west off U.S. 5 at exit 21

A 4½-acre former estate of the hybridizer Hulda Klager who worked with apples and lilacs for more than half a century. The garden contains a wide variety of plants and trees. Lilacs bloom first 2 weeks of May.

Daily, dawn-dusk, donation; (206) 225-8996.

CARSON

28 Wind River Nursery
Gifford Pinchot National Forest

This nursery grows 30 million seedlings annually for the national forests of Washington and Oregon. 16 species are grown. There are seedbeds and bedhouses. An arboretum established in 1912 is located nearby. Self-guiding tour booklets are available.

7:45-4:30 Mon-Fri; no admission charge; (509) 427-5679.

WEST VIRGINIA

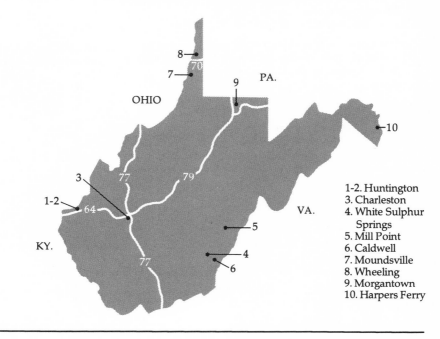

OHIO

PA.

KY.

VA.

1-2. Huntington
3. Charleston
4. White Sulphur
Springs
5. Mill Point
6. Caldwell
7. Moundsville
8. Wheeling
9. Morgantown
10. Harpers Ferry

HUNTINGTON

1 Huntington Galleries
8th St. Road

An art gallery set in fine grounds; a 2-mile walking trail leads through this area of native plants.

10-4 Tues-Sat, 1-5 Sun; closed Jan 1, Christmas; donation; (304) 529-2701.

2 Ritter Park R

A rose garden with more than 90 varieties planted in landscaped beds.

Daily, dawn-dusk.

CHARLESTON

3 Sunrise Garden Center ☆ A-HD-HH-R
746 Myrtle Rd.

This restored mansion serves many cultural purposes; it is set in a 16-acre estate with a fine iris garden; a rose garden with some 300 varieties. There are fine displays of perennials and annuals as well as rhododendron, azalea, dogwood, redbud, and crape-myrtle. The demonstration gardens deal with ground covers, small shrubs, and ornamentals.

10-5 Tues-Sat, 2-5 Sun; closed holidays; no admission charge to gardens; partial handicapped access; (304) 344-8035.

WHITE SULPHUR SPRINGS

4 Old White Garden A-L-S
Greenbrier Hotel

This famous spa hotel is set in lovely grounds which include some beautifully planted gardens. 2 miles west lies an area of rare plants which is marked; included are Box Huckleberry, Pimpernel, Swordleaf Phlox; also fine rhododendrons and azaleas.

For additional information call (304) 536-1110.

MILL POINT

5 Cranberry Glades Botanical Area W-WF
Monongahela National Forest, Rt. 102

A bog-like setting crossed by boardwalks which contains many rare plants including Snakemouth orchids, Pitcher plants, Bog rosemary, sundews, pink orchids. Spring and summer blooming periods.

Daily 9-6; no admission charge.

CALDWELL

6 Brooks Memorial Arboretum
Watoga State Park
Off U.S. 219

This 400-acre arboretum specializes in native plants.

Daily, dawn-dusk; no admission charge; (304) 799-4087.

MOUNDSVILLE

7 Prabhupada's Palace of Gold W
Limestone Palace Rd. off U.S. 250, east

An Indian style palace completed in 1980 as a memorial to Srila Prabhupada. This ornate colorful building is set in a series of gardens. They contain formal beds of annuals and perennials as well as lily ponds, fountains, Indian pergolas, and ornaments.

8-8 winter; 9-9 summer; (304) 843-1600.

WHEELING

8 Oglebay Park G
Rt. 88 north of I-70

Formal gardens as well as greenhouses are set in this 800-acre recreational park. There is a small collection of tropicals.

Daily 8-midnight; greenhouses 9-4 daily; (302) 242-3000.

MORGANTOWN

9 **Core Arboretum** FE-WF
West Virginia University
Evansdale Campus
Monongahela Blvd.

This 75-acre arboretum, which lies along the Monongahela River, was established in 1948. It emphasizes native trees and shrubs with 500 species represented. The arboretum contains a forest area, a flood plain, and a lagoon. There are special collections of viburnums, heaths, ferns, herbs, and wildflowers. A Chinkapin oak is the 3rd largest in the world.

Daily, dawn-dusk; (304) 293-3489.

HARPERS FERRY

10 **The Harper House and Gardens** HH
High St.

This house built in 1782 has a small antebellum garden.

Daily 8-5; no admission charge; (304) 535-6371.

WISCONSIN

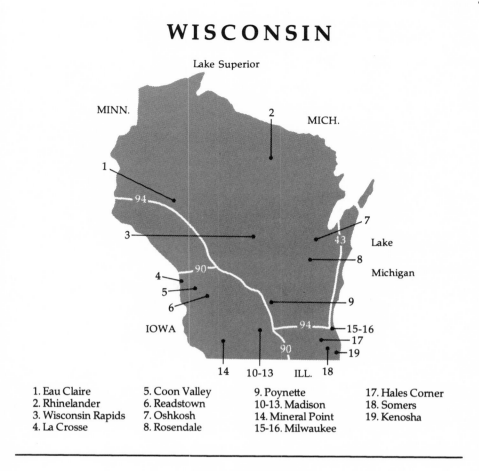

Lake Superior

MINN.

MICH.

Lake

Michigan

IOWA

ILL.

1. Eau Claire	5. Coon Valley	9. Poynette	17. Hales Corner
2. Rhinelander	6. Readstown	10-13. Madison	18. Somers
3. Wisconsin Rapids	7. Oshkosh	14. Mineral Point	19. Kenosha
4. La Crosse	8. Rosendale	15-16. Milwaukee	

EAU CLAIRE

1 Putnam Park G-HA-S
University of Wisconsin—Eau Claire

Much of this 230-acre tract lies along the banks of the Chippewa River adjacent to the university campus. In accordance with the donor's provisions, it has been kept in its natural state and displays more than 400 species of indigenous plants; many have been labelled. Trails wind through the park. There is a well-illustrated guidebook. The university greenhouses are also worth visiting.

Daily, dawn-dusk; greenhouses by appointment; handicapped access; (715) 836-4166.

RHINELANDER

2 Consolidated Papers Forest G-HA
Leith Rd. off Rts. 8 and 47, 10 mi. east

This well-marked road is designed to provide an 11 mile car tour through a portion of the Oneida Forest of the Consolidated Paper Company. This provides a good understanding of reforestation from greenhouse seedlings to full grown trees. Illustrated guide booklet available.

Daily, dawn-dusk, Memorial Day weekend-Sept 30; no admission charge; handicapped access; (715) 422-3878.

WISCONSIN RAPIDS

3   Consolidated Papers Forest
Eagle Rd., off Rt. 54, 1½ mi. east

A 1½-mi. walk through a forest on what was once a tree nursery. Many species of economically important trees may be viewed at various stages of growth. Self-guiding tour with illustrated booklet.

Daily, dawn-dusk; walk or cross-country ski; no admission charge; (715) 422-3878.

LA CROSSE

4   Hixon House   HH
429 N. 7th St.

This house, built at the end of the 19th century, stands in a small period garden.

Daily 1-5 by tour only, June 1-Labor Day; adults, under $3; children half; (608) 782-1980.

COON VALLEY

5   Norskedalen
Helga Gundersen Arboretum
Vernon Count Rd. 1, off U.S. 14 and 61

The arboretum operated by the University of Wisconsin-La Crosse covers 350 acres. Oak savanna, prairie grasses, native trees, and shrubs may be seen along with a restored pioneer homestead.

Daily 9-5; no admission charge; (608) 452-3424.

READSTOWN

6   Jones Arboretum   ☆   FE-HA-H-J-R-WF
U.S. 14, 3 mi. north

A fine arboretum of 128 acres, founded in 1974, with special collections of wildflowers, hostas, ferns, and lilies. There is a rose garden, a herb garden, a perennial garden, a Japanese garden planted with Japanese and American hardy plants, and a test garden for hardiness.

Daily 8-8, May 15-Sept 15; no admission charge; handicapped access; (608) 629-5553.

OSHKOSH

7   Paine Art Center and Arboretum   ☆☆   HA-H-HH-R-S-WF
1410 Algoma Blvd.

A Tudor House surrounded by 14 acres. 4 acres are designed as a formal 18th century English garden. This garden was established in 1920 and redesigned in 1970. These areas display 200 species of plants. There is a herb garden with 100 species, a rose garden with 50 varieties among its 150 bushes, a white garden, a rock garden, as well as a wildflower area and a prairie restoration area. Many spring bulbs, dwarf lilacs, junipers; specimen Burr Oak and ginkgo. An illustrated book is available.

1-4:30 Tues-Sun, Memorial Day-Labor Day; Tues, Thurs, Sat, Sun rest of year; closed Jan; adults, under $3; children free; under 14 must be accompanied by adult; handicapped access; (414) 235-4530.

ROSENDALE

8   **Sison's Peony Gardens**   HA-L-S
    1 block north, junction Rts. 23 and 26

More than 2,000 varieties of peonies have been planted in 4 gardens. They present a spectacular display in this beautifully landscaped setting. Mid-June is the best season for viewing blooming plants.

Daily 8-8, Memorial Day-July 4; no admission charge; handicapped access.

POYNETTE

9   **Mackenzie Environmental Education Center**   HA-S-WF
    East on Rts. CS and Q, off U.S. 51

This museum and center is located on 500 acres of land which include a model forest, an arboretum, a prairie and a small nursery. More than 300 species of indigenous and foreign trees are to be found here along with numerous wildflowers and grasses. Many marked trails with a dozen guide booklets.

Daily 8-4; museum closed weekends from mid-Oct to May; no admission charge; handicapped access; (608) 635-4498.

MADISON

10   **Olbrich Gardens**   H-HA
     3330 Atwood Ave.

A 12-acre arboretum established on former marshland; the garden center has been constructed and the gardens themselves are underway. A herb garden is open now; a dahlia garden is scheduled for 1984 with many others to follow. There is a library.

Daily 9-dusk, June 1-Oct 1; 9-5 Mon-Fri, rest of year; no admission charge; handicapped access; (608) 266-4148.

11   **University of Wisconsin Arboretum, Madison**   H-L-S
     1207 Seminole Highway

This 1,200-acre arboretum has developed 60 acres into special gardens with 2,000 species represented. The garden is arranged into 32 plant communities. There are special collections of flowering crab-apples, lilacs, and viburnums. The Longnecker Horticultural Gardens which are part of the arboretum contain more than 250 kinds of lilacs planted in a landscaped setting. Test and demonstration gardens. Restored tall-grass prairie; crab-apples bloom in early May, lilacs in mid-May, wildflowers in summer; There are greenhouses and a library.

Daily 7-10; McKay Visitor Center 12:30-4 except holidays; no admission charge; limited handicapped access; (608) 262-2746.

12   **Capitol Grounds**

The 7-acre park which surrounds the capitol building contains parterre gardens and formal beds with numerous designs done with perennials and annuals.

Daily, dawn-dusk.

13 Executive Residence HH
Lake Mendota

This Georgian style mansion stands in 2½ acres of formally landscaped grounds which include a fragrance garden for the blind.

12-3, 2nd and 4th Thurs of each summer month; (608) 266-7484.

MINERAL POINT

14 Shake Rag Alley
18 Shake Rag St.

An All-American Garden surrounds the oldest home in this area with perennials and annuals.

Daily 10-5, May-Oct 30; adults, under $3; 6-12 half; (608) 987-2808.

MILWAUKEE

15 Mitchell Park Conservatory ☆☆☆ C-G-HA-P-R-SU
524 S. Layton Blvd.

A 60-acre park with three striking geodesic dome conservatories which place 1½ acres under glass. A tropical house contains an Amazon rain forest with a lagoon; there is also an Australian section. The arid and desert plant house display a fine cactus collection. The flower show house features seven major themed floral displays. Outside there is a sunken rose garden and a mall planted with perennials.

Daily 9-8 except Fri 9-5, Memorial Day-Labor Day; 9-5 Mon-Fri, 9-8 Sat-Sun, rest of year; adults, under $3; under 16 half; handicapped access; (414) 278-4383.

16 Lowell Damon House HH
2107 N. Wauwatosa Ave.
Wauwatosa

A period garden lies on the grounds of this colonial style home built in 1847.

3-5 Wed, 1-5 Sun; no admission charge; closed major holidays; (414) 259-0372.

HALES CORNER

17 Alfred L. Boerner Botanical Gardens ☆☆☆☆ F-HA-H-R-RG-S-W-WF
5879 S. 92nd St.

This 680-acre arboretum contains 6 acres of formal gardens developed in 1939; they are outstanding and feature 13,000 species. A lilac garden of 401 species and 1,200 plants is surrounded by 50,000 tulips of 100 varieties; a formal rose garden contains more than 5,000 plants of 375 varieties; the walled tree peony garden contains more than 125 European and Japanese varieties. There is a rock garden with 456 different species; perennial and annual gardens feature day-lilies, 460 types of irises, 264 varieties of peonies, dahlias, tuberous begonias, and chrysanthemums; pools with hardy water lilies; bog gardens; prairie garden; a large intricately designed herb garden with 500 species and cultivars.

The gardens contain a fine collection of flowering crab-apples of 1,000 trees representing 327 cultivars. In addition there are test gardens, demonstration gardens, a pinetum, mulch exhibits, grass demonstrations, a wildflower garden, and nature trails. The collection of shade trees is good as is that of dwarf fruit trees. There is a library. Illustrated guide booklets.

Daily 8-dusk, summer; 8-4 Mon-Fri winter, but formal gardens are closed; no admission charge; children must be accompanied by an adult; handicapped access; (414) 425-1132.

SOMERS

18 **Hyslop Foundation**
Hawthorn Hollow

This arboretum was established in 1971; it contains a growing collection of trees, shrubs as well as beds of perennials and annuals. Trails lead through the grounds.

Daily, sunrise-sunset.

KENOSHA

19 **Lincoln Flower Gardens**
22nd Ave. and 70th St.

A small botanical garden is located in this public park.

Daily, dawn-dusk.

WYOMING

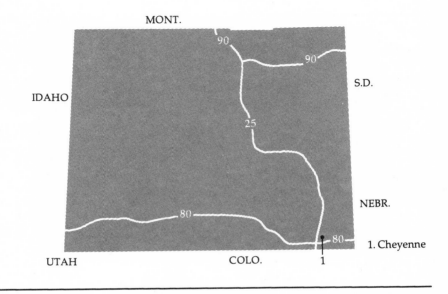

MONT.

IDAHO

S.D.

NEBR.

1. Cheyenne

UTAH   COLO.   1

CHEYENNE

1 Horticultural Field Station

Hardiness test plots for trees, shrubs, and vegetables are maintained at this station.
For hours call (307) 777-7321.

CANADA

ALBERTA

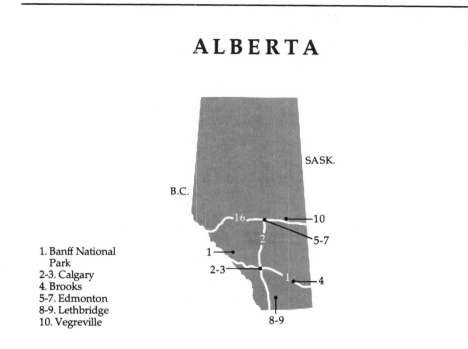

SASK.

B.C.

16
2
10
5-7

1. Banff National
Park
2-3. Calgary
4. Brooks
5-7. Edmonton
8-9. Lethbridge
10. Vegreville

1
2-3
1
4

8-9

BANFF NATIONAL PARK

1   **Cascade Rock Gardens**   RG
Administration Building

A series of small gardens connected by cascades; there are numerous shrubs,
flowering plants, rustic bridges. This rock garden features alpine plants primarily.

Daily; no admission charge; (403) 762-3324.

CALGARY

2   **Devonian Gardens**   ☆☆   G-HA-P
Toronto-Dominion Square

A completely enclosed 2½-acre tropical garden on top of the largest downtown
shopping center. It features a large selection of sub-tropical plants in an unusual
setting.

Daily; no admission charge; handicapped access.

3   **Calgary Zoo, Botanic Gardens, and Natural History Park**   ☆☆   BR-C-HA-O
Memorial Drive and 12th St. East, St. George's Island

This park, founded in 1929, contains a conservatory and aviary with more than
10,000 plants. There are collections of bromeliads, cacti, orchids, and tropical plants.

Daily 9-6, May 1-Aug 31; 9-4:30 Mon-Fri; 9-5:30 Sat-Sun rest of year; Adults, under $3; 12-17 half; under 12 nominal; handicapped access; picnic area; (403) 262-8144.

BROOKS

4   Alberta Horticultural Research Center   F-HD-R-S
3 mi. southeast, off Rt. 1

The center tests plants for the severe local climate. There is an All-American Selections garden, a rock garden, a rose garden, a juniper collection, a demonstration orchard, as well as beds of perennials and annuals. June to August are the best times.

Weekdays 9-5; no admission charge; (403) 362-3391.

EDMONTON

5   Devonian Botanic Garden   ☆☆☆   H-HA-HD-RG-S
University of Alberta

This 190 acre botanical garden was founded in 1959 and emphasizes herbaceous and alpine plants as well as shrubs and trees hardy in the area. More than 2,500 species of plants are grown. There is a herb garden, shrub and rock garden. Special collections of alliums, peonies (75 varieties), Tibetan poppies, irises, and primulas are maintained. The demonstration gardens test for hardiness. There is a library.

Weekdays 10-4, May-Sept; 12-6 Sat, Sun, holidays; no admission charge; handicapped access; (403) 987-3054.

6   Muttart Conservatory and Botanical Gardens   ☆☆☆   C-G-HA-P-SU
96 Ave. and 96A St.

4 large pyramid shaped greenhouses are divided into an arid house, a tropical house, a temperate house, and one for special displays. The fine collection of plants is augmented by good seasonal shows.

Daily 11-9; adults, under $3; over 65 and 13-18 two-thirds; 6-12 half; family rate, under $6; handicapped access; (403) 428-2939.

7   Legislative Buildings
109 St. and 97th Ave.

Well-landscaped grounds surround this legislative building with beds of perennials and annuals.

Daily 9-4; (403) 427-7445.

LETHBRIDGE

8   Brewery Gardens   ☆   HA
Sicks Brewery, off Hghway 3

These gardens, founded in 1901, include 8 areas which feature both annuals and perennials in beautifully designed beds.

24 hours daily; lighted at night; no admission charge; handicapped access; (403) 328-3511.

9 **Nikka Yuko Japanese Garden** ☆ HA-J
Henderson Park; Mayor Magrath Drive

A Japanese Garden in 5 traditional sections which include ponds, streams, pavillions, bridges, tea house, and bell tower from Japan and Taiwan. This well-scaled garden utilizes only hardy native plants and is authentic within those limitations.

Daily 8-9, May 19-Aug 15; 8:30-9 Aug 16-day before Labor Day; 9-5 Victoria Day, Labor Day, Thanksgiving; adults, under $3; Senior citizens, 12-17 half; handicapped access; (403) 328-3511.

VEGREVILLE

10 **Soil and Crop Substation**
Alberta Environment Center
2 km. west of town

Test and demonstration plantings for plant hardiness and production on saline soil.

8-4:30 Mon-Fri; no admission charge; (403) 632-6761.

BRITISH COLUMBIA

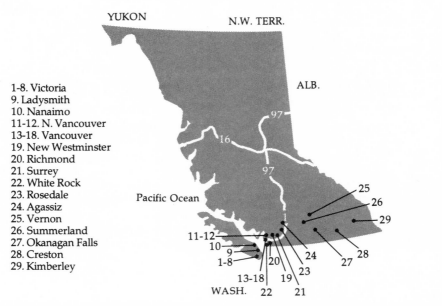

1-8. Victoria
9. Ladysmith
10. Nanaimo
11-12. N. Vancouver
13-18. Vancouver
19. New Westminster
20. Richmond
21. Surrey
22. White Rock
23. Rosedale
24. Agassiz
25. Vernon
26. Summerland
27. Okanagan Falls
28. Creston
29. Kimberley

VICTORIA

1   The Butchart Gardens ☆☆☆☆   HA-J-L-R-W
800 Benevenuto Blvd.
Brentwood Bay

This is among the most colorful gardens in North America with thousands of massed plants in large special gardens. Plantings include rhododendrons, primroses, delphiniums, poppies, myosotis, lupines, irises, foxgloves, hundreds of varieties of tulips, etc. Trees include Japanese Maples, Purple-leaf Plum, Variegated Box-Elder, madrone, Dove-Tree, redwoods. Plants are changed constantly so that all is at its peak constantly. Japanese garden, rose garden, Italian garden, sunken garden, lake garden, and fountains add to the beauty of this park. It is illuminated at night. There is a library.

Daily 9-11, July 1-Aug 31; 9-9 May 1-June 30 and Sept 1-30; March 1-April 30 and Oct 1-31; 9-4 rest of year; adults, under $6; 13-17 two-thirds; 5-12 nominal; handicapped access; (604) 652-4422.

2   Fable Cottage Estate
5187 Cordova Bay via Hghway 17

A fairytale home set in 3½ acres of lush gardens. There are well-kept flower beds of perennials and annuals. The estate includes a 2,000 pound revolving flower basket.

Daily 9:30-dusk, late March to late Oct; adults, under $6; senior citizens three-quarters; students two-thirds; 4-12 half; family rate, under $15; (604) 658-5741.

3   Government House Gardens ☆   R-W
1401 Rockland Avenue

Formal flower beds are set in 35 acres of grounds. There is a 7-acre sunken rose garden, a lily pond, and a waterfall. The garden displays perennials and annuals as well as ivies, heathers, rhododendrons, azaleas, and blooming shrubs which surround the government buildings.

Daily; no admission charge; handicapped access; (604) 595-1515.

4 Victoria's Enchanted Garden BO
Victoria Heritage Village
321 Bellefield St.

Waterfalls, ponds, and dollhouses are surrounded by gardens of shrubs, perennials, and annuals. There is a bonsai display.

Daily 8:30-10; somewhat shorter hours in winter; (604) 384-3232.

5 Crystal Gardens ☆ G
713 Douglas St.

This conservatory and aviary contains 150 species of exotic tropical plants, trees, winding walkways, streams, waterfalls, as well as 50 species of tropical birds. It is well planted and maintained.

Daily 10-9, July 1-Aug 31; 10-5:30 rest of year; adults, under $6; senior citizens, 6-16 half; family rate, under $9; live entertainment nightly July 1-Aug 31; (604) 381-1213.

6 Anne Hathaway's Cottage SH
429 Lampson St.

A replica of the home of Anne Hathaway, Shakespeare's wife, along with its garden has been created here as part of a 5-acre complex which includes an old English village.

Lily Pond, Butchart Gardens

Daily 9-9, June 1-Sept 30; 10-4, Oct 1-May 31; adults, under $6; children half; (604) 388-4353.

7   **Beacon Hill Park**
Douglas St. and Marine Drive

This 154-acre park contains old oaks and cedars. There are large beds of perennials and annuals.

Daily, dawn-dusk.

8   **Hatley Castle—Royal Roads Military College**   HA-J-R
Royal Roads

A house with gardens constructed at the turn of the century. This site is now a military college with 650 acres of lawns, gardens, and shrubbery. There are Italian and Japanese gardens, all placed in a beautiful setting.

Daily 10-4; no admission charge; handicapped access; (604) 388-1660.

LADYSMITH

9   **Crown Forest Industries Arboretum and Museum**
Rt. 1

The arboretum includes native and introduced species of trees, many planted more than 30 years ago. The museum displays logging equipment.

Daily 10-4:30; no admission charge; (604) 754-3206.

NANAIMO

10   **Harmac Arboretum**
Rt. 1, 7 mi. south

This arboretum established in 1956 seeks to discover exotic trees which would do well in the area. There is also a section of native forest.

Daily 7:30-4; no admission charge; (604) 753-1112, local 267.

NORTH VANCOUVER

11   **Capilano Suspension Bridge and Park**
3735 Capilano Rd.

The park includes gardens of perennials and annuals, waterfalls, and mountain scenery.

Daily 8-10:30, July, Aug; 8-5, Sept-June; adults, under $3; children less than half; (604) 985-7474.

12   **Park and Tillford Gardens**   ☆☆   A-G-HA-J-R
1200 Cotton Rd.
North Vancouver

This series of 8 special gardens includes a rose garden, an oriental garden as well as a fine selection of rhododendrons, annuals, and native trees and shrubs. There are excellent seasonal displays. The gardens cover an area of 2½ acres; there are greenhouses.

Daily 8-11; no admission charge; handicapped access; (604) 987-9321.

VANCOUVER

13 Bloedel Conservatory ☆☆☆☆ G-HA-P
Queen Elizabeth Park

A triodetic dome which contains more than 500 species of jungle and desert plants is located in a magnificent park. There is a good display of palms. Seasonal displays augment the collection. There is a library.

Daily 10-9:30, winter 10-5:30; closed Christmas; adults, under $3; Senior citizens and children less than half; handicapped access; (604) 872-5513.

14 Queen Elizabeth Park ☆☆☆ HA-L-R-RG
Cambie St. and W. 33rd Ave.

50 acres of magnificent gardens. There are rose gardens, perennial, and annual beds, a sunken garden, quarry gardens, and an arboretum. The views of the harbor, city and North Shore mountains are excellent.

Daily; no admission charge; handicapped access; (604) 872-5513.

15 Stanley Park ☆☆ A-HA-L-R-W
downtown Vancouver

This large park contains a fine rose garden as well as beds of perennnials and annuals. The plantings of dogwoods, azaleas, flowering cherries, and weeping hemlocks are particularly good. There is a lagoon with water lilies and a natural forest with walking trails.

Daily; no admission charge; handicapped access.

16 Vandusen Botanical Gardens—MacMillan Bloedel Place ☆☆ A-HA-L-T-W
5251 Oak St.

This 55-acre garden was established in 1971. It contains a good collection of rhododendron, holly, as well as ponds with water lilies. There is a Sino-Himalayan garden and a maze. Bloedel Place consists of a 'walk in the forest' museum. The structure, which cleverly utilizes forest and water, is exciting as are the exhibits. There is a library.

10-8 summer, 10-4 winter; adults, under $3; senior citizens and 6-18 half; groups rates; guided tours; handicapped access; (604) 266-7194.

17 Nitobe Memorial Garden ☆☆☆ HA-J-L
University of British Columbia
6501 Marine Drive

A 2½ acre Japanese garden which has been carefully designed to use native plants, trained in the Japanese fashion. It consists of a tea garden and a large garden surrounding a lake which include a waterfall and miniature mountain. There is a moss area and a good diplay of irises and Japanese cherries.

Daily 10-one hour before dusk; Good Friday-Thanksgiving; weekdays 10-3 rest of year; adults and children nominal; senior citizens free; handicapped access; (604) 228-3928.

18 Botanical Garden ☆☆☆ A-G-H-HA-HD-J-P-R-RG-S-T
University of British Columbia
6501 N.W. Marine Drive

This garden, established in 1916, is the oldest university botanical garden in Canada. 110 acres have been beautifully planted. The Asian garden reached through a

Chinese gate includes 30 acres of vines, rhododendrons, and magnolias. There is a fine rose garden with an important collection of hybrid roses. Economic plants important to the Indians have been planted in a special section.

A 'Physick' Garden presents medicinal plants in a 16th century design. An 8-acre arboretum emphasizes native shrubs and trees. There are special collections of woody Asian plants, alpines, heathers. A Contemporary garden emphasizes recently introduced hybrids and new flowering perennials. Greenhouses. There is a library.

Daily 10-one hour before dusk; admission, nominal; senior citizens, handicapped free; handicapped access; (604) 228-3928.

NEW WESTMINSTER

19   **Japanese Friendship Garden**   ☆   HA-J-W
Queens Ave near City Hall

This western interpretation of a classic Japanese garden is dedicated to the sister city of Moriguchi in Japan. 2½ acres of plantings including 100 Yoshino cherry trees; the garden mainly utilizes native plants. There is a water-lily pond.

Daily; no admission charge; handicapped access.

RICHMOND

20   **Bota Gardens**   ☆☆   A-R
10800 No. 5 Rd. at Steveston Highway

A fine 6 acre garden planted around a lagoon and on a small island. More than 200 varieties of tulips with 100,000 bulbs bloom in spring. There are also large groupings of rhododendrons, azaleas, dogwoods, Japanese cherries, and magnolias. In the summer the rose and lily gardens as well as annual beds are in bloom.

Daily 9-dusk; adults, under $6; Senior citizens three-quarters; 13-17 two-thirds; 6-12 half; guided tours; (604) 271-9235.

SURREY

21   **Woodland Garden**   A
172nd St.

This arboretum has several ponds, flowering cherries, and magnolias. The old rhododendrons are especially beautiful in May.

Daily; adults, under $3; check for hours (604) 536-9282.

WHITE ROCK

22   **Peace Arch Park**   HA-S
Rt. 99A on international border

This park is jointly operated by British Columbia and the State of Washington. Its Redwood Arboretum has a good collection of native and cultivated trees.

Daily, dawn-dusk; no admission charge; handicapped access.

ROSEDALE

23   **Minter Gardens**   ☆☆   A-FE-L-R
52892 Bunker Rd.

Nestled at the foot of 7,000 ft Mt. Cheam, are 10 large gardens which cover 27 acres with fine plantings of rhododendrons, azaleas, herbaceous plants, annuals, roses, and heather. The lake garden is especially beautiful as is the view of the mountains. There is also a good fern garden and a fragrance garden. The neighboring area near Aldergrove and Bradner contains many acres of flowering bulbs in spring; best viewed around Easter.

Daily 9-dusk, April 1-Oct 31; adults, under $6; over 64 and 13-18 three-quarter; 6-12 half; handicapped access; (604) 794-7191.

AGASSIZ

24 Agassiz Research Station
.6947 No. 7 Highway

There is a small arboretum with some good 90-year-old specimens. Research for hardiness on vegetables, turf, and flowers is conducted.

8-4:30 Mon-Fri; guided tours; no admission charge; (604) 796-2221.

VERNON

25 Japanese Garden HA-J
Polson Park
Highway 97 at 25th St.

A Japanese garden with a Chinese tea house in an Oriental setting. The garden also features a large floral clock composed of 3,500 plants.

Daily 9-10; no admission charge; handicapped access; picnic area.

SUMMERLAND

26 Agriculture Research Station

There are gardens of perennials and annuals. Hardiness test gardens.

Daily 7:30-8:30, April 1-Sept 1; 8-5, Oct 1-March 31; no admission charge; (604) 494-7711.

OKANAGAN FALLS

27 Memorial Rose Gardens R

This park contains a rose garden and a collection of more than 190 hybrid tea roses.

Daily 8-dusk, May-Oct; no admission charge; (604) 497-8416.

CRESTON

28 Blossom Festival

A festival is held each May.

For information call (604) 354-4831.

KIMBERLEY

29 Cominco Gardens

A 2½ acre park with fine beds of perennials and annuals.

Daily, dawn-dusk.

MANITOBA

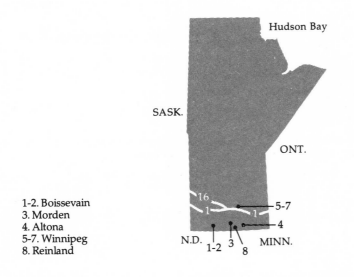

Hudson Bay

SASK.

ONT.

1-2. Boissevain
3. Morden
4. Altona
5-7. Winnipeg
8. Reinland

N.D.

MINN.

BOISSEVAIN

1 International Peace Garden ☆☆ L-R
Highway 10 and U.S. 281

The beautifully landscaped formal gardens are part of a 2,300-acre preserve established in 1932 on both sides of the American and Canadian border. There are terrace gardens and sunken rose gardens with more than 2,000 bushes. Fine beds of perennials and annuals are spread throughout the gardens. A floral clock. There is an arboretum.

Daily mid-May to mid-Sept; vehicle permit, under $3; partial handicapped access.

2 Manitoba Horticultual Association Arboretum
Canadian Loop Rd.

This small arboretum provides a well-labelled collection of native trees and shrubs. One must watch for the sign along the road closely.

Daily, all hours; no admission charge; (701) 263-4390.

MORDEN

3 Research Station and Arboretum G-HA-R

12 acres of gardens and 60 of arboretum contain some 3,000 species. Founded in 1915, it tests and develops plants for hardiness. There are large collections of ornamentals, hedges, roses, hardy fruit and shade trees including flowering crab-apples, flowering prunes, chrysanthemums, as well as grain and vegetable test sites. 3 greenhouses. There is a library.

Daily 8:30-5 during summer months; no admission charge; handicapped access; (204) 822-4471.

ALTONA

4 **Sun Flower Festival**

An annual festival is held here

For information call (204) 832-0167.

WINNIPEG

5 **English Garden** ☆☆ CH-HA-G-P-R
Assiniboine Park
Corydon Ave W. at Park Blvd.

A large rose garden is featured along with smaller plantings of perennials. The new conservatory has a palm house, a permanent floral display area, and an exhibition area. There are special seasonal flower shows; they include an Easter lily, chrysanthemums, and a Christmas display.

Daily 8-10; no admission charge; handicapped access; (204) 889-0007.

6 **Living Prairie Museum and Park** HA-S
2795 Ness Ave.

This park preserves 40 acres of prairie with more than 150 species of plants once common to the great plains. Trails and nature walks.

Daily 10-6, July, Aug; 9-1 Mon-Fri, 12-5 Sat, Sun, April, May, Sept; weekdays 12-5 other months; closed holidays; no admission charge; handicapped access; (204) 832-0167.

7 **Little Mountain Park** WF
½ mi. east of Sturgeon Rd off Inkster Blvd.

This park contains an aspen forest and a large selection of wildflowers which bloom during the summer months.

Daily, dawn-dusk; no admission charge; guided nature walks; picnic areas; (204) 832-0167.

REINLAND

8 **Village Gardens** HH
Rt. 243 near border

This small village contains many houses and farmsteads which have been restored to celebrate the centennial of the community. The grounds and gardens have been attractively restored to their original form.

Daily, dawn-dusk.

NEW BRUNSWICK

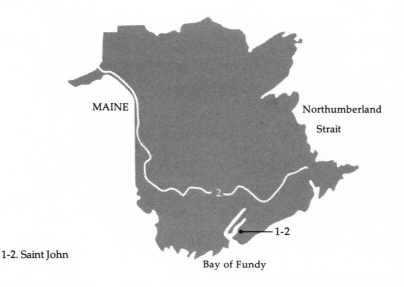

MAINE

Northumberland

Strait

2

1-2

1-2. Saint John

Bay of Fundy

SAINT JOHN

1 Horticultural Gardens
Seeley St.

A display of perennials and annuals along with flowering shrubs.

Daily, dawn-dusk.

2 Rockwood Park and Public Gardens

Gardens comprise 3 acres of this large park; there are lily ponds as well as 16 flower beds of perennials and annuals. Greenhouses.

Daily, dawn-dusk.

NEWFOUNDLAND

Gulf of
St. Lawrence

Atlantic Ocean

1. Holyrood
2. St. John's

HOLYROOD

1 Salmonier Nature Park
12 km. south on Hwy. 1 at Hwy. 90

This is a nature and wildlife preserve with a representative collection of local flora. There are boardwalks and nature trails.

Daily 12-7, June 1-Labor Day; adults and under 12 nominal; senior citizens free; picnic area; (709) 737-2816.

ST. JOHN'S

2 Memorial University Botanic Park at Oxen Pond ☆☆ HA-S
Pippy Park
Memorial University
Mt. Scio Rd.

This botanical garden of more than 80 acres, established in 1971, now possesses a large collection of plants native to Newfoundland and Labrador. There are a number of special gardens including a rock garden, a peat garden, a cottage garden, a vegetable garden, a heather garden, and a garden of flowers grown in old Newfoundland gardens. Trial and demonstration gardens test the hardiness of plants.

1:30-4 Mon-Fri; 10-5:30 Sun, May 1-Nov 30; no admission charge; handicapped access; (709) 737-8590.

NOVA SCOTIA

1-2. Annapolis Royal
3. Aylesford (and Kentville)
4. Kentville
5. Starr Point
6. Grand Pre National
Historic Park
7. Windsor
8. Truro
9. Halifax
10. Louisburg

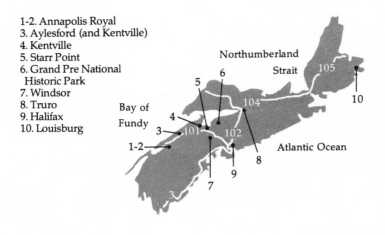

ANNAPOLIS ROYAL

1 **Annapolis Royal Historic Gardens** ☆☆☆ BX-HA-R-T
1 block south of junction Hwys. 201 and 1

4 beautiful sections make up this 10-acre garden which depicts the history of the area. The Acadian garden deals with the plants of the earliest settlers. The Governor's Garden is based on New England examples with boxwood and other typical plantings. The rose garden contains more than 1,600 plants and has a maze. The Victorian garden is romantic in nature.

Daily 9-dusk, June 1-Sept 30; adults, under $3; senior citizens half; under 12 free; handicapped access; (902) 532-5104.

2 **Runciman House** HH
St. George St.

This Georgian colonial house stands in a garden of shrubs, perennials, and annuals.

2-5, 7-9 weekends, June-Oct; no admission charge.

AYLESFORD AND KENTVILLE

3 **Apple Blossom Festival** A-F

Late May and early June find thousands of apple trees in bloom in this orchard country. The blooming rhododendron are also celebrated.

KENTVILLE

4 **Research Station** A

A large collection of rhododendrons and azaleas is tested for hardiness.

8-4:30 Mon-Fri; no admission charge; (902) 678-2171.

STARR POINT

5   **Prescott House**   HH-S
Town Plot Rd.

Charles Ramage Prescott, who introduced apples to Nova Scotia, built this house in 1799. The grounds contain some rare shrubs and trees, including acacias.

Daily 9:30-5:30, May 15-Oct 15; donations.

GRAND PRE NATIONAL HISTORIC PARK

6   **Acadian Village**   HH

Some of the ruins have been rebuilt along with their gardens.

Daily 9-6, June 1-Oct 15; no admission charge.

WINDSOR

7   **Haliburton House**   HH

A 25-acre estate surrounds this house built in 1836. A portion of the grounds have been developed into gardens of perennials and annuals.

Daily 9:30-5:30, May 15-Oct 15; donations; (902) 798-2915.

TRURO

8   **Nova Scotia Agricultural College**
Bible Hill

The college maintains a collection of trees, shrubs, and ornamentals as well as a display garden of perennials and annuals.

Call for hours (902) 895-1571.

HALIFAX

9   **Halifax Public Gardens**   ☆☆   HA-L-S-W
Spring Garden Road and Summer St.

This beautiful garden established in 1867, but based on gardens a century older, extends over almost 20 acres. It is filled with colorful flower beds, Lily ponds, and numerous trees and shrubs collected from many lands. Concerts are held during the summer months.

Daily 8-10, July 1-Aug 31; 8-dark May 1-June 30, Sept 1-Oct 31; no admission charge; handicapped access; (902) 422-5264.

LOUISBOURG

10   **National Historic Park**
3.2 km. west of town

The ancient fortress and portions of the town have been reconstructed. There is an 18th century French herb garden.

Daily 9-8, July 1-Labor Day; 10-6 June 1-30, Labor Day-Sept 30; adults, under $3; 5-17 half; under 5, Canadian senior citizens free; family rate, under $6; (902) 733-2280.

ONTARIO

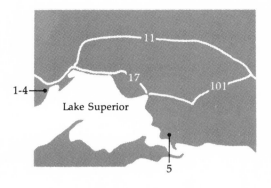

N.W. ONTARIO
1-4. Thunder Bay
5. Sault Ste. Marie

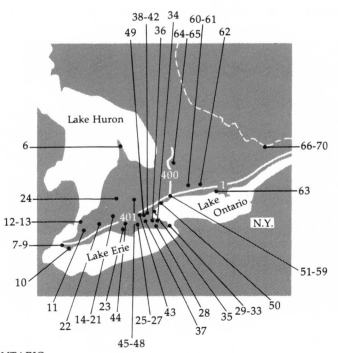

SOUTH ONTARIO

6. Tobermory	23. St. Thomas	36. St. Catherines	50. Etobicoke
7-9. Windsor	24. Stratford	37. Vineland	51-59. Toronto
10. Ruthven	25-27. Brantford	38-42. Hamilton	60-61. Whitby
11. Chatham	28. Welland	43. Dundas	62. Oshawa
12-13. Sarnia	29-33. Niagara Falls	44. Puslinch	63. Cobourg
14-21. London	34. Queenston	45-48. Guelph	64-65. Barrie
22. W. Lorne	35. Niagara-on-the-Lake	49. Milton	66-70. Ottawa

THUNDER BAY

1 Centennial Botanical Conservatory ☆☆ C-G-HA-P-SU
Balmoral and Dease Sts.

This large modern conservatory was constructed in 1967. It contains a good collection of tropical plants, cacti, and succulents. Seasonal flower shows are presented.

Daily 1-4; closed Good Friday, Dec 25-26; no admission charge; handicapped access; (807) 623-2711 ext. 351.

2 Lakehead University Arboretum   HA-S
Lakehead University

A 50-acre arboretum was established here in 1975. It displays collections of junipers, arborvitae, and hardy conifers. Test and demonstration gardens for woody ornamentals are grown. There is a small library.

Daily 9-5, May-Sept; no admission charge; handicapped access; (807) 345-2121.

3 Hillcrest Park
High St., between Red River and Oliver Rds.

This park lies high above the southern section of the city with a fine view of the harbor. It contains sunken gardens with perennials and annuals; approximately 70 varieties of flowers have been planted.

Daily, dawn-dusk; no admission charge.

4 International Friendship Garden   ☆
Victoria and Hyde Park Aves.

This international park was established in 1966 by various ethnic communities and it continues to expand. At present there is an Italian garden, a Canadian garden, a Slovakian garden, a Lithuanian garden, a German garden, a Polish garden, and a Ukranian garden.

Daily, dawn-dusk; no admission charge.

SAULT ST. MARIE

5 Great Lakes Forest Research Centre Arboretum   HA
1219 Queen Street East

The arboretum placed on 9 acres has developed a collection of native Canadian species suitable for the climate of the area. It was begun in 1978. There is a library.

Daily, dawn-dusk; no admission charge; handicapped access; (705) 949-9561.

TOBERMORY

6 Lake Whistle Gardens
Dyer Bay Rd., off Rt. 6

These gardens include a hundred varieties of shrubs, perennials, and annuals. There is a demonstration vegetable garden.

8-dusk Fri, Sat, Sun and holiday Mon, May 1-Sept 6.

WINDSOR

7   Coventry Gardens
Riverside Drive East and Pillette Rd.

This riverfront park contains a large floating fountain and a garden of perennials and annuals.

Daily, dawn-dusk.

8   Jackson Park Sunken Garden ☆☆   HA-R
Tecumseh and Ouellette Sts.

A war memorial garden has been established here around a Lancaster Bomber. There is a fine rose garden with 12,500 bushes representing 450 varieties; the collection continues to expand. 25,000 tulips bloom each spring. Many ornamental shrubs, as well as beds of perennials and annuals have been planted in the park.

Daily, dawn-dusk; no admission charge; handicapped access; (519) 255-6276.

9   Dieppe Gardens   R
Ouellette Ave.

The park along the riverfront contains a rose garden and a good display of colorful annuals.

Daily, dawn-dusk.

RUTHVEN

10   Colasanti's Tropical Gardens   C-P-SU
3 mi. east of Jack Miner Bird Sanctuary

These commercial greenhouses contain large collections of tropical plants, as well as cacti and succulents. They are well displayed. The nearby bird sanctuary is a migration site for Canadian geese in late Oct, early Nov and mid-March.

8-5 Mon-Sat; 10-5 Sun; no admission charge; (519) 326-3287.

CHATHAM

11   Jacee Gardens   H-R-W

A collection of alpine plants surround a sunken garden with its 8,000 annuals, a fountain, and a lily pond. A rose garden, herb garden, and arboretum are under construction at the McKenzie Ross Park. The small riverside B'nai Brith Collins Park downtown contains imaginative plantings of annuals.

Daily, dawn-dusk.

SARNIA

12   Centennial Park
Sarnia Bay

These gardens are planted with more than 50,000 annuals each year.

Daily, dawn-dusk.

13 Germain Park

A sunken garden of perennials, annuals, and shrubs has been planted here. A vine collection and an arboretum has been started.

Daily, dawn-dusk.

LONDON

14 Eldon House HH
481 Ridout St.

This 19th century home is the oldest residence of the city. It stands in a period garden planted in the Victorian style.

Daily 12-5, June 1-Aug 31; 2-5 March 1-May 31, Sept 1-Nov 30; closed New Year, Feb, March, Christmas; adults, under $3; senior citizens half; under 12 nominal; (519) 433-6171.

15 Victoria Park S
Dufferin and Wellington Sts.

A small park with specimen London plane, Tulip trees, Kentucky Coffee trees. There are extensive flower beds.

Daily 8-dusk.

16 Rose Garden R
Springbank Drive and Wonderland Side Rd.

A 6-acre rose garden has been planted with many varieties. There is a lily pond.

Daily, 8-dusk.

17 Sifton Botanical Bog W
Oxford St., directly south from Royal York Rd.

This 70-acre bog contains plants typical of the immense bogs of northern Canada. There is sphagnum moss, leatherleaf fern, pitcher plant, Sundew, several types of orchids as well as a variety of trees.

Daily 8-dusk.

18 Reservoir Park
West London

This park which overlooks the Thames River Valley contains a fine stand of native trees with good specimens.

Daily 8-dusk.

19 Elmo W. Curtis Gardens W
Springbank Drive and Wonderland Rd.

A formal garden has been planted in this 6-acre park which also contains a water lily pond and woodlands.

Daily, dawn-dusk.

20 Storybook Gardens and Springbank Park T
Banks of the Thames River

281 acres along the river are filled with colorful beds of perennials and annuals. There is a maze as well as unusual specimen trees.

Daily, dawn-dusk.

21   Fanshawe Pioneer Village   H-HH
Fanshawe Park

22 log and frame buildings seek to recapture the life of a community a century ago. There is an old-fashioned herb garden.

For hours call (519) 451-2800.

WEST LORNE

22   Swains Greenhouses   C-P-SU
Junction of Rt. 3 and 76 at Eagle

3½ acres of tropical plants, cacti, and succulents are shown in interesting displays by this large commercial greenhouse.

Weekdays 9-4; 10-4 Sat; (519) 768-1116.

ST. THOMAS

23   Waterworks Park   W

This picturesque park contains water lilies as well as beds of perennials and annuals in an informal design.

Daily, dawn-dusk.

STRATFORD

24   Centennial Gardens   ☆

Gardens have been planted on both sides of the Avon River and among a series of ponds. Ornamental shrubs, perennials and annuals are chiefly used.

Daily, dawn-dusk.

BRANTFORD

25   Glenhyrst Gardens
20 Ava Rd.

This 10-acre park contains gardens and landscaped grounds planted with perennials and annuals. The park overlooks the Grand River. The building on the ground is used for changing art exhibits.

10-8 Tues-Fri, 2-6 Sat-Sun; no admission charge; (519) 756-5932.

26   Lorne Park
Colborne St.

The park includes large beds of perennials and annuals planted in colorful designs.

Daily, dawn-dusk.

27   Alexander Graham Bell Memorial and Home
94 Tutela Heights Rd.

A small garden is part of this site.

Daily 10-4, June 15-Labor Day; closed Mon, rest of year; adults nominal (519) 756-5662.

WELLAND

28 Rose Festival

A 2 week rose festival is held in June.

For information call (416) 732-7515.

NIAGARA FALLS

29 Queen Victoria Park ☆☆☆☆ L-R-RG
Niagara Parkway, at the falls

This 200-acre park provides a grand view of the falls and provides a spectacular combination of a natural wonder and fine landscape design. 500,000 daffodils bloom in spring. There is a fine rose garden, a rock garden, as well as beds of perennials and annuals which are well maintained through the seasons. The park is lit at night.

Daily; concerts Fri eve, mid-June-Labor Day.

Queen Victoria Park

30 Niagara Park Commission Greenhouses ☆☆ CH-G-HA-P
½ km. south of Horseshoe Falls

The greenhouses contain palms and tropical plants; seasonal displays of flowers and foliage plants are presented. There is a chrysanthemum show in fall, a Christmas, and a spring show. A calendar of floral displays in the area is maintained.

Daily 9:30-4:15; extended summer hours; no admission charge; handicapped access; (416) 356-2241.

31 Oakes Garden Theater ☆ RG-T-W
1 km. north on Niagara Parkway

An amphitheater of the Roman style is set in rock gardens, terraces, and lily ponds. Topiary has been used. The gardens overlook the falls.

Daily; no admission charge.

32 Niagara Park Commission School of Horticulture ☆☆☆☆ HA-H-L-R-RG-S-W-WF
8 km. north on Niagara Parkway

The 100-acre campus garden is principally maintained by the students. More than 2,500 species are grown. Special gardens include an alpine garden, an aquatic garden, a herb garden, a rose garden, an ornamental formal garden, and a natural garden. There are large displays of lilacs, irises, peonies, wildflowers, vegetables, ornamental shrubs, and specimen trees. Demonstration gardens and a library have been established in this garden founded in 1936.

Daily; dawn-dusk; no admission charge; handicapped access; (416) 356-8554.

33 Floral Clock and Lilac Gardens ☆
9¾ km. north on River Rd.

The clock is maintained with 25,000 flowering plants from spring to the first frost with a series of interesting designs. The lilac gardens are new; 1500 shrubs representing 256 varieties have been planted.

Daily; no admission charge.

QUEENSTON

34 Laura Secord Homestead HH-R
Partition St.

A restored 1812 homestead is surrounded by a rose garden with some old roses as well as modern varieties.

10-6 Mon-Fri, 10-7 Sat, Sun; (416) 751-0500.

NIAGARA–ON–THE–LAKE

35 Home and Garden Tours HH

Historically interesting homes and gardens are open for tours for a few days in June

For information call (416) 468-3912.

ST. CATHERINES

36 Trial Gardens ☆
Stokes Seeds Inc.
Martindale Interchange from Queen Elizabeth Way

A 3-acre trial garden, near the large seed crop area, is devoted to flowers and vegetables; a half mile of annual beds lead to the site. July and August are the best time to visit.

Weekdays 8-4:30; no admission charge; (416) 688-4300.

VINELAND

37 Horticultural Experiment Station

There are 230 acres of orchards, vineyards, vegetables, and ornamental planting at this research facility. The ornamental flower beds are of general interest. Research on fruit trees is emphasized here.

There is an annual open house; by appointment only; (416) 562-4146.

HAMILTON

38 Royal Botanical Gardens ☆☆☆☆ A-G-HA-L-R-RG-P-S
Highway 2, west

2,000 acres of gardens have been established here since 1941 on varied terrain in this large park. There is a very large rock garden. The Centennial Rose Garden cover 2 acres with 2,800 modern hybrid roses and 450 shrub roses. The gardens include a trial garden of annuals, an iris garden, in which 250,000 blooms open in June, a lilac garden, and a children's garden. The gardens maintain good collections of rhododendrons, azaleas, crab-apples, clematis, day-lilies, peonies, hedges, weeping trees, avenue trees, native trees, dogwoods, redbuds, tulips, some 480 varieties of lilacs, and lilies.

Many different kinds of trees and shrubs are also represented and most plants are labelled. The woodlands form an arboretum which includes a pinetum. There are greenhouses with tropical plants and a 'Nature Interpretive Center. There is a library.

Daily 8-dusk; no admission charge; nominal parking fee; handicapped access; (416) 527-1158.

39 Gage Park ☆☆ CH-G-HA-P-R
Main St. East and Gage Ave.

This 70-acre park contains a rose garden with numerous varieties represented. The greenhouses have a tropical collection and mount a chrysanthemum show each November. 60,000 bloom represent 125 varieties

Daily, dawn-dusk; 9-8 during flower show; no admission charge; handicapped access; (416) 549-9285.

40 Sam Lawrence Park L-R
Jolley Cut, on top of Hamilton Mt.

This panoramic view of the entire area has been augmented by a garden of perennials and annuals as well as roses.

Daily, dawn-dusk; no admission charge.

41 Whitehern HH
Jackson Street West

This Georgian mansion has been restored along with its garden.

Daily 11-4, June 15-Labor Day; 1-4 rest of year; closed New Year, Christmas; adults, under $3; children half; (416) 522-5664.

42 Dundurn Castle HH
York St. and Dundurn

This restored Victorian mansion includes a small garden.

Daily 11-4, June 15-Labor Day; 1-4 rest of year; closed New Year and Christmas; adults, under $3; children half; (416) 522-5313.

DUNDAS

43 Ben Veldhuis Limited BR-C-G-P-SU
154 King Street East

These greenhouses contain 2 acres under glass and feature thousands of cacti, succulents, bromeliads, as well as tropical plants.

7-5 Mon-Sat; no admission charge; (416) 628-6307.

PUSLINCH

44 Kiln Farm Herb Garden H
Conc. 11 West, off Rt. 6

This old English herb garden displays 200 species of herbs. There are trails through nearby woods.

For hours call (416) 659-1001.

GUELPH

45 University of Guelph Arboretum ☆ HA-R-S
University of Guelph
Arboretum Rd.

This 332 acre arboretum was established in 1970; collections of roses, lilacs, dwarf conifers, native trees and shrubs have been developed. There is a demonstration garden for woody ornamentals.

Daily, dawn-dusk; no admission charge; handicapped access; (519) 824-4120 ex 2113.

46 Riverside Park
Woodlawn Rd.

This park contains beds of perennials and annuals as well as a large floral clock.

Daily, dawn-dusk.

47 Heritage Park
Speed River

Allan's Mill which has been restored in this park includes a garden of shrubs, perennials, and annuals.

Daily, dawn-dusk.

48 Col. John McCrae Birthplace Museum HH
108 Water St.

The home of the author of the poem, 'In Flander's Field', is a museum with an attached memorial garden of perennials and annuals.

1-5 Mon-Fri, 2-4 Sat, 2-4:30 Sun; adults, children nominal; (519) 836-6144.

MILTON

49 Ontario Agriculture Museum HH
Exits 312 and 320 off Hwy. 401

3 restored homes and 23 other buildings present exhibits on the development of agriculture in the province. There are both indoor and outdoor plant exhibits.

Daily 10-5, May 16-Oct 9; adults, under $3; 13-17 two-thirds; 64 half; 6-12 one-third; (416) 878-8151.

ETOBICOKE

50 Centennial Park Greenhouses ☆ C-HA-P-SU
Centennial Park
Elmcrest and Rathburn Rds.

This new greenhouse complex contains a tropical house, a southern house with cacti and succulents as well as a display house for flower shows.

Daily 10-5; handicapped access; (416) 626-4320.

TORONTO

51 Allan Gardens ☆ G-HA-P-R-W
Carlton and Jarvis Sts.

A 13-acre park along with greenhouses is located in the heart of the city. Roses, perennials, and annuals as well as water lilies are grown. The greenhouses have collections of tropical and subtropical plants.

Daily 10-5; no admission charge; handicapped access; (416) 947-7286.

52 China Court J
Spadina Ave. and Dundas St.

The Oriental pagodas and Chinese gardens in this commercial development have made it a new focal point of Toronto's Chinese community.

Daily, business hours.

53 Edwards Gardens ☆ G-L-RG
Exit 373 off Hwy. 401 at Lawrence Ave. and Leslie Sts.
North York

The park extends for 34 acres along the Don River; it began as a private garden. The site is planted with beds of annuals and perennials. There is a rock garden near the greenhouses. The Civic Garden Center lies adjacent.

Daily 10-9; no admission charge; partial handicapped access; (416) 445-1552.

54 James Gardens ☆
61 Edgehill Rd.
Etobicoke

10 acres of formal gardens are planted with thousands of tulips in spring and with annuals later. The ponds and streams are crossed by rustic bridges which also lead through a woodland.

Daily 10-9; no admission charge.

55 Metro Zoo ☆ HA-P
Meadowvale Rd.
Scarborough

The zoo is located on a 700-acre site and is built around a series of outdoor and indoor natural habitats. A large jungle and rainforest contains hundreds of tropical plants.

Daily 9:30-7, summer; 9:30-4:30 winter; adults, under $6; seniors and 12-17 half; children one-third; handicapped access; (416) 284-8181.

56 Guildwood Park WF
off Guildwood Parkway

The Guild Inn and its stone artifacts are set in a formal garden. There is a woodland with numerous wildflowers.

Daily 8-5.

57 Toronto Island Park
Ferry from Young Street

This park in the harbor includes an avenue of reflecting pools and formal mosaic beds of perennials and annuals. There are some fine specimen trees.

Daily 7:30-11:30; no admission charge; (416) 367-8193.

58 Humber Arboretum ☆ A-HA-WF
205 Humber College Blvd.

The arboretum is part of the college and was established on 300 acres in 1977. Good collections of rhododendrons, native trees, and wildflowers are maintained. There is a library.

Daily; no admission charge; handicapped access; (416) 675-3111 ex 445.

59 Victorian Gardens
Cathedral Church of St. James
106 King St. East

This small Victorian garden contains plantings of shrubs, perennials, and annuals.

Daily 10-4; no admission charge; handicapped access; (416) 364-7864.

WHITBY

60 Cullen Gardens and Miniature Village ☆☆☆ CH-L-R-RG-T
Taunton Rd., off Hwy. 12

Beautifully landscaped grounds are the setting for more than 100 historic Ontario buildings reproduced in miniature. Trees and shrubs have been carefully selected and shaped to create an effective illusion. There is some fine topiary. A wide variety

ONTARIO 335

of colorful plants has been used in these gardens. 80,000 tulips bloom in spring and more than 10,000 roses in summer. There is a good chrysanthemum display in fall.

Daily 9-10, April 1-Sept 30; 10-10 Oct 1-Dec 31; Wed-Sun 10-late afternoon (depending on weather), rest of year; closed Dec 25; adults, under $6; over 65 and students three-quarters; 3-12 half; April 10-Sept 20; adults, under $3; 3-12 half; rest of year; (416) 668-6606.

61 Marigold Festival

Held annually in mid-September, this festival sees more than 60,000 marigolds in bloom

For information call (416) 579-1311.

OSHAWA

62 Parkwood ☆ G-HH-L-P
270 Simcoe St. N., exit 417, off Hwy. 401

This 55-room mansion stands in a large formal garden which has been completely restored. There is an Italian garden with fountains and a pool. Greenhouses maintain collections of tropical plants. Flower shows are held during the summer along with concerts.

10:30-4:30 Tues-Sun, holidays, June 1-Labor Day; 1:30-4 Tues-Fri and Sun, mid-March-May and after Labor Day to mid-Dec; adults, under $3; over 62 two-thirds; 5-18 half; (416) 579-1311.

COBOURG

63 Victoria Park R
King St. E. at McGill St.

This 30 acre park and beach includes a 30 ft floral clock as well as beds of perennials and annuals. There is a rose garden.

Daily 8-dusk; no admission charge; (416) 372-8641.

BARRIE

64 Barrie Greenhouses P
165 Ferndale Drive

A display of tropical and sub-tropical plants is maintained here. There is a winter flower show.

Weekdays 9:30-12, 1-3; no admission charge; (705) 726-4242.

65 The Barrie Arboretum R-S

Begun in 1974, this arboretum has steadily grown; more than 100 types of lilacs have been planted along with smaller collections of trees. Good specimens of Kentucky Coffee tree, Japanese walnut, ginkgo, and Northern pecan may be seen here. There is a small rose garden with 42 varieties.

Daily, dawn-dusk.

OTTAWA

66 Dominion Arboretum ☆☆☆ C-CH-G-HA-HD-RG-P-S
Central Experimental Farm
Queen Elizabeth Driveway at Maple Dr.

This 85-acre arboretum was founded in 1886. There are 15 acres of gardens with good collections of irises, peonies, lilacs, and crab-apples. The arboretum contains numerous species of hardy trees and shrubs. There is a rock garden, a perennial and annual garden, a vegetable garden, a hedge collection as well as demonstration gardens. The greenhouses contain a tropical collection and mount seasonal flower shows. The autumn chrysanthemum show displays more than 3,000 bushes representing 100 varieties. There is a museum of agriculture on the grounds. There is a library.

Daily, dawn-dusk; different hours for greenhouses and museum; no admission charge; handicapped access; (613) 995-5287 or 995-5222.

67 Garden of the Provinces ☆
Wellington And Bay Sts.

The series of flag-poles with emblems of the provinces, including their flowers are surrounded by beds of perennials and annuals on these large grounds.

Daily; illuminated at night.

68 Rideau Hall ☆
Sussex Drive

This is the official residence of the Governor General of Canada. The extensive grounds contain formal gardens.

9-5 Mon-Fri; closed weekends and civic holidays; (613) 749-5933 ext. 48.

69 The Mackenzie King Estate HH
Swamp and Barnes Rds.

This estate of several hundred acres includes elaborate formal gardens, some with ruins in the English manner. Fine plantings of shrubs, conifers, perennials and annuals have been undertaken. There is a large wooded area with specimen trees.

Daily 9-4:30, spring thaw to first snowfall; no admission charge; (613) 827-2020.

70 Festival of Spring

The festival held annually in mid-May finds more than 3,000,000 tulips in bloom.

For annual information call (416) 965-4008.

PRINCE EDWARD ISLAND

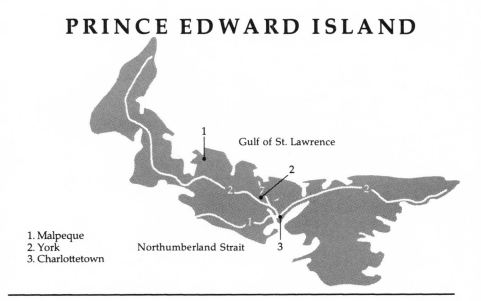

Gulf of St. Lawrence

1. Malpeque
2. York
3. Charlottetown

Northumberland Strait

MALPEQUE

1 Malpeque Gardens ☆☆ F-R-S
Hwy. 20, Cabot Park

Colorful flower beds, 2 rose gardens, sunken gardens, and the Anne of Green Gables gardens are found in this park. More than 400 cultivars of dahlias are grown. There is a dwarf fruit orchard on 4 acres of landscaped grounds.

Daily 9-dusk, June 25-Aug 31; 9-5 Sept 1-30; adults, under $3; 6-14 half; (902) 836-5418.

YORK

2 Jewell's Gardens and Pioneer Village HH
Rt. 25 on way to Charlottetown

The pioneer village is set in 5 acres of gardens of perennials, annuals, and fountains.

9-5 Mon-Sat, June 14-30 and Sept 1-Oct 11; 9-dusk July 1-Aug 31; closed Sun; adults, under $6; under 12 half; (902) 892-1503.

CHARLOTTETOWN

3 Ardgowan National Historic Park HH
Mt. Edward Rd. and Palmer's Lane

The home of W.H. Pope, one of the Fathers of the Confederation, is set in grounds restored to reflect the 1850's.

Daily 9-5; no admission charge.

QUEBEC

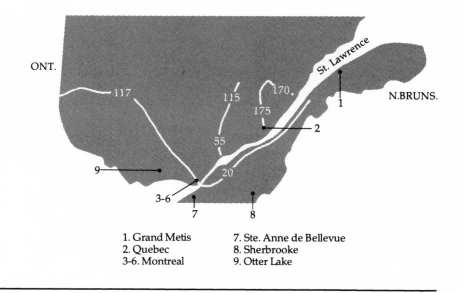

1. Grand Metis   7. Ste. Anne de Bellevue
2. Quebec   8. Sherbrooke
3-6. Montreal   9. Otter Lake

GRAND METIS

1 Parc Metis—The Redford Estate ☆☆ L-RG-S-W
Hwy. 132

This garden on the Gaspé Peninsula was the Redford Estate. It is beautifully landscaped with streams, flower beds, large plantings of shrubs and trees. Collections of Tibetian, Himalayan, and Alpine plants with more than 1,500 species not normally found so far north may be seen here. There are also unusual collections of lilies, rock plants, and shrubs. Native and aquatic plants have been planted as well.

Daily 8:30-10, June 5-Sept 10; adults, under $3; under 18, over 65 half; disabled free; parking fee; (418-775-3165 or 775-5080.

QUEBEC

2 Jardin Van den Hende
Laval Université

This botanical garden of the university presents a wide ranging collection of native and introduced species.

For hours call (418) 643-5349.

MONTREAL

3 Ile Ste-Hélène
Jaques Cartier Bridge

This park, landscaped with flower beds of perennials and annuals, is located on an island in the St. Lawrence River and is adjacent to the 'Man and His World' exhibit.

Daily; no admission charge; open-air trolleys provide rides within this large park.

4 Lafontaine Parc   HA
Rue Sherbrooke Est and Rue Parc Lafontaine

The 100 acres of well-landscaped parkland contain numerous flower beds of perennials and annuals around several lakes.

Daily; no admission charge; handicapped access.

5 Montreal Botanical Garden   ☆☆☆☆   BR-C-FE-G-H-HA-L-O-R-RG-S-SU-W
4101 est, Rue Sherbrooke

Among the very best botanical gardens of North America, this garden contains more than 22,000 species and cultivars on 190 acres as well as greenhouses. It combines research with beautiful displays and plantings. The park offers a rock garden, an Indian medicinal garden, an aquatic garden, a rose garden, an economic garden, an arboretum, and test gardens. There are special collections of alpines, cacti, ferns, succulents, begonias, bromeliads, orchids, and roses. There is a library. The outdoor displays are best mid-May to mid-June; the greenhouse displays change constantly.

Daily, gardens 10-sunset; greenhouses 9-6; adults, under $3; 5-7, senior citizens half; handicapped access; (514) 252-1173.

6 Westmount Floral Clock
Rue Sherbrooke and Ave. Landsdowne

This operating clock is decorated with 4,000 plants.

Daily.

ST. ANNE DE BELLEVUE

7 Morgan Arboretum   ☆   S
Macdonald Campus

This arboretum, which is operated by McGill University, covers 530 acres. Since its establishment in 1947, the collection has grown to more than 800 species of native shrubs and trees, as well as introduced species from the Northern Temperate Zone. Plantings are spaced to permit full natural growth. There are test and demonstration gardens as well as trails. There is a library.

Daily 8-5; admission, under $3 weekends only; partial handicapped access; (514) 457-2000.

SHERBROOKE

8 Parklets
Courthouse, King St. W

More than 50,000 perennials and annuals in interestingly arranged flower beds are planted throughout the city; many have been placed in a mosaic pattern.

OTTER LAKE

9 Belle Terre Botanic Garden   C-H-HD-P-R-RG-S

A number of gardens surround a historic house. They include a herb garden with 125 species, a rose garden, children's garden, a perennial garden, a rock garden, an old-fashioned garden, and vegetable and fruit trial gardens. There are collections of crab-apples, day-lilies as well as specimen trees. 2 greenhouses contain tropical plants, cacti, and succulents.

Daily, dawn-dusk; no admission charge; (819) 453-7334.

SASKATCHEWAN

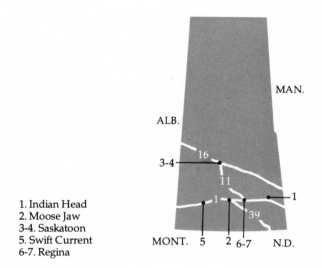

MAN.

ALB.

3-4

16

11

1

39

1. Indian Head
2. Moose Jaw
3-4. Saskatoon
5. Swift Current
6-7. Regina

MONT.   5   2 6-7   N.D.

INDIAN HEAD

1   PFRA Tree Nursery ☆ HA
Indian Head

A 26-acre arboretum along with 640-acre nursery which display a large selection of plants which are hardy on the plains. There are 200 species of poplars and willows as well as more than 225 species of other plants. Demonstration annual and perennial gardens. There is a library.

Daily 8-dusk; guided tours 8-4:30 weekdays; no admission charge; handicapped access; (306) 695-2284.

MOOSE JAW

2   Crescent Park HA
Civic Center

A war memorial garden with formal plantings is part of a larger park.

Daily, dawn-dusk; handicapped access; (306) 692-4471.

SASKATOON

3   Mendel Art Gallery and Civic Conservatory G-HA
950 Spadina Crescent between Queen and 25th St.

Large floral displays, which are changed seasonally, are the main feature of this conservatory. The botanical garden is good.

Daily 10-10; closed Good Friday, December 25; no admission charge; handicapped access; (306) 652-1910 or 664-9610.

4 Patterson Garden
University of Saskatchewan

Hardy trees, shrubs, and climbers have been planted.

Daily 8-dusk; handicapped access; no admission charge; (306) 244-4343.

SWIFT CURRENT

5 Prairie Life Interpretation Center
28 km. west on Hghway 1

A display area of prairie fauna and flora. Some exhibits are inside the buildings, others outside. There is a large collection of prairie plants as well as those introduced later. There are trails; guidebooklets and binoculars loaned free of charge.

Daily 9-5 May 15-Sept 30; no admission charge; (306) 674-2287.

REGINA

6 Wascana Center Production Greenhouses

A tour of large greenhouses of the area may be undertaken; they feature a wide range of plants. There are formal flower gardens as well as collections of trees and shrubs.

4pm Fri, Sat, Sun; tour leaves from Wascana Centre; (306) 522-3661.

7 Legislative Flower Garden
Capitol
Alberta St.

More than 100 acres of beautifully landscaped grounds surround this building. Both perennials and annuals are planted here.

Daily, dawn-dusk.

Index to Places

Index to Gardens, Arboreta, Conservatories and Other Sites